For Franny and Alex
with Thanks for
enfolding us in the
embrace of each other

God's Bounty

Much love from us both -
Judy and Pete

Katie Moose

Katie Moose

Conduit Press
Easton, Maryland

This book is dedicated to my sisters and brothers who know the Word and the Way, and have kept me on a path that leads only to our Lord and Savior Jesus Christ. Without them I could not have been inspired to write this book. God bless you all.

Front Cover Design:
Watercolor by Jerry Lee Canada, Easton, Maryland
Graphic design by Jean Harper Baer, Baltimore, Maryland

Published by Conduit Press, 307 Goldsborough Street, Easton, Maryland 21601

Library of Congress Cataloging-in-Publication Data

Printed and Bound by Victor Graphics, Inc., Baltimore, Maryland

ISBN: 978-0-9821069-0-7

Introduction

"He causeth the grass to grow for the cattle, and herb for the service of man: that he may bring forth food out of the earth; And wine that maketh glad the heart of man, and oil to make his face to shine, and bread which strengtheneth man's heart."

During our short lives there are those who are our building blocks, our saints, our angels. They light up the future, give us hope, courage and love. They are there when we need them, they can hug you, and make you laugh, and cry. We all have saints in our lives. Maybe we can't remember exactly who they are, or when they touched us. Sometimes it's just a phone call, a bouquet of flowers, a short note, or a pat on the back. In this book I highlight some that have touched me, some that have touched all of us with their words or music, and those that have changed the world. Always be open to finding that new saint or angel, or being one yourself. Like Christ we are fishers of men, women and children.

Each day is a new day. We do not know what will happen on a particular day. The only positive in our lives is that God is always with us. When we read the Bible we read the Wondrous Words of Life – "Flowers fade, but the Word endures forever."

Using favorite Biblical passages, poems, and hymns, I add inspirational thoughts and a special recipe for each day of the year. During our liturgical seasons I use appropriate favorite recipes. The personal stories are testaments to God's goodness and faithfulness. You will find some very uplifting and happy, others so tragic. That is life. But out of each story comes the power that is God. The God that is all loving, all knowing, reassuring, and always there.

Jesus Christ is Lord. Let this resound in your lives every single day. Never forget those words. When a former minister had his first child he asked the doctor to let him speak to his son first. His words were "Jesus Christ is Lord".

1

Years later when his father was dying his last words to him were "Jesus Christ is Lord." Alleluia

During the period the Bible was written we know the diet consisted of bread, barley, lentils, chickpeas, eggplant, artichokes, onions, garlic, yogurt, lamb, goats, herbs, spices, figs, grapes, and other foods that still abound today. I have used these throughout the book, not concentrating on foods of the Middle East, but throughout the world. I am particularly fond of the herbs and spices mentioned in the Bible.

Herbs of the Bible

Mint is an aromatic herb used to flavor tea, vegetables, cold drinks, fruits, salads, lamb, candies, jellies, and desserts.

Rosemary is also a member of the mint family and is a symbol of remembrance, affection, fidelity or constancy. Greek Students once wore garlands of rosemary in their hair while taking examinations as they thought it increased memory. The early colonists used it to scent soap. Rosemary is a strong, resinous flavoring for lamb, beef, chicken and other dishes. In early times it was used to mask odors on especially gamy meats. During the holidays rosemary wreathes and trees are popular decorations.

Coriander is the seed of the cilantro plant. Today we are more apt to use cilantro for flavoring than the seed. Mention of the seeds appears in Exodus and Numbers.

Garlic can reduce cholesterol levels and can be used as an antibiotic, anti-cancer and cardiovascular treatment. Garlic can be used in meat, potato, salad and vegetable dishes.

Mint, cumin, and dill are mentioned when Jesus scolds the Pharisees in Matthew 23:23 "Woe to you… tithe the mint, dill and cumin."

Cinnamon, myrrh, calamus, and cassia were used for the preparation of the oil in the tabernacle in Exodus 30:23-24.

"The meek shall eat and be satisfied: they shall praise the LORD that seek him: your heart shall live for ever." Psalm 22:26

May your days be filled with the Lord. May you eat from his abundant table. May his Light always shine upon you now and for ever.

January 1

"Amazing grace! How sweet the sound that saved a wretch like me! I once was lost, but now am found; was blind, but now I see. 'Twas grace that taught my heart to fear, and grace my fears relieved; how precious did that grace appear the hour I first believed. Through many dangers, toils, and snares, I have already come; 'tis grace hath brought me safe thus far, and grace will lead me home. The Lord has promised good to me, his word my hope secures; he will my shield and portion be, as long as life endures. Yea, when this flesh and heart shall fail, and mortal life shall cease, I shall possess, within the veil, a life of joy and peace. When we've been there ten thousand years, bright shining as the sun, we've no less days to sing God's praise than when we first begun."

"So for the second time they called the man who had been blind, and they said to him, "Give glory to God! We know that this man is a sinner." He answered, "I do not know whether he is a sinner. One thing I do know, that though I was blind, now I see."
John 9:24-25

The New Year starts with a favorite hymn known throughout the world that brings tears to eyes that have never heard the words or tune, or who know it by heart. When *Amazing Grace* is played on a bagpipe even more feelings well up. We are so thankful John Newton (1725-1807) came to know the Lord and foreswore his position as captain on a slave ship. He was ordained in 1764 and wrote "Amazing Grace" in December 1772. John Newton and William Wilberforce (1759-1883) led the fight for the Slave Trade Act of 1807 making slave trade illegal, and slavery abolition in 1833 in Great Britain. Emancipation did not occur in the United States until 1865.

Heavenly Pudding

Serves 6

½ cup sherry
4 egg yolks
2/3 cup sugar

2 cups cream
1 tsp. vanilla
½ cup sliced almonds

Stir the sherry, egg yolks, and sugar in a double boiler. Heat until thickened. Cool.
Fold in the cream, vanilla and almonds.
Serve in bowls with crushed macaroons.

January 2

"Onward, Christian soldiers, marching as to war, With the cross of Jesus going on before. Christ, the royal Master, leads against the foe; Forward into battle see His banners go!

Refrain: Onward, Christian soldiers, marching as to war, With the cross of Jesus going on before.

Crowns and thrones may perish, kingdoms rise and wane, But the church of Jesus constant will remain. Gates of hell can never 'gainst that church prevail; We have Christ's own promise, and that cannot fail. Refrain"

Onward, Christian Soldiers is one of the very first songs we learn as children. I can remember us marching around the parish hall holding high our banners and singing away, though I never could carry a tune. Soldiers of Christ are mentioned in the Bible – 2 Timothy 2:3 *Thou therefore endure hardness, as a good soldier of Jesus Christ*. I don't think as children we knew what that meant, but we did know about soldiers.

Sabine Baring-Gould (1834-1924) wrote the words for a Whit-Monday school festival in Yorkshire. Arthur Sullivan composed the music in 1871 and named the tune "St. Gertrude," for the wife at whose country home he composed the tune. The Salvation Army adopted the hymn as one if its processional tunes. The hymn was also played at the funeral of President Dwight D. Eisenhower at the Washington National Cathedral in 1969.

Herbed Green Beans

Serves 4

1 lb. green beans	2 tbls. fresh rosemary
½ stick butter	2 tbls. fresh basil
3 green onions, chopped	¼ cup fresh parsley, snipped
2 cloves garlic, crushed	Salt and pepper to taste
½ stalk celery, chopped	

Trim the beans and cook in boiling water for three minutes. Remove from pan. Melt butter in pan. Add onion, garlic and celery. Cook until tender. Add rest of ingredients and beans.

January 3

"And it came to pass, that, as he was praying in a certain place, when he ceased, one of his disciples said unto him, Lord, teach us to pray, as John also taught his disciples."
Luke 11:1

Each morning I read my "Day by Day" and the Bible passages associated with it. Sometimes I get down on my knees to pray, but more often I say a prayer before a meal that day. I might be by myself, or with others. In the spring and summer I thank God for the flowers that bloom and the birds that sing. I have to be more creative in the fall and winter. I do thank God every day for all the blessings of this life, for family and friends, for health and those that need to be restored to health. I also realize I need to change the way I pray, and I ask His guidance in choosing what I pray. Listen to the Lord. Don't always ask. Let Him tell you how to pray.

Grilled Chicken with Green Sauce

Serves 4

4 medium boneless chicken breasts   Salt and pepper
Olive oil

Rub the chicken breasts with olive oil and salt and pepper.
Grill on BBQ.
Serve with green sauce.
Chicken can be served warm or chilled.

Green Sauce

½ cup olive oil
2 tbls. white wine vinegar
½ cup mayonnaise
4 chives, snipped
¼ cup fresh parsley, chopped

½ bunch watercress, stems removed and chopped
2 tbls. dill, snipped
2 tbls. tarragon, chopped
2 green onions, chopped
½ small leek, chopped

Combine the ingredients in a bowl.

January 4

"All hail the power of Jesus' Name! Let angels prostrate fall; bring forth the royal diadem, and crown him Lord of all! Bring forth the royal diadem and crown Him Lord of all! Crown him ye martyrs of our God, who from his altar call; praise him whose way of pain ye trod, and crown him Lord of all! Praise him whose way of pain ye trod, and crown him Lord of all! Hail him the heir of David's line, whom David Lord did call, the God incarnate, Man divine, and crown him Lord of All! the God incarnate, Man divine, and crown him Lord of all!"

Jesus is our Lord, our King. He is the God who gives us life, breath and being. Each day praise Him, preach his word, and thank Him for all the blessings of life. Hail Him, kneel before Him, uplift your arms, and crown him Lord of all.

Edward Perronet was born in 1726 in Kent, England, the son of an Anglican minister. He worked with John and Charles Wesley. However, it is the beautiful hymn that we remember him for. *"All Hail the Power of Jesus' Name"* is one of my favorites, and a tune that is easily remembered. He is buried at Canterbury Cathedral in Kent.

Leek Soup

Serves 4

½ stick butter
1 medium onion, chopped
2 leeks, chopped
4 red Yukon Gold potatoes, peeled and diced

3 cups chicken stock
1 cup heavy cream
Garlic sourdough bread croutons
Snipped chives

Melt the butter in a sauce pan. Stir in onions, leeks and potatoes. Pour in the stock. Cover and bring to a boil. Simmer for 20 minutes, or until potatoes are tender.
Puree in a food processor.
Pour back into pan. Heat and add cream.
Serve in bowls garnished with croutons and chives.

January 5

"Behold that which I have seen: it is good and comely for one to eat and to drink, and to enjoy the good of all his labour that he taketh under the sun all the days of his life, which God giveth him: for it is his portion. Every man also to whom God hath given riches and wealth, and hath given him power to eat thereof, and to take his portion, and to rejoice in his labour; this is the gift of God."
Ecclesiastes 5:18-19

Twelfth Night celebrates the end of the Christmas season and the beginning of Epiphany. The tradition dates from Tudor England when it marked the end of a festival that had started on All Hallow's Eve. It is the time to take down Christmas decorations and get back to a normal routine after too many Christmas parties and presents. Be thankful for what you have, and for what is to come.

Roast Goose

Serves 4

1 goose (4-6 lbs.)   3 tbls. sea salt
4 cloves garlic, minced   1 cup water
1 tbls. Italian herbs

Preheat oven to 400°
Rub the outside and inside of goose with the garlic, seasoning and salt.
Prick legs and wings with a fork.
Pour water into uncovered roasting pan. Place goose in water. Cook 20 minutes
Turn oven down to 325°. Cook for 2 ½ hours.
Serve on a platter with red currant sauce.

Red Currant Sauce

1 jar currant jelly   2 tbls. fresh grated ginger
2 tbls. sherry

Combine the ingredients in a sauce pan. Serve in a bowl with the goose.

January 6 – Epiphany

"Make a joyful noise to the Lord, all the earth. Worship the Lord with gladness; come into his presence with singing. Know that the Lord is God. It is he that hath made us, and we are his; we are his people, and the sheep of his pasture. Enter his gates with Thanksgiving, and his own courts with praise. Give thanks to him, bless his name. For the Lord is good, his steadfast love endures forever, and his faithfulness to all generations."
Psalm 100

This was one of the first psalms, after Psalm 23, that I remember memorizing. I think it was because we used the old Book of Common Prayer, and dutifully followed the Sunday lessons prescribed for each week. There were certain psalms that were sung and this was one of them.

Epiphany comes from the Greek "to manifest or to show" and celebrates the human form of God in the coming of Christ. The magi came bearing gifts. Gifts that meant a lot in those long ago days. Gifts of gold, frankincense and myrrh.

"...ahead of them went the star...Until it stopped over the place where the child was. When they saw that the star had stopped, they were overwhelmed with joy."
Matthew 2:9-10

Black Beans and Rice

Serves 6

8 slices bacon, cooked and crumbled, save fat
2 tbls. olive oil
1 medium onion, chopped
2 cans black beans, drained
2 stalks celery, chopped
1 carrot, peeled and sliced
4 cloves garlic, minced

1 tsp. oregano
2 large tomatoes, chopped
2 jalapeno, seeded and diced
2 tsp. cumin
1 tsp. cayenne
1 tsp. hot sauce
1 tbls. Worcestershire sauce

Heat the bacon fat and olive oil in a sauce pan. Add onion and sauté till tender. Add other ingredients. Bring to boil. Simmer ½ hour.
Served over rice. Top with sour cream, chives or chopped green onions, and black olives.

January 7

"Jesus said to him, "I am the way, and the truth, and the life. No one comes to the Father except through me. If you know me, you will know my Father also. From now on you do know him and have seen him."
John 14:6-7

Knowing someone is easier than imaging how they might look or act. Yes, there are numerous images of Christ, but is he black, white, or what color? Does he have long hair and a beard? It doesn't matter. What matters is our understanding the Lord and what He stands for. The man who gave his life so that we can live without sin, that we can look forward to our rewards on earth and in heaven, and being with our heavenly Father. We do know Him and his Father. They are our being.

Chicken Paprika

Serves 4

4 boneless chicken breasts
½ cup flour
1 tsp. salt
1 tsp. fresh ground pepper
4 slices bacon
2 tbls. butter
½ red pepper, sliced

½ yellow pepper, sliced
1 tbls. medium Hungarian paprika
1 tbls. mild Hungarian paprika
1 cup chicken broth
2 stalks celery, chopped
½ cup fresh parsley, chopped
1 cup sour cream

Preheat oven to 350°
Combine ¼ cup flour, salt and pepper in a bowl. Dredge the chicken in flour.
Sautee the bacon in a large skillet. Remove bacon and add butter. Brown chicken on both sides, about 8 minutes per side.
In a large ovenproof covered dish, place chicken and drippings from skillet.
Add all other ingredients, except for flour and sour cream.
Cover and cook for ½ hour.
Combine sour cream and remaining flour in a bowl. Pour over chicken.
Cook chicken for ten minutes more.
Serve with noodles or rice.

"Let them praise his name in the dance; let them sing praises unto him with the timbrel and harp."
Psalm 149:3

"Therefore brethren, stand fast, and hold the traditions which ye have been taught, whether by word, or our epistle."
2 Thessalonians 2:15

An old tradition in Boston is the Waltz Evening held either at the Ritz or Copley Hotels. My mother attended years ago, and I have had the opportunity since. These glamorous evenings find gentlemen in white or black tie, ladies in long evening gowns and long gloves. Prior to the dance, dinners are given throughout the city. Maintaining traditions are important for us and generations to come. They instill in us a sense of familiarity, something that is ongoing. Yes, they can be changed, but when they are it doesn't feel the same. We like to know that on Christmas and Thanksgiving we'll eat turkey, that on a certain date a family reunion will occur, that on Christmas we celebrate the birth of Christ, and at Easter His glorious Resurrection. Think of your family's traditions and continue to maintain them.

Baked Brie with Apricots

1 package crescent rolls	½ cup pecans
1 small brie round	2 tbls. brown sugar
10 dried apricots, chopped	2 tbls. butter

Preheat oven to 400°
On a floured cutting board roll out crescent rolls into a roll pie shape.
Place the apricots, pecans and brown sugar in the center of the circle.
Put brie on top.
Fold dough sides together to form an enclosed circle around brie. Turn upside down and place in glass baking dish.
Pat with butter.
Bake for 15 minutes, or just browned.

January 9

"He shall cover thee with His feathers, and under His wings shalt thou trust."
Psalm 91:4

"But they that wait upon the Lord shall renew their strength; they shall mount up with wings as eagles; they shall run, and not be weary; and they shall walk, and not faint."
Isaiah 41:31

"And He will raise you up on eagle's wings,
Bear you on the breath of dawn,
Make you to shine like the sun,
And hold you in the palm of His Hand."
On Eagle's Wings

My husband and I visited Ballintubber Abbey in Ireland on a Friday just before a wedding was to take place. As I opened the church doors music floated out, a tenor practicing "on Wings of Eagles" and other songs for the wedding. Both he and the priest invited us to stay, but in travelling clothes we did not want to stand out among the stylishly dressed wedding guests.

I constantly hum the hymn and remind myself that the Lord will lift me up on wings of eagles. This is especially true if I am feeling a little low. I need that uplifting. I know that the Lord protects me, and will answer my prayers. I do trust in the Lord. Give yourself to Him.

Sauteed Carrots

Serves 4

2 tbls. butter
6 large carrots, sliced lengthwise and slivered

¼ cup honey
2 tbls. dill, snipped

Melt the butter in a skillet,
Saute carrots for 3 minutes, or until just tender.
Stir in honey and dill.

"Pilate therefore said unto Him, "Art thou a king, then?" Jesus answered, "Thou sayest that I am a king. To this end was I born, and for this cause I came into the world, that I should bear witness unto the truth."
John 18:37

Jesus did not seek power. He came into to this world to redeem its citizens who had gone astray. He came as the Son of God, preaching, healing, and teaching. We need Him to come again. These are sad times. Politicians gone amok, seeking power and believing they have the power. That they are above everyone else and the law. They seek to destroy others, confessing they believe in the Lord. They are hypocrites. Only when they are brought down, laughed at, shunned, do they truly know who is Lord and our King. Do not rise up and pretend to be something you are not. Believe in Christ and the Ten Commandments. Believe in what is right and just, not only for yourself, but for others.

"Blessed be the King that cometh in the name of the Lord, peace in heaven and glory in the highest."
Luke 19:38

White Bean Salad

Serves 6

2 cans chickpeas, drained
1 can artichoke hearts, drained
8 oz. kalamata olives, pitted
½ lb. sun-dried tomatoes

½ lb. mozzarella
Juice of 1 lemon
¼ cup olive oil
1 tbls. fresh oregano, chopped

Combine all ingredients in a salad bowl. Serve chilled.
Pine nuts can also be added
Feta cheese can be substituted for the mozzarella

January 11

"And God spake all these words, saying, I am the Lord thy God, which have brought thee out of the land of Egypt, out of the house of bondage. Thou shalt have no other gods before me. Thou shalt not make unto thee any graven images, or any likeness of any thing that is in heaven above, or that is in the earth beneath, or that is in the water under the earth."
Exodus 20:3

How many times are we tempted – tempted to steal, to lie, to hurt, to think that there is a better God? The temptations are everywhere – more money, more clothes, more shoes, more and more. But that is not what Christ asked us to do. He asked us to love God his father. We do not need material goods to do this. We need only to trust in Him. He will show us the way – the way to truth, a healthy and a happy life. Believe in our one and only God. There are no other gods.

As Luke (10:27) said, *"Thou shalt love the Lord thy God with all thy heart, and with all thy soul, and with all thy strength, and with all thy mind; and thy neighbor as thyself."*

Asparagus Risotto

Serves 4

3 tbl. butter
1 lb. asparagus, ends trimmed, slice into 1 inch pieces
2 green onions or 1 leek, chopped
4 cups chicken stock

2 cups Arborio rice
¼ cup dry white wine
Parmesan cheese
Fresh ground black pepper

Melt the butter in a large sauce pan. Add asparagus and green onions. Stir in rice. Slowly add stock.
When the rice has absorbed almost all of the stock, cover pan and turn heat off. Cover with heavy pan.
After about fifteen minutes, stir in wine.
Serve with parmesan cheese and black pepper.

January 12

"So whether you eat or drink or whatever you do, do it all for the glory of God.
1 Corinthians 10:31

My former husband's family was very involved with food and wine. His father was a former president of the International Wine and Food Society. Because of this we enjoyed gourmet meals and exquisite wines. Many Sundays after church, we would have the family for brunch. Sometimes I was told which type of wines would be brought, other times I would announce what I was cooking and the wines revolved around those dishes. His three brothers sometimes took part in the cooking. They loved to cook, to use every pan and bowl in the kitchen, and leave me to pick up. To this day I don't know how they could make such a mess. Of course, it was my house, and they were all still bachelors! Eat and do all for the Glory of God!

Salmon with Herb Sauce

Serves 12

1 8 package cream cheese
1 stick butter, softened
2 tsp. dill
2 tsp. parsley
2 tsp. tarragon

1 large clove garlic, crushed
12 salmon fillets or 4½ lbs. of salmon
Lemon juice

In a bowl combine the cream cheese, butter, dill, parsley, tarragon and garlic. Refrigerate at least 1 hour.
Preheat oven to 400°
Place the salmon on a large piece of aluminum foil in a baking dish. Sprinkle with lemon juice.
Make small balls out of the cheese mixture. Dot on salmon. Fold aluminum foil over salmon and seal.
Bake 20 minutes.
Serve with rice and a salad. Garnish with Lemon slices and more dill.

January 13

"And the peace of God, which passeth all understanding, shall keep your hearts and minds through Christ Jesus."
Philippians 4:7

Church services often conclude with these words. They are soothing. They tell us to depart in peace, that God is a peaceful entity and that our hearts and minds are always focused on the Lord.

Paul's letter to the Philippians exhorts them to be steadfast, joyful, doing things for Christ, not for themselves."*Rejoice in the Lord always, and again I say Rejoice.*" We must be steadfast in our Christian beliefs. We must be joyful in all our doings, but above all keep our hearts and minds through Christ.

Cinnamon French Toast

Serves 4

4 eggs
1 cup half and half
1 tsp. vanilla extract
1 teaspoon cinnamon
¼ tsp. nutmeg
¼ tsp. cloves
½ tsp. ground ginger

8 slices challah or French bread
Butter, cinnamon sugar, and maple syrup
Strawberries, blueberries, and blackberries

Combine the eggs, half and half, vanilla, nutmeg, cloves and ginger in a bowl. Place the bread on a cookie sheet. Pour the egg mixture over the bread. Cover and refrigerate overnight.
Heat some butter in a skillet and brown the bread on both sides.
Serve with cinnamon, sugar, maple syrup and fruit. Sausage and bacon are also good sides.

January 14

"Moreover, because I have set my affection to the house of my God, I have of mine own proper good, of gold and silver, which I have given to the house of my God, over and above all that I have prepared for the holy house."
1 Chronicles 29:3

A friend of my daughter's used to spend a lot of time with us in Newport. Her manners kept getting worse and worse. One day when she had not said thank you, or whatever it was, I went to the kitchen and baked cookies and scones. I set the table and made a pot of tea. Calling the girls I had them sit down for a proper tea and we went over proper etiquette. As soon as this friend got home she told her mother. Her mother immediately called to thank me. I never had a problem with her again, nor her parents. Now grown up, I hope she is teaching her children proper manners. They make all the difference whether you are dining out, going for an interview, or greeting someone. Politeness is a virtue.

Almond Scones

Makes 12

2 sticks butter
½ cup sugar
4 cups flour
2 tsp. baking powder
½ tsp. baking soda
¼ tsp. salt

1 cup heavy cream
1 tsp. almond extract
1 cup dried currants, raisins, or apricots
½ cup slivered almonds

Preheat oven to 375°
Cream butter in a bowl. Stir in sugar. Gradually add other ingredients.
 Add more cream, if not moist enough.
Roll dough out on a floured surface into a round circle. Cut into quarters. Cut each of these into 3 wedges.
Place on baking sheet. Brush with beaten egg and sprinkle with granulated sugar.
Bake 25 minutes, or until just browned.
Serve with clotted cream, butter and jams.

"A friend loveth at all times…"
Proverbs 17:17

When you least expect it, someone comes into your life, boosts your spirits, and is a kindred soul. Sharing mutual interests leads to finding a better spiritual life. Skiing and sailing become pastimes. Sadly when this person departs this world you have lost a best friend and often a mentor. Memories linger and you cannot forget the happy and sad times you have shared. Save a picture whether it be in your mind only, or a hard copy. Friends are too dear to ever lose. Let your friends know how much you appreciate them. Drop them a note, make a phone call, or stop by to see them. Ask them for tea, lunch, or just go for a walk. Friends can be of any age, in any place in the world, and of any religion. Touch them as Christ has touched us. The little gesture will probably mean the most.

"I do not cease to give thanks for you as I remember you in my prayers."
Ephesians 1:16

Pecan Tarts

Crust

1 3 oz. package cream cheese   ¼ cup cold water
1 stick butter   2 tbls. sugar
1 cup flour

Combine the ingredients in a food processor until a ball is formed. Make into 1" balls and press into ungreased muffin tins.

Filling

1 egg   1 teaspoon vanilla
¾ cup brown sugar   1 cup pecans
2 tbls. butter

Preheat oven to 350°
Combine egg, brown sugar, butter and vanilla in a bowl. Put a spoonful of pecans on top of each crust in muffin tin. Divide up the filling among the tins.
Bake 25-30 minutes.
Serve with clotted cream, whipped cream or ice cream.

January 16

"Go in peace to love and serve the Lord."

At the end of a service the rector may exhort you to go out into the world to serve the Lord, but also to serve others. Some people assist at food pantries, others in Sunday school, or day care, while others keep the spirit alive with the elderly. Whoever we are, we need to follow in the Lord's footsteps. *"feed my sheep."* Get out there and make a difference in the world. You don't have to be a Mother Theresa or Gandhi. But you can forgive, you can serve, and you can teach others to love the Lord. Peace means tranquility, keeping silent or quiet, and harmony in personal relationships. What better way to start the day then to find peace and serve the Lord.

Lamb Stew

Serves 8

3 lbs. boneless leg of lamb, cut in cubes
½ pint beer
2 small turnips, peeled and diced
2 carrots, peeled and sliced
1 leek, chopped

4 medium red potatoes, chopped
2 stalks celery, chopped
1 tsp. salt
1 tbls. pepper
1 cup cream
1 tbls. Worcestershire sauce

Place the lamb in a large pot with the bone. Just cover with water and beer. Bring to a boil and simmer one hour.
Add vegetables, salt and pepper. Cook for one hour more, until meat is tender. Remove bone.
Remove meat and vegetables. Reserve one cup stock. Discard remaining liquid.
Combine the 1 cup stock with cream and Worcestershire sauce in the pot. Add meat and vegetables. Just warm.
Serve stew with fresh chopped parsley, crusty bread and a salad.

January 17

"And the dove came to him in the morning; and lo, in her mouth was an olive leaf plucked off: so Noah knew that the waters were abated from the earth."
Genesis 8:11

Extreme flooding in the Midwest this year has taken a toll on thousands of people. They have lost their homes, their possessions, their crops, and loved ones. Only God can stop these torrential downpours. Man builds levees and dams, homes and businesses, only to have them swept away. Noah saved his family and animals, enduring endless days at sea, not knowing where they were headed and when the rains would stop. Finally a dove appeared with an olive leaf. Olive branches are a sign of peace and goodwill. Remember those who suffer from natural disasters and pray that God will offer them an olive branch and hope.

Tortellini Soup

Serves 4

2 tbls. olive oil
1 lb. Andouille sausage
1 medium onion, chopped
4 cloves garlic, minced
4 cups beef stock
2 large tomatoes, chopped
1 zucchini, chopped
2 carrots, peeled and sliced

½ red pepper, chopped
½ green pepper, chopped
½ cup red wine
¼ cup basil, chopped
1 tbls. oregano, chopped
10 oz. cheese tortellini
Fresh grated Parmesan cheese

Heat the olive oil in a large pan. Add sausage and onion, breaking up sausage into pieces. Add garlic. Stir in other ingredients, except tortellini and cheese. Cook 40 minutes.
Add tortellini. Cook 8 minutes, or until tortellini rise to top and are tender. Serves in bowls with cheese.

January 18

"Teach us to count our days that we may gain a wise heart."
Psalm 90:12

How often do we say to someone that we'd like to see them or do something with them, and then it keeps getting put off. A dear neighbor was dying of cancer. Going to work each day I would promise myself to stop by. One day I purchased a plant and said I would visit. By the time I got there, she had passed away. Don't keep making promises, do it. Take time to smell the roses. Take time to pick up the phone and call a friend or family member. Take time to visit the sick and needy. Tomorrow comes too quickly and you or that person might no longer be around.

Veal Thermidor

Serves 6

2 tbls. butter	½ lb. crab meat
2 tbls. olive oil	½ lb lobster meat
6 veal chops	

Heat the butter and olive oil in a skillet. Brown the veal chops on both sides to desired pinkness.
Divide the crab and lobster between the chops. Spoon lobster sauce on top and garnish with dill or parsley.

Cream Lobster Sauce

½ stick butter	½ cup grated parmesan cheese
¼ cup flour	½ lb. lobster meat
1 ½ cups cream	Fresh dill or parsley
1 tbls. Dijon mustard	
2 tbls. brandy	

Melt the butter in a pan. Stir in flour and cream, until just slightly thickened. Add mustard, brandy and cheese. Fold in lobster.

January 19

"Whenever you read the Gospel, Christ himself is speaking to you. And while you read, you are praying and talking with him."
St. Tikhon

As you sit and read the Bible find quiet time, so that you and the Lord can communicate. Turn off the TV, the phone, and find a comfortable chair so that the words resonate in your ears and eyes, that you know the true meaning of God's Word. You will learn wisdom, your heart will warm with love, and God will speak to you.

St. Tikhon of Moscow (1865-1925), born Vasily Ivanovich Bellavin, studied at the Pakiv Theological Seminary and graduated from the St. Petersburg Theological Academy. In 1891 he took monastic vows and was given the name Tikhon in honor of St. Tikhon of Zadonsk. He was consecrated Bishop of Lublin in 1897 and in 1898 became Bishop of the Aleutians and Alaska, and was made an American citizen. He established several churches in the United States, including St. Nicholas Cathedral in New York. In 1907, he returned to Russia, and was appointed Bishop of Yaroslavl. In 1917, he was elected the ruling bishop of Moscow by the Diocesan Congress of clergy and laity and was raised to the office of Metropolitan of Moscow. He was the Patriarch of Moscow and All Russia of the Russian Orthodox Church 1917 - 1925.

Barley Pilaf

Serves 4

1 cup pearl barley
1 stick butter
¼ cup pine nuts
4 green onions, chopped

½ cup fresh parsley, chopped
½ tsp. sea salt
1 tsp. pepper
3 cups chicken stock

Preheat oven to 350°
Rinse barley in water and drain.
Melt the butter in a skillet and brown pine nuts. Add onions and barley until just browned.
Combine all ingredients in a casserole dish. Bake 1 hour.

"Be not anxious about tomorrow."
Matthew 6:34

We are told we should not look back, but look to the future. However, our worries can be about our finances, being hurt, hurting someone, what will happen in our office, a sick relative or yourself, or just wasting time on trivialities. Look at the good things that are happening at this moment – the blue sky, flowers blooming, the noise of the surf, a dog barking, a child crying. Take your mind off these worries. Let Christ speak to you. God works in us, calms us, and assures us that there is a tomorrow, that there will be a sunrise. Let our joy be in what happens today. Let your mind be at peace. If today is a worrisome day, get through this day first.

One of my very oldest college friends is an investment banker on Wall Street. He survived Black Monday in 1987, and has continued to prosper during very trying times. I admire his willingness to continue when he might retire. However with one child in college, and another on the way, I am sure he has to be careful about the future. We have known each other for over forty years, and the fact our friendship continues speaks well for our relationship years ago. I sailed many lovely, and not so lovely days on Long Island Sound with him, and had the privilege of being in New York Harbor for Independence Day 1986. That day there didn't seem to be a worry on our minds, only the enjoyment of the parade of ships, good company, and the most incredible fireworks ever seen.

Stuffed Portabella Mushrooms

2 lb. portabella mushroom caps
¼ lb. fresh baby spinach
1 small round brie, finely crumbled
¼ cup pine nuts
2 scallions, chopped

2 tbls. parsley, chopped
2 tbls. dill snipped
2 tbls balsamic vinegar
Breadcrumbs

Preheat oven to 350°
Combine the spinach, brie, pine nuts, parsley, dill and vinegar in a bowl.
Divide between each of the mushroom caps. Sprinkle breadcrumbs on top.
Place on cookie sheet.
Bake 15 minutes. Can also be placed under broiler until just bubbling (watch closely)
Boursin or blue cheese can be substituted for the brie

January 21

"But Mary stood without at the sepulcher weeping: and as she wept she stooped down, and looked into the sepulcher. And seeth two angels in white sitting, the one at the head, and the other at the feet, where the body of Jesus had lain. And they say unto her, Woman, why weepest thou? She sayeth unto them, Because they have taken away my Lord, and I know not where they have laid him. And when she had thus said, she turned herself back, and saw Jesus standing, and knew not that it was Jesus...Jesus saith unto her, Touch me not; I am not yet ascended to my father: but go to my brethren, and say unto them, "I ascend unto my Father and your Father, and to my God and to your God."
John 20:11-17

Women are mentioned very prominently throughout The Bible and we see them constantly at our Lord's side during His life and the time of the Resurrection. As a women, I will highlight as many of these as possible in this book and the saints that followed.

St. Agnes who died c 305 was thirteen years old when she refused to marry, and instead dedicated her life to Christ. She was martyred in Rome. A church was later built on her grave c 354. Because of her youth she is known as the patron saint of young girls.

Spinach Frittata

Serves 4

3 tbls. butter
7 eggs
4 green onions, chopped
½ pound baby spinach

2 tbls. fresh chopped dill
1 cup grated parmesan cheese

Preheat oven to 400°
In a bowl beat the eggs.
Melt the butter in a large iron skillet. Add eggs, scraping sides so eggs do not stick. Cook for 4-5 minutes until eggs begin to set. Sprinkle with onions, spinach, dill and cheese.
Place skillet in oven. Bake for 10 minutes.
Remove and cut in 4 slices.
Serve with fresh parsley, bacon or sausage and pastries.

January 22

"Jesus loves me! This I know, For the Bible tells me so. Little ones to Him belong; They are weak, but He is strong.
Refrain: Yes, Jesus loves me! Yes, Jesus loves me! Yes, Jesus loves me! The Bible tells me so.
Jesus loves me! This I know, As He loved so long ago, Taking children on His knee, Saying, "Let them come to Me." Refrain Jesus loves me still today, Walking with me on my way, Wanting as a friend to give Light and love to all who live. Refrain Jesus loves me! He who died Heaven's gate to open wide; He will wash away my sin, Let His little child come in. Refrain Jesus loves me! He will stay Close beside me all the way; Thou hast bled and died for me,I will henceforth live for Thee .Refrain"

When we were children the first two songs we learned were *Fairest Lord Jesus* and *Jesus Loves Me*. How many now do you still hum these tunes? They can never stray far from our memories. They tell us how much Jesus loves us and that he is the fairest of all.

Anna Bartlett Warner (1827-1915) was born to a well-to-do New York family. Her father lost his fortune during the 1837 depression and the family moved to their summer home on Constitution Island in the Hudson River. Here Ms. Warner and her sister began their writing and taught Bible classes for the cadets at West Point. Today the Academy's Constitution Island Association maintains the property and Warner house as a National Registered Landmark. The site was important during the Revolution War when a chain was placed across the river to keep the British out.

Pound Cake

2 sticks unsalted butter
2 cups flour
2 cups sugar

1 tsp. almond extract
5 eggs
Powdered sugar

Preheat oven to 350°
Cream the butter and sugar in a bowl. Stir in flour. Add almond extract, and beat in eggs, one at a time.
Pour into a greased and floured bundt pan.
Bake 1 hour.
Cool. Slice and sprinkle with powdered sugar.

January 23

"As every man hath received the gift, even so minister the same one to another, as good stewards of the manifold grace of God."
1 Peter 4:10

We are all given gifts – gifts to serve, gifts to lean a shoulder on, gifts to heal, gifts to celebrate, and gifts to praise the Lord. But more importantly as stated in Romans we are given spiritual gifts that come from the Lord. *For I long to see you, that I may impart unto you some spiritual gift, to the end ye may be established; that is, I may be comforted together with you by the mutual faith, both of you and me.* Romans 1:11-12 And in Galatians *Having then gifts differing according to the grace that is given to us, whether prophecy, let us prophesy according to the proportion of faith.* Galatians 16:6 Let us show to others our gifts that the glory of God may be shown to its fullest.

Coffee Pudding

6 eggs, separated
1 cup sugar
1 cup strong coffee
3 tbls. unflavored gelatin

1/3 cup Irish whiskey
2 ¼ cups heavy whipping cream
¼ cup broken walnut pieces

Beat egg yolks with sugar until thickened.
Heat the coffee and dissolve the gelatin in it. Add to egg mixture. Heat over a double boiler until thickened.
Add whiskey. Beat until creamy.
Place the bowl over cracked ice and stir until it begins to set.
Whip 1 ¼ cups cream and fold in.
Beat egg whites until thickened. Fold into coffee mixture.
Pour into a mold with center well.
Chill to set.
Beat rest of cream. Fold in nuts.
Unmold the coffee pudding.
Put the cream and nut mixture in hole, or serve over top.

January 24

"Good Christian friends, rejoice with heart and soul and voice; Give ye heed to what we say: Jesus Christ is born today; Ox and ass before him bow, And he is in the manger now. Christ is born today! Christ is born today! Good Christian friends, rejoice With heart and soul and voice; Now ye hear of endless bliss: Jesus Christ was born for this! He has opened heaven's door, And we are blest forever more. Christ was born for this! Christ was born for this! Good Christian friends, rejoice with heart and soul and voice; Now ye need not fear the grave; Jesus Christ was born to save! Calls you one and calls you all to gain his everlasting hall. Christ was born to save! Christ was born to save!"

John Mason Neale (1818-66) was born in London, educated at Trinity College, and ordained a priest in 1842. Since his health was not good, he lived in Madeira for a while. He later founded the nursing Sisterhood of St. Margaret. Mr. Neale was proficient in numerous languages and authored over seventy books and hymns. His works include *Hymns of the Eastern Church* (1862), *Essays on Liturgiology and Church History* (1863), and *The History of the Holy Eastern Church* (1847-1873). *For Good Christian Friends* he used 7th century Latin words. He also wrote or translated *All Glory, Laud and Honor; Christ is Made the Sure Foundation; and Come Ye Faithful, Raise the Strain.*

Rice Pudding

Serves 4

1 cup uncooked basmati rice	¼ cup honey
2 cups milk	½ cup heavy cream
Zest of 1 lemon	¼ cup dark rum
Zest of 1 orange	¼ cup pistachios

In a saucepan bring the rice, milk, zests and honey to a boil. Turn off heat. Cover tightly for 20 minutes. Stir in cream and rum.
Serve garnished with pistachios.

January 25

"Giving thanks always for all things unto God and the Father, in the name of our Lord Jesus Christ."
Ephesians 5:20

Acquiring a son-in-law, particularly when your daughter is an only child, takes a little scrutiny and some poking around. Who is this man, where did he go to school, can he make enough money to take care of her, his family and friends, his upbringing and his relationship to God? These are all hard things to question, but we do want only the best, and above all for their complete happiness.

I was so fortunate. Ned is a lot older than Lucinda. However both are chefs, have high energy levels and are so suited for each other. They laugh a lot, talk alike, and enjoy the outdoors, and life. I am very thankful God brought Ned into her life. She had some bumps, he had some too. But when two people are brought together let no man put them asunder. Love overcomes all. May you be so blessed.

Coq au Vin

Serves 4

½ stick butter	1 tsp. pepper
2 leeks, sliced	1 tbls. sweet paprika
1 pint portabella mushrooms	4 boneless chicken breasts
2 cloves garlic, minced	1 tbls. tarragon
¼ cup flour	½ cup chicken stock
1 tsp. sea salt	1 cup red wine

Melt 2 tbls. butter in a large covered pan. Saute the leeks for 3 minutes. Stir in mushrooms and garlic. Place the vegetables on a plate.
Combine the flour, salt, pepper and paprika in a bowl. Dredge the chicken breasts in the flour until coated.
Add 2 tbls. butter to the pan. Brown the chicken on all sides.
Add vegetables and remaining ingredients to the pan. Bring to a boil. Cover tightly and simmer 30 minutes.
Serve over noodles.
The coq au vin can also be baked at 350° for 30 minutes.

"Finally, be strong in the Lord and in his mighty power. Put on the full armor of God so that you can take your stand against the devil's schemes. For our struggle is not against flesh and blood, but against the rulers, against the authorities, against the powers of this dark world and against the spiritual forces of evil in the heavenly realms. Therefore put on the full armor of God, so that when the day of evil comes, you may be able to stand your ground, and after you have done everything, to stand. Stand firm then, with the belt of truth buckled around your waist, with the breastplate of righteousness in place, and with your feet fitted with the readiness that comes from the gospel of peace. In addition to all this, take up the shield of faith, with which you can extinguish all the flaming arrows of the evil one. Take the helmet of salvation and the sword of the Spirit, which is the word of God. And pray in the Spirit on all occasions with all kinds of prayers and requests. With this in mind, be alert and always keep on praying for all the saints. Pray also for me, that whenever I open my mouth, words may be given me so that I will fearlessly make known the mystery of the gospel, for which I am an ambassador in chains. Pray that I may declare it fearlessly, as I should."
Ephesians 6:10-19

This is one of the most powerful passages in the Bible. We are asked to stand up for everything God has given us. We must continue daily to pray, to put on the armour – the Truth, to keep our faith, and use the Word of God, shout it out that all may hear. Do not be afraid. God gives us strength. We cannot fall down or fail Him. He hears our every word, sees our every movement, and knows everything about us. Do not fail the Lord.

Rice with Peppers

Serves 4

2 tbls olive oil	1 yellow pepper, chopped
2 leeks, chopped	1 tsp. cumin
2½ cups chicken stock	1 tsp. ground ginger
2 cups basmati rice	2 tbls. pignoli
2 cloves garlic, minced	¼ cup cilantro, chopped
1 red pepper, chopped	

Heat the olive oil in a pan. Stir in rice for five minutes. Add chicken stock, garlic, rice, pepper, cumin, and ginger. Bring to a boil. Let simmer 15 minutes, or until all water is gone and rice is fluffy.
Serve garnished with pignoli and cilantro.

January 27

"Grant them eternal rest, O Lord, and may perpetual light shine on them. Thou, O God, art praised in Sion, and unto thee shall the vow be performed in Jerusalem. Hear my prayer, unto Thee shall all flesh come. Grant them eternal rest, O Lord, and may perpetual light shine on them."
Mozart's *Requiem Introitus*

Wolfgang Amadeus Mozart (1756-91), born in Salzburg lived a short life, but during that time he composed some of the greatest music, including his Requiem in 1791 and never completed at his death. He began playing the clavier at age three and by age five was composing his first pieces. Beginning in 1773 he served as court musician in Salzburg, but finding the salary meager, resigned. Sadly he lived most of his life in debt, though he did return to Salzburg after traveling in Europe as court organist and concertmaster. His great ambition was to write operas. He eventually found work in Vienna, and went on to compose *Don Giovanni* and The *Marriage of Figaro*, and *The Magic Flute*, all very successful operas.

One Sunday, while visiting Paris, we arrived at Notre Dame Cathedral. Music filled the huge nave. It was Mozart's birthday and the whole service was comprised of his compositions. The weather outside was winter – dark and gloomy, but inside, the Cathedral resonated with joy, hope and praise for our Lord.

Pear Pie

1 pie crust	Zest of 1 lemon
½ cup sugar	2 tbls. lemon juice
½ cup brown sugar	1 tsp. cinnamon
1 stick butter	½ tsp. nutmeg
1 cup flour	1 tbls. fresh grated ginger
6 ripe pears, peeled and sliced	

Preheat oven to 400°
Bake pie crust for 10 minutes
Turn oven down to 375°
In a bowl cream the sugars and butter. Beat in flour until crumbly.
Line the pie plate, going in circles with the pears. Sprinkle with the zest, lemon juice, cinnamon, nutmeg and ginger.
Spread sugar butter topping over the pears.
Bake 45 minutes.
Serve with whipped cream or ice cream. Sprinkle with fresh grated nutmeg.

January 28

"Come you that are blessed by my Father, inherit the kingdom prepared for you from the foundation of the world; for I was hungry and you gave me food, I was thirsty and you gave me something to drink, I was a stranger and you welcomed me, I was naked and you gave me clothing, I was sick and you took care of me, I was in prison and you visited me."
Matthew 25:34-36

No matter where we are, the Lord is always with us. He never leaves us. Only we leave him. God does give us everything we need. We shall never want.

Thomas Aquinas (1225-74) came from a well-to-do family in Naples, Italy. At the University of Naples he secretly joined the Dominican friars. When his family found out, they kidnapped and imprisoned him for a year. Eventually he was allowed to study, and taught in Paris and Italy. His greatest work is the *Summa Theologia*, written in 1266, a book of theological questions and his answers.

Stuffed Mussels

24 mussels, scrubbed and beards removed
1 cup dry white wine
½ stick butter
1 leek chopped
2 shallots, chopped
2 cloves garlic, crushed

2 tbls. tarragon
2 tbls. parsley
2 tbls. basil
1 tsp. sea salt
1 tsp. pepper
¼ cup grated parmesan cheese

Cook the mussels in the wine until they open. Remove the mussels from the pan and place on a baking sheet.
Save one shell from each mussel. Reserve liquid.
Heat the butter in a skillet. Saute leeks, shallot and garlic until tender. Stir in tarragon, parsley, basil, salt and pepper. Add liquid and mussels.
Preheat oven to 350°
Place a mussel in each shell. Pour herbs and liquid over each mussel. Top with parmesan cheese.
Bake 10 minutes.
Instead of stuffing the mussel shells the mussels can be served over pasta, or with crusty bread.

January 29

"Charity and devotion differ no more from each other than fire does from flame; for charity is a spiritual fire, which, when inflamed, is called devotion. Hence it appears that devotion adds nothing to the fire of charity but the flame, which makes it ready, active, and diligent, not only in the observance of the commandments of God, but also in the execution of His heavenly counsels and inspirations."
Introduction to the Devout Life

As good Christians we are taught to give of ourselves to others and to be devout to our God. We do this through giving to the poor, building churches, and to assure those who are suffering that God is with them and their mind can be at peace. We are devout to God through prayer and meditation. He gives us inspiration, and by following his commandments we can lead a more godly life.

Saint Francis de Sales (1567 -1622) was Bishop of Geneva. He worked to convert Protestants, especially Calvinists back to Catholicism. He wrote two books to back up his religious views - *Introduction to the Devout Life* and *A Treatise on the Love of God*. The Saint was beatified by Pope Alexander VII in 1661 and canonized in 1665. He was declared a Doctor of the Church by Blessed Pius IX in 1877. He also helped St. Jane Frances de Chantal to establish the Sisters of the Visitation. He is the patron saint of writers and the deaf.

Potato Delight

Serves 12

4 lbs. red bliss potatoes, sliced
1 stick butter, melted
1 8 oz. package cream cheese
½ red pepper, chopped
½ green pepper, chopped
6 scallions, chopped

½ cup grated parmesan cheese
½ cup grated Swiss cheese
¼ cup milk
1 tsp. kosher salt
1 tsp. pepper
¼ cup basil, chopped

Preheat oven to 350°
Cook potatoes. Drain.
In a bowl combine all the ingredients, except potatoes.
Place the potatoes in a baking dish. Top with butter mixture.
Bake 25 minutes, or until just browned and bubbling.

January 30

"As the apple tree among the trees of the wood, so is my beloved among the sons. I sat down under his shadow with great delight, and his fruit was sweet to my taste."
Song of Solomon 2:3

"Who is this that cometh up from the wilderness, leaning upon her beloved? I raised thee up under the apple tree: there thy mother brought thee forth: there she brought thee forth that bare thee."
Song of Solomon 8:5

Apple trees were not common in ancient times, and it is now thought the apples mentioned in the Bible were most likely apricots. The climate would have been much too warm. Apples are mentioned six times in The Bible. The trees probably provided a fragrance, shade, and were beautiful to behold. This passage speaks of the virtues of the fruit, and his beloved, a virtuous woman, who is a sight to behold.

Apricots grow in abundance in the Holy Land. In Greece apricots are called golden apples. Apricots are delicious in the summer, eaten as is, in a dessert, or as juice.

Apricot Pudding

Serves 4

2 cups water   3 tbls. cornstarch
1 cup dried apricots   Whipped cream
¼ cup sugar

In a sauce pan bring the water and apricots to a boil. Simmer 20 minutes. Puree ½ cup liquid and apricots in a food processor.
Combine the sugar and cornstarch in the pan. Stir in apricot puree and remaining liquid. Bring to boil.
Serve in individual bowls with whipped cream.

January 31

"Behold thy cousin Elizabeth..."
Luke 1:36

"All the days of the afflicted are evil: but he that is of a merry heart hath a continual feast."
Proverbs 15:15

You are often closer to cousins than your own siblings. Aunties can be closer to their nieces and nephews than parents, and they often resemble each other. As the oldest of ten cousins I get teased about my age, especially by the next in line. We so close to each other, and have shared all of life's ups and downs. She rides, I'm afraid of heights. She's a stock broker. I'm helpless with numbers. She's a Scottish hoarder. My house has to be in order. I can write. She can count. You know what I'm talking about. However, communication between the two of us doesn't rely on numbers, or horses, who's wearing what, or how lousy the day is. We try to keep laughing, even when several old family friends die in the same week, and others have lost their jobs. Laughter keeps us going, keeps us happy, makes us smile and gives us a healthier cheery heart.

Bean and Corn Salsa

1 can black beans, drained	½ yellow pepper, chopped finely
1 cup fresh corn	¼ cup olive oil
2 large tomatoes, finely chopped	2 tbls. vinegar
1 cup cilantro, chopped	Dash cayenne
4 green onions, chopped	½ tsp. chili powder
2 cloves garlic, crushed	½ tsp. cumin

Combine ingredients in a bowl.
Serve with corn chips, or toasted tortilla triangles

February 1

"Rejoice ye pure in heart; Rejoice, give thanks, and sing; Your glorious banner wave on high, The cross of Christ your King.
Refrain Rejoice, rejoice, rejoice, Give thanks and sing.
Then on, ye pure in heart! Rejoice, give thanks and sing! Your glorious banner wave on high, The cross of Christ your King. Refrain Praise Him Who reigns on high, The Lord Whom we adore, The Father, Son and Holy Ghost, One God forevermore. Refrain"
Edward Plumptre

Rejoice in the Lord alway; and again, I say rejoice."
Philippians 4:4

Each day when you wake up rejoice in the Lord. Thank Him for all that He has given you. The day may be dark and dreary, or you may be having a hard time, but rejoice. He brought you into this world. Pray that each day will get better. Rejoice, give thanks and sing.

Edward Hayes Plumptre (1821-1891) graduated from Oxford, was ordained and became the Dean of Wells Cathedral. He also was a professor of Pastoral Theology at Kings College, London. This hymn was written for the Peterborough Choral Festival in May 1865 and was first sung in the Peterborough Cathedral.

Potato Muffins

Serves 4

2 large red bliss potatoes, cubed
¼ cup milk
½ stick butter
½ cup grated cheddar cheese
1 leek, chopped

½ tsp. salt
1 tsp. pepper
¼ tsp. nutmeg
1 egg, separated

Cook the potatoes in boiling water until tender.
Preheat oven to 400°
In a bowl mash the potatoes with the milk, butter, cheese, onions, salt, pepper, nutmeg and egg yolks.
In a separate bowl beat the egg whites until stiff. Fold into the potatoes.
Spoon the mixture into greased muffin tins. Bake 15 minutes.
The dough can also be formed into balls and sautéed in butter, or fried.

February 2

"Be of good courage and He shall strengthen thine heart."
Psalm 27:14

February used to be the month we honored our two most famous Presidents –
George Washington and Abraham Lincoln. Now the month honors Black
History and little mention is made of the Presidents. I truly wish they had chosen
a different month for Black History Month. Under each President a war was
fought, each forever changing our country. George Washington won freedom for
American citizens suppressed by the British. Abraham Lincoln won freedom for
slaves. We cannot forget these two great men. President Washington served two
terms as our first President before retiring to his plantation, Mount Vernon,
where he died three years later. President Lincoln was assassinated before he
could see the changes that would occur in this country after the Emancipation
Proclamation freed the slaves. Remember those who chose to do the right thing
for our country. Elect to public office those who know and follow the Lord.

Spoon Bread

3 cups corn
3 cups milk
1 tsp. salt
1 cup cornmeal
½ stick butter

1 leek, chopped finely
1 tsp. baking powder
3 eggs, separated
1 tbls. sugar
2 tbls. snipped chives

Preheat oven to 350°
Bring the corn and milk to a boil in a sauce pan. Slowly stir in salt and cornmeal
until thickened. Remove from heat and stir in butter, leek, baking powder and
egg yolks.
Beat egg white until peaks form.
Fold egg whites, sugar and chives into the corn.
Pour into a buttered casserole.
Bake 45 minutes.
Serve hot.

"All we like sheep have gone astray; we have all turned to our own way, and the Lord has laid on him the iniquity of us all."
Isaiah 53:6

I always knew the Yale Whiffenpoof song could be easily hummed, but I also thought it had Biblical origins. You know the little lost lambs. Well, I have now been straightened out, and have since found out the song comes from "Gentlemen Rankers", a ballad written by Guy Scull, Harvard class of 1898, although Judge Tod Galloway, Amherst 1885 may also have written it. Back when the Whiffenpoofs was founded they were called "The Growlers". By 1908-09 they became the Whiffenpoofs. If you ever have a chance to hear them sing you will be amazed and delighted as this group still holds forth, singing many of the songs from the original groups.

The words in the song are *"We're poor little lambs who've lost our way, Baa! Baa! Baa! Little black sheep who've gone astray, Baa-aa-aa!"*

So if you compare Isaiah and this you can see why I was confused. Anyway I love the words, and with many family members attending Yale I often find myself singing *"To the tables down at Mory's"* or *"we're poor little lambs."*.

My cousin was a member of the group when they made their 50th anniversary record. My parents played it over and over. Somehow I have got to make a copy on a CD. And at Mory's they may well have eaten mutton and had a few good beers!

Grilled Leg of Lamb

Serves 6

4½ lbs. boneless leg of lamb	¼ cup rosemary
¼ cup fresh ground pepper	1 tbls. cumin
2 tbls. garlic	¼ cup olive oil

In a bowl combine the pepper, garlic, rosemary, cumin and olive oil. Rub the lamb with the mixture.
Grill on BBQ until desired pinkness.
Serve with mint sauce made of mint, garlic, lime juice and sour cream.

"Only he who believes is obedient and only he who is obedient believes."
Dietrich Bonhoeffer

"That I may know him, and the power of his resurrection, and the fellowship of his sufferings, being made comfortable unto his death...Brethren I count not myself to have apprehended: but this one thing I do, forgetting these things which are behind, and reaching forth unto those things which are before, I press toward the mark for the prize of the high calling of God in Jesus Christ."
Philippians 3:10-14

A truly good Christian is one that believes and is obedient to the Highest, our Lord and God. We read his Word, accept it for the truth, and live our lives according to it. Straying only brings disillusionment, doubts, and darkness, not the light that shines from the Lord. Feel his presence, open your eyes, and pray. God is with you, and you are His.

The modern world lost a great theologian when Dietrich Bonhoeffer urged the church to stand by the Jews during the Second World War. He was killed for his convictions. Mr. Bonhoeffer (1906-45) was a Lutheran pastor and theologian.
He received his doctorate in theology from the University of Berlin at age 21 and then attended Union Theological Seminary. While in New York he visited the Abyssinian Baptist Church in Harlem and became acquainted with the African-American spiritual music. His best known books are *Cost of Discipleship, Letters and Papers from Prison*, and *Ethics*. He was active in the German Resistance and as a member of the Confessing Church, part of the planning group to assassinate Adolph Hitler. He was caught, imprisoned at Flossenburg Concentration Camp, and then hanged.

Spinach Soup

Serves 6

½ stick butter
2 leeks, chopped
1 lb. baby spinach
2 cloves garlic, minced

¼ tsp. nutmeg
4 cups chicken stock
2 cups heavy cream
Chives or dill, snipped

Melt the butter in a pan. Stir in leeks and spinach. Cook until just tender. Add garlic and nutmeg. Pour into a food processor until pureed.
Pour back into the pan. Add stock and cream. Heat
Serve in soup bowls with chives or dill as garnish

"Come unto Me, all ye that labour and are heavy laden, and I will give you rest."
Matthew 11:28

Winter seems to drag on, the snow falls, the streets ice, and our hearts and minds drag. We need some sunshine, something to lift our spirits. Reading a good book, looking at brochures on warmer climes, or lunching with a friend can change your frame of mind. But Lord, I am weary. I need something more. I need to find you so that you can guide me. I am lost not just weary from the winter. Too many troubling things are happening in my life. Friends are sick, or even dying. I lost my job. I lost my husband. I feel like I'm losing me. But Lord, I know you are there. You watch over me. You love me. Help me out of my distress. Lord I promise to set aside time each day for prayer, for singing, and finding time for you. I trust you Lord. I know the Word and you will answer my prayers. I will be made whole again. I will not fear.

"By prayer and supplication with thanksgiving. Let your requests be made known unto God."
Philippians 4:6

Lamb Soup

Serves 4

½ stick butter	1 tbls. paprika
1 lb. lamb, finely diced	¼ tsp. cayenne
2 carrots, sliced	1 tsp. cinnamon
1 onion, chopped	4 cups beef stock
1 leek, sliced	2 egg yolks
1 pint mushrooms, sliced	Zest of 1 lemon
2 cloves garlic, crushed	Juice of 1 lemon
¼ cup flour	Parsley

Melt the butter in a sauce pan. Stir in lamb, carrots, onions, leek and mushrooms. Saute for 10 minutes. Stir in flour. Add paprika, cayenne, cinnamon and stock. Bring to a boil and simmer 1 hour.
Just before serving beat the egg yolks. Slowly stir into soup, along with the zest and lemon juice.
Serve in bowls garnished with parsley. Good with crusty bread and a salad.

February 6

"But that ye may know that the Son of man hath power upon earth to forgive sins, (he said unto the sick of the palsy,) I say unto thee, Arise, and take up thy couch, and go into thine house. And immediately he rose up before them, and took up that whereon he lay, and departed to his own house, glorifying God. And they were all amazed, and they glorified God, and were filled with fear, saying, We have seen strange things to day."
Luke 5:24-26

Ever since I was a child my great love has been travel and meeting people of every nationality. In college I was a member of the International Club. Wherever I moved I belonged to or was president of the local international visitor center. I have not traveled as much I had hoped, but there are plenty of years left.

While living in Greenwich I met a group of international ladies who wanted to form a book group. However, with our varied interests, we would gather weekly and discuss one topic, not a book. One lady was a journalist from South Africa, who visited when Apartheid was unraveling and came back with a published story. Another was Japanese and headed up the Japan-America Society. Another, Chilean and a member of a mining family. We were also Americans with diverse backgrounds. Our host who founded the group was head of an educational placements service company. She lived in a gracious condo overlooking Greenwich and loved to entertain. She also realized if she were to maintain her lifestyle she would have to move into a smaller place. After residing there for several years she decided to move closer to her daughter who was a partner in her business. Just as she was about to move out the ceiling from the apartment above crashed into hers, crushing her legs. After surgery and agonizing therapy she once again can play tennis and golf. Her faith was strong. She had been an active church member, served with the Stephen Ministry, and in her new town found a Benedictine Monastery offering evensong. I have now twice attended this service with her. She is blessed to be alive and healed!

Salmon with Mango Sauce

Serves 4

4 salmon filets
1 large mango, peeled and diced
½ cup maple syrup

¼ cup lemon juice
2 tbls. mint

Grill the salmon on a BBQ.
Combine the mango, maple syrup, lemon juice and mint in a bowl.

February 7

How many times have you yearned to be rich? Is it to have a bigger house, more expensive car, to send your children to private schools, and to wear the latest Paris fashions? God gave each one of us gifts. What we must strive for are not the material riches of the earth, but to chose to see all the blessings of God. Each day that the flowers bloom, the birds sing, and the sun shines, that is a blessing that no money can pay for. Appreciate the beauty of the earth, preserve what God has given us. Make each moment count. Don't look down, always look up.

Peanut Butter Pie

Crust

½ box chocolate wafers   ¼ cup sugar
½ stick butter, melted

Combine the ingredients in a food processor. Press into a pie plate.

Filling

8 oz. cream cheese   1 cup heavy cream
1 cup chunky peanut butter   1 cup peanuts
½ cup sugar

In a bowl beat together the cream cheese and peanut butter.
In another bowl beat the cream until peaks form. Fold in sugar, cream cheese mixture and peanuts.
Pour into pie crust.
Refrigerate at least 2 hours.

Chocolate Sauce

4 oz. semi sweet chocolate   ½ cup sugar
½ cup heavy cream

Combine the ingredients in a saucepan. Heat until melted.
Drizzle over pie.

February 8

"And to know the love of Christ which passeth knowledge, that we might be filled with all the fullness of God. Now unto him that is able to do exceeding abundantly above all that we ask or think, according to the power that worketh in us, Unto him be glory in the church by Christ Jesus throughout all ages, world without end. Amen."
Ephesians 3:19-21

Throughout the Old Testament, God's people turned from him. They were stubborn, they disobeyed, even when Moses spoke to his people, even when he climbed the mount to receive the Ten Commandments. When we turn to the New Testament God's love shines through our Lord Jesus Christ. We turn to Him. When we find love, we also strengthen our relationship with God. Through Him he teaches us love. He teaches us to love our family, our friends, even our enemies. Thank Him for opening the door to finding courage to love.

Bread Salad

Serves 4

2 large onions, thinly sliced	1 lb. cherry tomatoes, cut in half
¼ cup balsamic vinegar	½ lb. feta cheese
½ lb. baby spring greens	4 slices ciabatta bread, cubed

Combine the ingredients in a bowl with the pesto dressing.

Pesto Dressing

1 large bunch basil leaves	¼ cup fresh grated parmesan cheese
2 large cloves garlic	2 tbls. lemon juice
¼ cup olive oil	½ tsp. salt
2 tbls. pignoli	½ tsp. pepper

Combine the ingredients in a food processor.

"A certain man went down from Jerusalem to Jericho, and fell among thieves, which stripped him of his raiment, and wounded him, and departed, leaving him half dead. And by chance there came down a certain priest that way: and when he saw him, he passed by on the other side. And likewise a Levite, when he was at the place, came and looked on him, and passed by on the other side. But a certain Samaritan, as he journeyed, came where he was; and when he saw him had compassion on him. And went to him, and bound up his wounds, pouring oil and wine, and set him on his own beast, and brought him to an inn, and took care of him."
Luke 10: 30-34

Friends happen in the most unexpected way. While living in Providence I met a lovely lady who had grown up in Philadelphia. Having lived in that city for 4 years I knew it well. We struck up a lively conversation. Not long after that she called to say she had to leave her husband, and needed a place to stay. With four bedrooms my daughter and I had plenty of room. After several weeks she moved to San Francisco to start a new life. Thank goodness she did, several years later meeting an exceptional gentleman. They are happily married, and our paths still cross. Now it is mainly when she comes East to see her brother who recently had a heart transplant. She still reminds me of that special time we spent together, and how I, almost a stranger, took her in. Good friends are for life.

Bourbon Cake

1 stick butter	¼ cup milk
1 cup sugar	¼ cup molasses
3 eggs	2 cups raisins or currants
1¾ cup flour	2 cups pecans or walnuts
1 tsp. baking powder	½ cup bourbon
½ tsp. nutmeg	

Preheat oven to 300°
Cream the butter in a bowl and stir in sugar and eggs. Mix in flour and other ingredients.
Pour into 2 buttered and floured pans. Cook for 2 hours.
Cool. Wrap and store in refrigerator. Add more bourbon while storing.

February 10

"Thy lips, O my spouse, drop as the honeycomb: honey and milk are under thy tongue; and the smell of thy garments is like the smell of Lebanon."
Song of Solomon 4:11

Valentine's Day is approaching, time to find a special gift for your favorite love. I love reading the Song of Solomon, how he sings praises to his love. This was written as poem of love. Solomon is not yet engaged to this young lady, but he sings of her charm, and she moves him. Eventually he wins her over and she becomes his wife. However if you look at the song carefully it sings of the love of God. God looks after his people, He is the King, He feeds his flock, and He loves us all. We, like the woman, in the poem are hesitant in our love. We don't need to be. Love is everywhere. Do not be afraid to share your love. You don't need to buy a present. Make something, cook a special meal, pick some flowers if you live in a warm climate, or go for a walk with your love. Hold that person in your arms, and give him or her, a long and loving kiss.

Pistachio Puffs

Makes 12

2 sticks butter, melted
1 cup unsalted shelled pistachios, chopped

1 cup almonds, chopped
¼ cup sugar
12 sheets phyllo

Preheat the oven to 400°
Combine the nuts and sugar in a bowl.
Brush each phyllo sheet with butter. Fold each sheet in half and brush the top with butter. Sprinkle each sheet with rest of butter and nuts. Shape the phyllo into a nest shape by folding edges over and then tucking in ends of dough. Arrange on a baking sheet. Bake 20 minutes.
Serve with Syrup.

Syrup

2½ cup sugar
1¼ cup water

Zest of ½ lemon
Juice of ½ lemon

Combine sugar and water in a heavy saucepan. Bring to a boil, add lemon rind and juice. Boil for 15 minutes. Cool and strain into a bowl. Chill.

Christ said, "That many shall come from the east and the west, and shall sit down with Abraham, and Isaac, and Jacob, in the kingdom of heaven."
Matthew 8:11

"For where two or three are gathered together in my name, there am I in the midst of them."
Matthew 18:20

Most years we give a Chinese New Year party. We invite friends of every nationality. I do the menu planning and all the cooking. One year, while living in Newport, we had a monstrous blizzard. I mean it did not let up. My co-host was an architect, who without consulting me, decided to cancel the party. I had to recall everyone on our list and say yes it was on. Park, walk, sled, but if you can, get to the house, the party is on. The food had been prepared, the house decorated, and I was ready. Everyone showed up.

Like the party the number of Christians in China continues to grow. They meet in offices, homes, churches, parks, wherever two or three can gather together. I admire them for their perseverance, their devotion to our Lord, when they could immediately be arrested, tortured, or even killed. Please pray for our brethren in China and elsewhere where there is repression. *"In Christ There is no East or West"*- hymn by William Dunkerley 1908

Chinese New Year Stir Fry

Serves 4

2 tbls. soy sauce
2 tbls. sherry
2 tbls. fresh grated ginger
4 small boneless chicken breasts, cut into strips
Sesame oil
½ red pepper, sliced
½ yellow pepper, sliced

4 green onions, sliced
4 stalks asparagus, sliced
1 large carrot, peeled and sliced
½ lb. snow peas
½ lb. mushrooms, sliced
½ cup fresh basil leaves
4 cloves garlic, minced

In a bowl combine the soy sauce, sherry, and ginger. Add the chicken. Cover and marinate for at least 1 hour.
Heat some sesame oil in a wok. Quickly cook the chicken. Remove.
Add more oil to the wok. Stir in vegetables, basil and garlic. Stir in chicken.
Serve with rice and extra soy sauce.

February 12

"Only be thou strong and very courageous, that thou mayest observe to do according to all the law, which Moses my servant commanded thee: turn not from it to the right hand or to the left, that thou mayest prosper whithersoever thou goest."
Joshua 1:7

On October 17, 1965 F4B Phantom Fighters were shot down over Vietnam. One of the first people I met through the Junior League of Providence was the wife of one of the pilots. For seven and a half years her husband was held prisoner. He along with John McCain and so many others endured torture beyond anything most people could imagine. He was released on February 12, 1973. Unlike some World War II veterans who do not discuss their combat duty, those released from POW camps in Vietnam have been more open. My friend's baby was born just months before he was shot down. For all those years she did not know whether he was dead or alive. These men had strength, even in isolation, to pray, to remember favorite hymns, and only hope that their fate would not be death. These men served their country, this great country of ours with honor. Thank you Lord for being with them, giving them strength that they might prosper.

Pasta and Smoked Salmon

Serves 4

½ stick butter
1 leek, sliced
½ lb. asparagus, trimmed and sliced in 1" pieces
2 shallots, minced
2 cloves garlic, minced
Zest of 1 lemon
2 tbls. lemon juice

1 lb. smoked salmon, cut into bite size pieces
1½ cups heavy cream
1 tsp. fresh ground pepper
1 lb. fettuccine
¼ cup dill, snipped
Parmesan cheese

Melt the butter in a sauce pan. Saute the leek, asparagus, and shallots until just tender. Stir in garlic, lemon juice, and zest. At last minute before serving add salmon, cream and pepper.
Cook the fettuccine according to instructions. Drain.
Spoon the fettuccine into pasta bowls. Top with salmon sauce.
Garnish with dill and parmesan cheese.

February 13

"My soul waiteth for the Lord more than they that watch for the morning: I say more than they that watch for the morning."
Psalm 130:6

My favorite part of the day is the early morning with the sun rising, the sky turning bright pink and yellow, and clouds billowing. The same can said about the end of day when the sky is more purple and pink. I feel vigorous, happy, and ready to thank the Lord for another day. Get up. Don't stay in bed. Life is a fleeting moment that must be savored to its fullest.

"Morning has Broken like the First Morning"

This hymn was written in 1922 by Eleanor Farjeon (1881-1965), an English author, poet, playwright and broadcaster. Her book *Martin Pippin in the Apple Orchard* became a bestseller and was the beginning of a series on Martin Pippin. The story is absolutely charming with lovely little sentences, rhymes, and songs, with illustrations by Richard Kennedy. Ms. Farjeon was first inspired to write the story while visiting Brittany in 1907, but didn't finish the story until years later. Step back into your childhood and enjoy.

Seafood Frittata

Serves 4

7 eggs	½ lb. crab meat
2 tbls. cream	½ lb. lobster meat
3 tbls. butter	½ cup grated parmesan cheese
1 leek, sliced	2 tbls. dill, snipped
1 pint mushrooms, sliced	2 tbls. parsley, chopped

Preheat oven to 400°
In a bowl beat the eggs and cream until fluffy.
Melt the butter in an iron skillet. Pour the eggs in. Scrape sides to keep from sticking.
As eggs begin to set, sprinkle the other ingredients on top.
Bake 10 minutes.
Divide into 4 sections. Garnish with extra dill and parsley.

February 14

"My flesh and my heart faileth, but God is the strength of my heart, and my portion forever."
Psalm 73:26

My heart hangs heavy today. It's supposed to be Valentine's Day, but I haven't gotten any Valentine's, not even from my daughter. Yes, we had gone and gotten them for her step sibling's and her father's family, but I didn't get anything. I felt lost, unhappy, and out of sorts. I couldn't concentrate. I could cry. I only wish then I had known the Lord as I do now. I could have reached out to Him, to let Him walk with me, to speak to me. Instead I sank into a pit that eventually led to the loss of my daughter, when my ex took custody of her. I had done nothing wrong. She wanted to live with a family, and I could not give it to her at this time.

St. Valentine is thought to be one of two people – a priest martyred in Rome c269, and a bishop of Terni, Umbria, who was also executed in Rome. Both of these men gave their lives for Christ. From ancient times it was thought birds chose their mates on February 14. The festival of Lupercalia, held at the same time, was to find fertility. I only hope that on this day families think about each other and exchange messages or signs of love. The Lord is our strength.

Chocolate Mousse

Serves 4

½ cup sugar	1½ cups heavy cream
4 tbls. espresso	1 tsp. Amaretto or Grand Marnier
4 oz. dark chocolate	1 pint raspberries
4 egg whites	Shaved chocolate

Heat the espresso and dissolve sugar. Add chocolate until melted.
Beat the egg whites until stiff.
Beat the cream until thickened.
Pour the chocolate into a greased soufflé dish. Fold in egg whites, cream and Amaretto.
Freeze.
Remove from freezer about ½ hour before serving.
Serve with raspberries and shave chocolate. Can also be served with whipped cream.

February 15

"But we appeal to you, brothers and sisters, to respect those who labor among you, and have charge of you in the Lord and admonish you; esteem them very highly in love because of their work."
1 Thessalonians 5:12

If you are like me, you thrill to know a bishop will be visiting your church. He (she) arrives in an alb (tunic) wearing a bishop's ring, pectoral cross and miter, and carrying a crozier. Even more incredible is to be at the installation of a bishop as Presiding Bishop when all are dressed in red inside a cathedral. Bishops are clergy who are elected to oversee a diocese and can ordain clergy and confirm.

Bishop Henry Whipple (1822-1901) was raised in the Presbyterian Church but became an Episcopalian through the influence of his grandparents and his wife, Cornelia. After his ordination he worked with poor immigrant groups in New York and Chicago. He was elected the first Episcopal bishop of Minnesota in 1859. He was a champion of Native American causes in Minnesota.

Bishop Whipple's Pudding

1 tbls. butter
2 eggs
½ cup sugar
2/3 cup flour
1 tsp. baking powder

½ tsp. vanilla
1 cup pecans
1 cup pitted dates
1 cup heavy cream
2 tbls. brandy or sherry

Preheat oven to 350°
Grease a soufflé dish with the butter.
In a bowl beat the eggs until fluffy. Beat in sugar, flour and baking powder. Add vanilla, nuts, and dates.
Pour into a soufflé dish. Bake 25 minutes. Remove from oven and let cool.
In a bowl beat the cream until peaks form. Stir in brandy or sherry.
Serve pudding with cream and brandy sauce.

February 16

"Master, which is the greatest commandment in the law? Jesus said unto him, Thou shalt love the Lord thy God with all thy heart, and with all thy soul, and with all thy mind. This is the first and greatest commandment. And the second is like unto it, Thou shalt love thy neighbor as thyself. On these two commandments hang all the law and prophets."
Matthew 22:36-40

A person is blessed when he or she can love. Love comes early from our parents, and when it is not there, children suffer. A void in young lives often lasts a lifetime, and that person may never learn to love. Through love we show empathy to others. We can hug or kiss, tell them we love them. Even though they may not tell or show us their love, love can be reflected in their actions, their eyes, or the unspoken word. If you really do love someone tell them. I'll never forget years ago when a dear friend told me she loved me. My daughter said, "Mom you love other women?" I said, as one of my oldest friends, I could tell her how much I love her. She was my soul mate, someone I could share my innermost thoughts with, which we still do after forty plus years. I know it is a deep, heartfelt love. I know my feelings come from the Lord. He loves me, and I Him. *"Love is patient and kind; love is not jealous or boastful...Love bears all things, believes all things, hopes all things, endures all things."* 1 Corinthians 13:4-7

Blue Cheese Salad

Serves 4

¼ cup olive oil
2 tbls. red wine vinegar
1 tbls. grainy mustard
1 tsp. fresh ground pepper

½ pound mixed spring greens
4 slices bacon, cooked and chopped
12 grape tomatoes
1 cup blue cheese or Gorgonzola
1 avocado, peeled and sliced

Whisk together the olive oil, vinegar, mustard and pepper in the bottom of a salad bowl.
Add other ingredients and toss. Serve immediately.

February 17

"God is our refuge and strength, a very present help in trouble."
Psalm 46:1

I hadn't been feeling well for several days. I was going to work, but getting painful headaches, blurriness in my eyes, and really feeling rundown. This was not my usual self. On Sunday morning my husband headed off to the yacht club for his weekly duties for the frostbite races. I started to dress for church, but no energy and the right side of my face didn't look too good. I ran to the computer to see if I could figure out what might be wrong. What appeared on the screen absolutely shocked me – brain tumor or stroke. I quickly drove the mile to the hospital, checked myself in, and luckily they hooked me up right away. No heart attack, but definitely TIAs. I called my husband who rushed home. Four days later, after every test possible they released me from the hospital. I stayed home for two weeks, just trying to rest. I was restless to return to work. That was a bad mistake and I ended up in the hospital twice more.

When our bodies tell us to slow down, we need to. Where I worked two government officials had died of heart attacks within a month of each other. I could have been next. Luckily I took precautions, though not quick enough, and I prayed a lot. Thank goodness for my support groups – a Bible Study and prayer group, and visits from some of their members. I am very thankful, Lord. You gave me strength when I was in trouble.

Lemon Squares

2 cups flour	Zest of 1 lemon
2 cups confectioner's sugar	¼ cup flour
2 sticks butter	½ tsp. baking powder
4 eggs	2 cups sugar
1/3 cup lemon juice	

Preheat oven to 350°
Cream flour, sugar and butter in a bowl. Press into a 9x13 baking dish.
Bake 20 minutes.
Combine other ingredients. Pour over baked mixture.
Bake 25 minutes.
Sprinkle with confectioner's sugar.

February 18

"Lord, who throughout these forty days For us didst fast and pray, Teach us with Thee to mourn our sins And close by Thee to stay. As Thou with Satan didst contend, And didst the victory win, O give us strength in Thee to fight, In Thee to conquer sin. As Thou didst hunger bear, and thirst, So teach us, gracious Lord, To die to self, and chiefly live By Thy most holy Word. And through these days of penitence, And through Thy passiontide, Yea, evermore in life and death, Jesus, with us abide. Abide with us, that so, this life Of suffering over past, An Easter of unending joy We may attain at last."

Claudia Frances Hernaman (1838-98) wrote this hymn which is usually sung on the first day of Lent. The music is from St. Flavian, *Day's Psalter*, 1563. *"Then was Jesus led up of the spirit into the wilderness to be tempted of the devil. And when he had fasted forty days and forty nights, he was afterward an hungred."* Matthew 4:1-2

Most of us give up things for Lent, but do not go into the wilderness. Here, Jesus, having survived this ordeal, is tempted by Satan. He will not give in, nor should you. *"Then Jesus saith unto him (Satan) ...Thou shalt worship the Lord thy God, and him only shalt thou serve."* Matthew 4:10 Jesus is always with us, he suffered for us, and through we must live by his Word. Never, no never give him up.

Broccoli Salad

Serves 6

1 cup mayonnaise	1 cup raisins
½ cup sugar	1 cup pecans
¼ cup white vinegar	1 cup fresh peas
2 lbs. broccoli flowerets	4 slices bacon, cooked and
1 large red onion, thinly sliced	crumbled

In a salad bowl combine the mayonnaise, sugar and vinegar.
Toss in the other ingredients.
¼ cup honey can be substituted for the sugar.

February 19

"Train up a child in the way he should go: and when (s)he is old, (s)he will not depart from it."
Proverbs 22:6

Mothers can love or hate daughters, and vice versa. This is not what the Bible has taught us, but somehow the animosity can simmer for years. This usually starts in the teenage years when mothers constantly criticize everything you do and set standards that almost no one can adhere to. During college the leash lightens a bit. Then you are out into the real world. Mother still can't let you alone. You can't date so and so, you're getting fat, don't marry that person even if he is smart. You can't pick up your room or house. But when your mother is still treating like you are fifteen, even though you are sixty, you begin to wonder where you went wrong. It's not you. It's your mother. Maybe her mother was the same way. Try not to do this to your daughter. Then your mother starts sending nasty notes to you and your husband. Doesn't she see this can break up a marriage. No one wonder mother-in-laws get such a bad rap. Or mother knows everything even if she thinks the hurricane season ends October 31! Peace in a family leads to stability and love - love of God, love of family, and love of friends. That is what we need to strive for, not stress and hatred, only love.

Sweet and Sour Meatballs

Makes about 4 dozen

2 lbs. ground beef	2 eggs
1 lb. ground pork or veal	½ cup milk
1½ cups bread crumbs	1 tsp. salt
1 onion, finely chopped	1 tsp. pepper
4 cloves garlic, minced	¼ cup parsley, chopped

Combine ingredients in a bowl. Make into small balls. Fry in a skillet, or bake for 25 minutes at 375°. Serve meatballs in a pan with a warmer. Pour sauce over them.

Sauce

2 cups ketchup	¼ cup vinegar
1 stick butter	½ cup water
½ cup molasses	

Combine the ingredients in a sauce pan. Bring to a boil. Simmer for 15 minutes.

February 20

"Be not forgetful to entertain strangers; For thereby some have entertained angels unawares. "
Hebrews 13:12

Over the years I have been very involved in international visitor centers across the United States. I served as President in Cleveland and Newport. Throughout the years I have taken hundreds of "strangers" into my home, sightseeing, or to professional appointments. I have loved every minute, and have kept all the records of those I have entertained. One time in Cleveland we had seven Japanese businessmen. In Japan and other countries, if a present is brought, you do not open it until after the guests have departed. Imagine receiving seven sets of a spoon set? They were cloisinee and beautiful. I kept one set, but over a period of time gave the others away as house presents. I am not so involved any more with the centers. I treasure the time I entertained complete strangers, welcoming them, and letting them have a taste of America. Open your heart to a stranger.

Spicy Chicken

Serves 6

6 boneless chicken breasts, cubed
2 tbls. soy sauce
2 tbls. sherry
1 tsp. water
2 tsp. sugar
2 tbls. sesame or vegetable oil

4 green onions, chopped
3 red chiles, remove seeds and dice
3 cloves garlic, crushed
2 tbls. fresh grated ginger
1 cup basil leaves
3 cups cooked rice

In a bowl combine the soy sauce, sherry, water, and sugar with the chicken. Refrigerate for at least one hour.
In a wok heat the oil. Stir in green onions. Add chiles and garlic.
Stir in chicken.
Serve with rice and garnish with basil leaves.

"Set your mind on God's kingdom and His justice before everything else, and all the rest will come to you as well. So do not be anxious about tomorrow; tomorrow will look after itself. Each day has troubles enough of its own."
Matthew 6:34

Too often we focus on the past, or the future and do not take today into account. Each day should be savored for its own merits. Find peace with yourself so that you aren't uptight or nervous about what will happen next. Keeping busy is good for you. Perhaps you are a stay at home mom, or have a fulltime job? Whatever you do, focus on yourself and others. As a mom think about your love for your family, how lovely your house is, and if you live in the South, or some place warm, isn't it time to work in the garden and pick a few flowers for the table? At work make a new friend, start up a conversation, or run up and down the stairs a few times to get rid of excess energy or pounds. Tomorrow will come. We don't know if it will be a good or bad day. Stay focused on today.

Focaccia

4 cups flour	3 tbls. olive oil
1 pkg. yeast	½ cup Kalamata olives, sliced
1 tsp. salt	1 onion, chopped
1 tsp. sugar	1 tbls. sea salt
1 cup hot water	2 tbls. rosemary

Place the flour, yeast, salt and sugar in a bowl. Make a well. Pour hot water and 1 tbls. olive oil. Knead well.
Place the dough in a large oiled bowl in a warm place. Let double in size, about 1 hour.
Punch dough down and knead for 4 minutes.
Oil a 13x9 shallow baking dish with 1 tbls. olive oil. Press the dough into the pan, or roll out into size of pan.
Cover and let rise for 30 minutes.
Preheat oven to 400°
Using your fingers make indentations in dough. Sprinkle dough with remaining olive oil, olives, onion, sea salt, and rosemary.
Bake 25 minutes, or until golden.
Sundried tomatoes can also be used.

February 22

"The Lord God took the man and put him in the garden of Eden to till it and keep it. And the Lord God commanded the man, You may eat freely of every tree of the garden; but of the tree of the knowledge of good and evil you shall not eat, for in the day that you eat of it you shall die."
Genesis 2:15-17

Temptation surrounds us. Utter a small lie, steal, cheat, we are only human. From the beginning of the Bible God exhorts us to do the right thing. But we rarely listen. We listen to only what we want. We get lost from God's message. Listen to Him. Read the Bible. The truth is there.

Cherry Pie

Pie Crust

1¼ cups flour   ½ cup almonds
¼ cup water   2 tbls. sugar
1 stick butter

Preheat oven to 400°
Combine all the ingredients in a food processor until a ball is formed. Roll out on floured board into pie shape. Put in pie plate and bake 10 minutes.

Filling

2 15 oz. cans tart red cherries   Zest of 1 lemon
¾ cup sugar   2 tbls. lemon juice
3½ tbls. cornstarch   ½ tsp. almond flavoring

Drain the cherries and reserve the liquid. In a saucepan combine the sugar and cornstarch. Slowly add cherry liquid, stirring until the mixture is thickened. Stir in zest, lemon juice and almond flavoring.
Pour into pie shell. Cover with topping. Bake 30 minutes.

Topping

½ cup flour   ½ tsp. nutmeg
½ cup sugar   ½ tsp. cloves
1 tsp. cinnamon   ½ stick butter

Combine the ingredients in a bowl.

"Joy to the world! The Lord is come: let earth receive her King; let every heart prepare him room, and heaven and nature sing, and heaven and nature sing, and heaven, and heaven and nature sing. He rules the world with truth and grace, and makes the nations prove the glories of his righteousness, and wonders of his love, and wonders of his love, and wonders, wonders of his love"
Words Isaac Watts; Music George Frederick Handel

I know it's long after Christmas, but as I write I love to listen to the carols, and *The Messiah*, which can be heard any time of the year. The music inspires my creativity, gets the juices roiling, and my mind set on the next project. If your day has not been the best play a CD of Christmas music. See how your mood will change.

George Frederick Handel (1685-1759) was born in Germany, but spent most of his life in England. He wrote some of our most glorious music, including *The Messiah*, using words directly from *The King James Bible*. By the age of nine he could perform on the harpsichord and pipe organ, and compose music. *The Messiah* was composed in 1741-42 and first performed in London in 1742. He wrote music for *The Royal Fireworks* and his hymns include *Joy to the World, Rejoice the Lord is King, Soldiers of Christ Arise*, and others. At Christmas as *The Messiah* is performed, be thankful he took the words of The Bible and put them to music. We know them by heart because they are The Word.

Syllabub

Serves 6

12 macaroons	Zest of 1 lemon
¼ cup Madeira	¼ tsp. cinnamon
¼ cup lemon juice	½ tsp. almond extract
6 tbls. sugar	2 cups heavy cream

Crumble the macaroons into 6 sherbet glasses.
In a bowl combine the Madeira, lemon juice, sugar, zest, cinnamon and almond extract. Beat in the cream until peaks form. Pour the mixture over the macaroons.
Chill before serving.

February 24

"In those days Peter stood up in the midst of the disciples and said Men and brethren, this scripture must needs have been fulfilled, which the Holy Ghost by the mouth of David spake before concerning Judas, which was guide to them that took Jesus. For he was numbered with us, and had obtained part of this ministry. Now this man purchased a field with reward of iniquity; and falling headlong, he burst asunder in the midst, and all his bowels gushed out...Wherefore of these men which have companied with us all the time that the Lord Jesus went in and out among us, beginning from the baptism of John, unto that same day he was taken up from us, must one be ordained to be a witness with us of his resurrection. And they appointed two, Joseph called Barsabas, who was surnamed Justus, and Matthias. And they prayed, and said, thou Lord, which knowest the hearts of all men, shew whether of these two thou hast chosen, that he may take part of this ministry and apostleship, from which Judas by transgression fell, that he might go to his own place. And they gave forth their lots, and the lot fell upon Matthias; and he was numbered with the eleven apostles."
Acts1:15-26

We all know the story of Judas' betrayal, but can you imagine Joseph and Matthias, and how they felt to be chosen an apostle? We were not there to know Joseph's disappointment, but we do know about Matthias, whose name means "gift of God". How right they were to choose this man.

Apple Raspberry Crisp

Serves 4

4 apples, cored and sliced	1 tsp. cinnamon
Juice of 1 lemon	¼ tsp. nutmeg
1 pint raspberries	1 stick butter, melted
½ cup flour	Whipped cream or ice cream
½ cup oats	
¼ cup sugar	
¼ cup brown sugar	

Preheat oven to 350°
Combine the apples, lemon juice, and raspberries in a baking dish.
In a bowl combine the flour, oats, cinnamon, nutmeg and butter. Sprinkle over the apples.
Bake 25 minutes, or until bubbling and browned.
Serve with whipped cream or ice cream

"Every good gift and every perfect gift is from above, and cometh down from the Father of lights, with whom is no variableness, neither shadow of turning. Of his own will begat he us with the word of truth, that we should be a kind of first fruits of his creatures. Wherefore, my beloved brethren, let every man be swift to hear, slow to speak, slow to wrath: For the wrath of man worketh not the righteousness of God. Wherefore lay apart all filthiness and superfluity of naughtiness, and receive with meekness the engrafted word, which is able to save your souls. But be ye doers of the word, and not hearers only, deceiving your own selves. For if any be a hearer of the word, and not a doer, he is like unto a man beholding his natural face in a glass: For he beholdeth himself, and goeth his way, and straightway forgetteth what manner of man he was. But whoso looketh into the perfect law of liberty, and continueth therein, he being not a forgetful hearer, but a doer of the work, this man shall be blessed in his deed. If any man among you seem to be religious, and bridleth not his tongue, but deceiveth his own heart, this man's religion is vain. Pure religion and undefiled before God and the Father is this, To visit the fatherless and widows in their affliction, and to keep himself unspotted from the world."
James 1:17-27

Are there days when you are just plain angry? Angry at the world, angry at your spouse, angry about your job – the list could go on and on. One of the best ways to relieve yourself of this madness is to take a long walk. Sort through what you are angry about. If you don't, a wrong decision could be made that could forever harm you or someone else. Yes, go scream. You can scream at God. He knows what you are thinking. Scream at the top of your lungs. Wow, what a relief to get that something off your chest. Bridle your tongue, not your heart. Let God in. Let him tell you what to do.

Coleslaw

Serves 6

1 medium head red or green cabbage, shredded
2 carrots, peeled and shredded
½ cup mayonnaise

¼ cup apple cider vinegar
1 tsp. cayenne
3 cloves garlic, crushed

Combine the mayonnaise, vinegar, cayenne and garlic in a salad bowl. Add cabbage and carrots. Toss. More vinegar can be added for flavor.

February 26

"The Lord God tends his flock like a shepherd: He gathers the lambs in his arms and carries them close to his heart; he gently leads those that have young."
Isaiah 40:11

This is one of the most tender passages in the Bible. The Lord cuddling the lambs, the warmness of his heart, his love as he envelopes you with his arms. God sent Jesus to comfort us, to forgive our sins. He is God's baby. He is the shepherd. He may lose his flock, but those who are true believers will always return. They too will find others. The flock will always grow.

New mothers are like this. Yes, nervous about holding a newborn, but so excited to take the baby in her arms. She holds him close, each feeling the warmth and love that brings them together. She looks at the baby realizing that God has given her a miracle, a being only God could form – so perfect and in his image.

Braised Lamb Shanks

Serves 4

4 lamb shanks	2 cups baby carrots
½ cup flour	1 red pepper, chopped
1 tbls. Italian herbs	2 stalks celery, chopped
1 tsp. garlic salt	2 medium tomatoes, chopped
½ tsp. sea salt	¼ cup fresh parsley, chopped
1 tsp. fresh ground pepper	2 bay leaves
2 tbls. butter	½ tsp. thyme
2 tbls. olive oil	½ tsp. oregano
4 slices bacon, cooked and crumbled	1 cup red wine
1 medium onion, chopped	2 cups beef stock

Preheat oven to 350°
In a bowl combine the flour, herbs, garlic salt, salt and pepper. Dredge the shanks in the flour mixture.
Heat the butter and olive oil in a large skillet. Brown the shanks, about 10 minutes each side. You might need to add more butter and oil.
Remove shanks and put in large covered baking dish. Pour any drippings left in the pan over the shanks. Put all other ingredients in dish.
Bake covered for 1½ - 2 hours, until the meat is almost falling off the bones.
Serve with couscous and baked pita bread.

"Out of Zion, the perfection of beauty, God hath shined."
Psalm 50:2

When I moved back to Long Island only a few of my friends remained there. I had vowed never to come back – the Long Island "Distressway", too many people, and just a general reluctance to live there. However my father had retired and my mother wanted someone take over her stationery business. One person was already helping out, but did not want to take it on full time. My daughter had gone to live with her father in Cleveland, I was without a job, and after carefully analyzing the situation decided to make the move. I settled in the delightful colonial and whaling town of Cold Spring Harbor. Through my mother's friends and her business I quickly made new acquaintances. I was asked to chair fundraisers, play bridge, and join a few organizations. I loved my time on Long Island and the special friends I made. One is a very talented artist who loves painting children and flowers. Her old house sits on a lovely wooded plot with a garden. Many hours we have partied together or just spent catching up on every topic possible. Luckily both of us read extensively, but she's had more time to join book clubs than I have. Sometimes we must return and look at a place in a new way. Our eyes are opened to the beauty that surrounds us. Block out the things we don't like. Look for what God has made.

Seafood Pizza

Serves 4

1 pizza dough
½ lb. shrimp, cooked, peeled and deveined
½ lb. scallops
½ lb. lobster meat

4 scallions, chopped
4 cloves garlic, crushed
2 large tomatoes, finely chopped
2 tbls. olive oil
1 cup parmesan cheese

Preheat oven to 500°. Turn down to 425°
Spread the dough on a pizza baking sheet. Bake 15 minutes.
Remove from oven and divide up the ingredients evenly on the dough, leaving a little bit of an edge.
Bake 5 more minutes, or until just bubbling.

February 28

"Christians awake, salute the happy morn whereon the Savior of the world was born; rise to adore the mystery of love, which hosts of angels chanted from above; with them the joyful tidings first begun of God Incarnate and the Virgin's Son."

John Byrom (1692-1763), an English inventor and developer of early shorthand, is best remembered for this Christmas hymn which he wrote for his daughter Dolly. He came from a well-to-do family graduating from Cambridge, then a fellow of Trinity, and later studied medicine at Montpellier in France. He patented his "New Universal Shorthand", taught at both Oxford and Cambridge Universities, and used by the clerk in the House of Lords. He is buried in the Jesus Chapel at Manchester Cathedral.

Awake every morning, renew your spirit, and bless the Lord.

Eggs Benedict

Serves 4

4 English muffins, cut in half
8 eggs
2 tbls. butter

½ lb. fresh baby spinach
1 lb. fresh crab meat

Toast the English muffins.
Poach the eggs.
Melt the butter and slightly warm the spinach and crab.
Spread some of the spinach and crab on each muffin.
Top with Hollandaise.
Serve immediately.

Hollandaise

¼ cup lemon juice
3 egg yolks
Pinch of cayenne

2 tbls. chives, snipped
2 sticks butter, melted

In a food processor blend the lemon juice, egg yolks, cayenne and chives. Slowly pour in the melted butter until thickened.

March 1

"The Lord is my light and my salvation, whom shall I fear? The Lord is the strength of my life, of whom shall I be afraid?
Psalm 27:1

"I am crucified with Christ: nevertheless I live; yet not I, but Christ liveth in me: and the life which I now live in the flesh I live by the Son of God, who loved me, and gave himself for me."
Galatians 2:20

During the forty days of Lent we should all look inside ourselves and give of more freely to the Lord. Jesus spent forty days in the desert, tempted by Satan, fasting, and praying(Matthew 4:2; Mark 1:13; Luke 4:2). Moses spent forty days on Mount Sinai with God (Exodus 24:18); Elijah spent forty days walking to Mount Horeb (1 Kings 19:8); Noah endured forty days of rain (Genesis 7:4); the Hebrews wandered forty years to find the Promised Land (Numbers 14:33); and Ninevah had forty days to repent (Jonah 3:4). Even with our busy schedules we too need time each day during Lent to be free of temptation and to think back on how our ancestors endured forty days – crossing the ocean, settling a new land, giving of themselves to God to succeed. And let us not forget Jesus' forty hours in the tomb, dying for us, and rising from the dead so our sins might be forgiven. Look to the risen Lord.

Baked Pancake

Serves 2

1 stick butter	2 eggs
½ cup milk	Fresh fruit
½ cup flour	Lemon juice
2 tbls. sugar	Confectioner's sugar

Preheat oven to 425°
Melt the butter in an iron skillet in the oven.
Beat together the milk, flour, sugar and eggs.
Pour into the skillet. Bake 20 minutes, until golden and puffed.
Remove from oven. Place on a large plate and dot with the fruit. Roll up and sprinkle with lemon juice and sugar.
Cut in half.

March 2

"Fight the good fight with all thy might; Christ is thy Strength, and Christ thy Right; Lay hold on life, and it shall be Thy joy and crown eternally. Run the straight race through God's good grace, Lift up thine eyes, and seek His face; Life with its way before us lies, Christ is the Path, and Christ the Prize. Cast care aside, upon thy Guide, Lean, and His mercy will provide; Lean, and the trusting soul shall prove Christ is its Life, and Christ its Love. Faint not nor fear, His arms are near, He changeth not, and thou art dear. Only believe, and thou shalt see That Christ is all in all to thee."
John Samuel Bewley Monsell (1818-75) was a Church of Ireland minister and poet.

"Fight the good fight of faith, lay hold on eternal life, whereunto thou also art called, and hast professed a good profession before many witnesses."
1Timothy 6:12

Every day we face new challenges – challenges in our lives, challenges in the world around us and challenges to our faith. Why, O God, does this have to happen to us? Why can't we lead a normal happy life? Why do there have to be so many steps, so many hurdles? Can't we just walk in a straight line? If we are so dear to you, Lord, open our hearts and let your face shine on us. Help us to learn to trust you, and to believe. Open my eyes and I will see. I love you Lord, even in my distress.

Rice Casserole

Serves 6-8

3 cups water	2 cups milk
2 cups uncooked basmati rice	4 eggs
2 leeks, chopped	¼ tsp. cayenne
1 red pepper, chopped	½ tsp. salt
1 green pepper, chopped	1 tsp. pepper
2 cups sharp cheddar cheese	½ cup parmesan cheese

In a sauce pan bring the water and rice to a boil. Turn down heat until almost all water is gone. Cover pan, and place heavy pan on top for 10 minutes.
Preheat oven to 350°
In a greased casserole combine the rice, leeks, peppers and cheddar cheese.
In a bowl beat the eggs, milk, cayenne, salt and pepper. Pour over the rice.
Sprinkle parmesan cheese on top.
Bake ½ hour or until bubbling and just browned.

"Let us now praise famous men, and our fathers that begat us. The Lord hath wrought great glory by them through his great power from the beginning. Such as did bear rule in their kingdoms, men renowned for their power, giving counsel by their understanding, and declaring prophecies: Leaders of the people by their counsels, and by their knowledge of learning meet for the people, wise and eloquent in their instructions: Such as found out musical tunes, and recited verses in writing: Rich men furnished with ability, living peaceably in their habitations; All these were honoured in their generations, and were the glory of their times. There be of them, that have left a name behind them, that their praises might be reported. And some there be, which have no memorial; who are perished, as though they had never been; and are become as though they had never been born, and their children after them. But these were merciful men, whose righteousness hath not been forgotten. With their seed shall continually remain a good inheritance, and their children are within the covenant. Their seed standeth fast, and their children for their sakes. Their seed shall remain for ever, and their glory shall not be blotted out. Their bodies are buried in peace; but their name liveth for evermore. The people will tell of their wisdom, and the congregation will show forth their praise."
Ecclesiasticus 44:1-15

On March 3, 1883 the United States Congress purchased Arlington House and its property from the Lee family. The mansion was built by George Washington Parke Custis whose daughter Mary Anna married Robert E. Lee. The mansion was built as a memorial to our first President. Today this historic plantation is the site of Arlington National Cemetery, burial place to thousands who gave their lives for our country. We may not even begin to know a few by name, but they served for peace in this world. May they all rest in peace. And may there be peace in this world.

Peanut Soup

Serves 4

½ stick butter	2 cups chicken stock
1 small onion, chopped	2 cups cream
2 celery stalks, chopped	1 cup peanut butter
2 tbls. flour	Salted peanuts

Melt the butter and sauté onion and celery. Stir in flour. Add stock and cream until slightly thickened. Stir in peanut butter.
Serve hot or chilled with peanuts for garnish.

March 4

"The fig tree putteth forth her green figs, and the vines with the tender grape give a good smell. Arise my love, my fair one, and come away."
Song of Solomon 2:13

Love is so tender, so fragile, so wonderful when it is found. No one can predict when it will happen. You can be a child, or an adult when your true love arouses in you feelings never before felt. One of my high school classmates met her husband when she was in the fourth grade on Long Island. Now forty years later they are still madly in love. My parents met on August 12, 1944 and on the 13th my father proposed. They were married six weeks later, still are in love and very much alive. Marriage is a covenant, entered into with trust, faith, love, and hope.

"And He (Jesus) answered and said unto them, Have ye not read, that he which made them at the beginning made them male and female, And said, For this cause shall a man leave father and mother, and shall cleave to his wife: and they twain shall be one flesh? Wherefore they are no more twain, but one flesh. What therefore God hath joined together, let not man put asunder."
Matthew 19:4-6

Figs In Honey

Serves 4

1 cup dry white wine	1 cinnamon stick
Zest of 1 lemon	4 cloves
½ cup honey	1 lb. ripe fresh figs
¼ cup sugar	Mint

Place the wine, zest, honey, sugar, cinnamon and cloves in a sauce pan. Bring to a boil. Reduce heat, and cook until amount is halved.
Add figs and cook for 10 minutes.
Serve immediately garnished with mint leaves.
Can also be served chilled.

"I am the true vine, and My Father is the vinedresser. Every branch of mine that bears no fruit, He takes away, and every branch that does bear fruit He prunes, that it may bear more fruit. You are already made clean by the word which I have spoken to you. Abide in Me, and I in you. As the branch cannot bear fruit by itself, unless it abides in the vine, neither can you, unless you abide in Me. I am the vine, you are the branches. He who abides in Me, and I in him, he it is that bears much fruit, for apart from Me you can do nothing. If a man does not abide in Me, he is cast forth as a branch and withers; and the branches are gathered, thrown into the fire and burned. If you abide in Me, and My words abide in you, ask whatever you will, and it shall be done for you. By this My Father is glorified, that you bear much fruit, and so prove to be My disciples."
John 15:1-8

Grapes, wine and raisins are mentioned throughout the Bible. Noah was the first to grow grapes (Genesis 9:20). The first miracle of Jesus Christ occurs in John when Jesus is asked by his mother to provide wine for a wedding in Cana of Galilee. Jesus replies to her *"Woman, what have I to do with thee? Mine hour is not yet come.* (John 2:4)

As long we do not abuse what we drink, and drink in moderation wine, especially red wine is good for your heart. Alcoholics Anonymous was founded so that alcoholics could regain control of their lives by reestablishing a relationship with God and the Bible through Jesus Christ. Some unfortunately do not commit themselves, others do so for life. If you know someone who has a drinking problem see if they can find their way through our Lord.

Sangria

Makes about 20 glasses

1 orange, sliced	1 quart club soda
1 lemon, sliced	2 cups brandy
2 fifths red wine	Strawberries
1 cup orange juice	Lemon slices
½ cup sugar	Orange slices

Combine the orange and lemon slices, wine, orange juice and sugar in a pitcher. Chill covered for several hours.
Pour in the club soda and brandy. Serve with strawberries, lemon and orange slices.

March 6

"In the beginning when God created the heaven and the earth...Then God said let us create humankind...God blessed them and said to them, Be fruitful and multiply...Then the Lord God said, See, the man has become like one of us, knowing good and evil; and now, he might reach out his hand and take also from the tree of life, and eat, and live forever."
Genesis 1-3

When visiting Rome or Florence, Biblical stories magically touch us through the most incredible and beautiful statues and paintings of Michelangelo. You sense the pain, the love, the hope, and strength whether it be the Pieta, David or his artwork in the Sistine Chapel. You can see pictures of these, but it is being right there to see the scars carved in marble or how a brush stroke can evoke such emotion. How any artist could recreate the life of our Lord in such a short period of time is almost unimaginable, but he did leave a legacy for all generations to come. I cannot wait to return.

Michelangelo di Lodovico Buonarroti Simoni (1475 –1564) and Leonardo da Vinci were the greatest Renaissance men. Michelangelo truly captured the Word of the Lord, perhaps in depictions and dress of his own time. No other artist could achieve his perfection, May God be praised that he gave us such a genius.

Divinity Candy

2 cups sugar
½ cup water
1/3 cup light corn syrup

2 egg whites
½ tsp. vanilla
1½ cups pecans, coarsely chopped

Combine the sugar, water and corn syrup in a pan. Bring to a boil. Stir until the sugar dissolves.
Cook for 10-15 minutes or until a candy thermometer reads 255°. Remove from the heat.
In a bowl beat the egg whites until peaks form.
Slowly pour the egg whites into the syrup.
Add vanilla and beat for 10 minutes, until thickened. Stir in pecans.
Drop candy by tablespoon onto wax paper. Let sit until firm.

"...the windows of heaven were opened."
Genesis 7:11

Raynham Hall in Oyster Bay, New York always held an annual benefit the first Saturday in March. These events took place in a gracious old home overlooking Long Island Sound. The couple that owned the house lent it out for special occasions, and were generous in doing so. Each year a different theme was chosen. During my tenure as benefit chairman they included "An Evening at the Hunt", an "Evening Regatta with Friends", and "A View of Oyster Bay" The Oyster Bay party highlighted the role the Tiffany had played on Long Island. We used the series of Tiffany stained glass windows as the invitation's cover.

The Tiffany Company produced some of the most beautiful stained glass windows ever made. Almost every church I have belonged to has had at least one Tiffany window. The colors are vibrant, the flowers so real, and the light coming through makes you feel as if you are part of the scene. The angels and our Lord reach out to you, drawing you ever closer to them. You cannot help but feel you are in paradise. They speak to you in many tongues. You cannot help but be uplifted. They praise the Lord. We praise the lord. I am sure in your community or one nearby you can find a Tiffany window. If not, go to the library or on online to search out these wonders.

Cheese Puffs

2 tbls. butter
1¼ cups water
1 cup flour
1 cup cheddar cheese
2 tbls. grated parmesan cheese
2 eggs, beaten

2 jalapeno, seeded and finely chopped
½ tsp. dry mustard
¼ tsp. cayenne
Oil

Heat the butter and flour in a sauce pan to a boil. Stir in the flour. Stir in cheeses. Remove from heat. Allow to cool slightly.
Stir in eggs, jalapeno, mustard and cayenne.
Heat oil in a skillet.
Form the dough into golf size balls. Fry in the oil until golden. Drain on a rack with paper towels.
Serve immediately.

March 8

"We remember the fish we did eat in Egypt freely... and the garlick."
Numbers 11:5

When we lived in San Francisco a Latino couple managed the building and lived in an apartment on the garage level. In the evening you had this unbelievable aroma of garlic, onions and tomatoes. Luckily for us there were several excellent Mexican restaurants nearby, if we didn't want to cook at home. I think it was during this time my love for garlic became more acute. Yes, I had spent a summer dividing time between Florence and Viareggio, but during those college days my host's family had a cook and I just enjoyed what was prepared.

Garlic is something we use almost daily in cooking. Garlic is good for hay fever, high blood pressure, cholesterol, coughs, asthma, and many other uses. Some people don't like the taste, but use it or substitute shallots, which aren't quite as strong.

Garlic Soup

Serves 4

2 egg whites, lightly beaten	2 egg yolks
4 slices French bread	½ tsp. salt
4 cups beef stock	½ tsp. pepper
¼ cup olive oil	½ cup parsley
8 garlic cloves	

Preheat the oven to 350°
Brush the bread slices with the egg whites. Place on a cookie sheet and bake in the oven until just slightly browned. Remove from oven. Cut into triangles.
Bring water to a boil in a pan. Add garlic cloves and boil for 15 minutes. Drain and peel.
In a bowl mash the garlic and add the egg yolks.
Using the same pan bring the stock to a boil. Stir in the garlic. Cook until thickened.
Season with salt and pepper.
Pour the soup into four bowls. Top with toast triangles and parsley.

March 9

"For an angel went down at a certain season into the pool, and troubled the water: whosoever then first after the troubling of the water stepped in was made whole of whatsoever disease he had."
John 5:4

There are times in our lives we need to be made whole again. Each day as I say my prayers I pray for the sick and wounded, naming those whom I know or have been asked to pray for. As I finish I ask God to make them whole again. I know he has done this for me, especially over the last year. Fortunately mine was deep hurt, not a physical affliction. Each day my list continues to grow –cancer, bad backs, a heart replacement, leukemia, Alzheimer's, and dementia. When will it stop? Never1 God made us as mortal beings, the end will come for each of us.

Frances of Rome (1384-1440) belonged to an aristocratic Roman family. At an early age she married Lorenzo Ponziano whose brother and sister-in-law Vanozza came to live with them. They believed in helping the poor and sick and went among them in Rome. Frances' gift of healing and being able to see at night led her to found the Oblates of the Tor de Speechi to care for the poor. When she died she had a strange light on her face and said these words *"The angel has finished his task: he beckons me to follow him."*

Veal Meatballs

Serves 4

2 slices bread, finely cubed
¼ cup milk
1 leek, finely chopped
1 clove garlic, minced
¼ cup parsley, chopped
1 egg, beaten
1 lb. ground veal

1 tsp. pepper
½ tsp. salt
½ tsp. oregano
½ tsp. paprika
¼ lb. chopped sundried tomatoes
½ cup raisins
Breadcrumbs

Soak the bread cubes in the milk. Combine all the ingredients, except breadcrumbs with the bread.
Shape into small balls. Coat with bread crumbs.
Heat the olive oil in a skillet. Brown the meatballs.
Serve with pasta or rice.

March 10

"Sing, my soul, his wondrous love, who from yon bright throne above, ever watchful o'er our race, still to us extends his grace. Heaven and earth by him were made; all is by his scepter swayed; what are we that he should show so much love to us below? God, the merciful and good, bought us with the Savior's blood, and, to make our safety sure, guides us by his Spirit pure. Sing, my soul, adore his Name! Let his glory be thy theme: praise him till he calls thee home; truth his love for all to come."
Words: Anonymous 1800; Music John Bacchus Dykes

John Bacchus Dykes (1823 - 1876) was an English clergyman and hymnist. At age 10 he became the assistant organist at St. John's Church, Hull, where his grandfather was vicar. He studied at Cambridge and cofounded the Cambridge University Musical Society. He was ordained in 1847 and for a short time was canon of Durham Cathedral, then precentor. He composed over 300 hymn tunes, including *Holy, Holy, Holy! Lord God Almighty!*; *Wir Pflügen*, harmonised by Dykes and commonly sung to the words *We plough the fields, and scatter*; *Melita*, sung to the words *Eternal Father, Strong to Save*; *O Perfect Love*; and *Dominus Regit Me*, sung to the words *The King of love my Shepherd is*. Sing out to the Lord. Sing a new song every day. Let Him hear you.

Venison Stew

Serves 4-6

4 slices bacon, cooked and crumbled, save drippings
2 lbs. boneless venison, cut into cubes
¼ cup flour
1 tsp. sea salt
2 tsp. pepper
1 tbls. Italian herbs

1 large onion, chopped
1 cup beef broth
1 cup red wine
2 carrots, peeled and sliced
¼ cup parsley
2 bay leaves
1 cup heavy cream
¼ cup Cognac

Preheat oven to 350°
Combine the flour, salt, pepper and herbs on a plate. Dredge the venison.
Heat the bacon drippings in a skillet. Brown the venison on all sides
In a Dutch oven or covered baking dish place the venison, bacon, onion, carrots, parsley, bay leaves, broth, wine and remainder of drippings.
Cook 1 hour.
Stir in cream and Cognac.
Serve over noodles.

"Set your troubled hearts at rest. Trust in God always; trust also in me."
John 14:1

"Are not five sparrows sold for two farthings, and not one of them is forgotten before God? But even the very hairs of your head are all numbered. Fear not therefore: ye are of more value than many sparrows. Also I say unto you, Whosoever shall confess me before men, him shall the Son of man also confess before the angels of God: But he that denieth me before men shall be denied before the angels of God. And whosoever shall speak a word against the Son of man; it shall be forgiven him; but unto him that blasphemeth against the Holy Ghost it shall never be forgiven...For the Holy Ghost shall teach you in the same hour what ye ought to say."
Luke 12:6-12

Whom can we trust? There are so many evil forces out there sometimes we do not know who to turn to. There is only one person we know for sure and that is God. Trust in Him. You will reap blessings and love. You will overcome hatred and ill thoughts, perhaps even those whom you cannot love or forgive. Trust in the Lord gives you hope and love. He tells you what to do and say.

Roast Pork with Avocado Salsa

Serves 4

2 lbs. pork tenderloin
2 tbls. pepper
1 tbls. sea salt

¼ cup lime juice
1 tsp. oregano

Preheat the oven to 350°
Rub the pork with the pepper, salt, lime juice and oregano.
Place in a baking dish and cook 45 minutes, or until desired pinkness.

Avocado Salsa

2 avocados, peeled, pitted and finely chopped
2 jalapeno, seeded and finely chopped
1 large tomato, finely chopped

¼ cup cilantro, chopped
2 tbs. olive oil
1 tbls. white vinegar
2 tbls. lime juice

Combine all ingredients in a bowl.

March 12

"O sacred head, sore wounded, defiled and put to scorn; O kingly head surrounded with mocking crown of thorn: What sorrow mars thy grandeur? Can death thy bloom deflower? O countenance whose splendor the hosts of heaven adore! Thy beauty, long-desirèd, hath vanished from our sight; thy power is all expirèd, and quenched the light of light. Ah me! for whom thou diest, hide not so far thy grace: show me, O Love most highest, the brightness of thy face. I pray thee, Jesus, own me, me...My days are few, O fail not, with thine immortal power, to hold me that I quail not in death's most fearful hour; that I may fight befriended, and see in my last strife to me thine arms extended upon the cross of life."

This hymn by Paul Gerhardt (1607-1676) is better known as the *Passion Chorale* by J.S. Bach. Mr. Gerhardt enrolled in the University of Wittenberg and was influenced by two teachers - Paul Röber and Jacob Martini, both Lutherans. Here he learned hymnody. When he later moved to Berlin he realized the tension between the Reformed clergy and the Lutherans. He called for several conferences with the two groups, but the Elector, Friedrich Wilhelm I of Brandenburg finally issued an edict against one of the Lutheran Confessions. Because of this, many of the Lutheran ministry were forced to leave their jobs. Mr. Gerhardt eventually became the archdeacon of Lubben, where he died. Through the words we get such a vivid picture of our Lord upon the cross, the crown of thorn, his countenance bright, and through it all showing his love and grace. We realize too that we must die, but without fear, and that the Lord is with us, and in his arms. Bold words, bold meaning, bold Christ whom we love so dearly.

Couscous Salad

Serves 4

1 cup chicken broth
1 cup couscous
¼ cup orange juice
Juice of 1 lime
¼ cup cilantro leaves

1 green onion, chopped
¼ cup pine nuts
1 cup dried apricots
1 cup dried cranberries

Bring the chicken broth to a boil in a saucepan. Stir in the couscous. Turn off heat. Let sit for 15 minutes. Fluff with fork. Stir in other ingredients.
Can be served warm or chilled.

"Be glad in the Lord, and rejoice, ye righteous."
Psalm 32:11

"Behold, I make all things new."
Revelation 21:5

My daughter was born in Alexandria, Virginia. I had always dreamed of moving back to the Washington area, and was fortunate to do so in 1995. I worked up on the Hill attempting to help Congressmen get education back to the State and Local level, now completely undone by the present administration and "No Child Left Behind" act. If I could, I would spend my lunch hour at the Washington National Cathedral's noon service, on Wednesdays followed by an organ concert. I rejoiced that God had brought me to this magnificent place, where I could find peace away from the bustle of Washington. I eventually moved to Annapolis and then the Eastern Shore. The Lord once again blessed me with an active religious community and neighbors that follow our Savior. He did make things new and better for my life. I rejoice always!

Pate

2 tbls. butter
1 medium onion, finely chopped
2 tbls. brandy
2 tbls. Madeira
¾ lb. ground pork
¾ lb. ground veal
2 cloves garlic, chopped
¼ cup toasted almond slivers
2 eggs

½ tsp. salt
½ tsp. thyme
½ tsp. allspice
¼ tsp. nutmeg
1 tsp. fresh grated pepper
Pork fatback
4 slices bacon
6 bay leaves

Preheat oven to 350°
Melt the butter in a skillet and sauté the onions, until just tender. Add brandy and Madeira. Remove from heat and add pork, veal, garlic, almonds, eggs, salt, thyme, allspice, nutmeg and pepper.
Line a pate pan with pork fatback. Top with ½ pate mixture. Cover with bacon and 3 bay leaves. Smooth out.
Add rest of pate. Top with pork fat and bay leaves. Cover pan with foil.
Put pan in a casserole dish filled halfway with water. Bake for 1½ hours.
Remove from water bath. Place brick on top. Refrigerate overnight.
Remove from pan and remove pork fatback before serving.
Serve with crusty bread.

March 14

"Whether therefore ye eat, or drink, or whatsoever ye do, do all to the glory of God."
1 Corinthians 10:31

I love to throw a party, and will do so even if I don't have an excuse. Sometimes it's dinner for four, or cocktails for forty. I'm careful about guests as I love mixing ages, different intellects and businesses, married or single. While living on Long Island and then Connecticut a number of my friends were single ladies. Single men seemed hard to come by, though I had met a few through church and a sailing group. A couple of bachelors appeared to want to remain that way. A couple of ladies decided to start a single's group. We would provide a venue, the men would bring the drinks and other guests a favorite dish. These parties grew in popularity, everyone wanted to bring a guest so our list grew. When I moved to Washington a lot of friends kept calling to keep us together. Many are still friends, but no more single's parties. Any way I am married now. But when you do gather for whatever occasion, bow your head and praise the Lord for what you receive. To the glory of God, Alleluia.

Roast Duck

Serves 4

1 5-6 lb. duck
1 orange, sliced

1 onion, thinly sliced
Sea salt

Preheat the oven to 500°
Place the duck in a casserole with the orange and onion in the cavity. Rub with the salt.
Turn the oven down to 350°
Bake 1 hour, or until browned and tender.
Serve duck on a platter with sauce in a gravy boat.

Warm Currant Sauce

2 tbls. butter
2 tbls. flour
1 cup currant jam

½ lb. chanterelle mushrooms, sliced
¼ cup Madeira
½ cup hazelnuts

Melt the butter in a sauce pan. Stir in flour and then jam. Add mushrooms and cook until just tender. Stir in Madeira and hazelnuts.

"Moreover the Father who sent me has testified on my behalf. But you have never heard his voice nor seen his form, and you do not have his word remaining in you, because you do not believe in the one whom he has sent."
John 5:37-38

Why do there have to be hypocrites in the world? People who profess belief, people who attend church, but do not have a Bible in their home, or say one thing and mean exactly the opposite. They can be your neighbor, your friend, or even a member of your family. They are the ones who, when you're about to sit down for a meal will say, "oh you do say grace before a meal?", though they never do at home. It can begin to get to you. Yet, if they are family you do want to enjoy time with them, and a good meal. Continue to say grace and pray that someday they too may know the Lord as you do.

Stuffed Peppers

Serves 4

4 red peppers
¾ lb. ground beef
2 cloves garlic, minced
4 green onions, chopped
¼ cup cilantro
1 cup corn

1 tsp. sea salt
2 jalapeno, seeded and chopped
1 cup Monterey Jack cheese, grated
½ cup sour cream

Preheat oven to 350°
Cook the ground beef in a skillet. Add the green onions, cilantro, corn salt and jalapeno.
Remove the stem from the peppers, slice the top off, remove the core and seeds.
Stuff the peppers with the beef mixture.
Place in a baking dish.
Bake in the oven for 30 minutes.
Remove from oven.
Sprinkle with cheese and sour cream. Cilantro can also be used as a garnish.

March 16

"Go and serve the Lord. Thanks be to God."

When I moved to Annapolis I was very fortunate to meet my husband within a week of the move. He had worked in the town for a few years, had close knit group of friends, most of whom he worked with in a marine supply business. They partied together, sailed, and shared in each others ups and downs. One couple lived nearby and we broke bread with them quite often, and still do since they also live on the Eastern Shore. When they found out George and I were to be married, they hosted an engagement party for us, at our age! What is so appealing about them is their devotion to their family, but also to the church and community. She actively serves on the altar guild, arranging flowers, washing linens, doing whatever needs to be taken care of in the little chapel. She also heads up the local mental health association, participating in aid to those who are in trouble. A growing concern is for those returning from war in Afghanistan and Iraq, and how to deal with the families and soldiers. We need to pray for those who serve.

Knowing that of the Lord ye shall receive the reward of the inheritance; for ye serve the Lord Christ."
Colossians 3:24

Red Cabbage

Serves 4-6

1 stick butter	½ cup currant jelly
1 large head red cabbage, shredded	2 bay leaves
1 large onion, sliced	¼ cup water
2 apples, cored and sliced	1/3 cup apple cider vinegar

Melt the butter in a sauce pan. Add all ingredients.
Bring to a boil.
Simmer for 1 hour, until cabbage is tender. Remove the bay leaves.
Serve warm.

March 17

"Bless the Lord, O my soul, and all that is within me, bless his holy name. Bless the Lord, O my soul, and do not forget all his benefits: who forgives all your iniquity, who heals all your diseases, who redeems your life from the pit, who crowns you with steadfast love and mercy, who satisfies you with good as long as you live, so that your youth is renewed like the eagle's."
Psalm 103:1-5

When I think of St. Patrick I am reminded that he has been attributed to the writing of the hymn *I Bind unto Myself Today*, a hymn that is sung on Trinity Sunday, but also at installations of bishops and priests into the church. This is a man who has given himself to God, to work for the better good of humankind, and knows the Lord will always be with him.

I am also reminded that this psalm is one of my favorites, and exemplifies all the good that St. Patrick did. How this man in the British Isles could be converted to Christianity c 400 and become Christ's missionary opens our eyes to the fact that all of us can be called. We do not know when or where. Like Paul it could be on the road to Damascus, or like St. Patrick in Ireland. The important thing is to serve our Lord, and to grow more and more like Him each day.

March 17 is also the birthday of one of America's most renowned stained glass designers. Rowan LeCompte's 45 windows at the Washington National Cathedral are breathtakingly beautiful. The Creation Rose is set above the west portal of the Cathedral and celebrates the beginnings of our universe. It is 25 feet in diameter and contains over 10,500 shards of glass.

Irish Bread

4 cups flour
2 sticks butter
2 cups raisins
Zest of 1 lemon
1 tsp. nutmeg
1 cup almonds

1 cup mixed dried fruit
¾ lb. brown sugar
1 bottle Irish ale
2 tsp. baking soda
4 eggs

Preheat oven to 350°
Sift the flour and cut in the butter. Add the raisins, zest, nutmeg, almonds, dried fruit, and brown sugar. Beat the eggs.
Heat the ale and pour it over the baking soda. Pour the stout and eggs over the floured ingredients. Mix well and beat for 15 minutes.
Bake in a well-greased pan for 2½ - 3 hours. Keep for a week before cutting.

March 18

"I am for peace, but when I speak, they are for war."
Psalm 120:7

President Bush decided to invade Iraq on this date. Sadly the excuse he used was to get rid of Saddam Hussein and find weapons of mass destruction. Hussein was found, but no weapons of mass destruction. Years later we are still involved in Iraq. War is not something you can just proclaim. War kills, war devastates, war maims, war is not good for anyone.

John Bakewell (1721-1819) died on this day. The words to his hymn resound in my ears *Hail, thou once despised Jesus*. We have our hates, but we must learn from Jesus that love is what should prevail. Jesus was hated too, so were the disciples. Many sacrificed their lives so that we might have a better world. Jesus gave his life for us. Please pray for love, hope and understanding among all peoples.

"Hail, thou once despised Jesus! Hail, thou Galilean King! Thou didst suffer to release us; Thou didst free salvation bring. Hail, thou agonizing Saviour, Bearer of our sin and shame! By thy merits we find favour; Life is given through thy name."

Braised Leeks

I love leeks. They are used in colcannon and other favorite Irish dishes.

Serves 6

3 pounds leeks
½ cup olive oil
1 large onion

2 cups water
½ cup uncooked rice
Lemon slices

Heat the oil in sauce pan. Add onions and cook until transparent. Stir in the water.
Add the leeks and rice. Simmer for 30 minutes.
Serve with lemon slices.

March 19

"Give, and it shall be given unto you; good measure, pressed down, and shaken together, and running over, shall men give into your bosom. For with the same measure that ye mete withal it shall be measured to you again."
Luke 6:38

Moving to a new town is always traumatic. You need a place to live, find schools for your children, support your husband with his new job, and get involved in the community. When my family moved to Birmingham, Michigan old friends from Wilmington, Delaware were getting settled in and expecting their first child momentarily. To have five of us descend on them in a small home was a bit much, but they took us in until we could move into our own house. The baby was born. Later another couple moved to Birmingham from Wilmington. Like the couple who had taken us in we became the wing to hang on to. Fifty years later we all continue an enduring friendship. We all gave to each other, we obeyed God's word.

Pork Stew

Serves 6

2 tbls. butter	½ lb. mushrooms
2 lbs. pork tenderloin, cubed	2 cloves garlic, minced
1 lb. smoked sausage	½ tsp. allspice
2 onions, chopped	¼ tsp. cloves
2 tomatoes, chopped	¼ tsp. thyme

Melt the butter in a pan. Sear the pork on all sides. Add the other ingredients. Simmer for about an hour, until meat and vegetables are tender.
Serve with polenta, dumplings, or over noodles.

March 20

"I will lift up mine eyes unto the hills, from whence cometh my help. My help cometh from the Lord, which made heaven and earth. He will not suffer thy foot to be moved: he that keepeth thee will not slumber...The Lord is thy keeper; the Lord is thy shade upon thy right hand. The sun shall not smite thee by day, nor the moon by night. The Lord shall preserve thee from evil: he shall preserve thy soul. The Lord shall preserve thy going out and thy coming in from this time forth, and even for evermore."
Psalm 121

How many times, besides repeating the 23rd Psalm do we look up to heaven and say these words? They are our solace, our hope. We know the Lord is with us. Remember Maria in the *Sound of Music* how when speaking to the Reverend Mother announced that she had sinned. How the Reverend Mother said *"when the Lord closes a door, somewhere he opens a window.'* There is a future for everyone so long as they dream and they hope. The lord does not slumber, he is always awake and with us.

Pasta with Clam Sauce

Serves 4

2 tbls. olive oil
¼ tsp. crushed red pepper
2 cloves garlic, minced
1 leek, sliced

1 red pepper, sliced
32 clams, chopped
6 tbls. butter
1 box angel hair pasta
Fresh parmesan cheese, grated

Heat olive oil, add the garlic, red pepper, leek, and pepper and saute for a few seconds. Add clams and butter, simmer briefly.
In the meantime, cook pasta separately, according to the directions.
Spoon the clams over the pasta.
Sprinkle with parmesan cheese.

March 21

"Listen, O my son, to the precepts of thy master, and incline the ear of thy heart, and cheerfully receive and faithfully execute the admonitions of thy loving Father, that by the toil of obedience thou mayest return to Him from whom by the sloth of disobedience thou hast gone away. To thee, therefore, my speech is now directed, who, giving up thine own will, takest up the strong and most excellent arms of obedience, to do battle for Christ the Lord, the true King..."
Prologue of The Rule of St. Benedict

St. Benedict was born at Nursia, Umbria, Italy (c 480- 547.) His twin sister Scholastica founded the Benedictine order of nuns. Both were raised as devout Christians. He went to study in Rome at the age of fourteen but left the city to become eventually became a hermit in the mountains. He organized twelve monastic communities. In c 530 he established a monastery at Monte Casino, and there wrote his Rule. The Rule is a book originally written for monks instructing them in wisdom, discipline, love and respect for others. Modern monasticism is based on poverty, chastity and obedience.

Also on this date Thomas Cranmer (1489-1556), leader of the English Reformation, Archbishop of Canterbury, and author of the first two editions of the Book of Common Prayer, was burned at the stake for supporting Lady Jane Grey, King Edward's cousin and a Protestant, instead of Mary, Henry and Catherine of Aragon's daughter and a Catholic.

Cashew Rice

Serves 6

2 cups basmati rice	¼ tsp. saffron
3 cups water	2 tbls. butter
½ tsp. cloves	1 cup cashews
1 tsp. cinnamon	1 cup raisins or currants

In a sauce pan bring the rice and water to a boil. Simmer for 3 minutes, or until water is almost gone. Turn off heat. Cover tightly and let steam.
Stir in other ingredients.
This is good served with lamb or chicken.

March 22

"And if your eye causes you to stumble, tear it out and throw it away; it is better for you to enter life with one eye than to have two eyes and to be thrown into the hell of fire."
Matthew 18:9

Today's sermons are so different from the ones I remember hearing about, particularly in the 17th, 18th and 19th centuries. Back then they were filled with talk of going to Hell, fire and brimstone. Today they are gentler – Jesus' love for us, stories of hope, and a gentle God.

Devil's Food Cake (Courtesy Ned Grieg)

Serves 12

4 cups flour	6 eggs, separated
½ cup cocoa powder	1 tbls. vanilla
1 tbls. baking powder	1½ cups buttermilk
1 tsp. kosher salt	8 oz. bittersweet chocolate, melted
3 sticks butter	and at room temperature
3½ cups sugar	8 white chocolate, grated

Preheat oven to 325°

Combine the flour, cocoa powder, baking powder and salt in a bowl. Cream the butter and 3 cups sugar. Add the egg yolks, one at a time. In another bowl beat together the vanilla extract and buttermilk. Now alternate adding the flour mixture and buttermilk to the butter mixture. Beat the egg whites and ½ cup sugar until stiff. Fold into mixture. Fold in melted bittersweet chocolate and white chocolate. Spray 2 nine in. round baking tins with Pam. Dust with flour or sugar. Distribute the batter between the pans. Bake 35-45 minutes, or until a toothpick comes out dry. Remove cakes from pans. Place one layer on a cake plate. Frost. Place other layer on top. Frost the rest of the cake.

Chocolate Baker's Frosting

4 oz. unsweetened chocolate	3 oz. cream
1 lb. powdered sugar	2 tbls. vanilla
1 stick unsalted butter	½ tbls. kosher salt

Melt the chocolate in a stainless steel mixing bowl over a pot of simmering water. Set aside and warm to room temperature. Cream together the unsalted butter, powdered sugar, cream, vanilla and salt. Add melted chocolate.

March 23

For many years my father was a Boy Scout leader. One of the annual trips he took the boys on was a camping trip in the middle of the winter. They'd pack up extra warm long johns, hiking boots, tents and sleeping bags. I never could understand why anyone would want to suffer through the night with severe cold, snow, ice, you know winter weather in New York! My mother, sister and I would stay home nice and warm. However, my father is a hardy New Englander. To this day he will wear only a light jacket, but then my parents do divide time between Florida and Nantucket. But up until just a few years ago he and my brother would hike out West, sometimes experiencing snowy or chilly weather. Mt brother still hunts in Montana, but with a bit more luxury. Thank goodness the boys, my father and brother were protected by the Almighty, and no evil befell them. The Boy Scouts offer an incredible training in survival. Please support them in your local area.

Chili

Serves 6

4 slices bacon
1 large onion, chopped
3 cloves garlic, crushed
3 jalapeno, seeded and minced
1 lb. ground beef
½ lb. ground pork
1 tbls. cumin

1 tbls. chili powder
1 tsp. cayenne
1 tbls. Italian herbs
1 15 oz. can kidney beans
1 28 oz. can diced tomatoes
½ can beer

Fry the bacon in a large pot. Remove bacon and crumble.
Cook the onion in the bacon fat until tender. Add garlic, jalapeno, beef, and pork. Cook until browned. Add other ingredients.
Bring to a boil and simmer for at least ½ hour.
Serve with toasted tortilla wedges, sour cream, grated Monterey Jack cheese, and sliced scallions.

March 24

"Only Thy presence, O Savior divine, Only Thy Spirit to witness with mine; Only Thine image of love on my breast, Seal of forgiveness, assurance of rest. Refrain: What tho' the billows like mountains may swell; All will be well; yes, all will be well; Under Thy shadow in peace I shall dwell; All, all will be well. Only Thy presence when wild is the gale, Only Thy presence when rent is my sail; Only Thy presence my vessel to guide Into the harbor and over the tide. Refrain"

Fanny Crosby (1820-1915) was blinded by a doctor when she was only six weeks old. However, during her long lifetime she composed over 8000 hymns. *All Will Be Well* was written in 1915, the year she died. The words are so optimistic, so uplifting. God is present for us at all times, and all will be well.

Coconut Coffee Cake

1 stick butter
1 cup sugar
2 eggs
1 cup sour cream
1 ½ tsp. baking powder

1½ cups flour
1 tsp. vanilla
1 cup coconut
1 cup walnuts or pecans

Preheat oven to 350°
Cream butter and sugar. Add other ingredients.
Pour into greased baking dish.
Pour topping over batter.
Bake for 45 minutes.
Apples, pears, craisins, or other dried fruit can be added for flavor.

Topping:

¼ cup sugar
¼ cup brown sugar

1 tbls. cinnamon

Combine ingredients in a bowl.

March 25

"Therefore we are buried with him by baptism into death: that like as Christ was raised up from the dead by the glory of the Father, even so we also should walk in newness of life."
Romans 6:4

A good friend had a tape (dates me) that he loved to listen to. One of his favorite hymns was *In the Garden*. After he died I realized the tape was in my glove compartment, and I too would play it, especially on long trips, listening to each hymn, and memorizing the words.

"I come to the garden alone", but I know that the Lord always walks with me, and each day if I wait He will listen to me and talk to me. Such precious words. I always know I am walking with my Lord, whether it be in my garden, or with him at the tomb with Mary Magdalene. Please Lord never leave me, and I will never stray from you. You are my Savior, my hope, my love. The hymn was composed by C. Austin Miles in 1912. Walk with the Lord every day. He is always with you.

Chicken Carbonara

Serves 4

4 cooked boneless chicken breasts
½ lb. broccoli
4 scallions
4 slices bacon, cooked and crumbled

¼ lb. sun-dried tomatoes
4 cloves garlic, crushed
¼ cup basil, chopped
1 lb. fettuccine, cooked and drained
Parmesan cheese sauce

In a large bowl toss all the ingredients. Serve warm.
Extra parmesan cheese and basil can be used to garnish the carbonara

Parmesan Cheese Sauce

1 stick butter
½ cup flour

2 cups cream
1 cup parmesan cheese

Melt the butter in a sauce pan. Stir in the flour and cream, until slightly thickened. Add parmesan cheese.

"When I survey the wondrous cross on which the Prince of Glory died; my richest gain I count but loss, and pour contempt on all my pride.
Forbid it, Lord, that I should boast save in the death of Christ, my God; all the vain things that charm me most, I sacrifice them to His blood.
See, from His head, His hands, His feet, sorrow and love flow mingled down; did e'er such love and sorrow meet, or thorns compose so rich a crown.
Were the whole realm of nature mine, that were a present far too small; love so amazing, so divine, demands my soul, my life, my all."
Isaac Watts 1707

Oh God, your son died for us. We did not witness his death. We know in our hearts He is the risen Lord, who died not in vain, but to save us, sinners all. Never let us forget his sacrifice. May we always listen to your Word. The Lord is risen indeed! Alleluia. Alleluia. Alleluia!

Paskha (Russian Easter Bread)

2½ lbs. large curd pot cheese
2 sticks butter
1 tsp. vanilla
1 cup heavy cream
5 egg yolks

2 cups sugar
½ cup candied fruit
½ cup chopped blanched almonds
¼ cup currants

Drain the cheese of all moisture by placing in a colander with cheesecloth. Weigh down with a brick or two.
Cream the butter and 1 cup sugar.
Beat the egg yolks and remaining sugar until almost white in color.
Combine the butter and yolk mixtures. Stir in cheese. Fold in fruit and nuts.
Beat the cream until peaks form. Fold into cheese mixture.
Line a clay pot with a dampened cheesecloth.
Pour the cheese mixture into the pot. Fold the ends of the cheesecloth over the top. Put weight on top.
Refrigerate at least 24 hours.
To unmold place a plate on top of mold. Invert. Let paskha slide out. Garnish with additional candied fruit, nuts and raisins.

"And He took bread, and gave thanks, and brake it, and gave unto them saying, This is my body which is given for you: this do in remembrance of me. Likewise, also the cup after supper, saying, This cup is the new testament in my blood, which is shed for you."
Luke 22:19-20

Each time we partake of the Lord's Supper we remember Jesus, alone in a room with his twelve apostles, knowing that one would betray him, and wishing for one last meal before suffering. He explains that he is a server, not a lord. He came among us as a human being. He died for us so that we might lead a sinless life, that Satan might not tempt us, that our faith "fail not". Drink this wine and eat this bread. They are the body and blood of our risen Christ. Take time to share a meal with family and friends. Don't sit in front of a TV. Set a fine table - good linens, china and silverware. Open a bottle of wine, eat simple food. Always say grace and thank the Lord for what He has given us. And remember his last meal.

Banana Bread

Makes 1 loaf

6 ripe bananas	1 tsp. salt
2 sticks butter	2 tsp. baking powder
1 cup sugar	1 cup pecans
4 eggs, beaten	¼ cup dark rum
2½ cups flour	

Mash the bananas in a bowl. Pour rum over the bananas. Cover bowl and refrigerate for at least 1 hour.
Preheat oven to 350°
In a bowl cream the butter and sugar. Add eggs, flour, salt, baking powder, and nuts. Stir in bananas and rum.
Pour into a loaf pan.
Bake 45-50 minutes, or until a toothpick comes clean.
Serve with cream cheese or honey butter.

March 28

"A man that hath friends must show himself friendly: and there is a friend that sticketh closer than a brother."
Proverbs 18:24

During my graduate year at the University of Pennsylvania I did not have a car. I frequently visited friends and partied in New York. The train gave me some time to read and relax. On one occasion I noticed another young lady with her Nantucket basket. We started chatting away, only to find out her parents were friends of my grandmother. We became instant friends, meeting each other in Philadelphia or Nantucket. Her mother always wore the most exquisite flowered dresses and real flowers. My friend enjoyed photography, and one of my favorite pictures is the one she took of my daughter and her mother in my grandmother's garden. We both still spend time on Nantucket, and she remains in Philadelphia. I wish we could see more of each other, but we both lead busy lives. Never lose touch with old friends. They are truly a blessing.

Lobster with Pasta

Serves 4

2 tbls. butter	¼ cup Cognac
2 large tomatoes, chopped	1 cup cream
1 red pepper, sliced	½ tsp. salt
2 cloves garlic, minced	1 tsp. fresh ground pepper
1 leek, sliced	1½ lbs. lobster meat
½ lb. portabella mushrooms, sliced	¼ cup fresh basil, chopped
8 asparagus, cut in 1" pieces	1 lb. linguine
2 tbls. shallots, minced	Parmesan cheese (optional)

Melt the butter in a sauce pan. Stir in tomatoes, pepper, garlic, leek, mushrooms, asparagus and shallots. Cook until just tender.
Stir in Cognac, cream, salt and pepper.
Fold in lobster and basil.
Cook the linguine according to the directions. Drain and keep covered.
Divide the linguine between 4 pasta bowls. Top with lobster mixture.
Serve plain or with parmesan cheese.

March 29

"For we were so utterly, unbearably crushed that we despaired of life itself."
2 Corinthians 1:8

The passage for this day completely changed my life and for a dear friend. I had gone into New York City for an event and spent the night of March 28th in town. I came home the next evening and opened the garage door. There was a smell of gasoline. After quickly turning off the engine of my car, I realized my companion's car was running while the garage doors had been closed. Panicked I opened all doors, turned off his car, called our minister and 911. He was rushed off to the hospital and spent the next week there recuperating and seeing therapists. Unbeknown to me was he had gone through all the money in his divorce settlement, and now had no job or income.

At the age of 64 he could not accept the fact he lived in a prominent Connecticut suburb and was almost penniless. I know each morning we would read our daily passages, and 2 Corinthians exposed the crushing blow of his helplessness I am sure that morning he prayed, but despair had taken over. I guess during this Tuesday in Holy Week he could not look beyond the Resurrection and a better life for himself.

Depression is a horrible sickness that can be cured. Suicide is often the alternative. If you suspect signs of depression in a loved one, friend, or even a co-worker try to find help. There are organizations, churches and counseling groups to assist. Suicide should not end a person's life. In some societies burial cannot take place in a church if death is by suicide.

Oriental Green Beans

Serves 4

1 tbls. sesame oil	1 pound fresh green beans, trimmed
1 small onion, chopped	2 cloves garlic, minced
1 red pepper, sliced	½ tsp. crushed red pepper

Heat the oil in a wok or skillet.
Add onion, pepper and green beans. Stir 1 minute. Add garlic and red pepper.
Can be served warm or chilled.

March 30

"And the Lord spake unto Moses, saying I have heard the murmurings of the children of Israel: speak unto them saying, At even ye shall eat flesh, and in the morning ye shall be filled with bread; and ye shall know that I am the You're your God. And it came to pass, that at even the quails came up, and covered the camp; and in the morning the dew lay round about the host."
Exodus 16:11-13

Throughout the Old Testament we constantly find God's people disobeying him. The more he gave them, the more they sinned. He saved them from the Egyptians taking them to a new land, yet they were unhappy. They could not find food, yet God rained manna and quail upon them. Do we sometimes feel this way? The more we have, the further from God we get. I trust not. I trust that material goods do not ruin your life. Let God be there in your heart. Trust him.

Quails are small migratory birds that provide a delicious meal for guests. They are members of the pheasant family. Interestingly some can travel for long periods of time.

Baked Quail

Serves 4

8 whole quail	¼ cup flour
1 stick butter	2 cups chicken stock
1 stalk celery	½ cup sherry
1 medium onion, chopped	1 tsp. salt
½ pint mushrooms, sliced	1 tsp. pepper
1 red pepper, chopped	

Preheat oven to 350°
Melt the butter in a skillet and brown quail on all sides.
Place the quail in a baking dish.
Stir the flour into the remaining butter. Add chicken stock. Heat until slightly thickened. Add sherry.
Spoon the vegetables and stock over quail.
Cover the baking dish. Bake 1 hour.
Serve with currant jelly or Madeira sauce.
Cornish hens can be substituted for the quail.

March 31

"Glorious things of thee are spoken, Zion, city of our God; he whose word cannot be broken formed thee for his own abode; on the Rock of Ages founded, what can shake thy sure repose? With salvation's walls surrounded, thou may'st smile at all thy foes."
Words: John Newton; Music Joseph Haydn

Joseph Haydn (1732-1809), an Austrian, was one of the most prominent composers in history. In fact he is called the "Father of Symphony". At age 6 he was apprenticed to Joann Mathias Franck, the choirmaster and schoolmaster in Hainberg, learned to play the harpsichord and violin, and sang treble in the church choir. Because of his voice he was asked to join the choristers at St. Stephen's Cathedral in Vienna, where he sang for nine years. Later he taught himself music theory and composition. His writing compositions took off, and he became Kapellmeister for the Esterhazy family where he served for 30 years. Eventually he was able to spend time in London where his music was making him famous. In 1795 he returned to Vienna where he began his religious compositions, including the two oratorios *The Seasons* and *The Creation*. In 1802 deteriorating health forced him to cut back on his writing, but he did compose *Gott erhalte Franz den Kaiser* which became the melody for the Austrian and German national anthems. Haydn was a devout Catholic and prayed before composing. We are thankful that he gave such heavenly music to be shared for all generations.

Dessert Pancakes

2 tbls. raisins	1 cup flour
¼ cup dark rum	5 egg whites
4 egg yolks	Unsalted butter
¼ cup sugar	Confectioners' sugar
2 cups milk	Fresh fruit
½ tsp. vanilla	

Soak the raisins in the rum for ½ hour.
Beat the egg yolks and sugar until eggs are thickened. Stir in milk and vanilla. Add the raisins.
Beat egg whites until stiff. Fold into batter.
Melt some butter in a large skillet. Pour about half of the batter into the skillet. Brown on one side. Remove and add more butter. Flip to the other side. Remove and keep warm. Add more butter and rest of batter, flipping as before.
Cut pancakes into wedges. Serve with fruit and confectioners' sugar.

April 1

"God is love; and he that dwelleth in love dwelleth in God, and God in him."
1 John 4:16

"God is love, and where true love is God himself is there".
James Quinn 1969

James Quinn translated the Latin hymn *Ubi Caritas* (*Where Affection Is*) into English. This is traditionally sung on Maundy Thursday *Holy Thursday* before Easter during the washing of feet. This commemorates the Last Supper of Jesus with his Apostles. After the meal Christ washed the feet of the Apostles. Today we commemorate Jesus' actions by having the rector or lay person wash the congregation's feet. The word *Maundy* comes from Middle English, and Old French *mandé*, from the Latin *mandatum*, the first word of the phrase "*Mandatum novum do vobis ut diligatis invicem sicut dilexi vos*" ("*A new commandment I give unto you, That ye love one another; as I have loved you*"), spoken by Jesus in the Gospel of John 13:34 when he explains to the Apostles the significance of washing their feet.

Roger Williams (1603-83), the founder of the Rhode Island, who died on this date, is remembered for his religious toleration, after being exiled from Massachusetts. He named Providence for "God's merciful providence to me in my distress" and founded the Baptist Church in that colony.

Applesauce Cake

1 stick butter	1 tsp. nutmeg
1 cup brown sugar	½ tsp. ground cloves
2 cups applesauce	½ tsp. ground ginger
2 cups flour	2 tbls. cider vinegar
1 tsp. baking soda	1 cup raisins
½ tsp. salt	1 cup walnuts
1 tsp. cinnamon	

Preheat the oven to 350°
Cream butter and sugar. Add other ingredients. Pour into greased tube pan.
Bake 25 minutes, or until a toothpick comes out clean.
Serve with powdered sugar.

Refrain *"All glory, laud, and honor to thee, Redeemer, King, To whom the lips of children made sweet hosannas ring!*
Thou art the King of Israel, thou David's royal Son, Who in the Lord's name comest, the King and blessed One! (r) The company of angels is praising thee on high; and we with all creation in chorus make reply. (r) The people of the Hebrews with palms before thee went; Our praise and prayer and anthems before thee we present: (r) To thee, before thy passion, they sang their hymns of praise; To thee, now high exalted, our melody we raise. (r) Thou didst accept their praises; accept the prayers we bring, Who in all good delightest, thou good and gracious King! (r)"
Theodulph of Orleans

On Palm Sunday we celebrate the Liturgy of the Palms singing during the Processional these ancient words penned by Theodulph of Orleans (760-821). He was born into a well-to-do Italian family, but found his calling in Christ. He served as an abbot in a Florence monastery. In 781 Charlemagne appointed him Bishop of Orleans, France. Charlemagne died not long after, and Louis the Pious, King of Aquataine, accused Theodulph of supporting Italy, not France in a time of much turmoil. Theodulph was imprisoned in Angiers, France. There he wrote *All Glory Laud and Honor*, and died in 821. His imprisonment has been compared to St. Paul's, a cold dreary prison, but the light of his faith never faltered. So as we sing this hymn remember all those who gave their lives for Christ, and He for us.

Haricots Verts

Serves 4

1 lb. fresh green beans, trimmed	1 cup toasted walnuts
4 slices bacon, cooked and crumbled, reserve drippings	½ tsp. salt
	½ tsp. pepper
¼ lb. blue cheese	

Bring a pan of water to boil. Blanch beans in pan for 3 minutes. Drain and rinse beans with cold water.
Saute the beans in the bacon drippings for 2 minutes. Remove from heat.
Place in serving bowl and toss with blue cheese, nuts, salt and pepper.
Butter can be substituted for bacon drippings.

April 3

"Thanks be to Thee, my Lord Jesus Christ For all the benefits Thou hast given me, For all the pains and insults Thou hast borne for me. O most merciful Redeemer, friend and brother, May I know thee more clearly, love thee more dearly, and follow thee more nearly; for ever and ever."
St. Richard of Chichester

Richard of Wyche was born in Worcestershire, England c 1197. He studied at Oxford, and there became regent master and chancellor of the diocese of Canterbury under Archbishop Edmund Rich. In 1244 he was elected Bishop of Chichester and consecrated by Pope Innocent IV at Lyons in 1245. He protected the clergy and their rights, the poor, the sick and the bereaved. When Henry VIII became king of England he had St. Richard's shrine at Chichester destroyed. However, in 2007 the shrine was re-established and in the Anglican Church his feast day is now celebrated on June 16. May we follow in his foot steps loving and worshipping the Lord more and more each day.

Vegetable Curry

Serves 4

¼ cup olive oil
1 tbls. coriander
1½ tsp. cumin
½ tsp. tumeric
2 tbls. curry powder
¼ tsp. cayenne
1 medium head cauliflower, cut into florets

6 red potatoes, cubed
1 carrot, sliced
1 cup chicken stock
1 cup peas
2 tomatoes, diced
1 red pepper, sliced
¼ cup coconut
½ cup cilantro, chopped

In a skillet heat the oil. Stir in spices.
Add cauliflower, potatoes, carrot and stock. Cook until the potatoes are tender.
Add more stock if necessary.
Add peas, tomato and pepper.
Cook 15 minutes.
Stir in coconut and cilantro.
Serve with rice.

April 4

"We shall overcome..."
Reverend Charles Tindley of Philadelphia

"I have a dream..."
Martin Luther King

There was shock and disbelief. How could such a godly man be shot down in cold blood? He had rallied Americans of every color around him. He held marches attended by thousands. He preached love, forgiveness and equality. And then in a moment he was gone. Martin Luther King (1929-68), a Baptist clergyman personified all that was good to make a nation a better place. He led the Montgomery Bus Boycott (1955–6) and helped found the Southern Christian Leadership Conference (1957), serving as its first president. In 1963 Dr. King delivered his *"I Have a Dream Speech"* during the March on Washington for Jobs and Freedom. In 1964, Dr. King became the youngest person to receive the Nobel Peace Prize for his work to end racial segregation and racial discrimination through civil disobedience and other non-violent means. He opposed the Vietnam War. Dr. King was assassinated on April 4, 1968, in Memphis, Tennessee. He was posthumously awarded the Presidential Medal of Freedom in 1977 and Congressional Gold Medal in 2004; Martin Luther King, Jr. Day was established as a U.S. national holiday in 1986. His last sermon was preached at Washington National Cathedral. Sadly even though Dr. King preached nonviolence, riots took place throughout the United States following his death, and included the burning of parts of several cities.

Succotash

Serves 4

2 tbls. butter	1 cup chicken stock
2 green onions, chopped	1 tbls. fresh thyme, chopped
1 shallot, minced	2 tbls. fresh dill, snipped
2 cups fresh corn	½ tsp. sea salt
2 cups lima beans	½ tsp. fresh ground pepper

Melt butter in a sauce pan. Add onions and shallot. Add other ingredients. Simmer until corn and beans are tender. Serve warm.

April 5

"He is risen, he is risen! Tell it out with joyful voice: he has burst his three days' prison; let the whole wide earth rejoice: death is conquered, man is free, Christ has won the victory. Come, ye sad and fearful-hearted, with glad smile and radiant brow! Lent's long shadows have departed; Jesus' woes are over now, and the passion that he bore-- sin and pain can vex no more. Come, with high and holy hymning, hail our Lord's triumphant day; not one darksome cloud is dimming yonder glorious morning ray, breaking o'er the purple east, symbol of our Easter feast. He is risen, he is risen! He hath opened heaven's gate: we are free from sin's dark prison, risen to a holier state; and a brighter Easter beam on our longing eyes shall stream."
Cecil Frances Alexander 1846

Cecil Alexander (1818-95), Irish hymnist and poet, began writing at an early age, and her hymns were included in the Church of Ireland hymn books beginning in the 1840s. She published *Hymns for Little Children*. Among my favorite hymns are *All Things Bright and Beautiful, There is a Green Hill Far Away,* and *Once in Royal David's City*. She married Reverend William Alexander, afterwards Bishop of Derry and Archbishop of Armagh. She helped build the Derry and Raphoe Diocesan Institution for the Deaf and Dumb, which was founded in 1846. Mrs. Alexander and her husband were both blessed with the gift of writing and giving of themselves. May we all follow in her footsteps.

Baked Trout

Serves 4

4 whole trout, cleaned and gutted	¼ cup parsley, chopped
½ stick butter	¼ cup basil, chopped
2 leeks, sliced	¼ cup slivered almonds
1 red pepper, chopped	2 tbls. lemon juice
1 cup bread crumbs	2 tsp. sea salt

Preheat oven to 350°
Melt the butter in a skillet. Add leeks and pepper. Saute until just tender. Stir in bread crumbs, parsley, basil, almonds and lemon juice.
Rub the inside cavity of the fish with the salt.
Place the fish in a greased baking dish. Stuff fish with crumb mixture.
Bake 30-35 minutes.
Serve with parsley and lemon slices.

"In my distress I called upon the Lord, and cried unto my God: he heard my voice out of his temple, and my cry came before him, even into his ears."
Psalm 18:6

"So that we may boldly say, The Lord is my helper, and I will not fear what man shall do unto me."
Hebrews 13:6

Stress and tension in an office environment can cause a heavy toll both mentally and physically on a person. It does not matter whether you are young or approaching retirement. Just don't let it happen. Your mind begins to get paranoid, your body may experience TIAs (minor strokes), or worse a stroke or heart attack. No person needs to undergo this, even if it means losing a job. The worse scenario is a boss who constantly criticizes or cannot stop pouring on the work. Either talk through the situation with the person or resign. Life is too short. The healing process does not happen overnight. A week, a month, perhaps years. Be good to yourself. Your mind and body need peace, not stress.

Risotto with Crab

Serves 4

2 tbls. butter	1 tsp. fresh oregano
1 leek, sliced	2 tbls.chives, snipped
4 cups warm chicken stock	2 tbls. chopped basil
2 cups arborio rice	1 lb. fresh crab meat
½ lb. chanterelle mushrooms, sliced	Parmesan cheese
½ lb. fresh peas	

Melt the butter in a sauce pan. Stir in leek and rice. Slowly add the water, stirring until water is almost absorbed. Turn off heat and cover pan tightly. Let sit for at least 10 minutes.
Stir in mushrooms, peas, oregano, chives, basil and crab.
Serve in pasta bowls garnished with parmesan cheese.

April 7

"But be glad and rejoice forever in what I am creating; for I am about to create Jerusalem as a joy, and its people as a delight. I will rejoice in Jerusalem, and delight in my people; no more shall the sound of weeping be heard in it, or the cry of distress."
Isaiah 65:18-19

Westminster Abbey in London dates back to 1045-50 and was built by Edward the Confessor, although a shrine was thought to have existed as early as the 7th c. The abbey housed Benedictine monks and did not become a cathedral until c 1550. In 1579 Queen Elizabeth made it a royal peculiar, a church responsible to the monarchy, not a bishop, and it became known as the Collegiate Church of St. Peter. In this majestic building almost all English monarchs have been crowned and then seated on St. Edward's Chair. The Archbishop of Canterbury is responsible for the crowning. Royal weddings and funerals take place here, among the more recent the funeral for Lady Diana in 1997.

Worship of God can take place anywhere and in any form. However creating a building, a cathedral, glorifies God with its towering spires, majestic windows, altars, sculptures, and the symbols of Christianity.

Honey Chicken

Serves 4

½ cup chicken stock
½ stick butter
¼ cup honey
½ cup orange juice
2 tsp. cornstarch
Zest of 1 orange

Zest of 1 lemon
4 boneless chicken breasts
½ cup slivered almonds
½ cup currants
1 tsp. cinnamon

Preheat oven to 350°
Heat the stock, butter, honey, and orange juice in a pan. Bring to a boil. Stir in cornstarch, until just slightly thickened. Stir in zests.
Place the chicken in a baking dish. Cover with almonds, currants and cinnamon.
Pour the sauce over the chicken.
Bake 40 minutes.
Serve with rice.

April 8

"For we are God's workmanship, created in Jesus Christ to do good works, which God prepared in advance for us to do."
Ephesians 2:10

Winchester Cathedral dates back to the 7th century but was begun in 1079. The bishops that served this cathedra were wealthy and influential in England. Bishop William of Wykeham, was twice Chancellor of England, and founder of Winchester College and New College Oxford. Benedictine monks lived on the close from the cathedral's earliest years. Jane Austen's tomb is located in the cathedral. Izaak Walton, the author of *The Compleat Angler* ,died in 1683 and is also buried here. The cathedral stands out on the plain as you drive into Winchester, its towering spires a regional landmark. Morning prayer with prayers for the world is still said, and evensong is sung daily by the Cathedral's choir. The cathedral is built to the glory of God. I am privileged to have visited at evensong and witnessed the power of the Word, the hymns of praise, the beauty of the stained glass windows, especially the west window which is made up of pieces of glass recovered after Cromwell's forces destroyed it during the Civil War in 1642. We are here to do good works and appreciate all that surrounds us.

Beef Hash

Serves 4

2 tbls. butter
2 tbls. olive oil
1 medium red onion, chopped
4 red bliss potatoes, diced
1 lb. leftover roast beef
½ lb. smoked ham, diced

¼ cup fresh parsley, chopped
1 tsp. sea salt
1 tsp. pepper
Snipped chives
Poached eggs

Preheat oven to 400°
Heat the butter and olive oil in an iron skillet. Stir in onion and potatoes. Cook until just tender.
Stir in beef, ham, parsley, sea salt and pepper.
Bake in oven for 20 minutes, or browned and crispy.
Serve with poached eggs, garnished with chives.

April 9

"Refrain: Hail thee, festival day! Blest day that art hallowed forever; day wherein Christ arose, breaking the kingdom of death.
Lo, the fair beauty of earth, from the death of the winter arising, every good gift of the year now with its Master returns. Refrain He who was nailed to the Cross is God and the Ruler of all things; all things created on earth worship the Maker of all. Refrain"

Venantius Honorius Clementianus Fortunatus (c. 530-c. 600), an Italian poet and hymnist, left Italy for Gaul in the mid 560s. C 600 he became Bishop of Poitiers. Two of his poems have become part of the liturgy of the Roman Catholic Church, the *Pange Lingua Gloriosi Proelium Certaminis* ("Sing, O tongue, of the glorious struggle. He also wrote *Vexilla Regis prodeunt* ("The banners of the King are lifted"), sung at Vespers during Holy Week. This poem was written in honor of a piece of the True Cross that had been sent from the Byzantine Emperor Justin II to Queen Radegunde of the Franks, who founded a monastery in Aquitaine. He also wrote *Welcome, Happy Morning*.

This hymn that we sing at Easter originally included sections for Easter, Ascension, Pentecost and Corpus Christi. The refrain and alternating verses carry different tunes, which sometimes makes it more difficult to sing and understand. The original was written in Latin, and has now been translated several times, and to different tunes.

Tsoureki (Greek Easter Bread)

2 packages yeast	12 cups flour
2 cups scalded milk	½ tsp. baking powder
2 sticks unsalted butter	½ cup slivered almonds
1½ cups sugar	½ tsp. vanilla
6 eggs	3 hard boiled eggs, dyed red
Zest of 1 lemon	1 egg beaten with 1 tbls. water

Dissolve the yeast in ½ cup milk. Put aside and let double.
Cream the butter and the sugar.
Beat the yeast, eggs and lemon zest in a bowl. Add the rest of the milk.
Slowly add the flour and baking powder. Knead the dough with a dough hook. Make into a ball, place in a bowl and cover until double in size. Punch dough and divide into 3 loaves. Divide these 3 once again. Braid dough. Place on greased cookie sheet(s), cover and let rise again until doubled.
Preheat oven to 350°. Brush the loaves with the beaten egg. Sprinkle with almonds and insert colored egg into each loaf. Bake 30 minutes, golden brown.

April 10

"At the name of Jesus every knee shall bow, every tongue confess him King of glory now; 'tis the Father's pleasure we should call him Lord, who from the beginning was the mighty Word. Humbled for a season, to receive a Name from the lips of sinners, unto whom he came, faithfully he bore it spotless to the last, brought it back victorious, when from death he passed; bore it up triumphant, with its human light, through all ranks of creatures, to the central height, to the throne of Godhead, to the Father's breast; filled it with the glory of that perfect rest. Name him, Christians, name him, with love strong as death, name with awe and wonder and with bated breath; he is God the Savior, he is Christ the Lord, ever to be worshiped, trusted, and adored. In your hearts enthrone him; there let him subdue all that is not holy, all that is not true; crown him as your Captain in temptation's hour; let his will enfold you in its light and power. Christians, this Lord Jesus shall return again, with his Father's glory o'er the earth to reign; for all wreaths of empire meet upon his brow, and our hearts confess him King of glory now."

Caroline Maria Noel (1817-77) wrote this hymn quoting from Philippians 2:10-11; Isaiah 45:23 and Romans 14:11. As the churches have become more progressive there is a lot less knee bending and heads bowing to our Lord. No longer do many people genuflect before the altar or entering a pew, or bow their heads when the cross is carried by. We do this for respect of our Lord. We daily need to bow our head heads in prayer and every word that shall be spoken is to His glory.

Tomato Bisque

Serves 4

¼ cup olive oil
4 cloves garlic, minced
2 leeks, sliced
2 tsp. cumin
¼ cup cilantro, chopped

2 cups chicken stock
8 medium tomatoes, sliced
1 tsp. sea slat
1 tsp. pepper
¼ tsp. cayenne or hot sauce

Heat the olive oil in a pan. Add the garlic and leeks. Cook 3 minutes. Stir in the other ingredients. Bring to a boil. Simmer 30 minutes. Let cool.
Place in a food processor until smooth.
Serve in bowls with croutons and cilantro.

April 11

"Our Father which art in heaven, hallowed by thy name. Thy kingdom come. Thy will be done on earth, as it is in heaven. Give us this day our daily bread. And forgive our debts, as we forgive our debtors. And lead us not into temptation, but deliver us from evil, for thine is the kingdom, and the power, and the glory forever. Amen."
Matthew 6:9-13
The Lord's Prayer

From an early age we are taught to pray to our Lord. We kneel beside our bed at night, kneel in church, and during the day hopefully find time to read lessons and pray. Without prayer there is little time to reflect on our lives and what is surrounding us. We need time to talk to God, he needs to talk to us. We must listen and be silent. We are obedient to our God who calls us to listen. Think of those who have listened – Abraham, Moses, Elijah, Isaiah, Mary, and Jesus Christ. Follow in their footsteps and be called. "Here I am."

Stuffed Grape Leaves

2 tbls. olive oil
1 small onion, chopped
½ lb. ground lamb
2 tbls. pine nuts
¼ cup currants
1 cup cooked rice
¼ cup parsley, chopped
2 tbls. mint, chopped

½ tsp. tumeric
½ tsp. salt
30 grape leaves
2 lemons, sliced
2 tbls. olive oil
2 tbls. water

Preheat oven to 325°
Heat the olive oil in a skillet and add onions. Stir until just tender. Add lamb, and cook until just browned. Drain any excess fat. Add the pine nuts, currants, rice, parsley, mint, turmeric and salt.
Divide up the meat mixture evenly on the grape leaves, about 1 tbls. each. Turn the stem end of leaf and fold, then do each of the other corners and roll into a cylinder shape. The dampness of the leaf should hold the it together.
Place the lemon slices in a baking dish.
Place the stuffed grape leaves on the lemons, seam side down. Sprinkle with olive oil and water. Cover baking dish.
Bake 50 minutes.
The leaves can also be cooked on the stove in a covered skillet for 50 minutes over low heat.

April 12

"Come, Thou almighty King, Help us Thy Name to sing, help us to praise! Father all glorious, o'er all victorious, Come and reign over us, Ancient of Days! Jesus, our Lord, arise, Scatter our enemies, and make them fall; Let Thine almighty aid our sure defense be made, Souls on Thee be stayed; Lord, hear our call. Come, Thou incarnate Word, Gird on Thy mighty sword, our prayer attend! Come, and Thy people bless, and give Thy Word success, Spirit of holiness, on us descend! Come, holy Comforter, Thy sacred witness bear in this glad hour. Thou Who almighty art, now rule in every heart, And ne'er from us depart, Spirit of power! To Thee, great One in Three, Eternal praises be, hence, evermore. Thy sovereign majesty may we in glory see, And to eternity love and adore!"

Felice de Giardini ((1716-96) wrote the music specifically for this hymn. The hymn itself is considered anonymous, but might have been composed by Charles Wesley. As a child Giardini was considered a musical genius, and was sent to Milan to study. He excelled on the violin, went on to play concerts throughout Europe, and eventually settled in London. There he became concertmaster and director for the Italian Opera. Unfortunately he later encountered financial difficulties, and trying to find his place again, died in Moscow.

This hymn is almost always sung on Trinity Sunday, the Sunday following Pentecost. Trinity Sunday is one of the seven feast days in the Episcopal Church. Trinity Sunday has the status of a Principal Feast in the Church of England and is one of seven principal feast days in the Episcopal Church. Thomas Becket (1118-70) consecrated as Archbishop of Canterbury on the Sunday after Whit Sunday, ordained the feast day.

Baked Onions

Serves 6

½ stick butter
6 large onions, peeled and sliced
¼ cup sherry
½ tsp. nutmeg

1 cup heavy cream
½ cup Swiss cheese
½ cup parmesan cheese

Preheat oven to 350°
Melt the butter in an iron skillet. Saute onions, until tender.
Remove onions and deglaze pan with the sherry. Put onions back in pan.
Combine with sherry. Stir in nutmeg, cream and Swiss cheese. Top with parmesan cheese. Bake 20-25 minutes, or until just browned.

April 13

"A merry heart doeth good like a medicine..."
Proverbs 17:22

When we lived in New Castle, Delaware my parents belonged to what they called the "Garbage Group". This was not long after World War II. The families did not have much money. Everyone was asked to bring a dish and a theme was chosen for the evening. The grownups smoked cigarettes and drank martinis. If it was at our house, we'd sneak down the stairs to peek at what was going on. The group obviously had a ball doing things together and what a mix of people. The women, as I remember did not work. Two couples had no children, and they were our adopted "aunts and uncles". The men were employed by Dupont, Playtex, GM, and included a hospital administrator, newspaperman, and other occupations. Sadly all, except my parents and one lady, have passed on to our heavenly Father. Life seemed so simple, carefree and such fun back then. I wish we had more of that in our lives now.

Jambalaya

Serves 8

¼ cup olive oil
1 onion, chopped
1 red pepper, sliced
1 green pepper, sliced
2 green onions, chopped
4 cloves garlic, crushed
2 stalks celery, sliced
½ cup parsley, chopped
3 cups chicken stock

2 bay leaves
1 tsp. thyme
1 tsp. cayenne
1 tbls. fresh ground pepper
2 cups basmati rice
1 lb. hot smoked sausage, thinly sliced and cooked
3 lbs. shrimp, cooked, peeled and deveined

In a large pot heat the olive oil. Saute the onion, peppers, green onions, garlic and celery, until just tender.
Stir in parsley, stock, bay leaves, thyme, cayenne, pepper and rice. Cook 30 minutes, covered.
Add shrimp and sausage until warmed.

"And he (Peter) said unto him, Lord, thou knowest that I love thee. "He said unto him, Feed my sheep."
John 21:17

Why do we doubt that God loves us, and we him? Yes, there are days when it seems nothing can go right, but let God hold you in the palm of his hand. Let him be in charge, not you. Let Him talk to you. Be silent and listen. Be still, my soul.

"Be still, my soul: the Lord is on thy side. Bear patiently the cross of grief or pain. Leave to thy God to order and provide; In every change, He faithful will remain. Be still, my soul: thy best, thy heavenly Friend Through thorny ways leads to a joyful end... Be still, my soul: when dearest friends depart, And all is darkened in the vale of tears, Then shalt thou better know His love, His heart, Who comes to soothe thy sorrow and thy fears. Be still, my soul: thy Jesus can repay From His own fullness all He takes away."

Katherina von Schlegel (1697-1768) was part of the ducal court in Kothen, Germany. She composed at least 20 hymns.

Grilled Lamb with Mint Sauce

Serves 6

1 boneless leg of lamb, about 6-7 lbs.
¼ cup fresh ground pepper

2 tsp. garlic salt
2 tbls. fresh rosemary

Rub the lamb with the pepper, garlic and rosemary. Cook on grill until desired pinkness, about one hour. Serve with mint sauce.

Mint Sauce

3 cloves garlic, minced
¼ cup apple cider vinegar
¼ cup packed cilantro leaves, chopped

½ cup packed mint leaves, chopped
½ cup olive oil
Juice of 2 limes or lemon

Combine all ingredients in a bowl. Serve with the lamb

April 15

"For I have received of the Lord that which also I delivered unto you, that the Lord Jesus the same night in which he was betrayed took bread: And when he had given thanks, he brake it, and said, Take, eat: this is my body, which is broken for you: this do in remembrance of me. After the same manner also he took the cup, when he had supped, saying, this cup is the new testament in my blood: this do ye, as oft as ye drink it, in remembrance of me. For as often as ye eat this bread, and drink this cup, ye do shew the Lord's death till he come."
1 Corinthians 11:23-26

Each time I hear this during Communion, I am reminded of Leonardo da Vinci's *Last Supper*. What could be a more poignant moment than seeing Jesus surrounded by his apostles and the one who would betray Him. He knew the last supper would be the last time all his apostles would be with him. None of them could ever realize his short life would be taken from them, so that he would die for our sins. Drinking the cup of wine and eating the bread of life should be a time of reflection, prayer and the power Christ has over us. *"Christ our Passover is sacrificed for us. Therefore let us keep the feast"*. Da Vinci (1452-1519) created his masterpiece from 1494-98 for the monastery of Santa Maria delle Grazie. The Mona Lisa is thought to have been painted between 1503-06.

Rosemary French Bread

1 cup warm water	2 tbls. olive oil
1 package yeast	1 tbls. sea salt
3 cups flour	2 tbls. rosemary

Dissolve the yeast in the warm water.
Place the flour in a food processor and slowly add the yeast and other ingredients until a ball is formed.
Put the dough in an oiled bowl. Cover with a cloth. Set in a warm place and let rise one hour, or doubled in size.
Oil a baking sheet and shape the dough into a long loaf. Let rise one more hour.
Preheat oven to 450°
Bake 15 minutes, or until golden brown.
Serve with olive oil or butter.

April 16

"Why died I not from the womb? Why did I not give up the ghost when I came out of the belly? Why did the knees prevent me? Or why the breasts that I should suck?"
Job 3:11-12

"By the rivers of Babylon, there we sat down, and there we wept when we remembered Zion. On the willows there we hung up our harps. For there our captors asked us for words of song, and our tormentors, for mirth: "Sing to us from the songs of Zion!" How could we sing the song of the LORD on an alien land? If I forget thee, O Jerusalem, may my right hand forget its skill, May my tongue cling to the roof of my mouth if I do not remember you, if I do not set Jerusalem above my highest joy. Remember, O LORD, against the sons of Edom the day of Jerusalem's fall, those who said: "Tear it down! Tear it down to its foundation!" O daughter of Babylon that will be devastated: Fortunate is the man who repays you what you have done to us; Fortunate is the man who will seize and dash your little ones against the rock!"
Psalm 137

To me these are some of the saddest lines in the Bible. Woe to poor Job who has lost everything, and woe to the captive Jews in Babylon. These were people long ago, but even today there are many lamenting their lives, especially with suicidal tendencies. For some this has run in the family – a father or mother committing suicide and a child now contemplating it. Help is out there. Please seek it for yourself, or someone you love. Life is worth living. Remember that all was restored to Job. Praise the Lord!

Ceviche

Serves 8

2 lbs. bay scallops
1 red pepper, diced
1 red onion, chopped
2 tomatoes, chopped
2 cloves garlic, minced
¼ cup cilantro, chopped

1 tsp. sea salt
1 tsp. pepper
1 cup lime juice
2 avocados, peeled, pitted and sliced thinly

Combine all ingredients, except avocado, in a bowl. Cover and refrigerate at least 2 hours.
Serve in martini glasses. Garnish with avocado slices.

April 17

"Hear my prayer, O Lord, and let my cry come unto thee. Hide not thy face from me in the day when I am in trouble; incline thy ear unto me: in the day when I call answer me speedily."
Psalm 102:1-2

Growing up my family moved several times, when I was ten and fourteen - difficult years. My mother was tall and elegant, my father tall and handsome. I was short, plump and terribly shy. I found it hard to make new friends. The schools I attended already had their cliques. I was sent to dancing class, which I loved; but get me into a modern dance class or Phys Ed, I was the most uncoordinated young lady. Luckily I enjoyed playing tennis, and when I spent summers on Nantucket could get out on the courts. I was never really that good, but it was a wonderful way to make friends and get some exercise. Over the years I walked a lot and now attend an aerobics class. Each morning is spent reading the Word and saying prayers. The Lord heard my cry and answered me. I am thankful for who I am.

Corn and Shrimp Chowder

Serves 4

2 tbls. butter
1 medium onion, chopped
1 carrot, peeled and sliced
2 cloves garlic, minced
2 cups chicken stock
2 cups corn

1½ lbs. shrimp, cooked, peeled and deveined
2 cups heavy cream
2 tbls. fresh dill, snipped
2 tbls. parsley, chopped
Paprika

Melt the butter in a large sauce pan. Add onion and carrot, cooking for about 5 minutes, or until tender. Add garlic.
Add stock and simmer for 20 minutes. Add the corn. Cook for 15 minutes.
Fold in the shrimp and cream.
Serve in bowls garnished with dill and parsley. Sprinkle paprika on the chowder.

April 18

"He is like a man which built an house, and digged deep, and laid the foundation on a rock; and when the flood arose, the stream beat vehemently upon that house, and could not shake it: for it was founded upon a rock."
Luke 6:48

St. Peter's Basilica, is located within Vatican City in Rome. Saint Peter, who, was the first Bishop of Antioch, and later first Bishop of Rome is buried here below the altar. There are over 100 tombs in the Basilica, and include 91 popes, St. Ignatius of Antioch, Holy Roman Emperor Otto II, and the composer Giovanni Pierluigi da Palestrina. Construction on the present basilica, over the old Constantinian basilica, began on April 18, 1506 and was completed in 1626. St. Peter's is not a cathedral, as it is not the seat of a bishop. The entrance to the east and the apse at the west end of the building are typical of early Roman churches. Michelangelo designed the dome of the basilica.

Eggs Florentine

Serves 4

4 English muffins, split and toasted
½ stick butter
¼ cup flour
½ cup half and half
½ cup heavy cream
¼ lb. baby spinach

½ cup parmesan cheese
15 oz. can artichoke hearts, drained and chopped
2 tbls. dill, snipped
8 poached eggs

Melt the butter. Stir in the flour, then half and half and cream. Fold in the spinach, parmesan cheese and artichoke hearts.
Divide spinach mixture between 8 English muffin halves. Top with poached eggs and Hollandaise sauce. Garnish with dill.
Crab can be substituted for spinach and artichoke hearts
Frozen creamed spinach can be substituted for creamed spinach mixture.

Hollandaise Sauce

3 egg yolks
1 stick butter, melted

¼ cup fresh lemon juice

Place the yolks in a food processor until blended. Slowly pour in the butter and then lemon juice. Process until thickened.

April 19

"I waited patiently for the Lord, and he inclined unto me and heard my calling."
Psalm 40:1

This has always been one of my favorite verses in the psalms. In this day and age everyone is moving so fast sometimes you can't catch your breath. Everything has to be instantaneous – the Internet, phone calls, work, play, even catching a few winks of sleep will disrupt what is going on. Life didn't use to be this way. Times were simpler. People had more time to enjoy each other's company, write a letter, sit down for a special meal, or just relax. If God wants to tell you where you are going, wait for Him to speak. Wait patiently. Good things will happen. Rushing gets you nowhere.

Patience is a virtue. Sometimes we want things to happen immediately. That is not God's plan. Waiting patiently does renew strength. Take time to think through a situation. Let God speak to you when he is ready. Rushing can only hurt, or make a mistake worse. Life is to be positive. God will tell you what to do.

Baked Trout II

Serves 4

2 cloves garlic, minced
1 leek, finely chopped
2 tsp. fresh thyme, minced
1 tsp. pepper
4 trout, about ¾ lb. each, cleaned

4 bay leaves
½ stick butter, melted
¼ cup lemon juice
Paprika

Preheat oven to 400°
In a bowl combine the garlic, leek, thyme, and pepper. Spread mixture in each trout cavity. Put in bay leaf.
Grease a baking tray and place fish on tray.
Pour butter on top of each fish.
Bake for 15 minutes. Remove bay leaves.
Sprinkle fish with lemon juice and paprika. Serve with rice.

April 20

"Mine house shall be called a house of prayer for all people."
Isaiah 56:7

Washington National Cathedral is one of the most incredible structures in the world. Built over a period of 100 years, the building will never be completed. More rosettes, stained glass windows, another chapel, always a work in progress, plus the maintenance that must continually be done to maintain this magnificent structure. During the year, State Days are celebrated with visiting dignitaries, bishops, rectors, choirs, and lots of banners. For ten years I served on the Cathedral Fund Committee and as a Lay Eucharistic Minister. Whenever I can return, I do so - Wednesdays for the noon organ recital, midday prayer, evensong, or a Sunday service. Each time I go back, I spot a new window, an old friend, or am touched by the beauty of the flowers and music. Worship can be anywhere. Being in a cathedral at evensong helps me through a day and prepares me for the next. English cathedrals do this more than American, but savor every moment. One of the banners near the high altar is embroidered with the above words. I have been in the Cathedral with all people – Christian, Muslim, Jew, and others. It is truly a house of prayer for all people!

Divine Bars

1 stick butter
1 cup graham crackers, crushed
1 cup coconut
1 package chocolate chips

1 package butterscotch chips
1 cup pecans or walnuts
1 cup dried cranberries
1 can sweet condensed milk

Preheat oven to 350°
Melt butter in 9 x 13 pan.
Sprinkle butter with graham crackers, then coconut, chips, nuts, and cranberries.
Pour condensed milk over the top.
Bake 30 minutes.
Remove from oven. Cool. Cut into bars.

April 21

"Lord, make me taste by love what I taste by knowledge, let me know by love what I know by understanding...I am wholly yours by creation; make me wholly yours in love."
Anselm, Archbishop of Canterbury c1033-1109

Anselm was born in Aosta, Italy and took his vows as a Benedictine monk at the Abbey of Bec in Normandy. He became prior of the abbey in 1063 and Archbishop of Canterbury in 1093. Anselm is considered the first true Christian theologian. He wrote about the importance of the existence of God in the *Proslogium* and *Monologium* and the necessity of atonement in *Cur Deus Homo* (Why God Became Man?), the reconciliation of God and man through the death of our Lord. He was opposed to the Crusades and forbade his monks to go forth on them. He devoted himself to prayer. Please make more time in your day for quietness and prayer.

Stuffed Veal

Serves 4

8 veal scaloppini, pounded thin
8 slices prosciutto
3 tbls. fresh parsley, chopped
3 tbls. rosemary, chopped
2 tbls. shallots, chopped

4 cloves garlic, minced
2 tbls. olive oil
2 tbls. butter
¼ cup Madeira or dry red wine

Preheat oven to 350°
Lay the veal flat and top with each slice with a piece of prosciutto. Sprinkle parsley, rosemary, shallots and garlic on prosciutto. Roll veal and tie with a light string or secure with a toothpick.
Heat butter and olive oil in an iron skillet. Brown veal.
Pour Madeira over the veal.
Bake in oven for 10 minutes.
Serve with pasta.

"Our soul waiteth for the Lord: he is our help and our shield. For our heart shall rejoice in him, because we have trusted in his holy name."
Psalm 33:20-21

Today I walk in Yorktown thinking of the sacrifices that my ancestors and others made during the Revolutionary War. There are monuments and the battleground, sacred territory to honor those who fought and won freedom for our country. I am proud to be an American.

However it is Earth Day. From the monuments overlooking the York River I stroll down to the beach, collecting my thoughts and breathing in the fresh sea air. Unlike further up the river or the nearby Chesapeake Bay, the water is clear. Dozens of large jellyfish lie dying. Where did they come from? In the Bay we have sea nettles, but these are too big and with larger tentacles. The day is cool, so I don't dip my feet in the water. As I wander along I think about those people who are walking along the waterways and other areas cleaning up. I stoop and do my part. There are a couple of wine bottles – someone must have been partying on the beach last night because they haven't filled up with sand or sea water. Then there is an old onion burlap sack. I walk back and forth to the trash cans doing my own little part to save our planet. I'm glad to have this quiet time, and gather my thoughts for the day. There will be book stores and gift shops, the Aquarium and other museums to sell my books. I sit down for a couple of minutes, and listen and wait for the Lord to speak to me. I know He is always there.

Couscous Salad II

Serves 6

2 cups chicken stock	4 green onions, chopped
2 cups couscous	1 cup dried currants
¼ cup olive oil	1 cup fresh peas
¼ cup lemon juice	1 cup pitted black olives
1 red pepper, sliced	¼ cup parsley or cilantro
1 yellow pepper, sliced	

Bring the stock to a boil. Stir in couscous. Turn off heat. Let cool. Add other ingredients.
Chill.
This can also be served warm.

April 23

"Now thank we all our God, with heart and hands and voices, Who wondrous things has done, in Whom this world rejoices; Who from our mothers' arms has blessed us on our way With countless gifts of love, and still is ours today. O may this bounteous God through all our life be near us, With ever joyful hearts and blessèd peace to cheer us; And keep us in His grace, and guide us when perplexed; And free us from all ills, in this world and the next! All praise and thanks to God the Father now be given; The Son and Him Who reigns with Them in highest Heaven; The one eternal God, whom earth and Heaven adore; For thus it was, is now, and shall be evermore."

Martin Rinckart (1586-1649) composed the hymn while a Lutheran minister in Eilenburg during the 30 Years' War. The Swedes had surrounded the walled city. Those inside perished from famine and plague, and much of the city was destroyed. Finally all the pastors died, leaving only Mr. Rinckart. When the Swedes demanded a huge ransom he left the city to meet with the Swedish commander who was so impressed by his faith and courage, the ransom was lowered. Catherine Winkworth translated the hymn into English.

Apple Pancakes

Serves 8

4 eggs
1 cup flour
2 tsp. baking powder
1 cup milk
½ tsp. salt

¼ cup sugar
1 tbls. cinnamon
½ stick butter
2 large apples, thinly sliced

In a bowl combine the eggs, flour, baking powder, milk salt, sugar and cinnamon.
Preheat oven to 400°
Please 2 large iron skillets in the oven, dividing the butter equally in each pan.
Melt the butter. Remove from oven and arrange the apple slices in the 2 pans.
Pour the batter over the apples.
Bake 25 minutes, until puffed and golden in color.
Sprinkle with powdered sugar. Serve immediately. Cut each pancake into four wedges.

April 24

"The Book of the generation of Jesus Christ, the son of David, the son of Abraham..."
Matthew 1:1

"To the Glory of God, and in grateful remembrance of those our ancestors who, through evil report and loss of fortune, through suffering and death, maintained stout hearts and laid the foundation of our country, we, The National Society of The Colonial Dames of America, pledge our loyal and affectionate allegiance to the flag. "
From the wall of the reconstructed church in Jamestown

As a member of the National Society of the Colonial Dames of America, I am proud of my heritage and that my ancestors were faithful to our Lord. The Society was founded in 1891 by a group of Philadelphia ladies who wished to preserve our history, patriotism and historic buildings. My ancestor Governor Thomas Dudley (1576-1653) became a Puritan in the 1590s. Because of religious tension and fear of persecution in England he came to Massachusetts in 1630. He served four terms as Governor of Massachusetts. He founded Cambridge in 1631 and in 1651 signed the charter for Harvard College. He was also one of the founders of the First Church of Boston, now located at Berkley and Marlborough Streets. Governor Dudley believed the state should be in control of the church.

Cream of Mushroom Soup

Serves 4

½ stick butter
1 lb. wild mushrooms
1 stalk celery, chopped
1 carrot, thinly sliced
2 scallions, chopped
½ cup parsley, chopped

2 cups chicken stock
2 cups cream
¼ cup sherry
½ tsp. salt
1 tsp. pepper
Nutmeg

Melt the butter in a pan. Add mushrooms, celery, carrot, scallions and parsley. Saute for about 5 minutes, or until tender.
Place half of mushroom mixture in a food processor and puree. Pour back into pan. Add stock and cream. Add sherry, salt, pepper and remaining mushrooms. Serve in bowls garnished with ground nutmeg.

April 25

"The Church's one foundation Is Jesus Christ her Lord, She is His new creation By water and the Word. From heaven He came and sought her To be His holy bride; With His own blood He bought her And for her life He died...O happy ones and holy! Lord, give us grace that we Like them, the meek and lowly, On high may dwell with Thee: There, past the border mountains, Where in sweet vales the Bride With Thee by living fountains Forever shall abide!"

Samuel John Stone (1839-1900) was an ordained minister in the Church of England. He wrote over fifty hymns, the most famous one being *The Church's One Foundation*. The words come from 1 Corinthians 3:11 *"For other foundation can no man lay than that is laid, Which is Jesus Christ"* and Ephesians 2:20 *"And are built upon the foundation of the apostles and prophets, Jesus Christ himself being the chief cornerstone."* Christ is our foundation, our cornerstone, and we are baptized with water and the word. We are a worldwide church, reaching out at all times to others. We also see schisms such as in the present Episcopal, Presbyterian and Methodist Churches, over homosexuality and ordination of women. This is not the way it should be. We need that one foundation, that one cornerstone, the trust we have in Jesus Christ our Lord.

St. Mark's feast day is celebrated on the anniversary of his martyrdom. Not only is he thought to be the author of the Gospel of Mark, but also was a companion of Saint Peter. He served as the first bishop and the first Pope of Alexandria. His symbol is the lion.

Honey Crullers

4 cups flour
4 eggs, beaten
¼ cup sugar
½ tsp. baking powder
Zest of 1 lemon
2 tbls. vegetable oil

Oil for frying
1 cup honey
1 tbls. water
Cinnamon
Coarsely chopped walnuts

Place the flour in a bowl and make a well. Pour in the eggs, sugar, baking powder, zest and oil. Knead until stiff.
Roll out on a floured board. Cut into strips.
Heat oil. Drop strips in oil, twisting them to form a circle. Fry until golden brown.
In a sauce pan bring the honey and water to a boil.
Pour the honey over the crullers and sprinkle with cinnamon and walnuts.

And all thy children shall be taught of the Lord: and great shall be the peace of thy children."
Isaiah 54:13

"I have no greater joy than to hear that my children walk in truth."
3 John 1:4

Daughters are a source of love. My daughter was conceived in San Francisco, but was born in Washington where we had moved only three weeks before. Because I was so pregnant I was not permitted to fly across the country. Instead my husband and I drove in our little Vega, stopping for Palm Sunday in Los Angeles with friends. Then on to Las Vegas, Shamrock, Texas, Tulsa, Saint Louis and finally Cleveland where his family lived. Each day we stayed one day ahead of a snow storm. I was praying awfully hard this baby would not arrive prematurely. Thankfully the storm hit us in Cleveland and we had to postpone our arrival in Washington by a day. Luckily through my doctor in San Francisco, he found an obstetrician and pediatrician who would take me in. Thank goodness my mother arrived for several days, and briefed me on the fundamentals of a new baby. For my daughter her paternal grandmother was more than delighted to have a little girl after four sons! Children and grandchildren are the greatest joy. Teach them to walk in the ways of the Lord.

Smoked Salmon Blini

1 cup sour cream
1 cup whipped cream

1 lb. smoked salmon
½ cup dill, snipped

In a bowl combine the sour cream and whipped cream.
Place the blini on a tray. Top each with a piece of smoked salmon. Top with a spoonful of sour cream mixture. Garnish with the dill.
At Christmas garnish with red caviar and dill.

Cornmeal Blini

2 cups white cornmeal
2 tsp. baking powder
1 tsp. salt

2 eggs
2 cups milk
Butter

In a bowl beat together the cornmeal, baking powder, salt, eggs and milk.
Melt butter in a skillet. Drop mixture by spoonful (size of large silver dollar) into a skillet. Turn and brown on each side. Remove to rack

April 27

"In that day shall there be upon the bells of the horses, HOLINESS UNTO THE LORD..."
Zechariah 14:20

Several generations of my family have attended the Maryland Hunt Cup. This steeplechase race is run the 4th Saturday of April in Glyndon, Maryland. Elaborate picnics are prepared, guests mill around the hillside and party until post time at 4PM. Afterwards we head to a friend's house for dinner and reminisce about the day – who raced, who won, and marvel at the beauty of the horses. Some still dress for the occasion, but with increasing casualness most appear in clothing fit for the day, which has been known to be quite warm, quite cool, or a lot of rain. You come prepared for anything. . Gone are the days of high heels, gloves and suits for the ladies; jacket and tie for the gentlemen. But that it still goes on over one hundred years later, attests to the enduring love of horses and tradition. I love being out on that hillside, marveling at all God has created – the lush fields, the sky, the horses, the bounty set before us, and the company we keep. Thank you Lord.

Lemon Bars

2 cups flour
½ cup confectioners' sugar
1½ sticks butter (at room temperature)

6 eggs
3 cups sugar
Zest of 2 lemons
Juice of 5 lemons

Preheat the oven to 325°
In a bowl combine 1½ cups flour, the confectioners' sugar and butter.
Press the mixture into a 13 x 9 inch baking dish. Bake 25 minutes, or until just browned. Remove from oven and cool.
Reduce oven to 300°
In a bowl beat the eggs, sugar, lemon zest and lemon juice, until thickened. Add ½ cup flour.
Pour the batter over the crust.
Bake for 35 minutes. Let cool. Sprinkle with powdered sugar.
Cut into bars.
Store in the refrigerator.

April 28

":Greater love hath no man than this, that a man lay down his life for his friends. Ye are my friends..."
John 15:13-14

In college I had two very close friends, one Iranian, the other Japanese. They shared the same birthday, April 28th. The Iranian had been educated in Europe, had travelled extensively and was very worldly. My Japanese friend had travelled a bit, but lived in a fairly protected family. Our freshman year we celebrated their birthdays at the local pizzeria. We downed a couple Cokes and ate pizza. For dessert someone suggested Grasshoppers. This drink is lethal – crème de cacao, green crème de menthe and vodka. It is very sweet, and one is enough. That night we had to carry our Japanese friend out of the restaurant, get her into a cab back to the dorm, and sneak her in past the dorm mother. No small feat back then! I don't remember the rest of us getting drunk, but obviously it left a lasting impression. The Bible in several passages teaches us that we should not drink, or at least be drunk, otherwise we *shall not inherit the kingdom of God.* (1 Corinthians 6:10) Since that time we have all managed to stay good people, and pray that we are God's people!

Grasshopper Pie

½ stick butter, melted
18 Hydrox cookies, crushed
25 marshmallows
½ cup milk

¼ cup green crème de menthe
2 tbls. white crème de cacao
1 cup whipped cream

Preheat oven to 400°
In the bottom of a pie plate combine the butter and cookies. Press into the plate. Bake in oven for 10 minutes.
In a sauce pan melt the marshmallows and milk until marshmallows are melted. Refrigerate for 1 hour.
Stir in crème de menthe, crème de cacao. Fold in whipped cream.
Pour into the pie shell. Freeze for 3-4 hours. Put in refrigerator for 2 hours before serving.

April 29

"Do not store up for yourselves treasures on earth, where moth and rust destroy and where thieves break in and steal. But store up for yourselves treasures in heaven...For where your treasure is, there will your heart be also."
Matthew 6:19-21

"How hard it is for those who have wealth to enter the kingdom of God."
Luke 18:24

As I drive through Greenwich I realize the wealth in this community, unlike any other place I have lived. Everywhere there are mega mansions, incredibly expensive cars, extravagant shops, a policeman at every corner, children sent to boarding or private school, and families owning one or more other homes. Does it bring happiness and knowledge of God into their lives? Do fathers (and mothers) have to work so hard to outdo the Jones that the reason for living is just work, or to be too rich? Sadly for some of these families there is no limit on how much they want and can spend. However, there are also families that regularly attend church, participate in Bible study groups, are actively involved in the community and charitable work, who truly know and serve the Lord. My fervent prayer is that those who seek only riches will come to know how hard it is to enter heaven.

Beef Tenderloin with Blue Cheese Sauce

Serves 4

4 beef tenderloin	2 tbls. rosemary, snipped
½ lb. blue cheese	2 tbls. basil, snipped
½ stick butter	½ cup pecans or walnuts

Take the butter and blue cheese out of the refrigerator about an hour before using.
Combine the blue cheese, butter, rosemary, basil and nuts in a bowl.
Cook the tenderloin on a grill or under the broiler until desired pinkness.
Serve the steaks with the blue cheese sauce.

April 30

"The heavens declare the glory of God; the skies proclaim the work of his hands."
Psalm 19:1

Driving across the Bay Bridge my husband and I notice not one, but two rainbows. The heavy rain had stopped and the sky lit up with God's majesty. All along Route 50 the rainbows persisted. Arriving home two rainbows again appeared, this time over the Episcopal Cathedral. Running inside to get his camera, George shot a few pictures. On looking at them, they could not capture what we had just observed. God had splashed the sky with color. Only the human eye could capture the awesome sight. The skies do proclaim God in all His glory, the work of His hands.

Shrimp/Crab Casserole

Serves 8

1 stick butter	½ cup Sherry or Madeira
½ cup flour	2 lbs. lump crab meat
2 cups cream	2 cans artichoke hearts, drained
1 tsp. fresh pepper	2 lbs. shrimp, cooked, peeled and
2 tbls. dill, snipped	deveined
2 tbls. parsley, chopped	½ cup cornflakes
½ pound Gruyere cheese	2 tbls. butter, melted

Preheat oven to 350°
In a saucepan melt the butter. Stir in the flour and cream until thickened.
Add pepper, dill, parsley, and Sherry.
Fold in crab, shrimp and artichoke hearts.
Pour mixture into a baking dish. Top with cornflakes.
Bake 20-25 minutes, until bubbling and just browned.

May 1

"I am the rose of Sharon and the lily of the valleys. As the lily among thorns, so is my love among the daughters."
Song of Solomon 2:1-2

May Day. A time to pick flowers for mother. We used to make a beeline for the garden as soon as we got up. It was usually violets or lilies of the valley. Then we would tie them with a bow and present them to my mother. Not a single cent spent, only love from the heart. Then off to school in our best party dresses to dance around the Maypole and enjoy a day outdoors. If only children still did this.

I have lived in towns where May baskets are proudly displayed on doors and blue ribbons given by the local garden club. I enjoyed winning a couple of times. Easton doesn't have this tradition, but I would like to start one. Perhaps your town or city could use some cheering up with May baskets. And if you haven't brought your mother flowers in a long time, or never, why not start now. Show your love and appreciation to her.

Walnut Cookies

1 lb. butter	4½ cups flour
½ cup confectioner's sugar	½ cup chopped walnuts
1 egg yolk	Extra confectioner's sugar
1 tsp. vanilla	

Preheat the oven to 350°
Cream the butter and sugar.
Add the egg yolk, vanilla and walnuts. Slowly add flour.
Form the dough into small crescents and place on ungreased cookie sheet.
Bake 15 minutes, or until slightly browned.
Cool the cookies and roll in confectioner's sugar.

May 2

"How sweet are thy words unto my taste; yea, sweeter than honey to my mouth."
Psalm 119:103

Strawberry season is here. The strawberries from the Eastern Shore of Maryland and the Northern Neck of Virginia are the sweetest, tenderest berries on earth. They are only harvested a short time in May. Marion, near Crisfield was once the strawberry capital of the United States. Trains daily went along the Shore and then up to Wilmington, Philadelphia and even to New York filled with these small, sugary delights. Each year they seem to get larger and sweeter.

When my husband was young and in school, a number of the teachers had grown up with his father in their small North Carolina town. One day he was told by one of these teachers if he brought in 2 quarts of his father's strawberries, he would be sure to get an A. Embarrassed he did so and got his A.

As you taste these sweet morsels be reminded of the words of the Lord. Words of wisdom, words of advice, words of love, come to us everyday from him. The words are the truth. Don't listen to any others. Follow only in his footsteps. Be true, be loyal, and He will show you the way. Bless Him every day.

Strawberry Salad

Serves 4-6

Juice of 1 large lemon	1 qt. strawberries, sliced
Zest of 1 lemon	1 small Bermuda onion, sliced
¼ cup honey or maple syrup	¼ pound Gorgonzola cheese
1 lb. baby spinach	1 cup candied pecans

Combine the lemon, zest and honey in a large salad bowl. Toss in the other ingredients.

Candied pecans

4 cups pecans	1 tbls. cinnamon
1 cup sugar	1 tsp. nutmeg
½ stick butter	

Preheat oven to 300°
Combine ingredients in baking dish. Bake 30 minutes. Cool.

May 3

"Eternal Father, strong to save, Whose arm hath bound the restless wave, Who biddest the mighty ocean deep Its own appointed limits keep; Oh, hear us when we cry to Thee, For those in peril on the sea!"

How often do you cry when you hear these words? Is it because you are at a funeral, or because they are so haunting? William Whiting (1825-78) wrote the words as a poem for one of his students leaving for America. He was head of the Choristers' School at Winchester College. Later it became the hymn of the U.S. Navy and the British Royal Navies. If you attend the incredibly beautiful domed Chapel at the United States Naval Academy this hymn is sung every Sunday. As the midshipmen carrying the flags leave the altar, first the Navy flag and then the U.S. flag are dipped before the altar. Above the altar is a stained glass Tiffany window depicting Christ in all his glory. Each year the number of midshipmen in the Chapel grows. May each one of these young men and women come to know the Lord more and more each day.

On Nantucket another verse has been added to this hymn. On August 15, 1958 a Northeast Airline plane crashed, taking 24 lives, including a cousin. Miraculously a baby survived, even though her mother was killed. So we pray for those in peril in the air. Verses have also been added for other members of the Armed Forces.

Rockfish in Tomato Sauce

Serves 4

2 lb. rockfish filets
2 large tomatoes, chopped
1 medium onion, sliced
1 red pepper, chopped
1 celery stalk, chopped
2 cloves garlic, crushed
½ cup white wine

¼ cup parsley, chopped
¼ cup basil, chopped
4 bay leaves
1 tsp. salt
1 tsp. pepper
2 bay leaves

Preheat oven to 350°
Place the fish in a greased baking dish.
Top with other ingredients.
Bake ½ hour.
Serve with rice. Garnish with feta cheese and parsley.

"Finally, brethren, farewell. Be perfect, be of good comfort, be of one mind, live in peace; and the God of love, and peace shall be with you. Greet one another with an holy kiss. All the saints salute you. The grace of the Lord Jesus Christ, and the love of God, and the communion of the Holy Ghost, be with you all. Amen."
2 Corinthians 13:11-14

Yes, like the strawberries, the Eastern Shore fresh thin asparagus is growing along the roadsides, or I can get them at the Farmers' Market. In season you can't seem to get enough. We have asparagus almost daily – grilled, roasted, blanched, or in soup. There are so many possibilities. It is like taking in an old friend. It also comes back every year. It is comfort food. The stalks might not be perfect and straight. We too are not perfect and we certainly ere from the way of God. But we know each year the stalks will appear. If we love God we know he is with us each day. He is the God of love and peace.

Asparagus Crab Casserole

Serves 4

½ stick butter	1 lb. crab meat
¼ cup flour	¼ cup dill, snipped
1½ cups half and half	½ cup gruyere cheese, grated
1 lb. asparagus	¼ cup parmesan cheese, grated
1 leek, sliced	

Preheat oven to 350°
Melt the butter in a sauce pan. Stir in flour and half and half.
Place the asparagus in a greased baking dish. Top with leek, crab and dill. Pour the sauce over the asparagus.
Sprinkle grated cheese on top.
Bake ½ hour, or until bubbling and slightly browned.
Serve with rice

May 5

"A faithful friend is a strong defence; and he that hath found such an one hath found a treasure...A faithful friend is the medicine of life..."
Ecclesiasticus 6:14, 16

While living in Cleveland some of my volunteer work was with the English-Speaking-Union. This group is dedicated to "international understanding and friendship through the use of the English language". Through this group I made longstanding friendships which continue throughout the world. One friend and I spent considerable time entertaining, traveling, and enjoying our children. I remember when *Brideshead Revisited* aired in 1981 inviting friends for champagne and strawberries. Several years later I spent a week at Oxford for the ESU International Relations Conference and then met this friend for a week of travel through Devon and Cornwall. Each afternoon we would make sure we were in a town with a church or cathedral to attend evensong. I cannot think of a more peaceful way to end the day – the music soothes the soul.

Strawberry Salsa

2 avocadoes, peeled, pitted and diced
1 pint strawberries, chopped
1 small red onion, chopped
3 jalapeno, seeded, and chopped

¼ cup cilantro, chopped
¼ cup lime juice
2 tbls. olive oil
½ red pepper, chopped

Combine all ingredients in a bowl.
Serve with tortilla or pita chips.
Also good with fish or chicken.

We are taught to honor and respect our mothers. Sometimes though there is intense tension between mothers and daughters. Mothers who only listen to what they want to hear, can easily change the conversation, and leave a daughter feeling lonely and unwanted. A daughter wanted to discuss with her mother that she was contemplating a divorce. The mother did not believe in divorce. Instead she turned the other ear, closing out her child, a person who desparately needed support during a very troubling time. She did go through with her divorce, but her parents never forgave her. The mother would write nasty notes, and often accuse her of doing things which she did not have any part in. Later the daughter remarried, and even though her mother loved the son-in-law, she now found excuses to accuse him of wrongdoing too. The marriage has held together, but there have been very intense times when the son-in-law even said he would never see his in-laws again. Mother-daughter relationships can be very loving, but also very strained. Pray that eventually the two can see eye to eye and can moderate their differences. Love one another, as I have loved you.

Zucchini Soup

Serves 6-8

½ stick butter
8 green onions, chopped
2 stalks celery, chopped
2 pounds zucchini, sliced, can leave skin on
3 cups chicken broth

¼ cup fresh basil, chopped
1 tsp. sea salt
1 tsp. fresh pepper
2 Tbls. fresh oregano
2 cups cream or half and half

In a large saucepan melt the butter and sauté the onions and celery. Add other ingredients, except cream. Cook ten minutes or until zucchini is tender. Cool.
Put into food processor and puree. Fold in cream.
Serve chilled in bowls garnished with a dab of sour cream, fresh chopped basil, parsley and chives.

May 7

"Blessed are they that mourn: for they shall be comforted. They that sow in tears shall reap in joy. They that go forth and weep, bearing precious seed, shall doubtless come again with rejoicing, bringing their sheaves with them."

Unlike Catholic Requiems which mourn the dead, Braham's Requiem comforts the living. I love this feeling that we are being healed, but we also mourn the dead.

Johannes Brahms (1833–1897) was born in Hamburg and later settled in Vienna. He began composing at an early age. In 1868 *Ein deutsches Requiem* (A German Requiem) debuted in Bremen. The music is from the Lutheran Bible. Robert Shumann, a close friend, died in 1856 Brahams' mother in 1865. These deaths probably inspired Mr. Brahams to write the Requiem. He also wrote cantatas and symphonies. In 1889 Theo Wangemann, a representative of American inventor Thomas Edison, visited the composer in Vienna and invited him to make an experimental recording. He played a Hungarian dance which was later released on a record.

Chicken Leek Mushroom Pie

Serves 4

½ stick butter
2 large leeks, sliced
1 pint portabella mushrooms, sliced
¼ cup flour
1 cup chicken stock
1 cup heavy cream

¼ cup basil, chopped
2 cooked boneless chicken breasts, cubed in small pieces
1 pie crust

Preheat oven to 400°
Melt the butter in a skillet. Saute the leeks for 3 minutes and add mushrooms.
Stir in flour and slowly add chicken stock until it thickens.
Stir in cream, basil and chicken.
Pour into a rectangular or round baking dish. Top with pie crust. Press the crust into the dish using a fork making marks all around the dish. If there is any leftover crust, make a couple of rosettes.
Bake 30 minutes, or until browned and bubbling.

"Prayer is not an idle occupation. It's a very powerful instrument of our work and love."
Saint Julian of Norwich

Dame Julian was born in 1342 in England. At the age of thirty she received a series of "Sixteen Shewings" which are in her *Revelations of Divine Love.* After this experience she retired to a hermitage in Norwich. *"Our faith cometh of natural love of our soul, and of the clear light of our reason, and of the steadfast mind which we have of god in our first making."*

Prayer is important in our daily lives. I start each morning using the Daily Office Lectionary found in *Day by Day.* Between the Biblical scripture and the meditations I have quiet time to ponder the day and the meaning of what I am reading. Sometimes the scripture or the meditations are quite appropriate for what is happening in my life. After this are my personal prayers. I realize how often I ask for certain things, rather than waiting for the Lord to reveal them to me. Take time for prayer and thought. Take time to let the Lord speak to you. He is the only one who knows your future. Vary your prayers. Think about what you are saying or asking God for. Perhaps it's time for a change, especially if you and God are not communicating.

Coffee Supreme

Serves 6-8

16 ladyfingers
1 cup strong espresso coffee
1 cup sugar
2 envelopes unflavored gelatin

3 cups cream
¼ cup Cognac
2 cups heavy cream whipped
Semisweet chocolate, shaved

Line a crystal bowl with the ladyfingers.
In a sauce pan heat the espresso, sugar and gelatin. Stir in cream until sugar is dissolved. Add Cognac. Chill.
Fold in whipped cream.
Pour over ladyfingers. Chill.
Serve with shaved chocolate

"The Lord is not slow in keeping his promise, as some understand slowness. He is patient with you, not wanting anyone to perish, but everyone to come to repentance.
2 Peter 3:9

Patience is a virtue we all should strive to incorporate into our busy lives. How can we, you ask? Every day is a whirlwind of appointments, phone calls, children, emails, crises – help? Remember it is God that has patience, not us. Think back on the trials of Job. .Job *was perfect and upright, and one that feared God, and eschewed evil."* (Job 1:1) He had seven thousand sheep, three thousand camels, five hundred yoke of oxen, five hundred she asses, sons and daughters, everything in abundance. Yet Satan came and everything was taken away from him. Each day he was tempted and had a reply. Finally when his patience was almost totally gone, Job gave himself to God."*I know that thou canst do everything, and that no thought can be witholden from thee...And the Lord turned the captivity of Job, when he prayed for his; also the Lord gave Job twice as much as he had before."* (Job 42:2, 10) Be steadfast in all you do, stick to a course with God, have patience with Him, and good things will happen.

Remember on this day, the Reverend George M. Docherty (1911-2008). In 1954 with President Dwight D. Eisenhower in the congregation of the New York Avenue Presbyterian Church in Washington, he preached a sermon that acknowledged "under God' should be included in our Pledge of Allegiance. On Flag Day of that year President Eisenhower signed it into law.

Baked Polenta

½ stick butter
1 cup water
1 cup chicken stock   2 tbls cilantro, chopped
1 cup cornmeal   2 tbls. basil, chopped
1 cup fresh grated parmesan cheese   1 jalapeno, seeded and chopped
   2 garlic cloves, crushed

Preheat oven to 350°
Put the butter in a skillet and melt in the oven. Remove as soon as butter is melted.
Boil water and chicken stock in saucepan. Stir in cornmeal until thickened. Add cheese, cilantro, basil, jalapeno and garlic.
Pour the batter into the skillet. Bake 20-25 minutes until browned on top.
Cut into slices. Serve warm or chilled. Serve with salsa.

"Be still and know that I am the Lord."
Psalm 46:10

Being quiet, like patience challenges us to take time each day to be with the Lord. If we do so we can feel his tenderness, his comfort, and his Word. Do you have to go so fast that life loses all meaning? Isn't better to connect with God, and know he is always with you? Can't we take a moment and just listen to him? Find a place – a comfortable chair by a window, a beach, a chapel or church where you can get down on your knees. Bow your head. Close your eyes. Be silent. Your body will not feel any tenseness or stress. Open your mind. Be still. Listen to his Word. The Lord is with you, now and forever. Peace be with you. Amen.

Brownies

2 sticks butter   1½ cups sugar
4 oz. semisweet chocolate   4 eggs
1 cup flour   1 tsp. vanilla
1 tsp. baking powder

Preheat oven to 350°
Melt the butter and chocolate in saucepan. Remove from heat. Stir in other ingredients.
Pour into greased baking dish.
Bake 25-30 minutes, or until toothpick comes clean.
Pour topping over brownies. Sprinkle with nuts and chips.

Topping

1 tbls. butter   ½ tsp. vanilla
½ cup cream   ½ cup pecans
4 oz. unsweetened chocolate   ½ cup chocolate chips
1 cup sugar

Heat the butter, cream and chocolate in a saucepan, until chocolate is melted. Stir in sugar and vanilla.

May 11

"Ask the animals, and they will teach you; the birds of the air, and they will tell you."
Job 12:7

The roses are bursting – the color, the fragrance, the multitude. Everywhere the garden blossoms. Here a yellow, there a shocking pink. Yes, I know I need to get someone in to tell me all the varieties we have. I am blessed. I inherited this garden, but each year we live here, we add our favorites, particularly herbs. I can't live without my herbs during the growing season. I use them everyday in my cooking. Herbs and spices. Yes, a bit of olive oil and a little butter. All this in moderation.

Everyday we read about all the weight people are gaining. Yes, we no longer do the manual labor of our ancestors, but there is no reason for so much obesity. People need to know how to control their eating habits. Eating out is not the solution, particularly at fast food joints. Learn to eat at home, and cook what is healthy, using fresh fruits, vegetables, and herbs and spices. Eat meat and poultry in moderation. Exercise daily, or at least a couple times a week. Even just a walk for 15 minutes or half an hour will rejuvenate the soul. And remember in the morning to stretch. Do as the animals do!

Tabbouleh

Serves 6

3 cups cracked wheat (burghul)
4 green onions, chopped
¼ cup lemon juice
1 cup parsley, chopped

1 tsp. salt
¼ cup olive oil
2 tbls. mint, chopped
2 large tomatoes, chopped

In a bowl soak the cracked wheat in water for 10 minutes. Drain well.
Combine all the ingredients in a bowl. Chill.

"Praise ye the LORD. Praise God in his sanctuary: praise him in the firmament of his power. Praise him for his mighty acts: praise him according to his excellent greatness. Praise him with the sound of the trumpet: praise him with the psaltery and harp. Praise him with the timbrel and dance: praise him with stringed instruments and organs. Praise him upon the loud cymbals: praise him upon the high sounding cymbals. Let every thing that hath breath praise the LORD. Praise ye the LORD."
Psalm 150

When I lived in San Francisco we were newly weds and many of the other young couples we met through the Junior League, the Council on World Affairs, or International Visitor Center were also newly married. We had a lot in common, and because most of us were Easterners, or from elsewhere we would celebrate our holidays together. Two of the ladies were quite musical, and one has gone on to perform internationally on the piano. For someone who cannot carry a note or play a musical instrument, yes I did have piano lessons, I am so impressed when someone can sit down and play. At least I know the tunes to most hymns, but am too embarrassed to sing out. I try anyway, and often get teased. Somehow I did spend one year in my school glee club, but only after putting much pressure on the director to let me in! If only I could come back in another life, that God would give me musical talent!

Clams in Wine Sauce

Serves 4

½ stick butter
2 leeks, chopped
2 cups dry white wine
36 small clams

¼ cup fresh tarragon, chopped
¼ cup parsley, chopped
Fresh ground pepper

Melt the butter in a large sauce pan. Add the leeks and sauté for 5 five minutes. Add wine. Bring to boil. Add clams until they just open.
Serve in pasta bowls with pasta or crusty bread. Top with parsley, tarragon and pepper.
Grated parmesan cheese can also be served with this.

"We went through fire and water, but you brought us to a place of abundance."
Psalm 66:12

Several fires swept through downtown Annapolis in a year's period. They could have destroyed the whole city. The narrow streets prevented equipment from easily getting through, but somehow the perseverance and bravery of the fire department saved a number of historic buildings. Nantucket too had a great fire in 1846. This was just before the end of the great whaling era when so many of Nantucket's grand homes were built. The fire started in Geary's hat shop on lower Main Street and quickly consumed the entire business district, waterfront warehouses and destroyed over four hundred buildings. I am thankful so many of the homes built by my family were spared. If only we still owned them! Fire is devastating, fire devours. Man can quench them. Only God knows what must be destroyed. Thank you Lord, for Nantucket, you brought my family to a place of abundance, a place we love and cherish, where we return every year.

Sauteed Bananas

Serves 4

4 ripe bananas, sliced lengthwise
½ stick butter
½ cup maple syrup
¼ cup dark rum

½ cup pecans
2 tbls. lemon juice
4 slices pound cake
Whipped cream

Heat the butter in a skillet. Add the bananas. Stir in the maple syrup, rum, pecans and lemon juice.
Serve over pound cake and with whipped cream.

"Christ is made the sure foundation, Christ the head and cornerstone, chosen of the Lord, and precious, binding all the church in one; holy Zion's help forever, and her confidence alone...Here vouchsafe to all the servants what they ask of thee to gain; what they gain from thee, for ever with the blessed to retain, and hereafter in thy glory evermore with thee to reign."
Christ is Made the Sure Foundation by John Mason Neale (1818-1866); Music tune Westminster Abbey by Henry Purcell (1659-1695). The words date from the 7th c. and were sung at the 100th anniversary of St. Carthage's Cathedral, Lismore on August 18, 2007.

Carthage, also known as Mochuda, was born in County Kerry, Ireland c 555. As a young man he was a shepherd and then became a monk. In 580 he built a hermitage which attracted numerous pilgrims. Two bishops forced him to close the hermitage. After serving in several cities he founded a monastery in Rahan and eventually a church in Lismore. He died in 637 and is known as the first bishop of Lismore and its patron saint. Today the lovely Cathedral, built between 1881-84 stands as a symbol of all that St. Carthage did for Christianity in Ireland. Lismore Cathedral, unlike many cathedrals, is a parish church with a congregation. The original crozier, now in the National Museum, was found in the walls in 1814 and dates back to the 12th century. The stained glass window by pre-Raphaelite artist Burne Jones is the only one of its kind in Ireland and depicts two virtues Justice (a man with sword and scales) and Humility (a woman holding a lamb).

Fruit Soup

Serves 8

1 cantaloupe	¼ cup lemon juice
1 quart strawberries	½ cup sugar
½ pound grapes	6 cups water
4 apples, peeled, cored and chopped	1½ cups orange juice
¼ cup lime juice	Mint

Remove the pulp from the cantaloupe skin. Chop finely.
In a sauce pan combine the cantaloupe, strawberries, grapes, apples, lemon and limes juices, orange juice, sugar and water. Bring to a boil. Simmer 15 minutes.
Cool. Pour into a food processor until smooth.
Serve in bowls with mint.
This is so good on a hot summer day.

"Trust in the Lord with all thine heart; and lean not unto thine own understanding. In all thy ways acknowledge him, and he shall direct thy paths."
Proverbs 3:5-6

The winter I spent on Nantucket brought new friendships and a much deeper love and relationship with God. I would walk on the beach, walk to the lighthouse, particularly in the evening, when there was barely a car or house light. A weekly Bible class became my core of friends. Our leader chose a theme – Hebrews, psalms, hymns and printed out a weekly sheet to guide us. We also spent time in prayer. One lady's husband owned a fishing boat which needed a new engine. The cost was about $100,000, well beyond their means. They homeschooled their seven children, but they still had to eat and be clothed, plus a roof over their head. God did bless them with a new engine. Our youngest member was pregnant with her first child, who arrived safely to the delight of all of us. Six years later our dear leader lost her son, aged thirty. Her faith has never stumbled. She has been steadfast in her belief and fervent in her prayer. May we all be blessed. *Trust in the Lord with all thine heart.*

Spaghetti

Serves 6

2 tbls. olive oil	1 tbls. Italian herbs
1 medium onion, chopped	1 tbls. chili powder
4 cloves garlic, crushed	1 tsp. oregano
1 red pepper, chopped	¼ tsp. cayenne
1 lb. ground beef	¼ cup fresh chopped parsley
½ lb. ground pork	1 tsp. pepper
2 tomatoes, chopped	1½ lb. spaghetti
1 15 oz. can tomato sauce	Fresh grated parmesan cheese

Heat the olive oil in a large pan. Stir in the onions until tender.
Add garlic, beef and pork. Cook until just browned. Add tomatoes, sauce, herbs, chili, oregano, cayenne, parsley and pepper. Bring to a boil and simmer for at least 20 minutes.
Cook the spaghetti according to the directions. Drain.
Divide up spaghetti between 6 pasta bowls. Pour sauce over spaghetti. Garnish with parmesan cheese.

"See then that ye walk circumspectly, not as fools, but as wise, redeeming the time, because the days are evil. Wherefore be ye not unwise, but understanding what the will of the Lord is."
Ephesians 5:15-17

A member of my Bible Study Group sent this passage to me in an email. Her wording was slightly different – "Ephesians 5:15 encourages us to "be very careful how you live, making the most of your time." Each one of us is going through tough times right now, but God is getting ready to bless you in a way that only He can. Keep the faith."

She said that she had picked four people to be blessed by God that day and I was one of them. She passed along a short prayer, and then asked us to forward the email to four more people. In these tough economic times when the population is going through this or terrible sicknesses, picking out four others was very easy. Pick out at least one person each day that you would like God to bless. Perhaps it is even you.

Lamb Kebabs

Serves 6

2 lbs. boneless lamb, cut into cubes
1 tsp. cinnamon
1 tsp. cumin
1 tsp. ginger
1 tsp. paprika
2 large onions, cubed

2 peppers, cut in chunks
½ lb. pitted figs or dates
1 pint cherry tomatoes

Rub the lamb with the cinnamon, cumin, ginger and paprika.
Using skewers alternate the lamb, onions, peppers, tomatoes and figs or dates.
Grill on a BBQ until desired pinkness of lamb.
Serve with hummus, grilled pita and couscous

"Ancient of Days, who sittest throned in glory, To Thee all knees are bent, all voices pray; Thy love has blessed the wide world's wondrous story With light and life since Eden's dawning day. O Holy Father, who hadst led Thy children In all the ages, with the fire and cloud, Through seas dry shod, through weary wastes bewildering; To Thee, in reverent love, our hearts are bowed. O Holy Jesus, Prince of Peace and Savior, To Thee we owe the peace that still prevails, Stilling the rude wills of men's wild behavior, And calming passion's fierce and stormy gales. O Holy Ghost, the Lord and the Lifegiver, Thine is the quickening power that gives increase; From Thee have flowed, as from a pleasant river, Our plenty, wealth, prosperity and peace. O Triune God, with heart and voice adoring, Praise we the goodness that doth crown our days; Pray we that Thou wilt hear us, still imploring Thy love and favor kept to us always."

The Right Reverend William Croswell Doane (1832-1913) was the first Bishop of Albany, New York. He wrote this hymn in honor of the bicentennial of Albany. The Biblical passage comes from Daniel 7:9 *"the thrones were set in place, and the Ancient of days did sit..."* The Bishop received honorary degrees from Oxford and Cambridge. He also wrote the biography of his father George Washington Doane, also a hymnist.

Beef with Portabella Sauce

Serves 6

6 beef tenderloins
2 tbls. fresh tarragon
2 tbls. fresh ground pepper
½ stick butter
1 large leek, sliced

8 oz. baby portabella mushrooms, sliced
¼ cup Corvoisier
¼ lb. blue cheese (Stilton, preferred)
Tarragon

Rub the beef with the pepper and tarragon. Cook on a grill until desired pinkness.
Melt the butter in a skillet. Saute the leeks and mushrooms, until just tender. Stir in the Corvoisier and blue cheese.
Pour the sauce on each tenderloin. Garnish with tarragon leaves.

"A poor widow came and put in two copper coins which are worth a penny. Then he called his disciples and said to them, "Truly I tell you, this poor widow has put in more than all of those who are contributing to the treasury. For all of them have contributed out of their abundance; but she out of her poverty has put in everything she had, all she had to live on."
Mark 12:42-44

A lovely woman I know does a great deal of volunteer work, and always has. She and her husband have never acquired much wealth, and even though she is working, she spends several hours a week giving her time to local organizations. Her good deeds have been spread through thrift shops, Meals-on- Wheels, her church, the Junior League, Waterfowl Festival, Hospice, women and children's organizations, anywhere some organization might need an extra hand. She can donate her time, which is just as valuable, if not more valuable, than money. Her thanks is received from the gratitude and the thank-you's she receives. Please find time each week, or at least once a month to volunteer. Your act of kindness will not go unnoticed.

Green Salad with Onion Vinaigrette

Serves 6

½ lb. mixed spring greens
2 large tomatoes, sliced
1 cucumber, sliced

15 oz. artichoke hearts, drained
½ pound mushrooms, sliced

Combine the ingredients in a salad bowl. Toss with the vinaigrette.

Onion Vinaigrette

2 tsp. Dijon mustard
4 scallions, finely chopped
½ cup parsley or cilantro, chopped

1 tbls. lemon juice
½ tsp. fresh ground pepper
¼ cup olive oil

Combine the ingredients in a bowl.

May 19

"I am creating new heavens and a new earth; everything of the past will be forgotten. Celebrate and be glade forever! I am creating a Jerusalem, full of happy people. I will celebrate with Jerusalem and all of its people...No child will die in infancy; everyone will live to a ripe old age. Anyone a hundred years will be considered young; and to die younger than that will be considered a curse...My chosen people will live to be as old as trees, and they will enjoy what they have earned...I the Lord have spoken."
Isaiah 65:17-25

As people live longer, they are an example to the younger generation on how to live life. Living to be 100 is no longer an impossibility. The wife of the doctor who delivered my husband just celebrated this milestone. Family and friends gathered in a small town in North Carolina to praise and remember her. Until recently, she still played bridge and golfed. Then her eyesight began to fail. Finally she had to give up all of this, and driving too! She's now living in assisted living, but did she hang out all those years on her own!

If only all of us can do this. Sometimes, it's a knee or hip problem, or something worse, such as lose of sight. Thank goodness for special computers that can allow the blind to be guided. Celebrate each day and try to live to an old and fruitful age.

Lemon Roasted Chicken

Serves 4

1 lb. asparagus	1 tsp. thyme
4 boneless chicken breasts	1 tsp. salt
Juice of 2 lemons	1 tsp. pepper
Zest of two lemons	½ stick butter
1 tsp. oregano	½ cup chicken stock

Preheat the oven to 350°
Place the asparagus and chicken breasts in a baking dish. Rub the chicken with the lemon juice, zest, oregano, thyme, salt and pepper. Divide up butter between the four breasts. Pour stock into pan.
Cover. Bake 45 minutes. Baste if necessary.
Serve with rice. Pour juice from chicken over rice. Garnish with lemon slices.

"The kingdom of heaven is like a grain of mustard seed, which a man took, and sowed in his field; Which indeed is the least of all seeds: but when it is grown, it is the greatest among the herbs, and becometh a tree, so that the birds of the air come and lodge in the branches thereof."
Matthew 13:31-32

This parable speaks of the grain of a mustard seed, something so small, yet its spiciness is used to season so many dishes. What is amazing, is the plant can grow to ten or fifteen feet in height. Like the small mustard seed Christianity began with small roots, but grew into branches that would spread throughout the world. Like the birds that lodge in its branches, so too Christ takes us in his arms. He opens them to us – warm and safe. Let those branches grow, let the mustard seeds spread. Spread the Word. Jesus Christ is Lord!

Green Beans with Mustard Seeds

Serves 4

½ stick butter
1 tsp. mustard seeds
1 small onion, chopped
2 tbls. fresh grated ginger
½ tsp. salt
1 tsp. pepper

¼ tsp. cayenne
1 lb. green beans, trimmed
¼ cup fresh grated coconut
2 tbls. cilantro
2 tbls. lemon juice

Melt the butter in a skillet. Add the mustard seeds.
 Add the onion, ginger, salt, pepper, cayenne, and green beans.
Cook 3 minutes.
Sprinkle with coconut, cilantro and lemon juice.
Serve warm, or can be chilled.

May 21

"It is more blessed to give than receive."
Acts 20:35

J. Hudson Taylor (1832-1905) was an English missionary to China. He founded the China Inland Mission which at his death included 205 mission stations with over 800 missionaries, and 125,000 Chinese Christians. He was a humble man who was called to minister to the Chinese. To the Christian Chinese who even now are being persecuted, imprisoned, killed for what they believe in. He spent five years translating the New Testament into the Ningpo dialect. He gave up the English countryside to help others, only in the end to be taken back to England as a very sick man. We must be thankful for Mr. Taylor and so many others who gave up creature comforts to follow in the footsteps of our Lord, and try to save others. For inspiration read Hudson Taylor's *Spiritual Secret*, published in 1989 by his son and daughter-in-law who were also missionaries in China, or his own books.

Crab Spring Rolls

2 oz. cellophane noodles
1 tbls. sesame oil
2 shallot cloves, chopped
2 garlic cloves, chopped
2 green onions, finely chopped
1 carrot, peeled and thinly sliced
½ cup bean sprouts, chopped

½ lb. crab meat
¼ cup cilantro, finely chopped
1 teaspoon sugar
¼ tsp. red pepper flakes
1 tbls. fresh grated ginger
14 spring roll wrappers

Cover the noodles with hot water. Let soak ten minutes. Drain. Cut into small pieces.
Heat the sesame oil in a wok. Stir in the shallot, garlic, green onion, carrot and bean sprouts. Cook for 1 minute. Remove from heat. Stir in the crab, cilantro, sugar, pepper flakes and ginger.
Divide the crab mixture between the 14 spring roll wrappers. Roll up and seal with a dab of water.
They can be served this way, or fried in hot oil.

Dipping Sauce

½ cup rice wine vinegar
½ cup sugar

3 tbls. fresh grated ginger
1 small mango, finely chopped

Combine the ingredients in a food processor. Serve with the spring rolls.

May 22

"And if I go and prepare a place for you, I will come again, and receive you unto myself; that where I am, there ye may be also."
John 14:3

Some people come into your life so unexpectedly and make such an impact you never, never forget them, even when they have been received into God's hands. While visiting Nantucket with my young daughter, a friend of hers and a neighbor's dog, I ran into a gentleman on the wharf. Immediately we struck up a conversation. He was there for the Fugawi Race, and his boat had won several times. We became fast friends, and over the years he taught my daughter to sail and ski, plus providing us with good laughs. The day my daughter was to have her tonsils out, her appendix burst. Since she had strep throat on top of that, they couldn't remove the appendix and tonsils at the same time. This dear friend came to visit us at the hospital. He sat in one of the children's chairs which immediately collapsed. Great roars! I don't know how many times my sides hurt from the things he said or did. He also was a good Christian, and one that God took much too early. He remains in my heart, and I am sure many others he touched.

Tomato Pie

Serves 4

1 unbaked pie crust	¼ cup fresh basil chopped
3 medium tomatoes, sliced	½ lb. mozzarella, thinly sliced
3 green onions, sliced	½ tsp. salt
1 cup mayonnaise	1 tsp. pepper

Preheat oven to 400°
Bake pie crust for 10 minutes.
Reduce oven to 375°
Combine the tomatoes, onions, mayonnaise, basil, cheese, salt and pepper in a bowl.
Pour into pie crust.
Cook for 45 minutes. Serve warm, or chilled.

May 23

"Then the same day at evening, being the first day of the week, when the doors were shut where the disciples were assembled for fear of the Jews, came Jesus and stood in the midst, and saith unto them, Peace be unto you. And when he had so said, he shewed unto them his hands and his side. Then were the disciples glad, when they saw the LORD. Then said Jesus to them again, Peace be unto you: as my Father hath sent me, even so send I you. And when he had said this, he breathed on them, and saith unto them, Receive ye the Holy Ghost: Whose soever sins ye remit, they are remitted unto them; and whose soever sins ye retain, they are retained. But Thomas, one of the twelve, called Didymus, was not with them when Jesus came."
John 20:19-24

Jesus had just been crucified, yet now he was here among his disciples. I cannot imagine how I would feel if someone had died on the cross, and then suddenly appeared alive, walking, and talking. No wonder Thomas doubted it was the Lord, even though he had been shown the Lord's hands and side. I am sure there are days we cannot trust what is happening in our lives. Yet, we must believe and we must trust the Lord. He gave his life for us, so that we can believe. We must be Thomas who with his own fingers felt the Lord's hands and side. "And Thomas answered and said unto him, *My Lord and my God.*" John 20:28

Vegetable Primavera

Serves 6-8

2 tbls. butter	1 pint cherry tomatoes
2 leeks, sliced	4 cloves garlic, crushed
1 red pepper, sliced	1¼ cups cream
½ lb. mushrooms, sliced	1½ lbs. fettuccine
1 lb. broccoli florets	½ lb. smoked Gouda, grated
1 cup fresh peas	Fresh basil leaves
½ lb. asparagus, trimmed	

Melt the butter in a large sauce pan. Stir in the leeks and pepper. Add the other vegetables. Stir in the cream just before serving.
Cook the fettuccine according to directions. Drain.
Place the fettuccine in a large bowl, or separate pasta bowls.
Spoon the vegetables on top. Garnish with Gouda and basil.

May 24

"God of grace and God of glory... For the facing of this hour."

In 1999, after losing my job writing hefty market research reports on telecommunications, I found a business class which would concentrate on writing a business plan. During the course I completely changed course with the collapse of the telecom industry. The idea of writing cookbooks started taking shape. During the class sessions I met several interesting people, all of whom had lost their jobs. One was a graphic artist who now does all my graphics. Several years ago she went through a terrible bout with cancer, but is whole again. Grant us courage in trying times.

The words to this hymn resonate through your mind as you repeat *grant us wisdom, grant us courage*. As Christians we need to remember them each day and *serve thee whom we adore*. Harry Emerson Fosdick (1878-1969) graduated from Union Theological Seminary and was ordained a Baptist minister. On May 21, 1922, he delivered a sermon "Shall the Fundamentalists Win?" at the First Presbyterian Church in New York. He preached that the Bible and above all Christians should be open minded and tolerant, and not stuck such as the Fundamentalists were. He was investigated by the General Assembly of the Presbyterian Church, but luckily his defense was led by John Foster Dulles. He eventually resigned from the church. He then was hired by John D. Rockefeller, Jr. as pastor at the Park Avenue Baptist Church. Mr. Rockefeller financially supported the building of the Riverside Church and Mr. Fosdick became the first minister there. The church has the largest carillon in the world.

Basil Parmesan Polenta

Serves 4

2 cups milk	2 cloves garlic, minced
1 cup cornmeal	¼ cup basil
1 cup parmesan cheese	½ stick butter

Preheat oven to 400°
Bring the milk to a boil in a sauce pan. Stir in cornmeal. Add cheese, garlic and basil.
Melt the butter in an iron skillet in the oven. Pour batter into the skillet.
Bake 25 minutes.
Serve warm.

"Paul, an apostle of Jesus Christ, by the will of God, according to the promise of life which is in Christ Jesus: To Timothy, my dearly beloved child. Grace, mercy and peace, from God the Father and from Christ Jesus our Lord. I am grateful to God, whom I worship with a clear conscience, as my ancestors did, when I remember you constantly in my prayers, night and day. Recalling your tears, I long to see you that I may be filled with joy. I am reminded of your sincere faith, a faith that lived first in your grandmother Lois and your mother Eunice and now, I am sure, lives in you."
2 Timothy 1:1-5

My grandmothers were called Little Ga and Big Ga. As the oldest grandchild I had named them. Little Ga was barely five feet, Big Ga was about 5'7". Their personalities were like night and day. Yet they had a common love for Nantucket Island and spent their summers there. Big Ga and my grandfather "Dega" had bought property on Island during the Depression. Overlooking Nantucket Sound we loved to spend time on the beach, or catching cool breezes on the wraparound porch. In the evening my grandparents would each have two old-fashion cocktails and then a formal dinner in the dining room. Sundays we were expected to be elegantly dressed and dined at one o'clock. Those were happy, carefree days. I wish we had them back, and not this immediacy to do everything. Life was much more simple then, and certainly less stressful.

Big Ga's Stuffed French Bread

3 three oz. packages cream cheese
3 tbls. capers
¼ cup grated onion
1 can anchovy filets, rubbed to a paste
4 tbls. chili sauce

1 tbls. Worcestershire sauce
3 dashes Tabasco sauce
½ tsp. salt
1 cup watercress, minced
1 stick butter, at room temp.
1 loaf French bread

Cream the cheese until smooth. Add anchovy paste, capers, chili sauce, onion, Worcestershire sauce, Tabasco sauce and salt.
Cream the butter. Add the watercress.
Split the bread lengthwise and remove the center. Fill the cavity of each half with watercress butter mixture. Press two halves together. Wrap in foil and chill. Cut in slices.
An alternative to this is chilling the watercress butter mixture. Place in nice serving bowl and serve with the French bread, cut in slices or cubes.
Back when my grandmother made this she added green food coloring. I prefer to have the color come from the watercress.

May 26

"And when they saw Him (on the mountain), they worshipped Him: but some doubted. And Jesus came and spoke unto them, saying, "All power is given unto me in heaven and in earth. Go ye therefore, and teach all nations, baptizing them in the name of the Father, and of the Son, and of the Holy Ghost. Teaching them to observe all things which I have commanded you: and lo, I am with you always, even unto the end of the world."
Matthew 28:17-20

These were Jesus' last words to his disciples. How more powerful can you get? Go teach others about me, but I am always with you. You can never forget me, I will never forsake you, I will always be with you. Times may be dark and gloomy, or they can be uplifting with the light shining in. Wherever you are, whatever you are doing, the Lord will always be with you. He is the King, the all present hope and light. Never ever forget Him.

"They took knowledge of them that they had been with Jesus."
Acts 4:13

Grilled Vegetables

Serves 8

2 large red onions, sliced	½ cup olive oil
1 pound asparagus	¼ cup balsamic vinegar
1 zucchini, sliced	4 cloves garlic, crushed
1 yellow squash, sliced	1 tbls. sea salt
2 large tomatoes, sliced	Juice of 1 lemon
1 eggplant, sliced	

Place all the vegetables in a large bowl.
In another bowl combine the olive oil, balsamic vinegar, garlic, salt and lemon juice. Pour over the vegetables.
Cook the vegetables in wire basket on a BBQ grill.
Reserve the remaining olive oil mixture. Pour over vegetables when cooked. Serve warm or chilled.
The vegetables can also be roasted in the oven - 350° for 20 minutes, or until tender.

May 27

"Mine eyes have seen the glory of the coming of the Lord; He is trampling out the vintage where the grapes of wrath are stored; He hath loosed the fateful lightning of His terrible swift sword; His truth is marching on. Glory! Glory! Hallelujah! Glory! Glory! Hallelujah! Glory! Glory! Hallelujah! His truth is marching on. In the beauty of the lilies Christ was born across the sea, With a glory in His bosom that transfigures you and me: As He died to make men holy, let us died to make men free; While God is marching on. Glory! Glory! Hallelujah! Glory! Glory! Hallelujah! Glory! Glory! Hallelujah! While God is marching on."

Two dear friends share this birthday. I got to know both of them the same year. One was a lovely Dutch lady who had served in the world's hotspots for the United Nations over a 25 year period. The other was an Episcopal minister, born of missionary parents in China. Recently he has been able to return to China and trace his family's roots there. He has also been instrumental in working with the Christian churches, bringing Chinese Christians to America, and helping build the faith in a country that still persecutes the faithful. When a mutual friend died, he was one of the presiding ministers. At the request of the deceased's family and this minister, the *Battle Hymn of the Republic* was sung at the funeral. The hymn was written by Julia Ward Howe (1819-1910) during the Civil War. She was a pacifist, woman's suffragette, and was the first to issue a proclamation for Mother's Day in 1870. Her husband Samuel Gridley Howe founded the Perkins Institute for the Blind.

Gazpacho

Serves 6

1 large tomato, chopped	4 cloves garlic
1 onion, chopped	4 cups V8 juice
1 medium cucumber, sliced	2 tbls. red wine vinegar
1 green pepper, seeded and quartered	Juice of 1 lemon
	1 tbls. sugar
1 red pepper, seeded and quartered	1 tsp. sea salt
1 celery stalk, chopped	1 tbls. Worcestershire sauce
¼ cup parsley	¼ tsp. cayenne or Tabasco sauce
4 chives	1 tbls. fresh ground pepper

Combine all ingredients in a food processor.
Serve in bowls. Garnish with snipped chives and croutons.

"We know that all things work together for good for those who love God, who are called according to his purpose."
Romans 8:28

There are people who give of themselves only to God and work out his purpose. One of those was Bernard of Montjoux (c996-c1081) who served for 42 years as the vicar-general of Aosta, Italy. The region contained numerous mountains, and part of his work was to help German and French pilgrims through the mountains on their way to Rome. He rid the passes of robbers, and founded hospices run by the Augustinian canons. The canons bred and cared for the dogs we now call St. Bernard's. Bernard is the patron saint of skiers and alpinists. We are thankful that when he saw paganism still being practiced in the Alps, he devoted his life to preaching the Gospels.

Grilled Chicken Penne

Serves 4

2 tbls. olive oil
2 cloves garlic, crushed
1 can white beans, drained
½ lb. baby spinach
8 sun-dried tomatoes
¼ cup fresh basil

1 large red pepper, sliced and roasted (can use small jar of roasted red peppers)
2 large chicken breasts, grilled and thinly sliced
4 slices prosciutto, diced
1 lb. penne
Parmesan cheese

In a sauce pan heat the olive oil. Stir in the garlic and beans.
Add spinach, until just wilted.
Stir in sun-dried tomatoes, basil, pepper, chicken breasts and prosciutto.
Cook penne according to directions. Drain.
Divide penne among 4 pasta bowls. Top with chicken mixture and parmesan cheese.
The penne can also be stirred into the chicken. Serve warm or chilled with the parmesan cheese.

"Love is the fulfilling of the law."
Romans 13:10

My other grandmother "Little Ga" was the one I stayed with the most. Like her, I was petite, but heaven knows what size she wore. We did like to try on her very old-fashioned bathing suits which were more like dresses. Each morning we helped her to get dressed and pulled the strings on her corset to tighten her middle. Then she put on the biggest pair of underwear I ever saw. Grandmothers don't dress like this anymore! In the evening we would go for a long walk, and she would talk about the history of Nantucket. She'd point out where our ancestors lived, or the time the jail keeper put her in the old gaol. It was only a joke, but she didn't think so. This was a time we could talk, but also look up at the stars and appreciate the beauty of our earth. We could breathe in the fresh sea air. After our walk we would head home for dessert – ice cream with blueberries, or perhaps Indian pudding with ice cream. Then it was time to change and say prayers. *"Now I lay me down to sleep. I pray the Lord my soul to keep. If I should die before I wake, I pray the Lord my soul will take."* Even today I can repeat every word. I love the Lord and praise him every day.

Seafood Chowder

Serves 4

2 tbls. butter
4 green onions, chopped
1 carrot, peeled and chopped
1 stalk celery, chopped
1 medium tomato, chopped
¼ teaspoon cayenne
2 cups milk

2 cups heavy cream
2 lbs. shrimp, cooked, peeled and deveined
1 lb. scallops
Salt and pepper
Fresh basil

Melt the butter in saucepan. Add the green onions, carrot, celery and tomato. Stir in the cayenne, milk and cream.
At last moment before serving, stir in shrimp and scallops until warmed. Add a small amount of salt and pepper.
Serve chowder in bowls with fresh chopped basil.
You can also add some dark rum or Sherry, or Bermuda Sherry Pepper Sauce.
Old Bay can be substituted for cayenne.
Halibut, cod, or other seafood can be substituted for the shrimp and scallops.

"God reigns over the nations; God is seated on his holy throne."
Psalm 47:8

Memorial Day began as "Decoration Day", a day to remember Civil War dead by decorating their graves with flags. Later wars led to a single commemoration on May 30th each year. In 1968 Congress moved a number of national holidays to the nearest Monday. This gave people an opportunity to take a long weekend, and for this one start off the summer. We must remember those who gave their lives during all the wars fought in this country and overseas. Pray for our troops.

We also remember on this day Joan of Arc (1412-31), "The Maid of Orleans", a peasant girl who led the French army to several victories during the Hundred Years' War. Her calling was from the archangel to take Charles VII to be crowned king of France. Her statue stands outside the Reims Cathedral where he was crowned. She was captured by the English, tried in an ecclesiastical court, and sentenced to be burned at the stake.

"And there was war in heaven: Michael and his angels fought against the dragon; and the dragon fought and his angels, And prevailed not; neither was their place found any more in heaven. And the great dragon was cast out, that old serpent, called the Devil, and Satan, which deceiveth the whole world: he was cast out into the earth, and his angels were cast out with him. And I heard a loud voice saying in heaven, Now is come salvation, and strength, and the kingdom of our God, and the power of his Christ: for the accuser of our brethren is cast down, which accused them before our God day and night. And they overcame him by the blood of the Lamb, and by the word of their testimony; and they loved not their lives unto the death."
Revelation 12: 7-11

Herb and Cheese Biscuits

2 cups flour	2 tbls. snipped chives
1 stick butter	2 tbls. snipped dill
1/3 cup cold milk	1 tsp. salt
2 tsp. baking powder	½ cup parmesan cheese

Preheat oven to 400°
Combine all ingredients in a food processor until a ball forms.
Roll out dough on floured board. Cut with round cutter.
Place on cookie sheet.
Bake 10-12 minutes, until just browned.

"Praise to the Lord, the Almighty, the King of creation! O my soul, praise Him, for He is thy health and salvation! All ye who hear, now to His temple draw near; Praise Him in glad adoration. Praise to the Lord, who over all things so wondrously reigneth, Shelters thee under His wings, yea, so gently sustaineth! Hast thou not seen how thy desires ever have been Granted in what He ordaineth? Praise to the Lord, who hath fearfully, wondrously, made thee; Health hath vouchsafed and, when heedlessly falling, hath stayed thee. What need or grief ever hath failed of relief? Wings of His mercy did shade thee. Praise to the Lord, who doth prosper thy work and defend thee; Surely His goodness and mercy here daily attend thee. Ponder anew what the Almighty can do, If with His love He befriend thee. Praise to the Lord, who, when tempests their warfare are waging, Who, when the elements madly around thee are raging, Biddeth them cease, turneth their fury to peace, Whirlwinds and waters assuaging. Praise to the Lord, who, when darkness of sin is abounding, Who, when the godless do triumph, all virtue confounding, Sheddeth His light, chaseth the horrors of night, Saints with His mercy surrounding. Praise to the Lord, O let all that is in me adore Him! All that hath life and breath, come now with praises before Him. Let the Amen sound from His people again, Gladly for aye we adore Him."

Joachim Neander (1650-80) was a Calvinist theologian and hymnist, composing about 60 hymns. He was born in Bremen, but later taught Latin in Dusseldorf. While there he enjoyed going to the Dussel River valley where he composed many of his poems and gave sermons. In 1856 the remains of the *Homo neanderthalensis* (Neanderthal Man) were found in the region, and named in honor of him.

Red Cabbage

Serves 8

½ stick butter
2 onions, sliced
2 large cloves garlic, minced
2 large apples, sliced
2 lbs. red cabbage
1 cup red wine vinegar
1 cup red wine

1 tsp. cinnamon
¼ tsp. ground cloves
2 tbls. grated ginger
1 cup dark brown sugar
1 tsp. salt
1 tsp. pepper

In a large pan heat the butter. Saute the onions, garlic, and apples. Stir in the other ingredients. Cook for one hour.

June 1

"I rejoiced with those who said to me, Let us go to the house of the Lord."
Psalm 122:1

Sunday in northern Maine, Bar Harbor to be exact. The day dawned sunny, and then the fog rolled in. Still a stroll along the harbor brought clean air into my lungs. After a small breakfast I attended St. Saviour's Episcopal Parish. This simple structure in downtown Bar Harbor contains 10 Tiffany windows and has a very faithful congregation, meeting all year round. The church is the oldest public building on Mount Desert Island, having been completed in 1878. The church however was established in 1613. The rector had just returned from a four month sabbatical, and this was his first Sunday back. During the service he greeted every person, including myself, the visitor. I was so touched. He was so welcomed back by everyone in the congregation – great hugs, laughter, tears. When we truly find a person of God he will envelop us in his arms, and we will take him into ours.

Lobster Stew

Serves 6

½ stick butter	3 cups half and half
1 large leek, sliced	3 cups cream
3 red bliss potatoes, sliced	¼ cup sherry
6 asparagus, sliced in 1 in. pieces	2 lbs. lobster meat
1 stalk celery, chopped	Paprika
¼ cup flour	Fresh basil leaves

Melt the butter in a sauce pan. Add the leek, potatoes, asparagus, and celery. Cook until the vegetables are tender.
In a food processor combine the vegetables into small chunks.
Put back into sauce pan. Heat and add flour. Stir in half and half and cream. Fold in lobster.
Serve in bowls garnished with paprika and basil.

June 2

"Then Samuel took a vial of oil, and poured it upon his head (Saul's)."
1 Samuel 10:1

On this date in 1953 Princess Elizabeth was crowned Queen of England. My parents, along with many other families back then did not own a TV. They rented one for this special occasion, and for President Dwight D. Eisenhower's inauguration. From the time the coronation came on, until it ended we savored every moment, pretending to be royal guests.

The ritual of British coronations in Westminster date back over 900 years. Queen Elizabeth took a coronation oath to serve her people and honor the laws of God. As symbols of her office she was given an orb, scepter, rod of mercy, a royal ring and then crowned with St. Edward's Crown. One of the most important parts of the service is her anointment with oil. The Anointing Oil contains oils of orange, roses, cinnamon, musk and ambergris. Usually a batch is made to last a few Coronations. In May 1941, a bomb hit the Deanery destroying the phial containing the anointing oil so a new batch had to be made. The pharmacy that had mixed the last anointing oil had gone out of business, but the recipe was found and the oil again produced.

Coronation Chicken Salad

Serves 8

8 boneless chicken breasts	4 apricots, peeled and chopped
1 tbls. olive oil	1 cup mayonnaise
2 leeks chopped,	1 tsp. salt
1 tbls. curry powder	1 tsp. pepper
1 tbls. tomato paste	½ cup heavy cream
1 cup red wine	1 cup macadamia nuts
2 bay leaves	1 cup currants
Juice of 1 lemon	Watercress

Heat the olive oil and sauté onion for 2 minutes. Stir in the curry, tomato paste, wine, bay leaf and lemon juice. Simmer for 10 minutes.
Puree the apricots, curry sauce and mayonnaise in a food processor.
Beat the cream until peaks form. Fold the apricot mixture and cream together.
Fold in the chicken, nuts and currants.
Serve on a bed of baby spinach with watercress as a garnish.

June 3

"Your beauty should not come from outward adornment, such as braided hair and the wearing of gold jewelry and fine clothes. Instead, it should be that of your inner self, the unfading beauty of a gentle and quiet spirit, which is of great worth in God's sight. For this is the way the holy women of the past who put their hope in God used to make themselves beautiful."
1 Peter 3:2-5

My daughter's oldest friend was born on June 3rd. She's just a year younger than Lucinda, and though she now lives in Colorado the girls keep in close touch. She has long reddish blonde curls, loves the environment and protecting it, and spends a great deal of time outdoors. When the girls were young I started designing children's clothing. My daughter was always in the 99th percentile, and very honestly there were not too many pretty dresses for her age. I designed party dresses out of taffeta, moiré silk, lush velvets, and Egyptian cotton. Most had a sash to compliment the color of the dress. These two little girls were my models. They're all grown up now. I still have the sample dresses, but will have to wait for a granddaughter! What I love about these two girls is their friendship has lasted forever, and they do not adorn themselves with outward material goods.

June 3rd is also my great uncle's birthday. He lived to be 104, and I attended his 100th in Seattle. He was so giving to his family and friends, an educator, and philanthropist. I am grateful for good family genes.

Hot Lemon Souffle

Serves 4

3 eggs, separated ½ stick butter
¾ cup sugar Juice of 3 lemons
3 tbls. flour Zest of 3 lemons
1 cup milk or cream Whipped cream

Preheat oven to 375°
Beat the yolks with ½ cup of sugar. Add the flour, milk and butter.
Beat the egg whites until stiff. Beat in ¼ cup of sugar. Add the lemon juice and zest to egg whites. Fold into the yolk mixture.
Butter a souffle dish and pour the mixture into the dish. Set in a pan of hot water and bake for 30 minutes. Remove from water bath. Put back in oven to slightly brown, about 5 minutes. Serve warm with whipped cream

June 4

"To every thing there is a season, and a time to every purpose under the heaven: A time to be born, and a time to die; a time to plant, and a time to pluck up that which is planted; A time to kill, and a time to heal: a time to break down, and a time to build up; A time to weep, and a time to laugh; a time to mourn, and a time to dance; A time to caste away stones, and a time to gather stones together; a time to embrace, and a time to refrain from embracing; A time to get, and a time to lose; a time to keep, and a time to cast away; A time to rend, and a time to sew; a time to keep silence, and a time to speak; A time to love, and a time to hate; a time of war, and a time of peace."
Ecclesiastes 3:1-8

My companion and good friend died in June 1994. As the church filled I reflected on his life and the fact he had taken it, leaving family, friends and a young daughter. How can anyone be so selfish? Only that person knows. We all try to live good and happy lives, but sometimes we are sidetracked. We lose a loved one, we lose a job, we're fat, we're just not in our right minds. When we get into trouble over these problems we often do not seek help, or if we do we deny it or even worse commit suicide .A natural death, or death in an accident we can possibly understand. But not when someone takes their own life. There can be signs of depression, hopelessness, disorientation, and heavy drinking. God taught us to live, not die. He died for us, so that we might live better lives. If only we could fervently believe in God, and hope this too will pass, and we can leave everything in God's hands. I chose to read Ecclesiastes 3 at his service.

"The Lord heals the brokenhearted and binds up their wounds."
Psalm 147:3

"Let nothing disturb you, Let nothing dismay you. All things pass; God never changes."
Saint Teresa of Avila (1515-1582)

Crab Spread

1 lb. fresh crab meat	½ cup mayonnaise
1 can sliced water chestnuts	2 green onion, chopped
2 tbls. soy sauce	

Combine all the ingredients in a bowl.
Serve with crackers.

June 5

""I have fought a good fight, I have finished my course, I have kept the faith."
Timothy 4:8

As I sit here writing this book I look back on the twenty-eight years since my divorce. When we grow up, we think everything will turn out perfectly. Life is not that way. I remember at a very young age being asked in class to draw the ideal family picture of what I wanted to be when I grew up. The picture is still so vivid in my mind, though I no longer can find it. The scene showed a white clabbered house with a fence, fields, children playing, and dogs and other animals. I am sure there must have been grownups too. I remember wanting five or six children. My sister ended up living in the white house with a picket fence and had four children, not the one or two of her dreams. I have only the one daughter. I've remarried and live in a lovely colonial house with a high white fence. I am a very different person. I have fought many battles, but I have kept the faith. Thanks be to God.

Cod with Tomatoes

Serves 4

3 medium tomatoes	3 cloves garlic, crushed
3 tbls. olive oil	1 tsp. salt
2 tbls. butter	1 tsp. fresh ground pepper
1½ lbs. codfish filets	¼ cup parsley, chopped

Bring a pan of water to boil. Drop the tomatoes in the pan. Remove immediately, and peel off the skins. Chop the tomatoes.
Heat the oil and butter in a skillet. Braise the codfish on each side until just golden. Put the fish on a plate.
Add garlic, salt, pepper and parsley to the skillet. Stir in the tomatoes. Put the fish on top of the tomato mixture. Just heat.
Place the fish on 4 individual plates. Spoon the tomato mixture over the cod. Garnish with more parsley.
Serve with rice or crusty bread and a salad.

"Jesus saith unto him (Thomas) I am the way, the truth and the life, no man cometh unto the Father, but by me."
John 14:6

A dear friend has so much inner strength. She grew up in a privileged family – private school, college, sailing, traveling and enjoying creature comforts. After her divorce she invested in real estate, little knowing the bottom would fall out. She lost everything. Her spirit, her laugh and her kind heart remained within her. Now living in a small apartment she manages to sail, enjoy her children and grandchildren, and in her seventies still works. She could have just lain down the gauntlet, but each day she wakes and is joyous in her life. When you think you are at your lowest, let the Lord enter your heart, take your hand, and let Him show you the way.

"In thee, O LORD, do I put my trust; let me never be ashamed: deliver me in thy righteousness. Bow down thine ear to me; deliver me speedily: be thou my strong rock, for an house of defence to save me. For thou art my rock and my fortress; therefore for thy name's sake lead me, and guide me. Pull me out of the net that they have laid privily for me: for thou art my strength. Into thine hand I commit my spirit: thou hast redeemed me, O LORD God of truth."
Psalm 31:1-5

Grilled Swordfish Kabobs

Serves 6

2 ½ lbs. swordfish, cubed	4 scallions chopped
½ cup mayonnaise	¼ cup fresh parsley, chopped
Juice of one lemon	¼ cup lemon juice
1 pint cherry tomatoes	¼ cup olive oil
1 large red onion, cubed	½ tsp. sea salt

Combine the mayonnaise and lemon juice
Place the swordfish on a platter. Coat on all sides with mayonnaise mixture.
Using 6 skewers, alternate swordfish, tomatoes, and onion.
Grill on BBQ, so that swordfish is golden.
In a bowl combine the scallions, parsley, lemon juice, olive oil and sea salt.
Serve the scallion mixture with the kabobs.

"In quietness and in confidence shall be your strength."
Isaiah 30:15

Be still, be quiet, be calm. So difficult to do? The news is troubling, the Stock Market is crashing, natural disasters strike every continent. A fellow brother has just written an email from the Baltics where he is visiting four countries, praying that the time he has spent with leaders in those countries will bring them and their citizens closer to our Lord. He was deeply troubled by an accident in Vilnius where he saw a young man zig and zag one too many times on a scooter. The man was hit by a semi-trailer loaded with cars, and killed instantly. Another young life lost. How can we be still? Take time each day to be quiet. Take a walk, curl up with the Bible or book, take the phone off the hook, stare out at the ocean. Do nothing. Just let the beauty of the earth surround you. Look up to the Lord, and be thankful.

Tomato Quiche

Serves 4

1 unbaked pie shell	2 eggs
4 medium tomatoes, sliced	1 cup cream
4 green onions, chopped	Salt and pepper
1 cup sharp cheddar cheese, grated	¼ cup fresh basil, chopped
1 cup mozzarella cheese, grated	

Preheat the oven to 400°
Bake pie shell for 10 minutes. Let cool.
In a bowl beat eggs, cream, salt and pepper together.
Place the tomatoes, onions and basil in pie shell. Top with cheeses. Pour cream mixture on top.
Bake for 45 minutes or until golden color.
Can be served warm or chilled.

June 8

"And thy seed shall be as the dust of the earth, and thou shalt spread abroad to the west, and to the east, and to the north, and to the south: and in thee and in thy seed shall all of the families of the earth be blest."
Genesis 28:14

Family reunions are a time to gather, share food, share stories, and be united under one roof, often after long periods of not seeing each other. Families drift apart, sibling rivalries develop, antagonism erupts when a person inherits and another does not. Reunions are joyous times. Set aside animosities and revel in what God has given you. Grandparents, aunts and uncles, and hopefully lots of cousins. Joy in the setting – an old family manse or barn, a park, or renting a compound or rooms. Joy in the food – old family recipes, new family recipes, or something even store bought. Share time with each member, reminisce and admire pictures. Catch up as though you had seen that person only yesterday, not thirty years ago. Family is so important, and those that can stay together are healthier and wiser. As you part from each other share in the hymn *"Blest be the tie that binds."*

Our hearts in Christian love;
the fellowship of kindred minds
Is like to that above.
When we asunder part;
It gives us inward pain;
But we shall be joined in heart,
And hope to meet again."
From: The Primitive Baptist Hymnal
Written by: John Fawcett, 1782

Tomato and Basil Flatbread

4 tomatoes, chopped
1 cup basil, chopped
Olive oil

1 pound mozzarella, thinly sliced
Flatbread or focaccia
Fresh grated parmesan cheese

Spread the mozzarella evenly over the bread. Top with tomatoes and basil. Drizzle olive oil on the tomatoes. Sprinkle with parmesan cheese.
Cut in bit size pieces. Serve immediately.

June 9

"The Lord will cover you with his feathers; And under his wings you find refuge."
Psalm 91:4

My niece was married in a lovely old New England church. Family and friends gathered for this elegant occasion, coming from San Francisco and places throughout the United States. The pastor was an old family friend. Her parents had owned a house almost across the street from my grandparents. Both summer homes are now sadly out of the families. What made this so special was not only the wedding which she presided over, but the pastor's story. She had grown up in a well-to-do family, but like many in the 1960s and 70s had lost her way to alcohol and drugs. One day, when she was at her lowest, she realized life was worth living. She saw the light, the light of our Lord. She has never swerved, and serves Him, her congregation, and the local community. May we also follow the true path.

"Thou wilt shew me the path of life; in thy presence is fullness of joy; at thy right hand there are pleasures for evermore."
Psalm 16:11

Clam Chowder

Serves 4

2 dozen hard shell clams	½ lb. pancetta
4 green onions, sliced	1 quart half and half
1 leek, sliced	1 tsp. pepper
4 large red bliss potatoes, cubed	1 tbls. sea salt
½ stick butter	¼ cup dill, snipped

Preheat the oven to 350°
Place the clams on a cookie sheet. Bake until the clams open.
Reserve the clam broth and put the clams aside.
Boil the potatoes until tender. Drain.
In a large pan melt 2 tbls. of the butter. Saute the pancetta for 2 minutes, until it just curls. Remove the pancetta.
Saute the green onions and leek in the pan. Add the potatoes, half and half, pepper, and salt. Bring to a boil. Turn down the heat and add the pancetta and clams.
Simmer until warm. Pour into bowls and top with a dash of butter and the dill.

June 10

"And he sent them to preach the kingdom of God and heal the sick."
Luke 9:2

My oldest friend called to say she had just been to her college reunion and was coming to see her sister, a couple of days before she planned. For the second time in her life she thought she might be losing another sister. Her oldest sister died several years ago, suffering from breast cancer, a heart attack and then lung cancer. Now the middle sister was suffering and in the ICU. I could console my friend and spend time with her, but the most important person was her sister. Her sister was hooked up to every possible machine, barely able to speak. Please God, heal the sick. Please be with my friend and her sister. (as a footnote, and as I finish up this book), this friend's sister is home, lost all her hair, but is back at work and acting her normal self. God be praised for miracles, and the miracle of prayer!

"Have mercy upon me, O Lord; for I am weak: O Lord, heal me for my bones are vexed."
Psalm 6:2

Spinach Salad

Serves 6

1 lb. baby spinach	1 cup pecans
1 large mango, peeled and diced	1 cup blue cheese
1 medium red onion, sliced	

Pour the dressing into a salad bowl. Toss in other ingredients.

Fruit Dressing

Juice of 1 orange	¼ cup honey
Juice of 1 lime	2 tbls. poppy seeds

Combine the ingredients in a jar. Shake hard.

June 11

"Hear, ye children, the instruction of a father, and attend to know understanding. For I give you good doctrine, forsake ye not my law. For I was my father's son, tender and only beloved in the sight of my mother. He taught me also, and said unto me, Let thine heart retain my words: keep my commandments, and live. Get wisdom, get understanding: forget it not; neither decline from the words of my mouth. Forsake her not, and she shall preserve thee: love her, and she shall keep thee."
Proverbs 4:1-6

On Father's Day 1997 I wrote the following: "I know Dad how hard it is to be a dad. But thank you for being who you are. Life does not always turn out the way we expect it to be. Instead there are ups and downs, and hopefully more ups than downs. I am so thankful for you and Mom. For being the wonderful parents you are – thoughtful, loving and generous to all. Thank you for the beauty and love of Nantucket and our strong heritage there and in other places in this country. But above all, thank you for just being you."

Baked Sole with Lobster Sauce

Serves 10

2 lbs. sole filets	1 lb. baby spinach
1 lb. large shrimp, cooked, deveined and peeled	2 large leeks, sliced
1 lb. scallops	1 lb. baby portabella mushrooms, sliced
1 lb. crab meat	

Preheat the oven to 350°
Place the sole in a buttered baking dish. Arrange the other ingredients on the sole. Pour the lobster sauce over the fish.
Bake ½ hour or until golden and bubbling.

Lobster Cream Sauce

1½ sticks butter	½ lb. Gruyere cheese
¾ cup flour	1 lb. lobster meat
3 cups cream	
¼ cup Madeira	

Melt the butter in a sauce pan. Stir in the flour, then cream, until thickened. Stir in the Madeira and Gruyere until the cheese is melted. Fold in the lobster.

June 12

"And when he was entered into a ship, his disciples followed him. And, behold there arose a great tempest in the sea, insomuch that the ship was covered with the waves, but he was asleep. And his disciples came to him, and awoke him, saying Lord, save us; we perish. And he saith unto them, Why are ye fearful, O ye of little faith? Then he arose, and rebuked the winds, and the sea; and there was a great calm." (Matthew 8:23-26) *"He maketh the storm a calm, so that the waves thereof are still. Then are they glad because they be quiet; so he bringeth them into their desired haven.*
Psalm 107:29-30

Only a week or so after I had met a lovely gentleman, he asked me to go sailing out of Westport Harbor, Massachusetts. We had taken a lovely sail and were heading back along Horseneck Beach when a tumultuous gale surprised us. The wind howled, the boat spun around as we quickly took the sails in. Every direction you looked, all appeared the same. There was no sense of direction. There was only the pelting rain, the wind and the raging sea. This friend, who was a seasoned sailor and knew these waters well, took my hands. We prayed, we wept, and we told each other how much we loved the other. This man was almost a stranger, but God had brought us into this situation and we prayed we would get back to the harbor safely.

To this day I don't remember how long the storm lasted. I do know we arrived back in Westport in the dark, soaking wet and chilled to the bone. We looked for a place to get a bite to eat, but everything seemed closed up. Finally we found a place to at least get some chowder and warm up. It was a long way back to Newport that night. But this friend and I remained true and loving friends until he died suddenly four years later. The shock was awful. How could he be taken away so young? I feel fortunate to have known him. He taught my daughter to sail and ski. He taught me to appreciate the sea, and how meaningful it is for God to be in our lives, no matter what the circumstances. May you also come to know the Lord more and more each day.

Crab Cream Cheese Dip

1 8 oz. package cream cheese	2 tbls. basil, chopped
1 stick butter, softened	½ tsp. thyme
½ lb. crab meat	1 tsp. dill, snipped
2 cloves garlic, crushed	
1 tsp. oregano	

Combine the ingredients in a bowl. Serve with crackers or French bread.

June 13

"Because they have no changes, therefore they fear not God"
Psalm 55:19

One of my college friends was born with an ear defect. She always wore hearing aids. A number of years ago a new brand came out. She was so excited, but on trying them, realized she preferred what she was wearing. The new ones brought new sounds into her life, too much change. Change can bring about marvelous new beginnings, but sometimes we want to cling to what we have.

During his time on earth Jesus was new, Jesus was change. People were ready for a Messiah, but only a few knew He was the one. Think of the Pharisees and Sadducees, the Herods and Pilates, the Romans who tortured and killed the Christians in the Colosseum. Religious intolerance continues today in Saudi Arabia and elsewhere. There could not be a king on earth and in the heavens. But there is God, Son and Holy Spirit, the three in one. Through Jesus came change and the redemption of our sins. We need him more than ever right now, right here.

Old Fashioned Baked Beans

1lb. dried beans (can be pinto, yellow eyed or navy beans)
6 cups of water
1½ tsp. dry mustard
1 tbls. salt
¼ tsp. pepper
2 large onions, sliced
¼ cup brown sugar
1/3 cup maple syrup
½ cup ketchup

Pick over the dried beans and rinse. Put the beans in a large bowl or kettle and add water. Let soak eight hours or overnight.
Drain and place in large pot with water and boil uncovered for 10-15 minutes.
Drain and put in an oven baking pot with all ingredients and bake at 300 degrees for 6-8 hours.
Check to see if more liquid is needed. Add a mixture of the water and maple syrup or brown sugar.
YUM!

"Stand fast therefore in the liberty wherewith Christ hath made us free, and be not entangled again with the yoke of bondage. For, brethren, ye have been called unto liberty; only use not liberty for an occasion to the flesh, but by love serve one another. For all the law is fulfilled in one word, even in this; Thou shalt love thy neighbour as thyself."
Galatians 5:1

June 14th is celebrated as Flag Day in the United States. In 1777 the Second Continental Congress passed a resolution proclaiming this day. In 1916 President Woodrow Wilson issued a proclamation for Flag Day. The citizens of the United States are so fortunate to have freedoms that are not known in other parts of the world. However to enjoy this they must respect the Declaration of Independence, the Constitution and seeing the flag flown. Burning the flag is not an option. When that happens hatred and disrespect are shown. You can only be a true American by respecting the flag and freedom associated with it. Stand fast for our liberty.

Red, White and Blue Pie

1 pie crust
1 pint strawberries
1 pint blueberries
Zest of 1 lemon
¼ tsp. nutmeg

2 tbls. orange juice
2 tbls. lemon juice
1 pt. whipping cream

Preheat the oven to 400°
Bake the pie crust for 10 minutes, or until just golden.
Combine the strawberries, blueberries, zest, nutmeg, lemon and orange juice in a bowl. Pour into crust.
Beat whipping cream until peaks form.
Top pie with whipped cream, and any extra berries.

"Children's children are the crown of old men; and the glory of children are their fathers."
Proverbs 17:6

I was asked to serve on the board of Justice for Children, a national organization dedicated to raising consciousness of our society to protect victims of child abuse and to provide legal assistance and treatment to those that have been abused. I have known about this organization for several years, but it is the impact the group has on assistance and legislation that made me realize this is something I needed to advocate for and support.

Children are so precious. You don't know what they will do or say next. One of the problems of modern society is programming them too much, and not allowing them time to imagine. Most children have imaginary people they talk to, confide in, and are their friends. Children need to read books, not sit behind a TV or computer screen all day. They need to get outside – swim, go to a playground, run around and play tag or spin the bottle or other games. Jumping rope, hopscotch and marbles are not a thing of the past. They are part of socializing and enjoyment of life. Competition is good to a certain point, but each child must be made to feel comfortable and praised no matter how well or poorly he (she) does. Never criticize, instead encourage, and give a loving arm or hug. Join Big Brother/Big Sister or become a mentor and friend. We all need hope for the future, and the children are the future. Christ loved children and surrounded himself with them. If it weren't for baby Jesus we would not have Christmas. Protect our children and love them with all your heart.

Shortbread

4 sticks butter   5 cups flour
1 cup sugar

Preheat oven to 350°
In a bowl cream the butter and sugar. Add flour one cup at a time.
On a floured board, roll the dough into a circle. Cut triangles of dough.
Place on a cookie sheet and cook 15 minutes, or until just browned.

June 16

"And if a house be divided against itself, that house cannot stand."
Mark 3:25

On June 16, 1858 Abraham Lincoln was nominated by the Illinois Republicans to run as Senator. Afterwards he addressed his fellow Republicans in one of his most famous speeches quoting directly from the Bible.

"Mr. President and Gentlemen of the Convention. If we could first know where we are, and whither we are tending, we could then better judge what to do, and how to do it. We are now far into the fifth year, since a policy was initiated, with the avowed object, and confident promise, of putting an end to slavery agitation. Under the operation of that policy, that agitation has not only, not ceased, but has constantly augmented. In my opinion, it will not cease, until a crisis shall have been reached, and passed. "A house divided against itself cannot stand." I believe this government cannot endure, permanently half slave and half free. I do not expect the Union to be dissolved -- I do not expect the house to fall -- but I do expect it will cease to be divided. It will become all one thing or all the other. Either the opponents of slavery, will arrest the further spread of it, and place it where the public mind shall rest in the belief that it is in the course of ultimate extinction; or its advocates will push it forward, till it shall become alike lawful in all the States, old as well as new -- North as well as South."

The Civil War tore apart this country three years later, ending with freedom for the slaves, but sadly the death of President Lincoln. This country is still divided whether it be race, politics, families, or regional differences. We cannot be a house divided, but a house united as one country, one people, living in a democracy under God!

Green Beans with Dill

Serves 6

2 lbs. fresh green beans
½ stick butter
2 shallots, minced
1 tsp. salt

1 tsp. pepper
¼ cup lemon juice
¼ cup fresh parsley, chopped
2 tbls. dill, snipped

Bring a pan of water to boil. Blanche the green beans for 4 minutes. Drain Remove the beans.
Melt butter in the pan. Stir in the shallots. Cook for 3 minutes. Add beans, salt, pepper, lemon juice, parsley and dill. Serve warm, or can be chilled.

June 17

"I'll praise my Maker while I've breath; and my voice is lost in death, praise shall my nobler powers. My days of praise shall ne'er be past while life and thought and being last, or immortality endures."
John Wesley

John Wesley (1703-91), an Anglican minister, was the founder of the Arminian Methodist movement, along with his brother Charles. They were both very attached to the Church of England, and used the Book of Common Prayer. Both brothers were educated at Oxford and traveled to Savannah, Georgia. On their return to England each received an inner conversion while attending a meeting in Aldersgate Street with a group of Moravians during the reading of Martin Luther's preface to the Epistle to the Romans. John founded the Kingswood School in 1748 to educate the children of his clergy. The words to *I'll Praise my Maker* are paraphrased from Psalm 146.

Also born on this date was James Weldon Johnson (1871-1938), author of the very joyous *Lift Every Voice and Sing*. He was a civil rights activist, involved in the Harlem Renaissance, and one of the first African-American professors at New York University. He also taught at Fisk University.

Stuffed Tomatoes

Serves 8

8 large tomatoes
¼ cup olive oil
1 medium onion, chopped
½ lb. baby spinach
1 cup fresh peas

½ tsp. salt
1 tsp. pepper
1 cup parmesan cheese
½ cup fresh basil chopped

Preheat oven to 350°
Cut the top off the tomatoes. Scrap out the tomato pulp.
Heat the olive oil in a skillet and add onions. Saute until just tender. Stir in the other ingredients.
Stuff the tomatoes with the mixture.
Bake 20 minutes, or until bubbly.

June 18

"The men of Dedan were thy merchants; many isles were the merchandise of thy hand: they brought thee for a present horns of ivory and ebony."
Ezekial 27:15

The year my daughter was born I was very involved with Meridian House in Washington. When diplomats arrive in this country they are briefed at Meridian House. Their wives and children are made welcome by learning American ways – shopping, housing, schools, cooking lessons, and sightseeing in and around DC. I also worked with the international visitors that came through the State Department programs. One of these was a lady from Mali. She was extremely tall and beautiful. As we chatted she took my baby daughter in her arms and then laid her out on her thighs. They were that long! Little did I know my daughter would grow to be 5'11", just like our guest from Mali. Later as our guest was leaving I asked about an ivory bracelet she was wearing. She told me it was made in Mali. With that she took it off and gave it to me. To this day I treasure and wear this symbol of her kindness. I have also learned when you admire something in another culture they will give it to you. Be careful in what you long for!

Chicken Stew

Serves 4

2 tbls. olive oil
2 tbls. butter
¼ cup flour
1 tbls. Italian herbs
1 tsp. salt
1 tsp. pepper
3 boneless chicken breasts
3 cloves garlic, crushed

1 cup tomato juice
1 cup peanut butter
4 medium tomatoes, chopped
1 small onion, chopped
10 oz. frozen okra
½ eggplant, peeled and chopped
2 jalapeno, seeded and chopped

In a bowl combine the flour Italian herbs, salt and pepper. Dredge the chicken breasts in the flour.
Heat the oil and butter in a large pan with a cover. Brown the chicken on both sides.
Combine all the ingredients in the pan. Bring to a boil. Simmer for 1 hour.
Serve with rice.
The stew can also be baked for one hour.

June 19

My sister's oldest friend has remained a good friend of mine. We attended each other's weddings, celebrated babies, and our parents are still close, though hers are in failing health. When her brother was in his teens he decided, rather than work for the family's printing business, he would sell pots and pans. No, not in a store, but he took them right into your living room and gave a demonstration on how strong they were. One of his gigs was to dance on each of them. We were uproarious. How could this cute kid be so funny? How could he even sell a pan? I truly don't know how many he sold, but he sure had fun doing it, and made a lot of people laugh. So when you're feeling sorry for yourself, think of something funny that has happened in your life. Or better yet, start the day the way I do, by reading the comics. You can't help but laugh. I don't care how long *Bettle Bailey*, *Dennis the Menace*, or *Family Circle* have been around, they still bring a smile to my face. And a great big chuckle!

Crab Dip

1 lb. fresh crab meat	½ cup parmesan cheese
½ cup cheddar cheese	2 green onions, chopped
1 3 oz. package cream cheese	1 tbls. lemon juice
¼ cup mayonnaise	½ tsp. Worcestershire sauce
¼ cup sour cream	½ cup fresh bread crumbs

Preheat oven to 350°
Combine all in ingredients, except breadcrumbs, in a buttered baking dish.
Cover with the bread crumbs.
Bake 20 minutes, or until bubbly.
Serve with crackers or French bread.
Artichoke hearts can also be added. Or substitute horseradish for Worcestershire sauce.

June 20

"From the fig tree learn its lesson: as soon as its branch becomes tender and puts forth its leaves, you know that summer is near. So also, when you see these things taking place you know that night is near, at the very gates. Truly I tell you, this generation will not pass away until all these things have taken place. Heaven and earth will pass away, but my words will not pass away."
Mark 13: 28-31

I love the spring and summer mornings. The sun rises early, the birds are humming, there is peace and quiet. Quiet like there must have been when God created the world. Forget about the Big Bang Theory. Think peace, think of the sky and the sun and stars and moon. Think happy thoughts, not the darkness which can enshroud you, take it off. if you cannot see the Light, see the way. The night should be like day – crystal clear and joyous. Sing to the Lord a new song, always.

Fig Pudding

Serves 4-6

1 lb. dried figs, stemmed and chopped
1¾ cups milk
¾ lb ground suet
1 cup sugar
3 eggs
1 ½ cups fresh bread crumbs

3 tbls. orange zest
1 ½ cups flour
2½ tsp. baking powder
1 tsp. cinnamon
1 tsp. nutmeg
½ tsp. salt

In a pan simmer the figs and milk for 20 minutes. Cool.
In a bowl cream the suet and sugar. Add the eggs. Stir in bread crumbs and zest. Stir in figs and milk. Then add flour, baking powder, cinnamon, nutmeg and salt.
Pour into a mold with a lid.
Put the mold into a large kettle. Fill the kettle halfway with hot water. Steam pudding for two hours. Cool.
Store adding brandy. Wrap in aluminum foil and store in refrigerator.
To serve, warm in oven at a low temperature.

June 21

"God grant me the serenity to accept the things I cannot change, courage to change the things I can, and the wisdom to know the difference."
Reinhold Niebuhr

Reinhold Niebuhr (1892-1971) was born in Missouri and went on to become one of the great theologians of the 20th century. He earned his Bachelor of Divinity Degree from Yale in 1914. He was ordained a pastor in the German Evangelical Church. His first parish was in Detroit, where the congregation grew from 65 to over 700 parishioners. As Detroit grew with automotive workers he took on their causes and even permitted union organizers to use his pulpit. He also spoke out against the Ku Klux Klan. Before leaving Detroit he wrote *Leaves from the Notebook of a Tamed Cynic.* He taught at Union Theological Seminary in New York, His best known theological work is the two-volume *"Nature and Destiny of Man."*

As we continue our war efforts in Iraq, Afghanistan and elsewhere please bear in mind these words of Dr. Niebuhr *"Democracies are indeed slow to make war, but once embarked upon a martial venture are equally slow to make peace and reluctant to make a tolerable, rather than a vindictive, peace."*

Remember also Laurence Tuttiett (1825-95) who wrote *Go Forward Christian Soldier* and died on this date. *"The Lord himself thy leader, shall all thy foes subdue."* Please Lord bring peace to this world.

Tomato Salsa

2 large tomatoes, chopped finely
1 can chickpeas, drained
1 small red onion, chopped
4 green onions, chopped
¼ cup cilantro, chopped
Zest of 1 lime

Juice of 1 lime
2 jalapeno, seeded and chopped
½ tsp. cumin
½ tsp. chili powder
¼ cup olive oil

Combine all ingredients in a bowl.
Serve with chips, or with grilled chicken, pork, or lamb.

June 22

"Pray one for another, that ye may be healed."
James 5:16

The mother of our Bible study group's leader was hospitalized this past winter after she broke her hip. She spent time in rehab and is now back home with my friend. We have prayed for her to be restored to health. During her stay in rehab, my friend was not sure she could cope with her mother at home. There were days when she thought it might be better if the Lord took her mother. As I talk to her now, her mother is doing very well. My friend is too. She even told me she was at peace if her mother were to leave her. I pray that we can all feel that way when the time comes for the Lord to take away our loved ones.

"By stretching forth thine hand to heal; and that signs and wonders may be done by the name of thy holy child Jesus."
Acts 5:30

Crème Brulee

Serves 4

2 cups heavy cream	Dash salt
¼ cup sugar	1 tsp. vanilla
4 egg yolks	½ cup light brown sugar

Preheat oven to 275°
Pour the cream into a double boiler. Heat, but do not boil. Add the sugar.
In a bowl beat the egg yolks till stiffened. Add salt and vanilla. Stir into cream.
Pour the mixture into individual custard dishes. Place these in a pan with boiling water.
Bake in oven for about 45 minutes, or until set.
Remove from oven. Chill.
Sprinkle some of the brown sugar on top of each custard. Place under the broiler, or use a kitchen torch until the sugar melts. Refrigerate until ready to serve.

"Who shall separate us from the love of Christ? Shall tribulation, or distress, or persecution, or famine, or nakedness, or peril, or sword? As it is written, For thy sake we are killed all the day long; we are accounted as sheep for the slaughter. Nay, in all these things we are more than conquerors through him that loved us. For I am persuaded that neither death, nor life, nor angels, nor principalities, nor powers, nor things present, nor things to come. Nor height, nor death, nor any other creature, shall be able to separate us from the love of God, which is in Christ Jesus our Lord."
Romans 8:35-39

As we go through life we experience so many distressing moments, but we can never forget it is the love of Christ for us that will get us through. Paul quotes Psalm 44:22 in this passage. *"Yes, for thy sake are we killed all the day long: we are counted as sheep for the slaughter."* We only have to look at all Paul suffered through to know that he understands what we go through. In those days Christians suffered more than those of today, and were persecuted more frequently. But we only have to look just beyond our nation to see persecution still taking place. We cannot hide from this fact. We cannot hide from our own sufferings. Instead we must never be separated from the love of Christ.

Herb and Cheese Biscuits

2 cups flour	½ cup heavy cream
2 tsp. baking powder	1 tsp. snipped dill
½ tsp. sea salt	1 tsp. rosemary
6 tbls. butter	½ tsp. tarragon

Preheat oven to 400°
Combine all the ingredients in a food processor until a ball forms.
Roll out dough on a floured board. Using a 2 inch round cookie cutter cut out dough circles.
Place on an ungreased baking pan.
Cook for 12-15 minutes, or until golden.

June 24

"And suddenly there came a sound from heaven as of a rushing mighty wind, and it filled all the house where they were sitting. And there appeared unto them cloven tongues like as of fire, and it sat upon each one of them. And they all were filled with the Holy Spirit and began to speak in other languages, as the Spirit gave them ability."
Acts 2:2-4

As an active Lay Eucharistic Minister at the Washington National Cathedral I loved to be part of the service on Pentecost. During the reading of Acts we were asked to speak in "foreign tongues". We could say whatever we wanted. At first I was a little shocked at the "noise", but I realized gathered in this glorious Cathedral we were all Christians. *"Therefore let all the house of Israel know assuredly, that God hath made that same Jesus, whom ye have crucified, both Lord and Christ."* Acts 2:36

Pentecost, the fiftieth day after Easter Sunday, was also the Jewish harvest festival of Shavuot or fifty days after the Exodus, on which God gave the Ten Commandments to Moses at Mount Sinai. For us Pentecost is the appearance of the Holy Spirit upon the Apostles and other followers of Jesus. Pentecost is also called Whitsun, Whitsunday, or Whit Sunday.

Grilled Chicken

Serves 4

4 boneless chicken breasts
Zest of 1 lime
Juice of 1 lime
2 cloves garlic, crushed
2 jalapeno, seeded and chopped

2 tbls. fresh grated ginger
¼ cup cilantro chopped
1 tsp. paprika
¼ cup olive oil

In a bowl combine all the ingredients. Cover and refrigerate at least two hours.
Grill chicken on the BBQ grill, reserving liquid from the bowl.
When the chicken is cooked, place on a platter or individual plates and pour the remaining sauce over the chicken.
Serve with basmati rice and a salad.

June 25

"Jesus said, if thou wilt be perfect, go and sell that thou hast, and give to the poor, and thou shalt have treasure in heave: and come and follow me...Then said Jesus unto his disciples, Verily I say unto you, That a rich man shall hardly enter into the kingdom of heaven."
Matthew 20:21, 23

This passage talks about the true Jesus. He asks that you give up everything for Him. This can be a difficult decision. Don't we love our material possessions – our house, our car, our garden, our jewelry, everything we own? But look how those that followed Him literally dropped everything they were doing or owned and followed him. They did not even question what they were getting into. They only knew they had found the Messiah, the living Lord. I want to follow Jesus. Sing or hum *I want to Walk as a Child*, the lovely hymn by Kathleen Thomerson (1934-). Have you found him, or are you still looking?

Salmon and Pasta

Serves 4

1½ lbs. salmon	2 tbls. dill, snipped
2 tbls. butter	¼ tsp. nutmeg
¼ cup white wine	1½ cups heavy cream
½ lb. baby spinach	1 lb. spinach pasta
4 cloves garlic, minced	Parmesan cheese

Cook the salmon on the grill to desired pinkness.
Heat the butter and wine in a skillet. Stir in spinach. garlic, dill and nutmeg.
When ready to serve gently fold in cream and salmon.
Cook the pasta according to the directions. Drain. Cover and keep warm.
Serve pasta with parmesan cheese.
Smoked salmon can be used instead of fresh salmon. Or substitute scallops, shrimp or other fish for the salmon.
Basil can be substituted for dill.

June 26

"Awake, my soul, stretch every nerve, And press with vigor on; A heavenly race demands thy zeal, And an immortal crown, And an immortal crown. A cloud of witnesses around Hold thee in full survey; Forget the steps already trod, And onward urge thy way, And onward urge thy way. 'Tis God's all animating voice That calls thee from on high; 'Tis His own hand presents the prize To thine aspiring eye, To thine aspiring eye. Then wake, my soul, stretch every nerve, And press with vigor on, A heavenly race demands thy zeal, And an immortal crown, And an immortal crown."

During our short span on earth many people pass by us. Some become friends, some only known by face, others just move on. When one realizes you are a Christian, arms open and you are taken into the fold. We are awakened, knowing this person holds our beliefs and values. We can discuss issues that might bring angry arguments from nonbelievers. We share sorrow and happiness. We pray together. We pray for each other when not together. We thank God that he has opened our eyes, that he calls us from on high. Alleluia, Jesus Christ is Lord.

Philip Doddridge (1702-51) was an English Nonconformist minister and hymn writer. His best known work *Rise and Progress of Religion in the Soul* (1745) was dedicated to Isaac Watts and has been translated into other languages. His many hymns include *Awake, My Soul, Stretch Every Nerve* and *O Happy Day.*

Banana Bread

5 bananas	1 tsp. baking powder
¼ cup dark rum	2 cups flour
1 cup sugar	½ tsp. salt
½ cup vegetable oil	1 tbls. milk
2 eggs	1 tsp. vanilla
1 tsp. baking soda	1 cup pecans or walnuts

Preheat oven to 350°
In a bowl mash the bananas. Stir in the rum. Refrigerate for at least 1 hour.
Add sugar, vegetable oil and eggs. Stir in other ingredients.
Pour into a bread pan.
Bake 1 hour, or until a toothpick comes out clean.

June 27

"Have I not commanded you? Be strong and courageous. Do not be terrified; do not be discouraged, for the Lord your God will be with wherever you go."
Joshua 1:9

What is there about water? The ocean can be so calm, but can also be so cruel. You don't want to mess with nature. During my years as an author and living in seaside towns and cities such as Newport, Annapolis, San Francisco and Nantucket, I have had the opportunity to meet sailors who defied nature, and survived tremendous ordeals. Sadly some such as Michael Plante lost their lives and were never found. Our family home on Nantucket was flooded during the "Perfect Storm" in 1991. God is with you wherever you are, but we, like Jesus, do not walk on water or control the churning seas. Have faith, but use common sense when on the water. Even the grandest and newest ships have sunk – the *Andrea Doria* off Nantucket in 1954 with friends on board and the *Titanic* in 1912. Let the Lord be with you wherever you go. Let Him take your hand and do not be discouraged.

Mussel Soup

Serves 6

¼ cup olive oil
1 large onion, chopped
2 cloves garlic, minced
¼ cup shallots, minced
3 stalks celery, chopped
3 tomatoes, chopped

1 red pepper, chopped
1 bottle dry white wine
¼ cup fresh basil, chopped
¼ cup parsley, chopped
2 tbls. tarragon, chopped
5 lbs. mussels, scrubbed

Heat the olive oil in a large pan. Stir in onions, shallots, garlic and celery. Cook until just tender. Add tomatoes and pepper.
Add white wine. Bring to a boil. Stir in mussels. Cook until shells open. Add basil and parsley.
Serve with crusty bread or rice, and a salad
Can also be served over pasta.

June 28

"Faith of our fathers! Living still in spite of dungeon, fire, and sword: O how our hearts beat high with joy, whene'er we hear that glorious word: Faith of our fathers, holy faith! We will be true to thee till death."

Frederick William Faber (1814-63) was educated at Oxford and is best known for the numerous hymns he composed. *Faith of our Fathers* and *There's a Wideness in God's Mercy* are two favorites. He was raised with Calvinistic views, but after traveling on the continent, became a follower of John Henry Newman. After studying Roman Catholicism he joined the Catholic Church in 1845. He founded a religious community at Cotton Hall, near Birmingham, England.

"My God how wonderful thou art, thy majesty how bright, how beautiful thy mercy seat, in depths of burning light."

Fruit with Rum Sauce

Serves 4-6

1 cantaloupe	1 pint blueberries
1 pint strawberries	1 pint blackberries

Make balls out of the melon. Combine cantaloupe, strawberries, blueberries and blackberries in a bowl. Pour rum sauce over the mixture, or serve in a separate pitcher.

Sauce

2/3 cup sugar	½ cup lime juice
¼ cup water	½ cup dark rum
Zest of 1 lime	

In a sauce pan bring the sugar and water to a boil. Simmer 5 minutes. Cool. Add zest, lime juice, and rum.

June 29

"By the rivers of Babylon, there we sat down, yea we wept, when we remembered Zion.
Psalm 137:1

My paternal grandmother had dinner on this night with my parents, my sister and her children on Nantucket. After dinner she went to bed. Later there was a huge crash. She fell, never to awaken again after a massive heart attack. She had laughed and giggled with the grandchildren, she had spent her last day on her beloved Nantucket, and she died believing in the Lord. Yes, we wept. She was our beloved Little Ga – Little Ga in the flowered dresses; Ga in her garden, or fixing a special treat, Ga taking us to church; Ga the light of our life. I still think of her constantly, and so many friends remind me of the special times they had with her. We remember her and we remember You, oh Lord. *"The lines are fallen unto me in pleasant places; yea, I have a goodly heritage."* Psalm 16:6

June 29 is also the feast day of St. Peter and St. Paul. Peter, the fisherman known as Simon was later named by Jesus as Cephas (Peter) or rock, the rock on which His church would be built. He denied Jesus three times, but he was also the first person to whom Jesus appeared after the resurrection. Jesus said to him, *"Feed my sheep."* May we all continue to feed our sheep. Paul's conversion along the road to Damascus promises us hope that we too can forever follow and obey our Lord.

Flounder with Vegetables

Serves 4

4 flounder filets
Juice of 1 lemon
2 tbls. olive oil
2 cups fresh corn
½ lb. baby spinach

1 pint grape tomatoes
2 green onions, chopped
¼ cup cilantro, chopped
Juice of 1 lime
Zest of 1 lime

Squeeze the lemon juice on the filets. Sprinkle with olive oil. Grill or broil flounder. Place on a platter.
In a bowl combine corn, spinach, tomatoes, green onions, cilantro, lime, and lime zest.
Serve the flounder on a bed of the corn mixture. Garnish with lime slices.

June 30

"Wherefore, sirs, be of good cheer: for I believe God, that it shall be even as it was told me. Howbeit we must be cast on a certain island.
Acts 27:25-26

"Preaching the kingdom of God, and teaching those things which concern the Lord Jesus Christ, with all confidence, no man forbidding him."
Acts 28:31

Halfway through the year, a good friend and I sit over lunch discussing our friends and how we can reach out to others. We were recently on Nantucket for the Spiritual Heritage Nantucket luncheon. Our speaker was inspirational, and that night spoke before the public with an audience mainly made up of young people. My friend mentioned that someone had asked her how the luncheon and speech had benefitted Nantucket. Nothing was mentioned about the spiritual aspect. Nantucket has gone through a number of teen suicides over the last year. By bringing in this speaker the group hoped to turn the tide, and show there is a way to look beyond the fog, and find one's way. He brought a lot to the Nantucketers and the Island, through faith and financially. We shouldn't think of the financial part, only how youngsters and people of all ages can turn to the Lord, to reach out, and know there is always a hand waiting to help. Open your eyes, feel Him, listen to Him, know Him. He does feed His sheep.

Brownies

2 sticks butter
4 oz. semi sweet chocolate
1 tbls. espresso powder
2 cups sugar
4 eggs, beaten
1 tsp. vanilla

1 cup flour
1 tsp. baking powder
1 tsp. salt
1 pkg. chocolate chips
1 cup pecans or walnuts

Preheat the oven to 350°
Butter a 9" square baking dish. Dust with flour.
In a sauce pan melt the butter and chocolate. Remove from heat.
Stir in the other ingredients.
Pour into a baking dish. Bake 25-30 minutes, or until a toothpick comes clean.

July 1

"The King of love my Shepherd is, Whose goodness faileth never, I nothing lack if I am His And He is mine forever. Where streams of living water flow My ransomed soul He leadeth, And where the verdant pastures grow, With food celestial feedeth. Perverse and foolish oft I strayed, But yet in love He sought me, And on His shoulder gently laid, And home, rejoicing, brought me. In death's dark vale I fear no ill With Thee, dear Lord, beside me; Thy rod and staff my comfort still, Thy cross before to guide me. Thou spread'st a table in my sight; Thy unction grace bestoweth; And O what transport of delight From Thy pure chalice floweth! And so through all the length of days Thy goodness faileth never; Good Shepherd, may I sing Thy praise Within Thy house forever."

This beautiful hymn is taken from the 23rd Psalm and has often been sung at funerals, including Lady Diana's on September 6, 1997. The hymn was written by Henry Williams Baker (1821-77). He also composed *O Praise Ye the Lord.* He came from a well-to-do English family, attended Cambridge and entered the ministry. Upon the death of his father he became the 3rd Baronet Baker. He was a contributor to *Hymn Ancient and Modern* published in London in 1861 to promote hymn singing in the Anglican Church.

Trifle

Serves 8

2 dozen lady fingers
1 cup Madeira
1 quart raspberries, plus 1 pint

2 cups heavy cream
1 cup toasted slivered almonds

In a large bowl arrange the ladyfingers around the side. Pour Madeira over them.
Spread 1 qt. raspberries around the bowl.
Pour custard over the berries. Refrigerate.
Whip the cream until peaks form and spread over custard. Garnish with almonds and remaining raspberries.

Custard

6 egg yolks
¼ cup sugar

3 cups heavy cream
1 tsp. vanilla

Whisk the eggs and sugar in a bowl, until thickened.
Heat the cream in the sauce pan. Pour eggs slowly into cream until thickened.
Refrigerate.

July 2

"Christ for the world we sing, The world to Christ we bring, with loving zeal, The poor and them that mourn, the faint and overborne, Sin sick and sorrow worn, whom Christ doth heal. Christ for the world we sing, The world to Christ we bring, with fervent prayer; The wayward and the lost, by restless passions tossed, Redeemed at countless cost, from dark despair. Christ for the world we sing, The world to Christ we bring, with one accord; With us the work to share, with us reproach to dare, With us the cross to bear, for Christ our Lord. Christ for the world we sing, The world to Christ we bring, with joyful song; The newborn souls, whose days, reclaimed from error's ways, Inspired with hope and praise, to Christ belong."

Samuel Wolcott (1813-86) attended Yale College and Andover Theological Seminary, and served as a missionary in Syria. He was a pastor at Plymouth Congregational Church, not far from where I lived in Cleveland. While living in Cleveland I served as President of the International Visitor Center and hosted the International Wives Group. I was fortunate enough to meet people from all over the world, some friendships still in place. One of them was a Romanian lady who defected while on a visit to the States. She worked for our embassy in Bucharest, but longed for a decent life here. Recently as we sat over lunch she told me how she and her family had kept their faith during those dark Communist days. They could not worship openly, but would as a family or secretly with friends. Now, living in Washington she attends the Romanian Orthodox Church, happy to openly display her affection for the Lord. *"Christ for the world we sing."*

Crab Quiche

1 pie crust
3 eggs
1½ cups cream
¼ tsp. nutmeg
½ lb. Swiss cheese, grated

¾ lb. crab meat
¼ lb. smoked ham, diced
1 leek, sliced
½ red pepper, chopped

Preheat the oven to 400°.
Bake the pie crust for 10 minutes. Let cool.
In a bowl beat together the cream, eggs and nutmeg.
Place the cheese, crab, ham, leek and pepper in the pie crust. Top with egg mixture.
Bake 40 minutes, or until browned and bubbling.

July 3

"O beautiful for spacious skies, For amber waves of grain, For purple mountain majesties Above the fruited plain! America! America! God shed His grace on thee, And crown thy good with brotherhood From sea to shining sea!"

Tomorrow we will celebrate the 4th of July, America's Independence Day. We are fortunate to live in a country with so much freedom. Others are not so lucky. They cannot vote, they cannot speak out on issues, they may not be able to live or work as they please, still live under a dictatorial government, or do not have the freedom to worship as they please. We must not take advantage of these freedoms. We must continue to maintain them for future generations. Remember freedom does not come free.

America the Beautiful was written as a poem by Katherine Lee Bates (1859-1929), an instructor at Wellesley College while on a trip to the top of Pike's Peak, Colorado in 1893. She also wrote a number of other poems, travel books and children's books. The poem is based on Psalm 33:12 *"Blessed is the nation whose God is the Lord."*

Lobster Salad

Serves 4

1 lb. lobster meat
¼ cup lemon juice
2 tbls. rice vinegar
2 tbls. olive oil
2 tsp. fresh snipped dill

½ lb. arugula
2 avocado, peeled, pitted and sliced
2 grapefruit, peeled and sectioned
½ cup toasted almonds

Combine the lobster, lemon juice, vinegar, olive oil and dill in a bowl.
Divide the arugula, lobster, avocado and grapefruit between 4 plates. Garnish with the almonds.
Serve with clam chowder, crusty bread and a summer dessert.

July 4

"You are a chosen people, a royal priesthood, a holy nation, a people belonging to God, that you may declare the praises of Him who called you out of the darkness into his wonderful light."
1 Peter 2:9

July 4th, our Independence Day. We spent many Fourth of Julys up on Nantucket, but more recently attend the Big Band concert at the Chesapeake Bay Maritime Museum in St. Michael's, Maryland. Everyone brings a dish. We listen to the music, dance and at dusk watch a spectacular fireworks display over the Miles River. Dear Lord, protect us this night, and protect this great country that our ancestors fought to keep free.

"My country,' tis of thee, sweet land of liberty, of thee I sing; land where my fathers died, land of the pilgrims' pride, from every mountainside let freedom ring! Our fathers' God, to thee, author of liberty, to thee we sing; long may our land be bright with freedom's holy light; protect us by thy might, great God, our King."

Samuel F. Smith (1808-95) graduated from Harvard, spent a period of time as a journalist, and after studying at Andover Theological Seminary became a Baptist minister. *He wrote My Country 'Tis of Thee* while a student at the Seminary. The hymn was first sung at Park Street Church, Boston on July 4, 1831.

Blueberry Sorbet with Limes

2 cups water
2 cups sugar
2 quarts blueberries

Juice of 1 lime
Zest of 1 lime

Bring the water and sugar to a boil in a sauce pan. Reduce heat and simmer for about 5 minutes, until sugar dissolves. Cool to room temperature.
Puree the blueberries in a food processor with ½ cup of the simple syrup. Stir in rest of simple syrup, lime juice and lime zest.
Pour the mixture into an ice cream maker. Mix until it thickens, about 20-25 minutes. Chill in freezer for at least two hours.
Serve in bowls with lime slices, or with cantaloupe.

"We believe in one God, the Father, the Almighty, maker of heaven and earth, of all that is, seen and unseen. We believe in one Lord, Jesus Christ, the only Son of God, eternally begotten of the Father, God from God, light from light, true God from true God, begotten, not made, of one Being with the Father; through him all things were made. For us and for our salvation he came down from heaven, was incarnate of the Holy Spirit and the Virgin Mary and became truly human. For our sake he was crucified under Pontius Pilate; he suffered death and was buried. On the third day he rose again in accordance with the Scriptures; he ascended into heaven and is seated at the right hand of the Father. He will come again in glory to judge the living and the dead, and his kingdom will have no end. We believe in the Holy Spirit, the Lord, the giver of life, who proceeds from the Father and the Son, who with the Father and the Son is worshiped and glorified, who has spoken through the prophets. We believe in one holy catholic and apostolic Church. We acknowledge one baptism for the forgiveness of sins. We look for the resurrection of the dead, and the life of the world to come. Amen."
The Nicene Creed

During the summer of 325 the Council of Nicea met to unify the Church and its teachings. Under the leadership of Emperor Constantine, disagreement about Jesus' relationship with his Father was debated and then put into writing. At the same time the Council agreed to celebrate the Resurrection on the first Sunday after the first full moon following the vernal equinox. In 381 the Creed was modified to the words we repeat today. As you say them, remember the Church is still divided on numerous topics, but by expressing our faith through the Creed we acknowledge the Holy Trinity and that there is only one God who rules the world.

Cucumber Dip

2 cups sour cream or yogurt	2 tbs. olive oil
1 medium cucumber, cut in small cubes	2 cloves garlic, minced
	½ tsp. salt
2 tbls. white vinegar	Parsley or mint

Combine all the ingredients, except the parsley in a food processor until just blended.
Serve as a side dish garnished with parsley or mint.
Can also be served with crackers.

July 6

"Stand up, stand up for Jesus, ye soldiers of the cross; lift high his royal banner, it must not suffer loss. From victory unto victory his army shall he lead, till every foe is vanquished, and Christ is Lord indeed. Stand up, stand up for Jesus, the strife will not be long; this day the noise of battle, the next the victor's song. To those who vanquish evil a crown of life shall be; they with the King of Glory shall reign eternally."

As I listen to the words of this hymn and *Onward Christian Soldiers* I realize that we are peaceful soldiers, rallying around us friends of like ilk, but also out there to bring victory for Jesus, King of Kings. We don't do this through battles, except with the devil. We do this through our prayers, our ability to convey to others that Christ is the risen Lord. He is our leader, our hope, our all. We must carry the cross.

The writer George Duffield (1818-1888) followed in his father's footsteps by becoming a Presbyterian minister. He graduated from Yale and Union Theological Seminary. His son Samuel Augustus Willoughby Duffield wrote several books including *English Hymns: Their Authors and History* (New York and London: Funk & Wagnalls, 1888) and *Latin Hymn-Writers and Their Hymns* (edited posthumously by Dr. R. E. Thompson), 1889.

Summer Shrimp

Serves 4

2 tbls. olive oil	1½ lbs. shrimp, cooked, peeled, and
1 leek, sliced	deveined
2 cloves garlic, minced	½ cup white wine
2 tomatoes chopped	¼ cup cilantro or basil, chopped
1 red pepper, sliced	¼ lb. feta, crumbled

Heat the olive oil in a skillet. Stir in leek, garlic, tomatoes and pepper. Cook until just tender.
Stir in shrimp and white wine.
Serve shrimp over rice, couscous or pasta. Garnish with cilantro and feta.

July 7

"Jesus said unto him, If thou canst believe, all things are possible to him that believeth. And straightway the father of the child cried out, and said with tears, Lord, I believe; help thou mine unbelief."
Mark 9:23-24

I sit today among my fellow sisters, hearing the word of the Lord and singing praises to His name. Each week on Nantucket a group gathers, prays and does a Bible lesson. For 8 weeks the group is focusing on idols and why we are attracted to them. We all laugh when the leader holds up a heart with "Elvis and me", her heartthrob from an early age. This demonstrates how easily we can be turned to idols, and not focused on our belief in God. Please Lord let us stay the course, not be swayed by material things and objects and idols. Let us know you are the path, the only path, and that all things are possible through You.

"Little children, keep yourselves from idols. Amen"
1 John 5:21

Potato Salad

Serves 12

12 red bliss potatoes, cubed	1 cup pitted Kalamata olives
2 large leeks, sliced	1 tsp. pepper
12 slices bacon, cooked and crumbled	1 tbls. sea salt
	½ cup sour cream
¼ lb. blue cheese, crumbled	½ cup mayonnaise
1 cup sliced roasted peppers	¼ cup dill
2 stalks celery, chopped	1 tbls. tarragon

Cook the potatoes until tender. Drain.
Combine all the ingredients in a salad bowl.
Garnish with dill and paprika.
Sliced red peppers can be substituted for the roasted peppers.

"Above all, maintain constant love for one another, for love covers a multitude of sins. Be hospitable to one another without complaining. Like good stewards of the manifold grace of God, serve one another with whatever gift each of you has received. Whoever speaks must do so as one speaking the very words of God; whoever serves must do so with the strength that God supplies, so that God may be glorified in all things through Jesus Christ. To him belong the glory and the power forever and ever. Amen."
1 Peter 4.8-11

Dad's birthday. Oh, what do we get him this year? He doesn't wear socks anymore, and ties only on special occasions. He's given up fishing, but will sail whenever possible. His hearty New England blood keeps him warm in the winter, even on the coolest days, though he does wear a jacket more often now. Get him on a plane to Europe, and you'll find him walking the moors of Scotland or Ireland, perhaps looking for an ancient ancestor.

Father's are special people. They leave a profound effect on you when growing up, especially little girls or teenagers. They can also be your bane when they tell you what time to be home, who can use the car, and very honest when it comes time to start dating. Make sure you try to find someone who is good looking, drives a neat car, and will pay for your dinner. Love your father, and mother. Thank you God for giving us such special people in our lives.

Grilled Scallops

Serves 4

1½ lbs. bay scallops
Olive oil
Lime juice
2 cloves garlic, crushed
¼ cup mint, chopped
½ lb. baby spinach

2 tomatoes, cut in wedges
4 new potatoes, cooked and diced
1 lb. thin asparagus, trimmed
2 avocado, peeled, pitted and sliced
Lime wedges

In a bowl combine the scallops, olive oil, lime juice, garlic and mint. Refrigerate for at least one hour.
Grill scallops on a BBQ. Reserve marinade.
Place the spinach on four plates. Divide up the scallops between the plates.
Serve with tomatoes, potatoes, asparagus, and avocado slices. Pour rest of marinade over salad. Garnish with lime wedges.

"And, behold a woman, which was diseased with an issue of blood twelve years, came behind him, and touched the hem of his garment: For she had said within herself, If I may but touch his garment, I shall be whole. But Jesus turned him about, and when he saw her, he said, Daughter, be of good comfort; "thy faith hath made thee whole." And the woman was made whole from that hour."
Matthew 9:20

Breast cancer can hit at any time, any age, and to any person. As the world gets more polluted certain places are more likely to have cancer in the air. Unfortunately I have lived in some of them – New York, Rhode Island, and Maryland. All three states have very high rates of breast cancer. I have lost several dear friends and others are now fighting courageous battles, two, more than once. One of my oldest Long Island friends kept us posted through email and pictures what she had to endure – losing her hair, eyebrows, and fingernails. When I went to visit her she had found a wig that almost exactly matched her long, curly hair. If she hadn't told me it was a wig I would never have guessed. Her hair, eyebrows and fingernails have grown back A grandson is on the way. She told me how much our prayers meant. I still include her every day.

Pray that we can find cures, and participate in the Susan K. Komen races, and other fundraising events. And please get yourself checked. One friend went in to have a knee operation. During the preliminary tests they found she had leukemia. She is in remission, but what a wakeup call!

Chicken Fried Rice

Serves 6

4 tbls. olive oil	1 pint mushrooms, sliced
2 eggs, beaten	3 cups cooked rice
1 small leek, finely chopped	1 cup chicken, cooked and diced
1 can sliced water chestnuts, drained	1 tbls. soy sauce

Heat 2 tbls. oil in a wok. Stir in eggs. Just slightly cook. Remove from wok.
Add remaining oil. Stir in vegetables. Add chicken and soy sauce. Fold in eggs.
Serve warm immediately.
Pork can be substituted for the chicken

July 10

"For the earth bringeth forth fruit of herself; first the blade, then the ear, after that the full corn in the ear."
Mark 4:28

During the summer the days are longer. If it's not unbearable you can sit outside for meals, or take a picnic somewhere fun. Beach picnics were always part of our time spent on Nantucket. Growing up my grandparents would pack us all up and take us to Miacomet. Then the beach got a reputation for being a nudist beach, so no more trips out there! After my divorce I met a lovely group of ladies, all married and all with children slightly younger than my daughter. I cannot even begin to count the beach picnics we planned. Luckily they are memorialized in photos and a cookbook. Now our picnics are rarer. The children are grown. They too are marrying, and having children. I look forward to planning picnics in the sunset once again. As the earth bringeth forth fruit, so too do we with binding friendships.

Cornbread

1 cup cornmeal
1 cup flour
1 tsp. baking powder
½ tsp. sea salt
1 cup Monterrey Jack cheese, grated
4 green onions, grated

3 jalapeno, seeded and chopped
3 eggs
1 cup sour cream
1 cup corn
½ stick butter

Preheat oven to 400°
In a medium size wrought iron skillet, melt the butter in the oven.
In a bowl combine the cornmeal, flour, baking powder, salt, cheese, onion, jalapeno, eggs, sour cream and corn.
Pour the cornmeal mixture into the skillet.
Bake for 25 minutes or until a toothpick comes clean.

July 11

"Let the peace of God rule in your hearts to the which also ye are called in one body; and be ye thankful. Let the word of Christ dwell in you richly in all wisdom; teaching and admonishing one another in psalms and hymns and spiritual songs, singing with grace in your hearts to the Lord. And whatsoever ye do in word or deed, do all in the name of the Lord Jesus, giving thanks to God and the Father by him."
Colossians 3:15-17

We have so much to be thankful for, yet there are days no prayers are said to thank the Lord for our abundance. No matter where you are, take a moment to give thanks for rest, for love, for hope, for a sick person, for a beautiful day, for children and grandparents, or for those in need. Thank God for all the blessings in this life. Find peace with yourself and with God.

I spent some time in the hospital due to a very stressful work situation. While there a man who leads a prayer group brought me *The Practice of the Presence of God* by Brother Lawrence. As I read this book I am astonished at the wisdom of this 17th century monk, who could pray in the kitchen or in a cathedral. *"The time of business does not with me differ from the time of prayer, and in the noise and clatter of my kitchen, while several persons are at the same time calling for different things, I possess God in as great tranquility as if I were upon my knees at the blessed sacrament."* May we all learn to pray and be thankful.

Cucumber Salad

Serves 6

2 medium cucumbers, sliced
4 green onions, chopped
1 tsp. salt
¼ cup cider vinegar

1 tbls. sugar
1 tsp. medium paprika
1 tsp. fresh ground pepper

Combine all ingredients in a bowl.
Serve chilled.

"All thy garments smell of myrrh, and aloes, and cassia."
Psalm 45:8

My daughter just called to say her husband had terrible sun poisoning on his legs after our recent trip to Nantucket. My first reaction was to suggest aloe. Not having any, she had to purchase it for him. Aloe is a type of fragrant East Indian tree. Aloe vera is also a member of the lily family. Aloe vera as a gel soothes and heals burns. The ozone layer is quickly thinning and the less time you spend in the sun, the better off your skin will be. Putting on suntan lotion does not keep rays from harming you.

Crab Cakes over Corn Salsa

Serves 4

Crab Cakes

1 pound jumbo lump crab meat	1 teaspoon mustard
2 tbls. bread crumbs	2 tbls. mayonnaise
1 egg	Dash of Old Bay
1 tsp. Worcestershire sauce	Butter

With a fork combine all the ingredients, except butter.
Melt the butter in a skillet.
Saute the crab cakes on each side until browned
Mound salsa on four plates. Top with crab cake.
Serve with crusty bread and a crisp white wine.

Corn Salsa

2 cups fresh corn	2 cloves garlic, crushed
½ cup cilantro, chopped	½ red pepper, diced
¼ cup olive oil	2 green onions, chopped
2 jalapeno, seeded and diced	2 tbls. vinegar
Juice of ½ lime or lemon	Salt and pepper to taste

Combine all ingredients in a bowl.

"My God will fully satisfy every need of yours according to his riches in glory in Christ Jesus."
Philippians 4:19

Every where we look there is an abundance of wealth in this country. But underlying it all there are those who suffer from deprivation. Even in the small town I live, there are people wandering the streets, bearing all they own with them. I spoke to our minister about a shelter. He said they have tried, but either a place could not be found, or there was no funding. The churches used to take them in, but with vandalism and drugs, they could no longer keep their doors open. However, that is about to change, and a new home will be open shortly. I am thankful to the Lord that we have been provided a roof over our heads, food on the table, good health, a large close family, and you dear Lord. Thank you for all you have blessed us with. I do not need more, just love and hope for the future.

Chicken over Fettuccine

Serves 4

4 boneless chicken breasts, cooked and cubed
2 tbls. olive oil
2 tbls. butter
4 green onions, chopped
2 medium tomatoes, chopped
4 cloves garlic, minced

¼ cup fresh basil, chopped
½ cup pitted Kalamata olives
½ tsp. salt
1 tbls. fresh ground pepper
1 cup cream
1 pound fettuccine
Fresh grated parmesan cheese

In a sauce pan heat the butter and olive oil. Stir in green onions and tomatoes.
Add garlic, basil, olives, salt, pepper, and cream. Stir in chicken.
Cook fettuccine according to directions. Drain.
Serve fettuccine on 4 separate plates. Place chicken mixture on top. Sprinkle with parmesan cheese.
The chicken breasts can also be served whole. Place on fettuccine, drizzle sauce over them, and top with parmesan cheese.
Sundried tomatoes can be substituted for tomatoes.

"Crown Him with many crowns, the Lamb upon His throne.
Hark! How the heavenly anthem drowns all music but its own.
Awake, my soul, and sing of Him who died for thee,
And hail Him as thy matchless King through all eternity.

Crown Him the Lord of Heaven, enthroned in worlds above,
Crown Him the King to Whom is given the wondrous name of Love.
Crown Him with many crowns, as thrones before Him fall;
Crown Him, ye kings, with many crowns, for He is King of all."

The words to this hymn were inspired by Revelation 19:12 *"His eyes were as a flame of fire; and on his head were many crowns; and he had a name written, that no man knew, but he himself."* When you sing this hymn you think of Jesus dying for us on the cross with his crown of thorns. The picture is so vivid, though it might only have been the Jesus we last saw in a picture in this position. We want to cry out for him, we want him off the cross with us. He died for us, us sinners, us humans whom God created, but always failing. We are not failures we only have to live more like Christ.

Matthew Bridges (1800-94) was raised as an Anglican, but converted to Roman Catholicism in 1848. He lived in Quebec, Canada, for some years, and then returned to England. He wrote the first six stanzas to this hymn. Godfrey Thring (1823-1903) completed the other verses.

Orzo Salad

Serves 6

¼ cup lemon juice
¼ cup olive oil
2 cups cooked orzo
1 cup fresh peas
1 pint cherry tomatoes

½ red pepper, sliced
½ yellow pepper, sliced
4 green onions, chopped
¼ cup fresh parsley
¼ cup fresh mint

Whisk together the lemon juice and olive oil in a salad bowl.
Toss in the other ingredients.

July 15

Great causes can sometimes end up with terrible consequences. Originally the Crusades were planned as military maneuvers by European Christians to recapture Jerusalem and the Holy Land from the Muslims. However other groups were soon targeted including pagan Slavs, Jews, Russian and Greek Orthodox Christians, Mongols, Cathars, Hussites, Waldensians, Old Prussians and anyone thought to be an enemy of the pope. On this date in 1099 Christian soldiers on the First Crusade captured Jerusalem after a month of battles and seized the Church of the Holy Sepulchre. They killed over 40,000 people and burned mosques and synagogues! Eight more Crusades followed. Those that agreed to serve on these Crusades took vows and were granted an indulgence for their past sins. Sadly as we look back on the Crusades not much seems to have changed in the Middle East. Christians still invade these countries. Muslims, Jews and Christians must learn to get along. Remember we are all descended from Abraham.

Orange Beets

Serves 4

4 medium beets	Zest of 1 orange
½ cup sugar	Juice of ½ lemon
¼ cup honey	¼ cup orange juice
2 tsp. cornstarch	2 tbls. butter
½ cup boiling water	

Cook the beets in boiling water until tender. Peel and slice the beets.
In a sauce pan combine the sugar, honey, cornstarch and boiling water. Stir until slightly thickened. Add the other ingredients.
Pour over the beets.
Serve warm.

July 16

"Now you have observed my teaching, my conduct, my aim in life, my faith, my patience, my love, my steadfastness..."
2 Timothy 3:10

Have there been people in your life that have inspired you? Have they inspired you to go into a profession you might not otherwise have chosen? Have they inspired you to believe in the Lord? Or have you done something you might not otherwise undertaken. Sometimes there is a fork in the road, and we do not know which one to take. But if there is a person who can lead you in the right direction take it.

Katharine Kennedy Brown was one of those people. She grew up in Dayton, Ohio in a well-to-do family. She attended boarding school in the East and later married. However her husband died only a year later. Instead of despairing she took it upon herself to give. She founded the Junior League of Dayton and the Colonial Dames chapter. She became involved in politics and for thirty-six years was head of the Republican Party in Ohio. She inspired others to go on and dream, but also to fulfill those dreams. Her name is still remembered by several generations.

The family house she lived in, Duncarrick, has been sold to the Salvation Army. After extensive renovation the organization hopes to turn it into a community center. The Salvation Army is dedicated to Christian principles, helping those in need and doing good in this world. May we all follow in the paths of Mrs. Brown and support the work of the Salvation Army. Mrs. Brown was my great aunt. Meringues were one of her favorite desserts.

Meringues

1 tbls. cornstarch
2 tbls. cold water
½ cup boiling water
1 tsp. vanilla extract

3 egg whites, at room temperature
¾ cup white sugar
Pinch of salt

Preheat oven to 350°
Combine the cornstarch and cold water in a saucepan. Add boiling water, and cook until thickened. Cool.
Beat the egg whites until stiff. Add the sugar.
Add salt and vanilla, and slowly stir in cornstarch mixture.
Drop by large spoonful onto baking sheet.
Bake for 10 minutes.

"O God, our help in ages past, Our hope for years to come, Our shelter from the stormy blast, And our eternal home. Under the shadow of Thy throne Thy saints have dwelt secure; Sufficient is Thine arm alone, And our defense is sure. Before the hills in order stood, Or earth received her frame, From everlasting Thou art God, To endless years the same. Thy Word commands our flesh to dust, "Return, ye sons of men:" All nations rose from earth at first, And turn to earth again. A thousand ages in Thy sight Are like an evening gone; Short as the watch that ends the night Before the rising sun. The busy tribes of flesh and blood, With all their lives and cares, Are carried downwards by the flood, And lost in following years. Time, like an ever rolling stream, Bears all its sons away; They fly, forgotten, as a dream Dies at the opening day. Like flowery fields the nations stand Pleased with the morning light; The flowers beneath the mower's hand Lie withering ere 'tis night. Our God, our help in ages past, Our hope for years to come, Be Thou our guard while troubles last, And our eternal home."

Isaac Watts (1674-1748), is considered the father of English hymns and wrote over 750 of them. During his time at King Edward VI School he learned Latin, Greek and Hebrew. He was brought up as a Nonconformist, meaning he did not adhere to the rules of the Church of England. Most of the hymns up until this time had come from the Psalms. Examples of the words can be seen in *Joy to the World* and From *All that Dwell Below the Skies. When I Survey the Wondrous Cross* and *Jesus Shall Reign Where'er the Sun* are other favorites. *Our God, Our Help in Ages Past* is paraphrased from Psalm 90.

Orange Salad

Serves 4

¼ cup honey
Juice of 1 lemon
½ tsp. cinnamon
½ lb. spring greens

4 oranges, peeled, seeded and sectioned
½ cup almonds
½ cup pitted dates, sliced
¼ cup coconut

In a salad bowl combine the honey, lemon juice and cinnamon.
Add the other ingredients and toss.

"When evening came, his disciples went down to the sea, got into a boat, and started across the sea to Capernaum. It was now dark, and Jesus had not yet come to them. The sea became rough because a strong wind was blowing. When they had rowed about three or four miles, they saw Jesus walking on the sea and coming near the boat, and they were terrified. But he said to them, "It is I; do not be afraid." Then they wanted to take him into the boat, and immediately the boat reached the land toward which they were going."
John 6:16-21

"You have changed my sadness into a joyful dance, You have taken away my sorrow And surrounded me with joy."
Psalm 30:11

Have you ever been to Cuttyhunk Island? This small island off Massachusetts is home to only a few year round residents. During the summer boaters come for a day or several nights. There's not much to do on the island – a couple of places to stay and eat, but good sailing, swimming, fishing and socializing. In the evenings a boat comes around selling seafood. Oh, those clams, mussels and lobsters! So fresh, so good! I loved to sail over to the island, but also you can take a small ferry. Arriving, take a walk around the island and see what's there. I'll never forget walking by a couple of people, who looked at us and burst out laughing. "No dancing in the aisles." That was the first time I had heard that expression. On another trip we were about to leave the harbor, but glancing to the East, saw a massive cloud bank. Scurrying back into the harbor we survived a major squall. Thank goodness we turned back, even if it meant spending the night without extra clothes and a toothbrush. Anyway, we were sailors!

Mussel Soup II

Serves 4

24 mussels, cleaned
2 tbls. butter
4 green onions, chopped
½ red pepper, chopped
½ yellow pepper, chopped

1 tbls. fresh grated ginger
1 tbls. curry powder
2 cups coconut milk
Garnish with mint or cilantro leaves

Melt the butter in a large sauce pan. Stir in green onions and peppers until just tender. Add ginger and curry. Stir in coconut milk. Add mussels and cook until open they open.
Ladle into bowls and garnish with mint or cilantro.

July 19

"May there always be work for your hands to do, May your purse always hold a coin or two. May the sun always shine warm on your windowpane, May a rainbow be certain to follow each rain. May the hand of a friend always be near you, And may God fill your heart with gladness to cheer you."
Old Irish Blessing

A surprise 85th birthday was held for one of my father's old Navy buddies. This gentleman has known me since I was born. I have always affectionately called him "Uncle", as I did many of my parent' friends - uncle or aunt, rather than Mr. and Mrs. I still like this formality, rather than everyone being called by their first name. We were asked not to bring presents to the party, but ourselves, an old picture, or a momento. I chose to read the Irish blessing, of which I had made a copy for dad's friend. He was very touched by this. I have always loved it – work for us to do, sunshine and may the hand of a friend always be near you. He has been Dad's friend for over 60 years!

Seafood with Newburg Sauce

Serves 4

1 pound bay scallops
2 pounds codfish
½ pound sliced mushrooms

1 red pepper, diced
2 green onions, chopped

Preheat oven to 350°
Place all ingredients in a nice baking dish that can be served at the table. Pour the Newburg sauce over the fish. Top with Parmesan cheese.
Bake 20 minutes or until bubbling and just browned.
Serve with rice.

Sauce

½ stick butter
¼ cup flour
1 cup heavy cream

¼ cup dry sherry
1 tsp. sweet paprika
½ cup grated parmesan cheese

Melt the butter in a saucepan. Stir in flour until smooth. Stir in cream until slightly thickened. Add sherry and paprika.

July 20

"Lord of all hopefulness, Lord of all joy, Whose trust, ever child-like, no cares could destroy, Be there at our waking, and give us, we pray, Your bliss in our hearts, Lord, at the break of the day. Lord of all eagerness, Lord of all faith, Whose strong hands were skilled at the plane and the lathe, Be there at our labours, and give us, we pray, Your strength in our hearts, Lord, at the noon of the day. Lord of all kindliness, Lord of all grace, Your hands swift to welcome, your arms to embrace, Be there at our homing, and give us, we pray, Your love in our hearts, Lord, at the eve of the day. Lord of all gentleness, Lord of all calm, Whose voice is contentment, whose presence is balm, Be there at our sleeping, and give us, we pray, Your peace in our hearts, Lord, at the end of the day."

This hymn has always spoken to my heart. The words are warm and huggy, they linger all day, and they do bring hope. Children trust, and we must be like them in our faith. Always trust in the Lord. He is always with us too! Lord, give us peace in our hearts always.

Jan Struther (1901-53) was the pen name of Joyce Anstruther, later Joyce Maxtone Graham, then Joyce Placzek. She is remembered for her character Mrs. Miniver and a number of hymns, including *"Lord of All Hopefulness"* and *"When a Knight Won His Spurs"*. In the 1940s Ms. Struther was a frequent guest panelist and one of the few women on the American radio quiz show *Information Please*.

Crab Souffle

Serves 4

½ stick butter	1 lb. fresh crab meat
¼ cup flour	2 green onions, chopped
1 cup half and half	½ green pepper, chopped
1 cup Gruyere or Swiss cheese	2 tbls. pimento, or chopped red
4 eggs, separated	pepper

Preheat oven to 350°

Melt the butter in a sauce pan. Stir in the flour and then half and half. Add cheese until melted. Turn off heat. Stir in egg yolks. Add crab meat, onions and peppers. Beat egg whites until fluffy. Grease a soufflé dish. Gently fold the crab mixture and egg whites into the dish. Bake for 45 minutes.

July 21

"The righteous are like trees planted by streams of water, which yield their fruit in its season, and their leaves do not wither."
Psalm 1:3

As I look out my office window the crepe myrtle are in full bloom. Pink, purple, white, so many colors of the rainbow. The petals fall to the ground covering it with a carpet of velvet. All along the Eastern Shore this year they seem to be more brilliant than ever. Have I not noticed them before? Is it the rain which fell so abundantly in the spring? Or is it because my eyes open even wider now to enjoy the beauty that God surrounds us? The days are hot and humid. We need rain. The trees remind us that they need water too. Let us feed them as God feeds us.

BBQ Pork Chops

Serves 6

1 small onion, chopped	1 tsp. celery seed
1 can tomato sauce	1 tsp. pepper
½ cup water	½ tsp. cayenne
¼ cup vinegar	1 tbls. paprika
2 tbls. Worcestershire sauce	½ tsp. cinnamon
1 tbls. chili powder	¼ tsp. cloves
1 tsp. salt	6 pork chops

Combine onion, tomato sauce, water, vinegar, Worcestershire sauce, chili, salt, pepper, celery seed, cayenne, paprika, cinnamon and cloves in a saucepan.
Bring to a boil. Simmer until thickened.
Pour ½ sauce over pork chops.
Grill pork chops until desired pinkness. Remove from grill.
Serve on a platter with the rest of the BBQ sauce.
Ribs can be substituted for the pork chops.

July 22

"And certain women, which had been healed of evil spirits and infirmities, Mary called Magdalene, out of whom went seven devils."
Luke 8:2

"Now there stood by the cross of Jesus his mother, and his mother's sister, Mary the wife of Cleophas, and Mary Magdalene."
John 19:20

"And when the Sabbath was past, Mary Magdalene, and Mary the mother of James, and Salome had brought sweet spices, that they might come and anoint him. And very early in the morning the first day of the week, they came into the sepulcher at the rising of the sun. And they said among themselves, who shall roll us away the stone from the door of the sepulcher? And when they looked they saw that the stone was rolled away: for it was very great. And entered into the sepulcher, they saw a young man sitting on the right side, clothed in a long white garment, and they were affrighted. And he saith unto them, Be not affrighted: Ye seek Jesus of Nazareth, which was crucified: He is risen; He is not here; behold the place they laid him."
Mark 16:1-6

The woman most devoted to Jesus was Mary Magdalene. She watched him on the cross, his burial, and later found his tomb empty. It was Mary who also anointed Jesus' feet with oil, and who sat at his feet while her sister served. Mary Magdalene is an example for all women. She loved and worshipped her Lord. She gave of herself freely and was a witness to His life and resurrection.

Tarragon Green Beans

Serves 6

2 lbs. fresh green beans, trimmed
¼ cup tarragon vinegar
¼ cup olive oil

4 green onions, chopped
2 cloves garlic, minced
2 tbls. fresh tarragon, chopped

In a skillet boil 2 cups of water. Add green beans and blanche 3 minutes. Drain.
In a salad or vegetable bowl combine all the ingredients.
Can be served warm or chilled.
If served chill add a dollop of sour cream.

July 23

"And Jesus said unto them, I am the bread of life: he that cometh to me shall never hunger; and he that believeth on me shall never thirst."
John 6:35

"I am the Bread of life;"
Suzanne Toolan

Bread has always been the staff of life. If there has been nothing else to eat there has been bread. But Jesus considered the bread His body. When one takes Communion, one is eating in remembrance of Him and with Him. We do this with respect and love, knowing that He is always there for us. He forgives our sins, finds our paths, and brings us together in fellowship. Never hunger, lift yourself up to the Lord; let Him feed you.

Mercy Sister Toolan (1927-) composed the hymn which has been translated into over 20 languages. She is very involved with the Taize ecumenical community.

Raisin Bread

1 packet yeast	Zest of 1 orange
1¼ cups warm milk	1 cup sugar
½ cup raisins	½ tsp. salt
½ cup currants	1 stick butter
½ tsp. nutmeg	3 cups flour
½ tsp. cinnamon	1 egg, beaten
1 tbls. brandy	

Combine the yeast and ½ cup milk in a bowl. Let stand 15 minutes.
In a bowl combine the raisins, currants, nutmeg, cinnamon, brandy and zest.
In another bowl beat together the remaining milk, sugar, salt and ½ stick butter.
Add the yeast mixture. Gradually stir in the flour.
Knead the bread on a floured board. Place in a greased bowl and let rise for 2½ hours in a warm spot. Punch down the dough and let rise another 20 minutes.
Grease 2 bread pans.
Preheat oven to 400°
On a floured board divide the dough in 2. Roll out into 2 large triangles. Melt the rest of the butter and brush the dough. Sprinkle the nut mixture on top. Roll tightly and place in bread pans.
Brush the bread with the egg.
Bake 20 minutes. Lower temperature to 350°. Bake 25 minutes more.

July 24

"For we brought nothing into this world, and it is certain we can carry nothing out...For the love of money is the root of all evil, which while some coveted after, they have erred from the faith, and pierced themselves through with many sorrows."
1 Timothy 6:7, 10

Each time I arrive in Nantucket I am deeply saddened to see the changes taking place on my beloved Island. Everywhere there are new houses, each bigger than their neighbors. There are too many cars, too much excess, little thought to preserving the Island. Just more and more! Growing up there everyone lived in cottages, not large ones, some very small. You did not talk about money, and you did not know a person's wealth. I wish these were simpler times like my youth. Everything is too fast, too big and too expensive. Think about what St. Paul said, *we bring nothing into this world and we take nothing out.* Live a gentle, simple life. There is nothing wrong with that. It will bring much more happiness.

Crab and Lobster Cakes

Serves 4

4 slices cooked and crumbled bacon	1 tbls. fresh dill, snipped
1 leek, sliced thinly	3 tbls. butter
2 cups mashed potatoes	Tomato slices
½ lb. crab meat	Avocado slices
½ lb. lobster meat	Parsley

In a bowl combine the bacon, leek, and potatoes.
Fold in the crab, lobster and dill.
Melt the butter in a skillet.
Make the crab and lobster into 4 patties. Saute on both sides until golden brown.
Serve with tomato and avocado slices and garnish with parsley.

"For the kingdom of heaven is as a man traveling into a far country, who called his own servants, and delivered unto them his goods."
Matthew 25:14

Today we celebrate the feast day of St. Christopher Offero, who was tempted by the devil, but decided to seek the Lord. He was asked by a hermit to carry a small child across a river. As he did so his burden increased until he almost could not lift the weight. On reaching the other side the child revealed that he was Jesus Christ. He was told his name would now be Christopher (Christ bearer). St. Christopher is the patron saint of travelers, and at this time of year when so many vacation, they should be reminded of the person he carried. Let all of us travel safely knowing that our Lord is always with us.

"They that wait upon the Lord shall renew their strength."
Isaiah 40:31

Shrimp Casserole

Serves 4

1½ lb. shrimp, cooked and deveined
½ stick butter
¼ cup flour
1½ cups heavy cream
¼ cup white wine
2 cloves garlic, crushed

2 shallots, finely chopped
1 leek, sliced
1 tsp. tarragon
1 lb. asparagus, trimmed
Seasoned bread crumbs

Preheat oven to 350°
Melt the butter in a pan. Stir in the flour and then cream, until thickened. Add the wine.
Stir in garlic, shallots, leeks, and tarragon.
Place the asparagus in a buttered baking dish. Top with shrimp. Pour the sauce over the shrimp. Sprinkle with bread crumbs
Bake 20 minutes, or until bubbling and golden.
Serve with rice.

July 26

"And he lifted up his eyes, and saw the women and the children; and said, who are those with thee? And he said, The children which God hath graciously given thy servant."
Genesis 33:5

Dear friends called to say they were nearby and wanted to stop in to see us. We were just about to sit down for dinner after a long day at the log canoe races. I could not turn them down, particularly when I heard they had just put their seventeen year old dog to sleep. As tired as we were I ran out to get more steaks. Luckily they were drained too, and after a lovely dinner we all collapsed. However it was just not the same without the little dog. Their other dog knew it and so did we. Pets are part of the family and must be treated so. Some people have pets and not children, others the other way around. We are all God's children.

Chicken in Tomato Sauce

Serves 6

6 boneless chicken breasts
Salt and pepper
½ stick butter
¼ cup olive oil
1 large onion, chopped

3 cloves garlic, minced
6 medium tomatoes, finely chopped
1 cup chicken stock
1 tbls. ground cinnamon

Sprinkle the salt and pepper on the chicken breasts.
Heat the butter and oil in a large skillet. Add the breasts and cook on each side until just browned. Remove from skillet and set aside.
Add the onions and garlic to the skillet and stir until transparent.
Stir in the tomatoes, chicken stock and cinnamon. Bring to a boil.
Add the chicken and cook for 30 minutes.
Serve over pasta or rice.

"And six years thou shalt sow thy land, and shall gather in the fruits thereof; But the seventh year thou shalt let it rest and lie still; that the poor of thy people may eat: and what they leave the beasts of the field shall eat. In like manner thou shalt deal with thy vineyard, and with thy olive yard."
Exodus 23:10-11

I will never forget visiting Italy, Greece and Turkey for the first time and seeing hillsides dotted everywhere with olive trees. I didn't realize until then how many different types of olive abound. In the wind the olive leaves look silvery. The trees are gnarled and have unusual shapes. The olive fruit is harvested when green or allowed to darken for black olives.

Olives are a staple in Middle Eastern life. They have been raised for thousands of years, probably beginning in the 4th millennium BC. When harvested, olives can be used for different types of olives and olive oil.

Olive oil does not contain saturated fats and can be substituted for butter in numerous dishes. Adding herbs to the oil can give it unique flavors. Your diet will be healthier, and may add a few years to your life.

Hummus is a Middle Eastern favorite. Serve with pita bread or pita chips. Instead of ketchup or mustard serve a lamb or beef burger with hummus.

Hummus

1 can chickpeas, drained
2 tbls. sesame seeds
2 tbls. olive oil
3 green onions, chopped
½ cup fresh parsley

3 cloves garlic, minced
2 tbls. lemon juice
½ tsp. salt
4 slices roasted red pepper

Combine the ingredients in a food processor. Serve with pita bread.

July 28

"Jesu, joy of man's desiring, Holy wisdom, love most bright; Drawn by Thee, our souls aspiring Soar to uncreated light. Word of God, our flesh that fashioned, With the fire of life impassioned, Striving still to truth unknown, Soaring, dying round Thy throne. Through the way where hope is guiding, Hark, what peaceful music rings; Where the flock, in Thee confiding, Drink of joy from deathless springs. Theirs is beauty's fairest pleasure; Theirs is wisdom's holiest treasure. Thou dost ever lead Thine own In the love of joys unknown."

Johannes Bach (1685-1750), the German composer and organist, was educated at St. Michael's School in Luneburg. After graduation he became a court musician in a chapel in Weimar and then St. Boniface's in Arnstadt where he began writing organ music. In 1708 he became the concert master and court organist at the ducal court in Weimar. He was a devout Lutheran and used the Word in his compositions. The *St. Matthew Passion* and *St. John Passion* tell the Easter story. He also composed fugues, oratorios, cantatas, chamber music, choral works, and lute music. One of his grandest undertakings was the *Mass in B Minor*. My favorite is *Jesu, Joy of Man's Desiring*. Every time I hear it I get goose bumps. It is so moving and beautiful.

Apple Fritters

2 cups flour
2 cups beer
5 apples
1 cup sugar

1 tbls. cinnamon
Vegetable oil
Confectioners' sugar

In a bowl make a well in the flour. Slowly stir in the beer. Let rest 3 hours
Combine the sugar and cinnamon in a shallow bowl.
Peel and core the apples. Slice thinly.
Dip the apple slices in the cinnamon and sugar, then the batter.
Heat the oil in a skillet. Fry the apples until just browned on both sides.
Place on a platter and sprinkle with confectioners' sugar.

"Now it came to pass as they went, that he entered into a certain village, and a certain woman named Martha received him into her house. And she had a sister called Mary, which also sat at Jesus' feet, and heard his word. But Martha was cumbered about much serving, and came to him and said, Lord dost thou not care that my sister hath left me to serve alone? Bid her therefore that she help me. And Jesus answered and said unto her, Martha, Martha, thou art careful and troubled about many things. But one thing is needful: and Mary hath chosen that good part, which shall not be taken away from her."
Luke 10:38-42

I have always been a lot like Martha, the one who always seems to be serving, wishing I could be sitting at Jesus' feet. However we all have roles, we must look beyond the hurts, the putdowns to what really matters, and that is, we all serve our Lord. We must keep our households running, our children off to school, and our husbands happy. Martha was jealous, but she is also so faithful to our Lord, that we must be reminded she is truly a saint, and the patron saint of housewives. May we be so faithful too.

Leek Tart

Pastry

1¼ cups flour   ½ tsp. salt
1 stick butter   1 tbls. snipped fresh dill
¼ cup cold water

Preheat oven to 400°
Combine all the ingredients in food processor until a ball is formed.
Roll out on floured board into pie shape. Place in pie dish. Bake 10 minutes.

Filling

6 slices bacon   ¼ tsp. cayenne
1 large leek, including green part,   4 eggs
sliced   1 8 oz. package cream cheese
1 tbls. Dijon mustard

Cook the bacon in a skillet until crisp. Remove from pan. Stir leeks into bacon fat until just tender. In a bowl combine the mustard, cayenne, eggs and cream cheese. Add the leeks and crumbled bacon.
Pour the mixture into the pie crust. Bake 35-40 minutes, or until just browned.

July 30

"Beareth all things, believeth all things, hopeth all things, endureth all things."
1 Corinthians 13:7

When a child comes into this world you pray for its well being and care and love. Sometimes parents can't give all of this. They're druggies, alcoholics, insane, cruel, and ungodly. They have not learned to respect themselves or others. They are selfish and mean. But children need tender loving care. They are innocent, unblemished and should not be harmed by the faults of their parents. Some of these children survive and become successful. Others follow in their parent's footsteps. Generation after generation can falter. When a child can survive and bring himself (herself) up by his (her) bootstrap we need to shout for joy. For he (she) needs all our support and the support of God. One of these blessed children who endured a harmful environment is now a Navy SEAL! Both parents have passed on, but he is that shining light that there is good in the world, that you can succeed, that there is hope in the future.

Birthday Cake

2 sticks butter	½ tsp. salt
2 cups sugar	3 tsp. baking powder
½ tsp. almond extract	1 cup half and half
1 tsp. vanilla extract	4 eggs, separated
3 cups flour	

Preheat oven to 350°
Cream the butter and sugar. Stir in almond and vanilla, flour, salt, baking powder, and half and half. Stir in egg yolks.
Beat egg whites until peaks form. Fold in egg whites.
Pour batter into 2 buttered and floured cake pans.
Bake 35-40 minutes, or until a toothpick comes clean.
Place 1 layer of the cake on a cake plate. Frost with icing, raspberry jam, or 12 oz. melted semisweet chocolate and 1 cup heavy cream.
Put other layer on top. Frost top and sides.
Garnish cake with shaved chocolate or coconut.

Icing

1 stick butter	6 tbls. cream
1 box confectioner's sugar	1 tsp. vanilla

Cream the butter and confectioner's sugar. Stir in cream and vanilla.

July 31

"One of the young men answered, I have seen a son of Jesse the Bethlehemite who is skillful in playing, a man of valor, a warrior, prudent in speech, and a man of good presence; and the Lord is with him."
1 Samuel 16:18

I lived in the beautiful sailing town of Annapolis for ten wonderful years. During that time I was privileged to meet some of the most incredible graduates of the United States Naval Academy. One of them was a retired rear admiral who had founded the ocean sailing program at the Naval Academy, served in World War II, and was commanding officer of the *Barb* under Admiral Fluckey. The heroism of these two men and their crew who sank numerous vessels off the China coast during nighttime raids and served in the Pacific during the War earned them the honor and respect of all citizens. Read *Thunder Below!* You will never stop marveling how these men survived. We are so thankful for their devotion to God and country. God bless our armed services. Keep them out of harm's way. Protect them, dear Lord. These are men of valor.

Mussel Salad

Serves 6

36 mussels
1 cup white wine
1 red pepper, sliced
1 yellow pepper, sliced
1 orange pepper, sliced
1 large red onion, sliced, rings separated

½ medium fennel bulb, cored and sliced lengthwise
½ cup olive oil
¼ cup cilantro, chopped
½ red cabbage, sliced
¼ lb. frisee

Bring the white wine to a boil in a large pot.
Stir in peppers, onion, fennel and olive oil. Add the mussels and steam them until they open.
Arrange the cabbage and frisee on 6 plates.
Pour mussels and vegetables on top.
Garnish with cilantro.

August 1

"I also, with my brethren and my servants, am lending them money and grain. Please, let us stop this usury! Restore now to them, even this day, their lands, their vineyards, their olive groves, and their houses, also a hundredth of the money and the grain, the new wine and the oil, that you have charged them."
Nehemiah 5:10-11

We always think of 1492 as the year Christopher Columbus discovered America. Columbus, a Roman Catholic from Italy, sailed from Spain under the sponsorship of King Ferdinand and Queen Isabella. Sadly a little mentioned fact is that on this date, also in 1492, the king and queen expelled all the Jews and Muslims who had not converted to Catholicism from Spain. They accused them of proselytizing and usury among the Christians. This is so ironic as usury is forbidden in the Muslim religion, although interest is not. Those who participate in it are sent to hell according to the Koran. The other irony is that when the king and queen needed money to finance Columbus' expedition it came from the Jews! The Bible too speaks against usury. Today usury is so much a part of our lives. Just look at your credit card statement!

Beef Fajitas

Serves 4

1½ lbs. sirloin
1 tbls. pepper
1 tsp. garlic
½ stick butter
2 large onions
¼ cup sugar
2 tbls. olive oil
1 large red pepper, julianned

1 green pepper, julianned
2 large cloves garlic, minced
2 jalapeno, seeded and chopped
8 tortillas
½ lb cheddar cheese, grated
½ lb.Monterey jack cheese, grated
½ cup sour cream

Rub the steak with the salt and pepper. Grill the steak on a BBQ. Slice thinly.
Melt the butter in a skillet. Saute the onions until tender. Stir in sugar. Remove onions and place in a bowl.
Using the same skillet heat the olive oil. Saute the peppers until tender. Stir in the garlic and jalapeno.
Warm the tortillas in a 350° oven for 3 minutes.
Divide up the steak, vegetables, and onions between the 8 tortillas. Roll up tortillas.
Serve with cheeses and sour cream.

"The earth is full of Thy riches."
Psalm 104:24

Dear Lord, everywhere we look we see what you have created. You created the sky, sun and moon, the stars, and our planet earth. The earth is full of life – the trees and flowers, birds and animals, and human beings. I am in awe of what you have given us. You only God have given us all this. Our hands did not fashion it. You, our creator, made the beauty of the earth. You open our eyes to see what is around us. You let us breathe the air to sustain us. You feed us so that we can work for you. You offer hope and love, and life everlasting. Amen.

Cherry Cobbler

Topping

1 stick butter	¼ tsp. salt
1 cup flour	½ cup milk
2 tbls. baking powder	

Combine all ingredients in food processor.
Place on board and roll into a square. Cut into latticework strips to fit the size of a 9x12 baking dish.

Filling

2 cans sour pitted cherries	½ tsp. nutmeg
1 cup sugar	½ tsp. cinnamon
2 tbls. cornstarch	½ tsp. cloves
2 tbls. lemon juice	¼ cup bourbon or rum

Drain cherries and pour the juice in a saucepan. Heat the juice with sugar, cornstarch and lemon juice, stirring until thickened. Add spices, rum and cherries.
Preheat oven to 375°
Pour filling into a buttered 9x12 baking dish. Make a lattice top crossing strips of dough. Sprinkle with sugar.
Bake 35 minutes, or until dough is browned.
Serve with whipped cream or your favorite ice cream.

August 3

"Wake up! Do something Lord! Why are you sleeping? Don't desert us forever. Why do you keep looking away? Don't forget our sufferings and all of our troubles. We are flat on the ground, holding on to the dust. Do something! Help us! Show how kind you are and come to our rescue."
Psalm 44:23-26

Alexander Solzhenitsyn (1918 - 2008) is best remembered for his tireless effort to educate the world about the former Soviet Union and the Soviet Gulag. As a teenager he became a Communist. In 1945 he was arrested and found guilty of "anti-soviet agitation and propaganda." As a child he was raised in the Russian Orthodox Church. During his eight year imprisonment he returned to his faith. In Russia and the former Soviet Republics religion was repressed for years. Yet followers continued to meet or pray on their own. This was so similar to the early Christian Church when oppression was rampant. We must be thankful the faithful persevered, even though tortured, killed and ostracized. Today and always we know that Jesus Christ is with us.

The Lord heals the brokenhearted and binds up their wounds."
Psalm 147:3

Stroganoff

Serves 6

¼ cup flour
1 tsp. Italian herbs
1 tsp. sea salt
1 tsp. pepper
2 lbs. beef tenderloin, sliced thin
2 tbls. butter
2 leeks, sliced

2 cloves garlic, crushed
1 pint mushrooms, sliced
2 tbls. tomato paste
1 cup beef stock
1 cup sour cream
¼ cup sherry or Madeira

In a bowl combine the flour, herbs, salt and pepper. Dredge the beef in mixture.
Melt the butter in a skillet. Brown the beef. Remove beef. Add a little more butter if necessary.
Saute the leeks until just tender. Stir in garlic and mushrooms. Cook for 2 minutes.
Add beef, tomato paste, and stock. Heat. Stir in sour cream and sherry. Just warm.
Serve over noodles.

"And herein do I exercise myself, to have always a conscience void of offense toward God, and toward men."
Acts 24:16

Though this is a hot summer day, I arrive at the Y at 7 for my morning exercise class. Several days I take aerobics, others it's stretching and muscles. My body needs this. As an author I spend too many days at the computer, or traveling – delivering books, or vacation. Not only does the body need exercise, the mind does too. But we do need peaceful moments to relax.

Towards the end of the Industrial Revolution in England, and in the United States, living conditions for many of the workers were deplorable. They often slept at work, in tenements, and worked long hours. In 1841 George Williams came to London to work in a draper's shop. He organized the first YMCA in 1844 to aid these workers, mainly to give hope and renewal of life through the Bible. The Y concept spread to Canada and the United States, where today they are a backbone of our communities. They offer child care, athletic and exercise programs, lectures, and still maintain a Christian base, some having fellowship such as a man's fraternity meeting. I learned to swim at the Y in Wilmington, Delaware. Today I exercise and make new friends, some very strong Christians. Did you know that volleyball was invented at the Holyoke, MA YMCA in 1895 by William Morgan; racquetball in 1950 at the Greenwich, CT YMCA by Joe Sobek; and softball was given its name by a motion of Walter Hakanson of the Denver YMCA in 1926? Please continue to support the YMCA in your area. And do get some exercise.

Artichoke Dip

2 cans artichoke hearts, drained and chopped	½ cup sour cream
	½ cup mayonnaise
1 leek, chopped finely	2 cloves garlic, minced
2 cups grated mozzarella cheese	1 cup grated parmesan cheese

Preheat oven to 350°
Combine ingredients in baking dish. Bake for 20-25 minutes, or until bubbling. Serve with crackers or sliced French bread.

August 5

"Your wife will be like a fruitful vine within your house; Your children will be like olive shoots around your table. Thus shall the man be blessed who fears the Lord."
Psalm 128:3-4

Did you ever know three people (three different couples) who were married on the same day, but different years? Who all got divorced, and yet their paths kept crisscrossing?

Marriage is something I truly believe in. It is the union of a man and woman for life. However, when times become so unbearable then perhaps a way should be found to end the union. When a man beats his wife not long after their marriage, cannot say something nice to her after eight years, breaks three of her ribs, and only when the divorce is almost final tells her he loves her, and that for the first time, then something should be done.

People often stay in bad marriages out of fear, or for the sake of children. But now with so much abuse taking place, and the courts not handling cases correctly, other means of defense must be found. Children and wives should be separated from abusive husbands. And there are cases where the wife is the abuser. You must look at all sides, and do what is fair. We cannot let a father kill his children for revenge on his wife. That is why we need organizations like CASA and Justice for Children, and judges who will do what is right and just. We live in a cruel world, but each of us must make an effort to make it better and safer for all to live in, particularly for our children

Swordfish Almondine

Serves 4

2 lbs. swordfish
¼ cup mayonnaise
Juice of 1 lemon

¼ cup fresh parsley, chopped
½ cup toasted slivered almonds

Coat the swordfish with the mayonnaise and lemon juice. Cook on grill to desired tenderness.
Garnish with parsley and almonds.
Serve with rice pilaf and a salad.

August 6

"The Lord said, Do not oppress an alien; you yourselves know how it feels to be aliens, because you were aliens in Egypt."
Exodus 23:9

Five ladies sit around a bountiful table for lunch and conversation. Three of them have come from Eastern Europe, one a defector. Each has her own story, but the one thing they are proudest of now is that they are American citizens and will vote in the upcoming elections. One will not leave for her homeland until the day after the election. And yet a high percentage of Americans will not vote. When you have been exiled, when you know what oppression is, you long for freedom and hope. These ladies have all done that with successful careers both in their repressed country, and in the United States. They could not have done it on their own. They learned English, they worked hard, and one had to start completely over. They only now feel like aliens in their former countries, not here. Take someone, legally here, and help them to feel welcome in this great country of ours.

Baked Rockfish (Striped Bass)

Serves 6

2½ lbs. rockfish filets	6 small red bliss potatoes, sliced
½ cup dry white wine	½ lb. baby carrots
1 pint cherry tomatoes	¼ cup fresh parsley, chopped
1 zucchini, sliced thinly	¼ cup fresh basil chopped
1 yellow squash, sliced thinly	4 cloves garlic, crushed

Preheat the oven to 350°
Place the rockfish in a buttered baking dish. Top with other ingredients. Seal with tin foil or top.
Bake 30 minutes. Serve with herb garlic butter

Herb Garlic Butter

1 stick butter, room temperature	¼ cup parsley, chopped
3 cloves garlic, crushed	2 tbls. tarragon, chopped
¼ cup basil chopped	

In a bowl combine the ingredients.
Fashion into six balls. Chill

August 7

"Though he had commanded the clouds from above, and opened the doors of heaven, And had rained down manna upon them to eat, and had given them the corn of heaven. Man did not eat angels' food: he sent them meat to the full. He caused an east wind to blow in the heaven: and by his power he brought in the south wind. He rained flesh also upon them as dust, and feathered fowls like as the sand of the sea: and he let it fall in the midst of their camp, round about their habitations. So they did eat, and were well filled: for he gave them their own desire."
Psalm 78: 23-29

During the dog days of summer, we often wish God would rain manna upon us. Too hot to cook, too many things to get done, and perhaps too hot to go to the beach. Instead sit back, find a comfy chair and read a good book, and let the air conditioning cool your body and mind. Be thankful you are not in the desert with nothing, nothing to eat, nothing to cloth you, only the knowledge God will come through and save you. Our God is a good God, now and forever. Sing his praises. Jump for joy. Stay cool.

Strawberry Bread

3 cups flour
1 tsp. soda
½ tsp. salt
3 tsp. cinnamon
2 cups sugar

4 eggs
1¼ cups vegetable oil
2 cups strawberries, sliced
1 cup pecans or walnuts

Preheat oven to 350°
Combine the flour, baking soda, salt, ground cinnamon and sugar in a bowl.
Beat together the eggs and oil and pour them into the dry ingredients. Stir until just blended.
Fold in the strawberries and nuts.
Pour mixture into 2 greased bread loaf pans.
Bake 1 hour, or until toothpick comes clean.
Serve with fresh strawberries and cream cheese.

"Go ye into all the world and preach the Gospel."
Mark 16:15

"Go in peace to love and serve the Lord."

Sadly the conflict between the Russians and Georgians has picked up. Because many Russians settled in Georgia, the conflict has also divided the Georgian Orthodox and Russian Orthodox churches. Neighbors fighting against each other, yet members of the Orthodox church who should love each other, and work together in the name of the Lord. We need to pray for conflicts like these, which sometimes can not only destroy neighbors, but families. Since the Cold War no longer hovers over us, and religion has returned to the former Soviet Republics, we pray the two Orthodox churches and their leaders can bring unity to these divided groups. No more genocide, no more bombing, no more hatred, just love and respect that our Lord has taught us. The Georgian Orthodox Church dates from the 4th century, and is thus one of the oldest Christian countries. When the Russians took over Georgia in 1801 they abolished the monarchy, the Patriarch of the church, and almost the language, attempting to force Russian culture on the Georgian people. Pray for peace in Georgia and in the world.

Berry Salad

Serves 6-8

¼ cup orange juice
Juice of 1 lime
¼ cup honey
½ cup fresh mint, chopped
1 pint blackberries
1 pint raspberries

1 pint blueberries
1 pint strawberries
2 bunches watercress, stems removed
1 cup macadamia nuts

Combine orange juice, lime juice, honey and mint in a bowl.
Add the other ingredients and toss.

August 9

"Trust in the Lord, and do good: so shalt thou dwell in the land, and verily thou shalt be fed. Delight thyself also in the Lord; and he shall give thee the desires of thine heart. Commit thy way unto the Lord; trust also in him; and he shall bring it to pass."
Psalm 37:3-5

When the earliest settlers came to America they had to have strong religious convictions to leave a native country, and come to an unknown one. They had no idea what lay in store for them. Most were men coming from European cities. They had never tilled the land or hunted, or even built a home. Many starved, were killed, and a few returned to their homeland. Those that stayed trusted in their Lord.

Captain John Smith explored the Chesapeake Bay from 1607-09. In 1608 he visited Shrewsbury Church just after the death of its chaplain Reverend Robert Hunt. He read prayers and the 37th Psalm. In attendance were those on board his shallop and members of the Tockwogh tribe. Today the Captain John Smith Memorial Chapel at Shrewsbury Church commemorates this historic visit to the Eastern Shore of Maryland by one of America's earliest explorers. In fact the map that Captain Smith published of the Chesapeake Bay is still considered one of the finest of the area.

Maryland Crab Imperial

Serves 4

1½ lbs. crab meat	1 tbls. Dijon mustard
½ stick butter	1/8 tsp. cayenne
2 tbls. flour	1 tsp. pepper
1 cup cream	½ tsp. celery salt
1 egg yolk, beaten	2 tbls. milk
1 tbls. lemon juice	2 tbls. mayonnaise
½ tsp. Worcestershire sauce	1 tsp. paprika
1 tbls. mayonnaise	

Preheat oven to 400°
Melt the butter in a sauce pan. Stir in flour and cream until slightly thickened. Stir in egg yolk, lemon juice, Worcestershire, mayonnaise, mustard, cayenne, pepper and celery salt. Fold in crab. In a bowl combine the milk, mayonnaise and paprika. Put crab mixture in shell ramekins or a casserole. Sprinkle with milk mixture. Bake 10 minutes, or until just browned and bubbling.

"How bright appears the morning star, With mercy beaming from afar! The host of Heav'n rejoices! O righteous Branch! O Jesse's Rod! Thou Son of Man, and Son of God! We too will lift our voices Jesus! Jesus! Holy, holy! yet most lowly! Draw Thou near us: Great Emmanuel! stoop and hear us! Rejoice, ye heav'ns, thou earth, reply! With praise, ye sinners, fill the sky! For this His incarnation! Incarnate God, put forth Thy power, Ride on, ride on, great Conqueror, Till all know Thy salvation. Amen, amen! Alleluia, alleluia! Praise be given Evermore, by earth and Heaven."

Philipp Nicolai (1556-1608) was a Lutheran pastor, poet and composer. While he was pastor in Westphalia in 1597 many of his parishioners died from the plague. It was during this time he wrote his two most famous hymns The first hymn was, "*Wake, awake, for night is flying*" (Wachet auf, ruft uns die Stimme). The words come almost directly from Biblical passages - the awake, awake and the watchman in Isaiah 52:1 and 8 and is always sung at Advent. The second hymn was, "*How bright appears the morning star*" (Wie schoen leuchtet der Morgenstern). The hymn praises our glorious Lord, and how appropriate at the dawn of day.

John Athelstan Laurie Riley, author of *Ye Watchers and Ye Holy Ones* was born on this date in 1858, and died in 1945. We all must watch and wait, but the Risen Lord is here, now and forever.

Asparagus Souffle

Serves 4

½ stick butter
¼ cup flour
1 cup half and half
4 eggs, separated

½ lb. asparagus, trimmed and cut in 1" pieces
1 leek, sliced
1 cup fresh grated parmesan cheese
¼ tsp. nutmeg

Preheat oven to 400°
Melt the butter in a sauce pan. Stir in flour and then half and half until thickened. Stir in the egg yolks.
Beat the egg whites until peaks form. Fold into egg yolk mixture.
Fold in the asparagus, leek, cheese and nutmeg.
Pour into a greased soufflé dish.
Bake 35-40 minutes until golden.

August 11

"Rock of Ages, cleft for me, let me hide myself in thee; let the water and the blood from thy wounded side that flowed, be of sin the double cure, cleanse me from its guilt and power."
Augustus Montague Toplady 1763

Jesus is our rock, upon which stands our Christian religion. *"And I say also unto thee, That thou art Peter, and upon this rock I will build my church; and the gates of hell shall not prevail against it."* Matthew 16:18

God is also mentioned as the rock in Samuel and Deuteronomy. *"The Lord liveth; and blessed be my rock; and exalted be the God of the rock of my salvation."* Samuel 22:47 *"He is the Rock, his work is perfect; for all his ways are judgment: a God of truth and without iniquity, just and right he..."* Deuteronomy 32:4

Augustus Toplady (1740-1778) was an English clergyman, poet and hymnist. He graduated from Trinity College, Dublin and in 1759 published his first book, *Poems on Sacred Subjects*. He believed Calvinism was the basis of the Church of England and was in complete opposition to John Wesley. Sadly he died at a very young age of tuberculosis.

Corn Relish

4 cups corn
1 large onion, chopped
2 cloves garlic, crushed
½ red pepper, diced
½ green pepper, diced
1 stalk celery, chopped
1¼ cups light brown sugar

1½ tbls. sea salt
2 tbls. dry mustard
2 tsp. celery seed
1 tsp. tumeric
½ tsp. cayenne or Tabasco Sauce
2 cups cider vinegar

Combine the ingredients in a sauce pan. Bring to boil. Turn down heat. Simmer 30 minutes.
Ladle into hot, sterilized jars. Seal tightly.

August 12

"Whoever can be trusted with very little can also be trusted with much, and whoever is dishonest with very little will also be dishonest with much."
Luke 16:10

Another politician is in the news! Why is it politicians think they are above everyone else and can abuse their power? They are people just like all the rest of us. Except they think they can do whatever they please. They accept bribes, they're adulterers, philanderers, and embezzlers. This is not to say history is not filled with these cheats, but why so many now? They are not from one political party, but both. Rarely do you hear a female politician committing these misdeeds, usually the men. O God punish them, and let them see how they have hurt their wives, children and You. Bring them back to your loving way, that they may love as you do. *"The Kingdom of God will be taken away from you and given to a people that will produce its fruit."* Matthew 21:33-46

Grilled Vegetable Pizza

Pizza Dough

1 cup lukewarm water	1 tsp. sea salt
1 package yeast	1 tbls. thyme
3 cups flour	1 tbls. oregano
1 tbls. olive oil	1 tbls. basil

Dissolve the yeast in the water. Place all the ingredients in a food processor until a ball forms.
Set in an oiled bowl. Let rise 1 hour.
Stretch dough on an oiled pizza pan, sprinkled with cornmeal. Spread to all edges. Let rise ½ hour.

1 large zucchini, thinly sliced	¼ cup fresh basil, chopped
1 eggplant, thinly sliced	3 tbls. olive oil
1 large onion, sliced, rings separated	1 cup mozzarella, grated
2 large tomatoes, thinly sliced	1 cup parmesan cheese, grated

Preheat oven to 500°
Turn oven back to 452° just before baking pizza
Arrange the vegetables on the dough. Sprinkle with basil and olive oil. Top with cheeses.
Bake 15-20 minutes until just browned and bubbling.

August 13

"Man goeth forth unto his work and to his labour until the evening. O LORD, how manifold are thy works! in wisdom hast thou made them all: the earth is full of thy riches. So is this great and wide sea, wherein are things creeping innumerable, both small and great beasts. There go the ships...I will sing unto the LORD as long as I live: I will sing praise to my God while I have my being."
Psalm 104-23-26

The Chesapeake Bay has many traditional boats that are not seen elsewhere in the world. These include bugeyes, buyboats, skipjacks and log canoes. The log canoes were once used to transport products, but today are raced during the summer. These boats range in size from about 30 to 60 feet and a crew of 5-13 people. The boats are top heavy with sails that billow in the breeze, pushing the boats as fast as they can go. Several of the boats are 100 years old, some much newer. Even so they are wooden and fragile, easily tipped, but probably one of the most incredible sights you can see when they race. With the sky and clouds like a painting these boats seem to float on the water and reflect on the past, when sailing boats and ships plied the Bay.

Being out on the water, especially on a lovely day soothes the soul. You breathe the fresh air, notice the clouds and color of the sky and water. You listen for the geese and other birds flying gracefully overhead, or the squawk of a seagull. The boats race by, leaving a wake. How can you not admire the work of God? Sing praises to His name.

Pesto Haddock

Serves 4

2 lbs. haddock filet	Juice of 1 lemon
1 large bunch basil	¼ cup pignoli
1.4 cup olive oil	½ cup parmesan cheese

Place the basil, olive oil, pignoli and cheese in a food processor.
Grill the haddock until desired color.
Serve haddock with pesto sauce.
You can substitute swordfish, tuna, or cod for the haddock.

"A land of wheat, and barley, and vines, and fig trees, and pomegranates."
Deuteronomy 8:8

After all the Israelites went through to come to the Promised Land, they now found the abundance of God. Moses exhorts them to obey and keep God's Commandments. If they do so they will be fed with manna. *"Man doth not live by bread only, but by every word that proceedeth out of the mouth of the Lord doth man live."* Deuteronomy 8:3 God now has given them everything. They are in the Promised Land and must be thankful. We in this country must be thankful for what we too have. Yet if you look on street corners and grates the homeless stare back at us. We are not a land of milk and honey. We too must feed the poor and starving. Reach out and support your local soup kitchen, or volunteer for Meals on Wheels. God will fulfill your needs.

Barley Soup

Serves 4

½ cup pearl barley
1 lb. ham hocks
1 tsp. salt
1 tsp. pepper
2 ½ cups water
2 leeks, chopped

1 celery stalk, chopped
1 small onion, chopped
1 carrot, chopped
2 cloves garlic, crushed
2 red bliss potatoes, cubed
1 cup heavy cream

Place all the ingredients, except cream in a heavy pot. Bring to a boil. Cover and simmer for two hours, stirring frequently.
Add cream just before serving.
Beef can be substituted for ham hocks.
Use beef bouillon and no meat for a vegetarian soup.

"And there was war in heaven: Michael and his angels fought against the dragon; and the dragon fought and his angels, And prevailed not; neither was their place found any more in heaven. And the great dragon was cast out, that old serpent, called the Devil, and Satan, which deceiveth the whole world: he was cast out into the earth, and his angels were cast out with him."
Revelation 12:7-9

When we think of St. George we picture him on his way to the Holy Land and having to battle a dragon. The story tells about the city of Silene, Libya, which is being threatened by a dragon living in the marsh. The citizens agreed to feed him two sheep a day. But not being satisfied the dragon demanded two children, and then the king's daughter, Cleolinda. On the day chosen, she walked towards the dragon dressed in her bridal attire. Along the way she met George who promised to save her through his belief in our Lord. He drew his sword, attacked the dragon, and led him into the city, and then killed him. The citizens of Silene were so grateful, all 15,000 men were baptized that day. George became the patron saint of England in the 14th century.

My husband is also George. He does not go out and slay dragons, but he can cut a mean swath on the water sailing, fixing rigging or doing a splice. Working with one's hands is an art. I truly hope people will continue to learn these trades like Joseph the carpenter, and be strong in their belief of the Lord like St. George.

Shrimp and Scallop Scampi

Serves 4

½ stick butter
4 cloves garlic, minced
4 green onions, chopped
½ lb. baby spinach
1 lb. shrimp

1 lb. scallops
¼ cup wine
Juice of 1 lemon
¼ cup fresh parsley, chopped
1 lb. angel hair pasta

Melt the butter in a large skillet. Saute the garlic and green onions. Remove from pan and put in a bowl. Saute spinach for 1 minute. Remove from pan.
Put the garlic and onions back in the pan. Stir in the shrimp, scallops, wine, and lemon juice.
Cook the angel hair pasta according to the directions.
Divide up the angel hair pasta among four pasta bowls. Divide up shrimp and scallop mixture. Serve garnished with parsley.

August 16

"O Lord my God, When I in awesome wonder,
Consider all the worlds Thy Hands have made;
I see the stars, I hear the rolling thunder,
Thy power throughout the universe displayed.

Then sings my soul, My Saviour God, to Thee,
How great Thou art, How great Thou art.
Then sings my soul, My Saviour God, to Thee,
How great Thou art, How great Thou art!

When through the woods, and forest glades I wander,
And hear the birds sing sweetly in the trees.
When I look down, from lofty mountain grandeur
And see the brook, and feel the gentle breeze."

Carl Boberg (1859-1940) was a Swedish poet, writer and served in Parliament for 20 years. He wrote *How Great Thou Art* after a thunderstorm, when looking over a bay where he heard church bells. A British missionary Stuart Hine first heard the song in the Ukraine in 1933, and translated it into the English words we sing today. Mr. Boberg published more than 60 hymns, poems and gospel songs. This hymn is considered one of twenty most popular hymns today. Sing out to the Lord, how great Thou art!

Tomato Cucumber Bisque

Serves 4

1 cucumber, peeled and seeded
1 red pepper, chopped
4 scallions, chopped
4 cloves garlic, crushed

4 cups V8 juice
1 cup heavy cream
4 tbls. dill, snipped
Croutons

In a food processor combine cucumber, pepper, scallions and garlic. Add V8 juice and cream.
Serve chilled with croutons and dill.
Tomato juice can be substituted for the V8 juice.
Sour cream or yogurt can be substituted for cream.

August 17

"And in the fourth watch of the night Jesus went unto them, walking on the sea. And when the disciples saw him walking on the sea, they were troubled, saying, It is a spirit; and they cried out for fear. But straightway Jesus spake unto to them, saying, be of good cheer; it is I; be not afraid. And Peter answered him and said, Lord, if it be thou, bid me come unto thee on the water. And he said, Come. And when Peter was come down out of the ship, he walked on the water to go to Jesus. But when he saw the wind boisterous, he was afraid; and beginning to sink, he cried, saying, Lord save me. And immediately Jesus stretched forth his hand, and caught him, and said unto him, O thou of little faith, wherefore didst thou doubt? And when they were come into the ship, the wind ceased. Then they that were in the ship came and worshipped him, saying, Of a truth thou art the Son of God."
Matthew 14:25-33

A miracle happened today. Michael Phelps won 8 Gold Medals at the Beijing Olympics, beating out Mark Spitz' record from 1972. This 23 year old is incredible! Yes, I know I cannot compare him to the miracles Jesus performed, but he has done the impossible in only a few days. Yes, there will probably be others who will top his record. I only hope they are as nice and affable as Michael. We must all trust in God. He gives us courage to achieve, to reach our rainbow, to live our dreams. Have faith in the Lord. He will lead you in the right direction.

Crab Quiche

Serves 4

1 pie crust

1 pound crab meat	1½ cups cream
½ red pepper, diced	3 eggs
1 leek, sliced including green	½ tsp. Old Bay seasoning
½ lb. Gruyere cheese, grated	

Preheat oven to 400°
Bake the pie crust in oven for 10 minutes.
In a bowl beat the cream, eggs and Old Bay.
Place the crab, pepper, leek and cheese in the pie crust. Pour the cream mixture on top.
Bake 40 minutes, or until set and slightly browned.
Serve with a green salad.

"Thou rulest the raging of the sea: when the waves thereof arise, thou stillest them."
Psalm 89:9

The Chesapeake Bay is a sorry mess. Only fifty years ago there was such an abundance of crab and oysters, they were shipped all over the country. Now the Bay is so polluted there are almost no crab and oysters. When you go to market much of the seafood comes from North Carolina, Texas, Louisiana, and even as far away as Thailand. The governors, the U.S. government and others meet periodically to find a way to fix the Bay. Sadly the only way this might happen is to have a tidal surge so great the whole Delmarva Peninsula would be engulfed and then you'd have to find a way to force clean ocean water up the Susquehanna, Monongahela and Delaware Rivers. We'd all be gone, but there might be another pristine bay to support wildlife and shellfish again. What man hath wrought, he hath destroyed!

Seafood Casserole

Serves 8

Sauce

1 stick butter	¼ cup sherry
½ cup flour	1 tsp. dry mustard
1 cup half and half	1 tbls. curry powder
1 cup heavy cream	1 tbls. Worcestershire sauce
2 cups Gruyere or cheddar cheese, grated	Juice of ½ lemon

Melt the butter in a sauce pan. Stir in flour. Add half and half and cream. Stir in Sherry, mustard, curry, Worcestershire sauce and lemon juice.

1 15oz. can artichoke hearts, drained	2 lbs. jumbo shrimp, cooked, peeled, and deveined
½ lb. mushrooms, sliced	
1 leek, chopped	2 lbs. lump crabmeat
½ lb. baby spinach	

Preheat oven to 350°
Place the artichoke hearts, leeks, mushrooms and baby spinach in a 13x9 casserole. Top with shrimp and crabmeat. Pour sauce over top.
Bake for 20 minutes, or until bubbly. Serve with rice, crusty bread and a salad.

August 19

"We know that all things work together for good for those who love God, who are called according to his purpose."
Romans 8:28

A dear friend and I became very involved with one of the house museums in Annapolis. After speaking with the director we realized we needed a major fundraising effort to restore the garden and the house. The original plans for the garden had been discovered in a chimney during Hurricane Floyd in 1999. Alden Hopkins was working in Williamsburg and at UVA, and finished the garden in Annapolis in 1949. Today they are back to the original plans. The fundraiser we started is now an annual event. The Secret Garden Tour has grown from an afternoon event to a two day extravaganza. God was looking down on us to do a good deed. He gave us direction so that we could prepare a garden in his honor and for all to enjoy.

Lobster Souffle

Serves 4

½ stick butter
¼ cup flour
1 cup half and half
1 cup Gruyere cheese

Pinch of cayenne
Pinch of nutmeg
4 eggs, separated
½ lb. fresh lobster meat

Preheat the oven to 375°
Melt the butter in a sauce pan. Stir in flour, and then half and half. Add cheese and cayenne, nutmeg and egg yolks.
Beat egg whites until stiff.
Fold egg whites and lobster into the egg mixture.
Pour into greased soufflé dish.
Bake 35-40 minutes, or until golden. Do not open the oven.

"O God, thou hast taught me from my youth: and hitherto have I declared thy wondrous works."
Psalm 71:17

Old Nantucket friends had a yearly party on the beach where they served a vodka punch in a watermelon. We were just of age to drink. Even though I wasn't particularly fond of vodka except in Bloody Mary's this punch was sweet enough for anyone that age to enjoy. Don't forget this was back in the days of rum and coke, bourbon and ginger ale, Tom Collins, and other sweet drinks. I have no idea what was in the recipe, so the one below is my concoction. Somehow I can't remember how they got the punch in the watermelon, but I think there was only a small opening with a spigot to pour. Maybe too, it was only a watermelon with lots of vodka and nothing else! My habits have certainly changed since then! I always loved going to this big house on the beach, gorgeous views out over Nantucket Sound and memories of the host's son being my first Nantucket crush. Now he's still handsome, very gray, and looks exactly like his father. But then so does my husband! Oh those sunsets on the beach! How I love thy wondrous works, O Lord!

Vodka Punch

Makes about 20 cups

1 fifth vodka
1 qt. cranberry juice
1 can frozen limeade
1 large bottle ginger ale

1 pint strawberries, stems removed
1 pint raspberries
1 orange, sliced
1 ice ring

Combine the vodka, cranberry juice, limeade and ginger ale in a punch bowl.
Float the ice ring, strawberries, raspberries and orange on top.
Serve in punch cups.

August 21

"And he (Jesus) answered and said unto them, Have ye not read that he which made them at the beginning made them male and female, And said, For this cause shall a man leave father and mother, and shall cleave to his wife: and they twain shall be one flesh? Wherefore they are no more twain, but one flesh. What therefore God hath joined together, let no man put asunder."
Matthew 19:4-6

Attending a wedding, or even being a bridesmaid or groomsman allows a person to be an active participant in a ceremony that binds two people together forever. These vows need to be taken seriously and understood by both parties. No wonder counseling has become such an important role in the churches. If two people are not suited for each other, how can they live together, produce children, and stay loyal? Life is but a fleeting moment, but God has taught us that love is above all else. *"This is my commandment, That ye love one another, as I have loved you."* John 15:12

Beef Tournedos

Serves 10

4 lbs. beef tenderloin, cut into 10 steaks
1 stick butter
10 thin slices of French bread
½ pint mushrooms, chopped

2 green onions, chopped
2 cloves garlic
½ cup heavy cream
10 artichoke bottoms

Cook the tenderloin on a BBQ to desired pinkness.
Melt ½ the butter in a skillet. Toast the French bread on each side in butter.
Melt the rest of butter. Saute the mushrooms, green onions, and garlic until just tender. Add the cream.
Place the beef on each slice of French bread. Place one artichoke heart on each beef tenderloin.
Spoon the mushroom sauce into each heart.
Serve the rest of sauce in a gravy boat.

"Forget what happened long ago! Don't think about the past. I am creating something new. There it is. Do you see it? I have put roads in deserts, streams in thirsty lands. Every wild animal honors me, even jackals and owls. I provide water in deserts – streams in thirsty lands for my chosen people. I made them my own nation, so they would praise me."
Isaiah 43:18-21

Too often we do dwell in the past. We can't seem to focus on today, tomorrow, or what the future will bring. Maybe it is the heat, the dog days of summer, or something is bothering you. Get it out in the open and enjoy what you have. Do not fret. God is always here with us. He provides for us, even when we think there is nothing left. You may not always think He is here when you are most down. Take a walk, call a friend, think happy thoughts. Pray to the Lord. He will answer your prayers, maybe not the way you wanted it. He knows what is deep in your soul. He knows your feelings. He knows we are weak. Let Him lift you up on wings of eagles. Soar like the birds. He is in charge.

Blueberry Salad

Serves 4

2 cups blueberries
¼ lb. blue cheese or gorgonzola

2 large bunches watercress
1 cup pecans

Toss the ingredients in a salad bowl with the chive dressing.
Dried blueberries can be substituted for fresh blueberries.

Chive Dressing

2 tbls. olive oil
2 tbls. lemon juice
¼ cup chives, snipped
1 clove garlic, crushed

1 clove shallot, crushed
2 scallions, chopped
½ tsp. salt

Combine the ingredients in a bowl. Mix well.

August 23

"And he said unto them, Ye will surely say unto me this proverb, Physician, heal thyself: whatsoever we have heard done in Capernaum, do also here in thy country."
Luke 4:23

When I was fourteen, my parents moved to Long Island. Eleven years later they moved further out on the island so my father would not have to commute so far. Across the street from them lived a lovely Greek couple, both doctors. They had no children, but were very involved with their work, and traveled frequently. When my father did not feel well and no tests showed any problems, our doctor friends suggested he go out to Stony Brook where the research for Lyme's Disease was in full swing. Luckily they found my father had the disease and probably had it several times. He was put on antibiotics, and later, because it had affected his heart gave him a pacemaker. We are forever grateful to this loving couple who became so much a part of our lives. When the whole family visited Athens a few years ago they took every one of us out for the best Greek dinner we ever had, or will have. Blest be the physician. Thank you Luke.

Greek Salad

Serves 8

Juice of one large lemon
¼ cup olive oil
½ tsp. salt
½ tsp. fresh ground pepper
1 head Boston lettuce, leaves separated
4 large tomatoes, sliced

2 scallions, chopped
1 large cucumber, sliced
½ lb. Kalamata olives
1 15 oz. can artichoke hearts, drained
½ pound feta cheese

Combine the lemon juice, olive oil, salt and pepper in a salad bowl.
Toss in the other ingredients.

"In God is my salvation and my glory: the rock of my strength, and my refuge in God. Trust in him at all times; ye people, pour out your heart before him: God is a refuge for us. Selah. Surely men of low degree are a lie; to be laid in the balance, they are altogether lighter than vanity. Trust not in oppression, and become not vain in robbery; if riches increase, set not your heart upon them. God hath spoken once, twice have I heard this; that power belongeth unto God. Also unto thee, O Lord belongeth mercy: for thou renderest to every man according to his work."
Psalm 62:7-12

William Wilberforce (1759-1833) was born to an affluent Yorkshire family and educated at Cambridge. He was elected to the House of Commons in 1780. In 1785 he underwent a conversion and became an evangelical Christian. He fought for many conservative causes including the Society for Suppression of Vice, British missionary work in India, the creation of a free colony in Sierra Leone, the foundation of the Church Mission Society and the Society for the Prevention of Cruelty to Animals.

If you have not seen the movie *Amazing Grace* which came out in 2007, I suggest you do so. This all powerful story focuses on John Newton and William Wilberforce and how they influenced the British Parliament to abolish slavery. He died one month before Parliament passed the Emancipation Bill and is buried at Westminster Abbey. Trust in God at all times, and not in oppression.

Onion Tart

Serves 4

1 pie crust	3 eggs
2 red onions, sliced	½ tsp. nutmeg
1 stick butter	1½ cups cream
2 tbls. flour	1 cup Gruyere

Preheat oven to 400°
Bake the pie crust in oven for 10 minutes.
Melt the butter in a skillet. Saute onions until tender.
In a bowl beat the eggs. Add flour, nutmeg and cream. Stir in onions and cheese
Pour into the pie crust.
Bake 35 minutes, or until set and just browned.

August 25

"The sea is his, and he made it: and his hands formed the dry earth."
Psalm 95:5

The summer has been long, hot and without much rain. I realize even with watering some of the boxwood, holly and other plants might not make it, as hard as we have tried to save them. However we have made sure the birdbath is always filled. The birds and squirrels sit playfully on the side, dunking themselves into the water and then flitting to the ground to shake off. I love watching them, as they talk among themselves, seemingly cheerful and happy to be alive. We are lucky to have the sea and water, but we also needed the land to live on.

"Thanks be unto God for his unspeakable gift."
2 Corinthians 9:15

Stuffed Rockfish

Serves 6

4 tbls. butter
4 cloves garlic, crushed
3 medium tomatoes, chopped
1 medium onion, chopped
¼ tsp. dried thyme
1 tbls. oregano
2 tbls. basil
¼ cup parsley, chopped

½ red pepper, diced
4 slices smoked bacon, cooked and chopped
1 tsp. salt
1 tsp. pepper
2 ½ lbs. rockfish filets
2 tbls. lemon juice

Preheat oven to 350°
Melt the butter in a skillet. Stir in garlic, tomatoes, thyme, oregano, basil, parsley and pepper. Cook until onion is just tender. Add bacon, salt and pepper.
Place the filets in a buttered baking dish. Top with tomato sauce. Sprinkle with lemon juice.
Bake for 20 minutes, or until just bubbling.
Serve with rice and garnish with fresh parsley.
Bluefish, salmon, or other types of fish can be substituted for the rockfish.
Substitute olive oil for the butter.

"Be patient therefore, brethren, unto the coming of the Lord. Behold the husbandman waiteth for the precious fruit of the earth, and hath long patience for it, until he receive the early and latter rain."
James 5:7

As children spending summers on Nantucket we loved to go berry picking near Alter Rock, or elsewhere on the Island. We'd fill our pails, eating half of them before being reunited with family. I guess that is why one of our favorite books is *Blueberries for Sal* by Robert McCloskey. Of course, our very favorite by him is *Make Way for Ducklings*. In the evening we might have blueberries and ice cream, blueberry muffins, or blueberry cobbler. Each year a friend now gathers them and makes the berries into jam. It's been a while since I've been blueberry picking. Happy memories, and a great way to entertain children. Just watch out for the poison ivy! Be patient and the Lord will give you a great harvest.

Blueberry Salad

Serves 4

¼ cup lemon juice
¼ cup honey or maple syrup
8 large mint leaves, chopped
½ lb. spring greens

2 cups blueberries
1 cup blue cheese, crumbled
1 cup toasted almonds or pecans

Combine the lemon juice, honey and mint leaves in a salad bowl.
Toss the rest of the ingredients with the dressing.

August 28

"Give what Thou dost command, and command what Thou wilt"
"Love the sinner and hate the sin"
"Nothing conquers except truth and the victory of truth is love"
"To sing once is to pray twice"
"God, O Lord, grant me the power to overcome sin. For this is what you gave to us when you granted us free choice of will. If I choose wrongly, then I shall be justly punished for it. Is that not true, my Lord, of whom I indebted for my temporal existence? Thank you, Lord, for granting me the power to will my self not to sin. "
"Christ is the teacher within us"

The next time you cannot think of how to pray open the words of Augustine of Hippo and let his words surround you with the Word of our Lord. They will uplift and grant you the power to be in the Lord's hands.

Augustine of Hippo (354-430) was born in Algeria to a pagan father and Christian mother. He studied, and then taught rhetoric. In Milan he met Ambrose, bishop of the city. He was baptized in 386. He then spent time in a monastic community, was ordained, and appointed bishop of Hippo in 394. He was a strong defender of the faith till his death. His writings include the *Confessions* and *City of God.* His body lies at rest in San Pietro Church in Ciel d'Oro.

Baby Greens Salad

Serves 6-8

1 lb. mixed baby greens	1 red onion, sliced
1 cup pistachios, shelled	¼ lb. Gorgonzola cheese, crumbled

Toss the ingredients with the vinaigrette in a salad bowl.

Vinaigrette

¼ cup white wine vinegar	1 tsp. fresh ground pepper
Zest of 1 lemon	1 tsp. sugar
1 tbls. Dijon mustard	½ cup olive oil
¼ tsp. salt	Juice of 1 lemon

Combine ingredients in a jar and shake well.

"Waters flowed over mine head; then I said, I am cut off. I called upon thy name, O LORD, out of the low dungeon. Thou hast heard my voice: hide not thine ear at my breathing, at my cry. Thou drewest near in the day that I called upon thee: thou saidst, Fear not."
Lamentations 3:54-57

A day of great destruction that no one in the United States, or around the world will ever forget as the Louisiana, Mississippi and Alabama coastlines were devastated by Hurricane Katrina in 2005. Following the hurricane I attended the National Day of Remembrance at the Washington National Cathedral on September 16th. Sitting with a group from Houston, who were finding shelter and food for those left homeless, I was overwhelmed by what they were going through, and giving of themselves day and night. They were of every religion, every background, but all had come together when a natural disaster struck. I couldn't help but think, even if they were Jewish or Muslim or Christian, or whatever, that those gathered here had come as a testimony to the Resurrection, and that life would go on, no matter how difficult things seemed at the time. Continue to testify and be a witness to others.

August 29th is also the feast day of John the Baptist "the *voice crying in the wilderness.*" How appropriate for those still suffering after Katrina, and now Gustav, and other hurricanes.

Spoon Bread II

1½ sticks butter
4 ears corn, shucked and corn removed
3 cups milk
1 tsp. salt
1 cup cornmeal

3 eggs, separated
2 tbls. sugar
2 tsp. baking powder
2 jalapeno, seeded and chopped
Dash cayenne

Preheat oven to 350°
In a large skillet melt ½ stick butter in the oven. Remove from the oven.
In a sauce pan heat the corn, milk and salt, bringing to a boil.
Slowly pour in the cornmeal. Simmer until thickened, stirring to keep from sticking. Remove from heat and add remaining butter.
Beat egg whites until stiff.
Stir the egg yolks into corn mixture. Add the sugar, baking powder, jalapeno and cayenne. Fold in egg whites.
Pour into a skillet. Bake 35-40 minutes, until top is golden brown.

August 30

"Praise ye the Lord, Sing unto the lord a new song, and his praise in the congregation of saints... Let them praise his name in the dance; let them sing praises unto him with the timbrel and harp... Let the saints be joyful in glory; let them sing aloud upon their beds. Let the high praises of God be in their mouth..."
Psalm 149:1-6

Have you ever walked into a party and recognized someone because you know a member of his or her family? Many years ago at a New England Society dance I did just that. On the dance floor I kept glancing over at this distinguished looking gentleman. Finally I could stand it no longer, and went over and asked if he was related to so and so. Yes, he was his son. The two were drop dead look alikes – twins. Since that time we have almost always celebrated our day and year apart birthdays. Sadly it's not every year now, as he lives in Hong Kong. Somehow we do try, and have a lobster feast on Nantucket.

This man also has one of the most beautiful voices, whether he sings at church, with the Blue Hill Troop, or the Hong Kong Welsh Male Voice Choir. Let the angels sing to you a new song. Open your heart to a new friend.

Lobster and Scallop Pie

Serves 6

1 stick butter	½ tsp. nutmeg
1 leek, chopped	2 tbls. fresh parsley, chopped
¼ cup flour	1 tbls. tarragon, chopped
2 cups heavy cream	½ lbs. bay scallops
¼ cup Cognac	1 ½ lbs. lobster meat
¼ tsp. cayenne	½ cup seasoned bread crumbs

Preheat the oven to 350°
Melt the butter in a sauce pan. Stir in the leek for 2 minutes. Add flour and slowly stir in cream, until slightly thickened. Add Cognac, cayenne, nutmeg, parsley and tarragon. Fold in the scallops and lobster.
Pour into a buttered baking dish. Sprinkle with bread crumbs. Parmesan cheese can also be used.
Bake 20 minutes, until golden and bubbling.
Serve with rice.

August 31

"Almighty and everlasting God, who kindled the flame of your love in the heart of your servant Catherine: Grant to us, your humble servants, a like faith and power of love; that, as we rejoice in her triumph, we may profit by her example; through Jesus Christ our Lord, who lives and reigns with you and the Holy Spirit, one God, now and for ever. Amen."
(The Collect for Saint Catherine)

Being named Katherine, I am honored to have received this name. Catherine of Siena was born in 1347 and dedicated her life to Christ. She ministered to the poor and sick, and in 1375 received the marks of Christ's wounds in her hands, side and feet, the stigmata. She was canonized in 1461 and in 1937 Pope Pius XII proclaimed she and St. Francis patrons of Italy.

Today as I celebrate my birthday I hope I can become more like her and all the saints. I am a humble servant, and I will try my best to be a faithful witness of God, keepings his precepts and walking in his footsteps.

Lobster Crepes

12 crepes

Crepes

1 cup flour   1½ cups milk
3 eggs   ¼ tsp. salt
2 tbls. butter, melted

Combine the ingredients in a bowl.
Melt some butter in a skillet.
Pour batter by a large spoonful into the skillet. Brown on both sides.

Filling

1 cup heavy cream   ½ lb. baby spinach
¼ lb. Gruyere cheese   2 tbls. chopped dill
1 lb. lobster meat   ½ lb. mushrooms, sliced

Combine the ingredients in a sauce pan. Heat until just warmed
Divide up lobster mixture between 12 crepes. Roll crepes.
Garnish with dill or parsley.
Some of the lobster sauce can be reserved to serve as garnish also.

September 1

"Behold how good and pleasant it is for brethren to dwell together in unity."
Psalm 133:1

These words are inscribed above the altar in the beautiful 'Sconset Union Chapel on Nantucket Island. When people enter the Chapel they stand awed by its simplicity. Services have been held here since July 15, 1883. The church is listed in the National Register, and has been the scene not only of worship services, but many weddings, christenings, and funerals. I love going here on Sunday morning. The music is so uplifting, the windows open, birds singing and the exuberance of the congregation. Stanley Johnson, who was the Chaplain at the University of Pennsylvania when I was in graduate school, served as summer rector for forty-two years. He and his wife Sally, were not only a beloved couple at the chapel, but active members of the 'Sconset community as well. Time marches on, but we always retain our memories. And when we can do it surrounded by others who believe in unity, the world is a better place. The weekend the Chapel closes in the fall, the congregation sings *"God Be With You Till We Meet Again"* by Jeremiah Rankin (1882). The words *"Behold how good and pleasant it is for brethren to dwell together in unity"* is emblazoned above the simple altar.

Lobster Bisque

Serves 6

Puff pastry	½ tsp. paprika
½ stick butter	Dash of cayenne
2 tbls. flour	¼ cup sherry
3 cups half and half	1 lb. lobster meat
3 cups heavy cream	2 tbls. fresh dill, snipped
½ tsp. salt	1 egg, beaten with 1 tbls. water

Preheat oven to 400°
Melt the butter in a sauce pan. Stir in flour, half and half and cream, until slightly thickened. Add salt, paprika, cayenne and sherry. Fold in lobster and dill. Divide the bisque among six oven-proof bowls. Brush each bowl rim with the egg wash.
Cut the puff pastry into six rounds to fit the top of the bowls, leaving a little extra. Press down on sides with fork. Brush pastry with egg wash.
Bake 12-15 minutes, or until pastry is puffed and golden.
Serve garnished with additional dill.

"And the word of God increased; and the number of disciples multiplied in Jerusalem greatly; and a great company of the priests were obedient to the faith."
Acts 6:7

From the time the disciples gathered around Jesus to those priests who followed after him, the Christian flocks grew. Today as Islam and other religions spread we must continue to grow our flock. I have been very thankful over the years to have known many inspirational ministers whose congregations continue to grow. They are warm, compassionate, and obedient to their faith.

"Let the words of my mouth, and the meditation of my heart, be acceptable in thy sight, O Lord, my strength and my redeemer."
Psalm 19:14

Stuffed Chicken with Basil Sauce

Serves 6

6 boneless chicken breasts	12 leaves basil chopped
6 pieces prosciutto	½ cup flour
6 oz. mozzarella cheese, sliced	2 eggs
3 cloves garlic, crushed	1 cup panko

Pound the chicken until thin. Place one piece of prosciutto and cheese on each chicken. Sprinkle garlic and basil on top. Roll up chicken and secure with toothpick.
Using three plates put flour in one, egg in another, and lastly the panko. Dip the chicken first in the flour, then egg and then panko. Place chicken in baking dish. Refrigerate chicken for 1 hour.
Preheat oven to 400° Bake chicken for ½ hour.
Serve with rice and basil sauce.

Basil Sauce

½ stick butter	1 large bunch basil, chopped
¼ cup flour	3 cloves garlic, crushed
1 ½ cups cream	

Melt the butter in a sauce pan. Stir in flour, then cream, until slightly thickened. Add basil and garlic.

September 3

*"Lamb of God, you take away the sin of the world, have mercy on us.
Lamb of God, you take away the sin of the world, have mercy on us.
Lamb of God, you take away the sin of the world, grant us peace. "*
Agnus Dei

Gregory the Great (c540-604) was born in Rome to a Roman senator. He became a perfect of the city, but also decided to devote his life to God. He sold most of his worldly belongings to found six monasteries in Sicily and one in Rome. He became a monk and in 590 pope. At that time Rome was ravaged by the plague, poverty, and war. He began converting Lombards, Visogoths, and Anglo-Saxons to Christianity. He wrote many homilies and the *Pastoral Care* to explain the duties of bishops. The *Gregorian Chant* is named for him. His other works include *The Kyrie, Gloria, Credo, Sanctus, Benedictus* and *Agnus Dei.*

Lamb with Fruit

Serves 6

2 tbls. olive oil
2 lbs. boneless leg of lamb, cubed
1 tsp. cinnamon
1 tsp. cumin
¼ tsp. ground cloves
Zest of 1 lemon
1 cup almonds

1 cup pitted prunes
1 cup dried apricots
1 cup dried currants
¼ cup cilantro
½ cup red wine
1 cup water or beef stock

Preheat oven to 350°
Melt the olive oil in a Dutch oven. Brown the lamb.
Add the other ingredients.
Cover and bake 1 hour, or until lamb is very tender.
Serve with couscous.

September 4

"Even a child is known by his doings, whether his work be pure, and whether it be right."
Proverbs 20:11

From the time I was a small child I dreamed of being a teacher. I loved children, and from the age of twelve on, babysit for local families, and spent summers on Nantucket mother helping. Back in those days the hourly wage was 25 cents an hour, or fifty dollars a week. When I got to college I was very fortunate to study under Dr. Myrtle McGraw. I didn't know at the time that she was a world famous leader in child development and growth, dating back to the 1930s and 40s. She brought to light the motor development of infants mainly through swimming. When we moved to Cleveland years later and joined a local club, I remembered this and got my daughter in the water at ten months. My daughter joined swim teams, and still swims when she can. Thank you, Dr. McGraw for being a wonderful mentor and stimulating further my love for children. And now I'm a grandmother! Treasure every moment with your children, let their imagination run free, and let them know the Lord.

Chocolate Chip Cookies

2 sticks butter	1 tsp. baking powder
1 cup brown sugar	1 tsp. baking soda
½ cup sugar	½ tsp. salt
2 eggs	8 oz. chocolate chips
1 tsp. vanilla	1 cup walnuts or peanuts
2 cups flour	Hershey's Kisses
1½ cup oats	

Preheat oven to 350°
Cream the butter and sugars. Beat in eggs, vanilla, flour, oats, baking soda and salt. Fold in chips and nuts.
Drop by spoonfuls onto ungreased cookie sheet.
Bake 12-13 minutes.
As Let cool slightly and place a kiss in each one.

"How firm a foundation, ye saints of the Lord, Is laid for your faith in His excellent Word! What more can He say than to you He hath said, You, who unto Jesus for refuge have fled? ...Fear not, I am with thee, O be not dismayed, For I am thy God and will still give thee aid; I'll strengthen and help thee, and cause thee to stand Upheld by My righteous, omnipotent hand...The soul that on Jesus has leaned for repose, I will not, I will not desert to its foes; That soul, though all hell should endeavor to shake, I'll never, no never, no never forsake."

Whenever I hear this hymn it is not only the first few lines I recall, but the end of the hymn. *I'll never, no never, ne never forsake*. Oh, Lord you are always with us. I have gone up hills and down into the valleys, but you have always been with me. I might not have thought so. I trusted not in myself. Thank goodness I found you Lord. You are the true rock, the foundation on which all life, all being is based. Lord, you test me, but I will be steady in my faith. Above all I will be a testimony to you so that others may come to know you. This I do believe!

John Rippon (1751-1836) was an English Baptist minister and in 1787 published, *A Selection of Hymns from the Best Authors, Intended to Be an Appendix to Dr. Watts' Psalms and Hymns*, now known as *Rippon's Selection*.

Chicken Salad

Serves 4

3 large boneless chicken breasts, cooked and cubed
1 medium cucumber, cubed
1 cup black olives
½ cup fresh parsley, chopped
½ cup sour cream
½ cup mayonnaise
2 cloves garlic, crushed

1 tsp. oregano
Spring greens
1 cup feta cheese
2 tomatoes, sliced
4 hardboiled eggs, quartered
1 large avocado, peeled, pitted, and sliced

In a bowl combine the chicken, cucumber, olives, parsley, sour cream, mayonnaise, garlic and oregano.
Place some of the spring greens on a plate. Divide up chicken salad into 4 portions on spring greens.
Sprinkle feta on top. Surround with tomatoes, hardboiled eggs and avocado.

"Thy plants are an orchard of pomegranates, with pleasant fruits; camphire and spikemnard."
Song of Solomon 4:13

Like the author of the Song of Solomon, my oldest friend is a poet. She often attends workshops, has several groups she meets with frequently, and enjoys a writer's retreat. She has shared her poetry with me, sending favorite pieces, books, and on her Christmas cards. Her grandfather was my godfather, a very beloved military figure who presented me with my first *Book of Common Prayer* on my first birthday.

Lovage

Like celery, but fiercer,
a gift of lovage takes on the herb bed
with rhubarbian tenacity.
Cut back to the ground, frozen, drenched
or left to fry, no matter. Each spring,
it offers pungent new leaves without reproach.
Whatever it is that lovage does,
we should be thankful.
© Q. Hallett

Salmon on the BBQ

Serves 4

1½ lbs. salmon filet
1 tbl. sea salt

2 tbls. olive oil
2 tbls. lemon juice

Rub the salmon with the salt, olive oil and lemon juice.
Smoke or BBQ the salmon. Serve with mustard sauce.

Mustard Sauce

1 cup olive oil
3 tbls. balsamic vinegar
2 tbls. Dijon mustard
1 egg yolk

1 tbls. sugar
2 tbls. fresh snipped dill
1 tsp. sea salt

Combine the ingredients in food processor or jar.

September 7

"Come, labor on! Who dares stand idle, on the harvest plain While all around him waves the golden grain? And to each servant does the Master say, "Go work today." Come, labor on! Who dares stand idle, on the harvest plain While all around him waves the golden grain? And to each servant does the Master say, "Go work today."

Living on the Eastern Shore surrounded by farms and fields, we appreciate the beauty of our country. Sadly development is taking over, but still the empty space abounds. During the summer tomatoes, corn and cantaloupe nourish our bodies. Now as fall approaches the soy beans are in abundance. The fields are green and lush, though a good rainfall would help. Geese fly overhead, and squirrels wiggle their tails and hide their nuts. The days are cooler, and the nights sleepable. Time to get back to fall schedules at church, and time to till the earth. *"Come labor on."*

Jane Laurie Borthwick, a Scotswoman, (1813-1897), along with her sister Sarah Findlater published a book of translations of German hymns titled *Hymns from the Land of Luther*. While living in Switzerland, she produced another book of translations called *Alpine Lyrics*. She was active with the Edinburgh House of Refuge and the Moravian Mission in Labrador.

Whisky Fudge

8 oz. dark chocolate
1 can condensed sweetened milk
½ tsp. vanilla

½ cup nuts
¼ cup whisky

Melt the chocolate in a sauce pan. Stir in condensed milk. Stir in other ingredients.
Grease a square baking dish. Pour chocolate into dish.
Refrigerate at least 2 hours.

"Who can find a virtuous woman? for her price is far above rubies. The heart of her husband doth safely trust in her, so that he shall have no need of spoil. She will do him good and not evil all the days of her life...Strength and honour are her clothing; and she shall rejoice in time to come. She openeth her mouth with wisdom; and in her tongue is the law of kindness. She looketh well to the ways of her household, and eateth not the bread of idleness. Her children arise up, and call her blessed; her husband also, and he praiseth her. Many daughters have done virtuously, but thou excellest them all."
Proverbs 31:10-29

From the time we were quite young my mother filled her days with attention to us, my father, volunteer work, and making ends meet by selling stationary and substitute teaching. She volunteered for the Flower Mart, the Junior League, the Colonial Dames, and numerous other organizations. She always remembers everyone's birthday, anniversary, or a special event. She has opened her heart to those who have lost their parents, and become a surrogate mother to several of my friends. She has been the virtuous woman to all of us.

Lobster Casserole

Serves 6

2 tbls olive oil	2 cloves garlic, crushed
2 lbs. lobster meat	½ cup bread crumbs
1 pint mushrooms, sliced	

Preheat oven to 350°
Heat the olive oil in a skillet. Saute lobster, mushrooms and garlic for 2 minutes. Pour into a buttered casserole. Pour tomato cream sauce on top. Sprinkle with bread crumbs. Bake 20 minutes, or until golden and bubbling.

Roasted Tomato Cream Sauce

2 large tomatoes	2 cups cream
½ stick butter	3 green onions, chopped
¼ cup flour	

Cut tomatoes in quarters. Roast on BBQ or in oven. Puree in a food processor.
Melt the butter in a sauce pan.
Stir in flour and cream. Add green onions and tomato puree.

September 9

"What Child is this who, laid to rest On Mary's lap is sleeping? Whom Angels greet with anthems sweet, While shepherds watch are keeping? This, this is Christ the King, Whom shepherds guard and Angels sing; Haste, haste, to bring Him laud, The Babe, the Son of Mary."

Christmas is still several months off, but as I travel I enjoy picking up appropriate presents for people. September is one of the nicest times to be on Nantucket, or as we have done several times recently, traveled in Europe. The crowds are gone, summer sales are on, and the days are warm enough to enjoy long walks, swim, or sightsee. On these trips we visit as many churches as possible. The stained glass windows depict times in the life of Christ, and almost always show a baby Jesus and Mary. Now as a grandmother, I treasure those moments laying my eyes on my peacefully resting grandson, keeping watch over him, and singing a hymn or lullaby. How glorious it is to share a new baby. Thank you Lord for giving us a new life.

William Chatterton Dix (1837-1898), born in Bristol, England went on to manage a marine insurance business in Glasgow. His great love, though, was writing hymns. He composed over forty hymns, including *What Child is This? With Gladness, Men of Old, Alleluia! Sing to Jesus! His the Scepter His the Throne*, and *To You, O Lord, Our Hearts We Raise*.

Braised Pork Chops

Serves 4

4 boneless lean pork chops	2 tbls. butter
¼ cup flour	½ cup balsamic vinegar
1 tsp. pepper	1 tbls. sage leaves
1 tsp. salt	1 cup black olives
2 tbls. olive oil	

In a bowl combine the flour, pepper, and salt. Dredge the chops in the flour mixture.
Heat the butter and olive oil. Brown the pork chops on both sides. Remove pork chops.
Add balsamic vinegar to the pork drippings. Stir until reduced by ½. Stir in sage and olives. Then add pork chops until just warmed.
Serve with pasta or roasted sweet potatoes.

"Thou shalt seek them, and not find them, even them that contended with thee: they that war against thee shall be as nothing, and as a thing of nought, For I the Lord thy God will hold thy right hand, saying unto thee, Fear not, I will help thee."
Isaiah 41:12-13

Seven years ago I drove home from Nantucket to Annapolis. The battery in the car had gone, so I didn't have the code to start the radio. There was not a cloud in the brilliant blue sky. I drove over the George Washington Bridge and onto the New Jersey Turnpike. Having made this trip so many times I always remember searching for the Empire State Building and the Twin Towers, while keepings my eyes pinned to the road. Now these years later, I have no recollection of seeing them. The Twin Towers are gone. Swept away in a few moments by the most ghastly accident on American soil. My mind is blank, yet I recall the sky and driving without a radio. How different that day would have been if it had been September 11th and I had gotten to New York, only to see the smoke. I cannot even imagine. My heart aches for those who were lost, including some of my own acquaintances. The world will never be the same again.

Vegetable Tart

Serves 8

2 pie crusts
1 yellow squash, sliced
1 zucchini, sliced
1 red onion, sliced
2 cloves garlic, crushed
2 tomatoes, sliced
¼ lb. baby spinach
1 red pepper, sliced

1 yellow pepper, sliced
1 green pepper, sliced
¼ cup parsley, chopped
½ lb. Guyere cheese, grated
6 eggs
¼ cup sour cream
3 cups cream
¼ tsp. cayenne

Preheat oven to 400°
Mold the pie crusts into a 9x13 baking dish. Bake for 10 minutes in oven.
Layer the vegetables in the dish. Sprinkle cheese on top.
In a bowl beat together the eggs, sour cream, cream and cayenne. Pour over the cheese.
Bake 40 minutes.
Swiss or cheddar cheese can be substituted for the Gruyere.

September 11

"Just then a lawyer stood up to test Jesus. "Teacher", he said, "what must I do to inherit eternal life?" He said to him, "What is written in the law? What do you read there?" He answered, "You shall love the Lord your God with all your heart, and with all your soul, and with all your strength, and with all your mind; and your neighbor as yourself." And he said to him," You have given the right answer; do this and you will live." But wanting to justify himself, asked Jesus, "And who is my neighbor?" Jesus replied, " A man was going down from Jerusalem to Jericho, and fell into the hand of robbers, who stripped him, beat him, and went away leaving him half dead. Now by chance a priest was going down that road; and when he saw him, he passed by on the other side. So likewise a Levite, when he came to the place and saw him, passed by on the other side. But a Samaritan while traveling came near him; and when he saw him, he was moved with pity. He went to him, and bandaged his wounds, having poured oil and wine on them. Then he took him on his own animal, brought him to an inn, and took care of him. The next day he took out two denarii, gave them to the innkeeper, and said, "Take care of him; and when I come back, I will repay you whatever more you spend." Which of these men, do you think, was a neighbor to the man who fell into the hands of the robbers?" He said, "The one who showed him mercy." Jesus said to him, "Go and do likewise."
Luke 10: 25-37

None of us can over forget 9/11. This horrific day in American history caused many changes in our attitude toward the Middle East, towards Muslims, and safety in our beloved country that is used to so much freedom. But there was an outcry from almost all over the world. We were not left like the man in the road. Our friends came to our aid, because it was not only Americans who were killed in New York, Pennsylvania and at the Pentagon, but people of many nationalities. The greatest country in the world had been attacked! The good Samaritans were the firefighters, police and everyone who came to the rescue. Many lives could not be saved that day.

We have a lovely next door neighbor in Annapolis. She is kind, smart, and walks in the footsteps of our Lord. She constantly takes a dish to a sick person or someone who has lost a loved one. She volunteers in the church office and elsewhere in town. If my Day by Day was about to end, a new one would appear in the mail slot. She never would tell us when her birthday was, until 9/11. She had celebrated it in a retreat in Massachusetts, as she had done for so many years. Now we know, and can call her, send a card, or even entertain her if she has arrived home after spending the summer in Vermont. I love God, but I also love my neighbor. *"Love thy neighbor as thyself."*

Salmon Pizza

Pizza Dough

1 cup lukewarm water	1 tsp. rosemary
1 package yeast	1 tbls. olive oil
3 ½ cups flour	½ tsp. sea salt
1 tsp. oregano	

Dissolve the yeast in the water.
Combine all the ingredients in food processor until a ball is formed
Place in an oiled bowl and let rise one hour.
Roll out the dough into a circle the size of a pizza cooking sheet.

Sauce

2 tbls. olive oil	3 cloves garlic, crushed
1 leek chopped	¼ cup basil, chopped
3 ripe tomatoes chopped	2 tbls. fresh parsley, chopped

In a saucepan sauté the leek in olive oil. Add garlic, tomatoes, basil and parsley.
Simmer for 20 minutes, or until tomatoes are tender.
Preheat the oven to 500°
Turn down oven to 425°
Pour the sauce over the dough. Bake 15-20 minutes until tomato mixture is bubbling. Remove from oven.

Topping

½ pound smoked salmon, cut in pieces	½ cup, or more, sour cream
	¼ cup fresh dill, chopped

After the pizza has been removed from the oven sprinkle the salmon over the sauce.
Garnish with sour cream and dill.
Can be served warm or at room temperature.
Crabmeat or other smoked fish can be substituted for the salmon.

September 12

"He that seeketh findeth."
Matthew 7:8

Starting on this date I spent time on Nantucket trying to regroup after my companion's death. I walked the beaches, prayed, met with friends and family. I made the decision to stay on the Island for a while longer. How long I did not know. Fall became winter, and as March approached I knew I could not stay here forever. I made the decision to move to Washington, DC. I had lived there twenty years ago, had friends, and wrote a newsletter on international business, I decided this was where I wanted to be.

During that winter I healed, made very special friends, belonged to St. Paul's Church and served as a Lay Eucharistic Minister. I did a lot of reading and entertaining. Money was running out and I needed a job. Each day I walked, often to the lighthouse. Listening to the foghorn or waves, or at night looking up at the stars, made me feel ever closer to God. I knew in my heart he was helping me get through a terrible tragedy, but also letting me find where I should go. For this I am ever thankful. When you seek something you too will find a way to attain it through God. Listen and let Him speak.

Seafood Chowder

Serves 4

2 tbls. butter
2 leeks, sliced
1 cup corn
1½ cups milk
16 shrimp, cooked, peeled and deveined

½ lb. crab meat
2 cups cream
1/8 tsp. cayenne
Snipped chives

Melt the butter in a large sauce pan. Saute the leeks until tender. Stir in corn. Add milk. Fold in shrimp, crab and cream. Simmer until warmed.
Serve in bowls garnished with chives.

"And God looked upon earth, and, behold, it was corrupt for all flesh had corrupted his way upon the earth...And behold, I, even I, do bring a flood of waters upon the earth, to destroy all flesh, wherein is the breath of life, from under heaven...
Genesis 6:12, 17

"And God remembered Noah, and every living thing, and all the cattle that were with him in the ark: and God made a wind to pass over the earth, and the waters asswaged."
Genesis 8:1

O God, why have you again brought such disaster to this country? I know we are corrupt people, but to bring such misery to millions in Texas with Hurricane Ike. I am praying for them all, and hoping the wind and rain will subside. To let them see the sun and your light, your hope for a brighter and dryer future. Our country may be the greatest in the world, but when nature strikes we know there is a far greater power out there. Only you, O God, can bring relief among the cries. Pray for those who lose everything, often a loved one, not just material possessions. We know what it is like to lose. We must keep the faith and let God restore hope in each of us.

Halibut with Vegetables

Serves 6

½ stick butter
2 lbs. halibut
2 dozen clams
1 carrot, sliced
1 celery stalk, chopped
1 leek, sliced

2 cloves garlic, crushed
½ lb baby spinach
2 tomatoes, diced
1 tsp. chervil
1 tsp. tarragon
½ cup white wine.

Preheat oven to 350°
Melt the butter in skillet. Saute the halibut, two minutes on each side.
Place the fish in a baking dish. Cover with vegetables, herbs, clams and white wine. Cover.
Bake 20 minutes, or until clams open.
Serve with rice.
Striped bass, cod, or other firm fish can be substituted for the halibut.

September 14

"What a Friend we have in Jesus, all our sins and griefs to bear! What a privilege to carry everything to God in prayer! O what peace we often forfeit, O what needless pain we bear, All because we do not carry everything to God in prayer. Have we trials and temptations? Is there trouble anywhere? We should never be discouraged; take it to the Lord in prayer. Can we find a friend so faithful who will all our sorrows share? Jesus knows our every weakness; take it to the Lord in prayer. Are we weak and heavy laden, cumbered with a load of care? Precious Savior, still our refuge, take it to the Lord in prayer. Do your friends despise, forsake you? Take it to the Lord in prayer! In His arms He'll take and shield you; you will find a solace there..."

A friend is someone on whose shoulder you can lean, someone who will listen, someone who truly cares. That person for us is Jesus, our devoted friend.

Joseph Scriven 1820-1886) was born in Ireland and at twenty-five moved to Canada. He led a difficult life, losing his wife-to-be only hours before they were to be married. She was thrown from her horse into a river and drowned. Another bride-to-be also died. He gave of himself by helping others for the rest of his life. In 1857 he wrote this hymn for his mother.

Chicken with Dumplings

Serves 6

2 tbls. olive oil	1 tbls. paprika
2½- 3 lb. chicken, cut into pieces	1 tsp. salt
2 leeks, chopped	1 tsp. pepper
1 tomato, chopped	1 cup water

Heat the olive oil in a skillet. Braise chicken on all sides. Add other ingredients and bring to boil. Cover and cook for at least ½ hour.
Serve chicken with the dumplings and pour sauce from skillet on top.

½ cup cornmeal	2 tbls. vegetable oil
½ cup flour	1 tsp. baking powder
¼ cup milk	½ tsp. sea salt
1 egg	4 cups chicken stock
2 green onions, chopped	

Combine the ingredients in a bowl. Drop by spoonful into boiling chicken stock. Simmer for 10 minutes. Drain.

September 15

For almost a month riots against Christians have been occurring in the state of Orissa, India and sporadically elsewhere, including Bangalore, Mangalore and Kerala. The reports coming in say a Catholic nun was raped, others murdered, and churches, shops, homes and orphanages burned. Christians worship in great secrecy, unable to even speak to neighbors about their religious beliefs. Hindu hardliners are behind these atrocities, attempting to crush Christianity. Troops were called in, but people were told unless they converted to Hinduism their lives were not safe. A number of Christians have fled their homes, leaving behind everything except their faith. India is 80% Hindu, but with over 2,000 ethnic groups, and a caste system still in place, there appears to be little toleration for other religions. Sad, when you think St. Thomas was thought to have visited the country almost 2000 years ago. Please pray for Christians here and elsewhere in the world that are being persecuted. Let the Lord show he gracious and full of compassion.

Cucumber Soup

Serves 6-8

3 cups yogurt
½ cup sour cream
2 tbls. white vinegar
3 cucumbers, peeled and finely chopped, or grated
½ cup currants

4 scallions
¼ cup fresh mint
¼ cup fresh dill, snipped
2 cloves garlic, crushed
½ cup walnuts

In a bowl combine the yogurt, sour cream, and vinegar. Stir in other ingredients. Chill.
Serve in bowls garnished with dill and mint.
Pomegranate seeds or dried cranberries can be substituted for the currants.

September 16

"Let your light shine before others, so that they may see your good works and give glory to your father in heaven."
Matthew 5:16

The summer of 1983 was one of the most enjoyable of my life. My daughter and I were residing in the historic sailing capital - Newport, Rhode Island. Each day we had house guests, either to see the America's Cup races, or just to visit. By the time summer was over my daughter mentioned we had visited the mansions at least fourteen times! What made the summer special were the elegant parties-the America's Cup Ball, a Bonnie Raitt concert, sailing, picnicking, and meeting new friends. A couple of local friends served on the International Race Committee, and through them we were able to meet some of the rival Aussies. I love these people. They are so easy going, laugh a lot, drink a lot, and appear to love life. Two of those friends have returned to Australia, but we still keep in touch. I would have loved to have seen the America's Cup stay in Newport, but Australia claimed victory that year. My Newport friends claimed it was because I became too cozy with them! New technology led to our defeat, and it is still changing. The America's Cup will never be the same. At least Newport still has a fleet of Twelve Meter boats – so graceful, so sparkling on the water. I miss my days there, in a city that has allowed religious tolerance for over 300 years! Let your light shine on others.

Rockfish (Striped Bass) Delight

Serves 6

2 ½ lbs. rockfish filets
1 lb. crabmeat, preferably lump
4 oz. prosciutto
3 scallions, chopped
1 red pepper, chopped

1 pint cherry tomatoes
½ lb. portabella mushrooms, sliced
3 tbls. shallots, minced
1½ cups heavy cream
¼ cup sherry

Preheat oven to 350°
Butter a baking dish. Place filets in dish. Cover with crabmeat, prosciutto, scallions, pepper, tomatoes, mushrooms and shallots.
Pour cream and sherry over fish.
Bake 25 minutes, or until just bubbling and slightly browned.

September 17

"For the word of God is living and active. Sharper than any double-edged sword, it penetrates even to dividing soul and spirit, joints and marrow; it judges the thoughts and attitudes of the heart."
Hebrews 4:12

On September 17, 1787 forty-two of the fifty-five Delegates to the Constitutional Convention met to sign the Constitution of the United States. This valuable document has kept the country together for more than two hundred years. The words have been tested and amended, and fought over. We are a solid nation, even in dire economic times and variable world situations. Yet our country is the most powerful and long lasting. The words our ancestors wrote are not as powerful as the Bible, but we know deep in our hearts they were inspired by the Word. God bless America.

"We the People of the United States, in Order to form a more perfect Union, establish Justice, insure domestic Tranquility, provide for the common defence, promote the general Welfare, and secure the Blessings of Liberty to ourselves and our Posterity, do ordain and establish this Constitution for the United States of America... "

Eggplant Casserole

Serves 4

8 baby eggplant, cut in half lengthwise
4 cloves garlic, crushed
2 large tomatoes, chopped
1 cup basil, chopped

¼ cup olive oil
Juice of 1 lemon
1 cup parmesan cheese
¼ cup parsley, chopped

Preheat oven to 350°
Place the eggplant in a casserole skin side down. Sprinkle with garlic. Top with tomatoes, basil, olive oil, lemon juice, cheese and parsley in that order.
Cover with foil.
Bake 30 minutes, or until eggplant are just tender.

"With great power the apostles continued to testify to the resurrection of the Lord Jesus, and much grace was upon them all."
Acts 4:33

"For the kingdom of God is not meat and drink; but righteousness, and peace, and joy in the Holy Ghost. For he that in these things serveth Christ is acceptable to God, and approved of men."
Romans 14:17-18

One of the earliest churches in Ireland is St. Mary's Collegiate Church in Youghal. St. Declan is thought to have had a monastic settlement here as early as c 450. He was a bishop and abbot who may have preceded St. Patrick. In fact he was considered to be the patron saint of Ireland since St. Patrick was not born there. The church was rebuilt in the Norman style c 750 and the Norman nave c 1220. The building is in a cruciform shape - Christ died on the cross. Saints such as Declan testified to the resurrection and brought Christianity to Ireland. Pray that the church will continue to grow in this Emerald Isle.

Lamb with Currant Sauce

Serves 8 or more

6-7 lbs. boneless leg of lamb	2 tbls. sea salt
2 tbls. rosemary	1 tbls. garlic salt
2 tbls. pepper	

Rub the lamb with the rosemary, pepper, sea salt and garlic salt.
Grill on the BBQ until desired pinkness.

Currant Sauce

Zest of 1 lemon	½ cup currant jelly
Zest of 1 orange	2 tbls. cornstarch
1 tsp. sugar	1 tbls. cold water
½ cup Port	2 tbls. rosemary

In a sauce pan heat the zests, sugar, port and jelly. Bring to a boil. Reduce heat. Combine the cornstarch and water in a bowl. Stir into currant mixture, until just thickened. Add rosemary. Serve in a gravy boat with the lamb.

September 19

"The flood continued forty days on the earth; and the waters increased; and bore up the ark, and it rose high above the earth. The waters swelled and increased greatly on the earth; and the ark floated on the face of the waters... And all flesh died that moved on the earth, birds, domestic animals, wild animals, all swarmimg creatures that swarm on the earth, and all human beings... Only Noah was left, and those that were with him in the ark...In the six hundred first year, in the first month, the first day of the month, the waters were dried up from the earth... Then Noah built an altar to the Lord, and took of every clean animal and of every clean bird, and offered burnt offerings on the altar. And when the Lord smelled the pleasing odor, the Lord said in his heart, "I will never again curse the ground because of humankind, for the inclination of the human heart is evil from youth; nor will I ever again destroy every living creature as I have done. As long as the earth endures, seedtime and harvest, cold and heat, summer and winter, day and night, shall not cease."
Genesis 7:17-8:22

No one could foretell that a massive hurricane would come roaring up the Chesapeake Bay. Hurricane Isabel was predicted to go out to sea, the winds would die, and there would be little damage. How many times do we hear this, and then awake in the middle of the night to find the alarm company calling? So it was at 2:30AM on the night of the 19[th,] 2003. Annapolis was sleeping, but with the tide coming in, a massive surge started racing up the Bay. By 6:30 that morning downtown Annapolis was under 4four feet of water. The media arrived, and we received phone calls and emails from friends and family around the world wanting to know if we were OK. We couldn't even get close to the dock where our boat was moored, and my husband's company was in the midst of the flood. All along the shoreline hundreds of people lost businesses and homes. Four years later some families were still living in FEMA trailers, and still not able to collect insurance on damage. The Bay area was much more fortunate than the southern states that were damaged by Hurricane Katrina. However we must remember that we are still sinners, and God gives, and God takes away. I pray there will never be another flood like in the days of Noah.

Easy Crab Dip

8 oz. cream cheese   3 tbls. horseradish
1 lb. crab meat   ½ cup ketchup

In a bowl combine the ketchup and horseradish.
Soften the cream cheese and put in a flat bowl. Top with the crab, then horseradish mixture. Serve with crackers or pita chips.

September 20

Ask, and you will receive; seek and you will find; knock, and the door will be opened to you."
Matthew 7:7

For fifteen years I had been a single lady, then an old friend called, just two weeks after my arrival in Annapolis. We hadn't seen each other in years, but he had dated my sister and cousin, and I remembered him well. After a few minutes he asked if I would be interested in a date. I said I might be. He came over two nights later. We chatted, caught up and checked each other out. Two nights later we met at the Annapolis Yacht where he introduced me to George. A year and a half later George and I were married. If you wait patiently and let the Lord do the seeking, you will find the doors opened. This I do know and can testify to.

Cheese Ravioli with Clams

Serves 4

2 dozen clams
1 lb. three cheese ravioli
2 tbls. butter

½ pound shitake mushrooms, sliced
1 lb. chorizo, sliced

Preheat oven to 350°
Place the clams on a baking sheet. Put in oven until the clams open.
Cook ravioli according to directions.
Melt the butter in a skillet and sauté mushrooms for 2 minutes. Remove from pan.
Brown chorizo in the skillet. Add clams and mushrooms.
Divide ravioli between 4 pasta bowls. Spoon chorizo, clams and mushrooms on top. Pour brandy balsamic cream over clams.

Brandy Balsamic Cream

2 tbls. butter
3 shallots, chopped finely
¼ cup brandy

½ cup cream
2 tbls. balsamic vinegar
¼ cup parsley

Melt the butter in a sauce pan. Stir in shallots until tender. Add brandy, cream, vinegar and parsley.

"And he went forth again by the sea side; and all the multitude resorted unto him, and he taught them. And as he passed by, he saw Levi the son of Alphaeus sitting at the receipt of custom, and said unto him, Follow me. And he arose and followed him. And it came to pass, that, as Jesus sat at meat in his house, many publicans and sinners sat also together with Jesus and his disciples: for there were many, and they followed him. And when the scribes and Pharisees saw him eat with publicans and sinners, they said unto his disciples, How is it that he eateth and drinketh with publicans and sinners? When Jesus heard it, he saith unto them, They that are whole have no need of the physician, but they that are sick: I came not to call the righteous, but sinners to repentance."
Mark 2:13-17

Jesus constantly reminds us that not only should we entertain our friends, but we need to feed *"the poor, the crippled, the lame, and the blind."* (Luke 14:13) He also dines with sinners and tax collectors. Matthew was first known as Levi the Roman tax collector. When he joined Jesus as a disciple, he took the name Matthew (the gift of Yahweh). Like Matthew, can we too be a gift of God, preaching that Jesus Christ is Lord, the Messiah who came to save us?

Veggie Pasta Salad

Serves 4

¼ cup rice wine vinegar
¼ cup soy sauce
4 tbls. grated ginger
4 cloves garlic, minced
1 tsp. sugar
1 tsp. fresh ground pepper

1 lb. angel hair pasta, cooked according to directions
½ pound fresh snow peas
4 scallions, chopped
1 red pepper, sliced
½ cup toasted almonds
¼ cup cilantro, chopped

In a salad bowl combine the vinegar, soy sauce, ginger, garlic and sugar.
Toss in pasta and vegetables.
Top with nuts and cilantro.

September 22

"Just as I am, without one plea, But that Thy blood was shed for me, And that Thou bidst me come to Thee, O Lamb of God, I come, I come. Just as I am, and waiting not To rid my soul of one dark blot, To Thee whose blood can cleanse each spot, O Lamb of God, I come, I come. Just as I am, though tossed about With many a conflict, many a doubt, Fightings and fears within, without, O Lamb of God, I come, I come. Just as I am, poor, wretched, blind; Sight, riches, healing of the mind, Yea, all I need in Thee to find, O Lamb of God, I come, I come. Just as I am, Thou wilt receive, Wilt welcome, pardon, cleanse, relieve; Because Thy promise I believe, O Lamb of God, I come, I come. Just as I am, Thy love unknown Hath broken every barrier down; Now, to be Thine, yea, Thine alone, O Lamb of God, I come, I come. Just as I am, of that free love The breadth, length, depth, and height to prove, Here for a season, then above, O Lamb of God, I come, I come!"

This hymn should be an inspiration to all of us. Charlotte Elliott (1789-1871) went to a party in London and was asked by Cesar Malan if she was a Christian. She preferred not to answer the question. About three weeks later she saw him again. She asked how she could come to Christ. He answered "Just come to him as you are." From that point on she was inspired in her poetry, music and hymns. Come to the Lord. Let it be in the morning, at noon or night, anywhere, anytime. He is always there!

Roasted Beet Salad

Serves 4

4 medium beets, greens trimmed, leave about ¼ "on beets	½ lb. spring greens
2 tbls. butter	¼ lb blue cheese, crumbled
¼ cup balsamic vinegar	½ cup candied pecans

Preheat the oven to 425°
Place the beets in a covered dish. Add ¼ cup water.
Bake 40 minutes, or until the beets are tender.
Remove beets, peel skins and slice thinly. Stir in butter and balsamic vinegar.
In a salad bowl toss the beets, spring green, blue cheese and pecans.
Goat cheese can be substituted for the blue cheese; walnuts or toasted sliced almonds for the pecans.

"Then was our mouth filled with laughter, and our tongue with singing...The Lord hath done great things for them."
Psalm 126:2

When I moved to Greenwich I knew a few people, but they were mainly old Nantucket friends and a couple of college friends. After several weeks I was speaking on the phone to someone whom I had not met. We suddenly realized that we had both graduated from Briarcliff College, she being much younger, but her sister had been my big sister. Our paths had not crossed in years, but our parents knew each other. My new friend was tall and elegant, a Jackie O look alike. She and her husband sort of adopted me, and we ended up spending much time together and celebrating holidays. At Easter they would trek down to Astoria for the lamb, and at Thanksgiving we cooked two turkeys. My friend was not a cook, but somehow her husband and I managed. She could keep my daughter, nieces and nephew in stitches, and still remembers them as teenagers quite vividly. Laughter makes each day seem better. Even if you can't tell a joke, keep laughing.

Lamb with Port Sauce

Serves 8

6-7 lbs. boneless leg of lamb
2 tbls. pepper

2 tbls. garlic salt
¼ cup rosemary

Rub the lamb with the pepper, salt, and rosemary.
BBQ to desired pinkness. Can also be roasted in 350° oven 20 minutes to pound.

Port Sauce

2 tbls. butter
2 shallots, chopped
½ pint mushrooms
2 tbls. flour

2 tbls. balsamic vinegar
1 cup Port
2 tbls. rosemary

Melt the butter in a sauce pan. Stir in shallots and mushrooms, until just tender. Add the flour, balsamic vinegar and Port. Stir until slightly thickened. Add rosemary.
Serve in a pitcher with lamb.
Mint can be substituted for the rosemary.

"The Lord shall preserve thy going out and thy coming in from this time forth, and even for evermore."
Psalm 121:8

"I have laid the foundation and another buildeth thereon."
I Corinthians 3:10

My paternal grandparents were married when my grandmother was twenty-four and he was fifty-eight. His first wife had died during childbirth. My father was born the following year. Their marriage lasted twenty-six happy years. Sadly he died while my father was serving during the Second World War. I never met my grandfather. One of my nieces was born on their anniversary and good friends also celebrate the date. While visiting my grandmother on Nantucket, I remember the sunroom always had books, and contained several Bibles. As she became blinder she would order the large print Reader's Digest, or sit and listen to music. Each night she made sure we would say our prayers. At home we would say prayers and go to church. However I never remember a Bible in the house. I was given The Book of Common Prayer by my godfather, and still treasure this red leather bound book that sits on my bedside table. Teaching children at an early age that Jesus Christ is Lord and reading his Word will strengthen them throughout life. Thank you for grandparents and parents who reinforce this every day.

Beef Tenderloin

Serves 4

4 oz cream cheese
1 clove garlic, crushed
1 shallot, crushed
2 tsp dried dill

2 tsp. dried parsley
4 beef tenderloin
4 slices smoked bacon
Fresh parsley

In a bowl beat together the cream cheese, garlic, shallot, dill and parsley. Make into four small balls. Refrigerate.
Preheat broiler.
Wrap the bacon around the tenderloin. Place on baking sheet. Cook under broiler until desired pinkness.
Serve the beef with cheese balls and garnished with parsley.

"Love is patient; love is kind; love is not envious or boastful or arrogant. It does not insist on its own way; it is not irritable or resentful; it does not rejoice in wrongdoing, but rejoice in the truth. It bears all things, believes all things, endures all things. Love never ends... And now faith, hope, and love abide, these three, and the greatest of these is love."
1 Corinthians 13:4-8, 13

My parents had somewhat known each other through participation in college glee clubs. On August 12, 1944 they met while waiting in the Sunday newspaper line at the Hub on Nantucket. The next day my father proposed and they were married on September 25. Those were war years. Times were tough. My mother followed my father to several bases, and then he was sent off to the Pacific. She and her sister moved to Los Angeles. Dad returned in December 1945 and I was born nine months later! Today, sixty plus years later they are in great health, divide time between Florida and Nantucket and travel to Europe, or elsewhere for several weeks. They are an inspiration to us all. My parent's lucky numbers, and ours too, have always been 13 and 31.

Honey Cake

1 cup sugar
1 cup honey
½ cup vegetable oil
4 eggs
2 tbls. lemon zest
2 tbls. lemon juice
2 tbls. brandy
3½ cups flour
1½ tsp. baking powder
1 tsp. baking soda

½ tsp. salt
1 tsp. ground cinnamon
½ tsp. ground ginger
¼ tsp. ground nutmeg
¼ tsp. ground cloves
1 tbls. instant coffee
1 tbls. boiling water
½ cup slivered almonds
½ cup raisins

Preheat oven to 350°
In a bowl combine the sugar, honey, oil, eggs, zest, lemon juice and brandy.
Stir in the flour, baking powder, baking soda, salt, spices, coffee and water. Fold in the almonds and raisins.
Pour the batter into a greased tube pan.
Bake 1 hour and 15 minutes, or until toothpick comes out clean. Cool.

September 26

"Make a joyful sound unto the Lord, all ye lands. Serve the Lord with gladness; come before his presence with singing. Know ye that the Lord he is God: it is he that hath made us, and not we ourselves; we are his people and the sheep of his pasture. Enter into his gates with thanksgiving, and into his courts with praise; be thankful unto him, and bless his name. For the Lord is good; his mercy is everlasting; and his truth endureth to all generations."
Psalm 100

The Dalmatian Coast is truly a romantic getaway. Mountains rise up from the Adriatic, small towns lie nestled in coves and on the islands, and cities are built on foundations dating back thousands of years. The sea is blue green in contrast to the starkness of the mountains. In each locale the dominating structure is the church spire. Each church is more magnificent than the last one visited. Feast days are observed with church processions. Children sing and are rewarded with fruits and sweets. Music and folk dance are an intricate part of life, along with local costumes. Fortresses protected the peoples of long ago, and during the recent war. Happily the country is almost unspoiled with little development, and the preservation of the past. After years of Marshall Tito and Communism, this country is blessed that its citizens know the Lord, and can sing anew. Much of the population is Catholic and there are churches everywhere. Altars are often along the side of the church, not just prominently in the front of the nave. Lace making is still done by the Benedictine sisters who sit Vermeer like on the island of Hvar. The beauty of the earth is reflected everywhere here. Make a joyful sound unto the Lord. Sing praises to His name!

Dalmatian Coast Vegetables

Serves

¼ cup olive oil
1 lb. green beans
2 zucchini, sliced
1 yellow squash, sliced
1 eggplant, sliced
2 carrots, peeled and sliced
4 garlic cloves, minced

1 tomato, chopped
½ cup white wine
12 slices pancetta
1 tbls. sea salt
1 tbls. pepper
¼ cup fresh parsley
Parmesan cheese

Heat the olive oil in a large pot. Stir in beans, zucchini, squash, eggplant, carrots, and garlic. Saute for 3 minutes. Add tomato, white wine and pancetta.. Cook for 10 minutes, or until vegetables are tender. Add salt and pepper.
Serve warm in a bowl. Garnish with parsley and parmesan cheese.

"And when he had considered the thing, he came to the house of Mary, the mother of John, whose surname was Mark; where many were gathered together praying."
Acts 12:12

The first landmark you spot when coming into Venice is the towering spires of St. Mark's Basilica. Getting closer you cannot miss the incredible façade with its gorgeous mosaics, gold inlay, and domes. Between that and the Doge's Palace you are overwhelmed with artwork that you have seen on Christmas cards and in art history books. St. Mark's was built in 828 in the Doge's Palace and housed the relics of St. Mark the Evangelist stolen in Alexandria, Egypt. The church and campanile have been rebuilt several times since. The present building dates from 1063 with extensive alterations. Until 1807 the basilica was considered a "state church" and was not under the auspices of the bishop whose cathedral was San Pietro di Castello. Since then is has been the seat of the Patriarch of Venice, and now a cathedral. St. Mark's bones lie in peace in a sarcophagus in the basilica.

Scallops, Shrimp and Angel Hair Pasta

Serves 4

2 tbls. olive oil	¼ cup white wine
1 tbls. ginger	3 tbls. lemon juice
2 cloves garlic, crushed	2 tbls. parsley
1 lb. scallops	2 tbls. tarragon
1 lb. shrimp, cooked, peeled and deveined	1 lb. angel hair pasta

Heat the olive oil and stir in ginger and garlic. Add scallops and shrimp, stirring so they are just warmed. Stir in white wine and lemon juice.
Cook pasta according to directions.
Serve pasta with the shrimp and scallops in four pasta bowls.
Garnish with parsley and tarragon.

September 28

"He watereth the hills from his chambers: the earth is satisfied with the fruit of thy works. He causeth the grass to grow for the cattle, and herb for the service of man: that he may bring forth food out of the earth; And wine that maketh glad the heart of man, and oil to make his face to shine, and bread which strengtheneth man's heart.
Psalm 104:13-15

Living in San Francisco we were able to visit the wineries at harvest time. The hillside vines were laden with grapes. Some of our friends volunteered to assist with the harvest. We opted to do an overnight, visiting as many wineries as we could fit into two days. At lunch we would buy some salami, cheese, French bread and fruit, and sit outside at one of the wineries with a bottle of wine. We were young and giddy then. Yes, we knew the consequences of driving drunk, and that was one reason we would spend the night instead of driving back to the city. As the sun lowered off toward the Pacific we would dine on local produce and perhaps fish or meat. Shrieks of laughter would ring out, friends would toast, and all seemed to be well in the world. How naïve we were! However, we were thankful for all that we had been given, and for a bountiful harvest.

Winery Sandwiches

Serves 4 or more

½ lb. Genoa salami
½ lb. Cappy ham
½ lb. Pepperoni
½ lb. Provolone cheese
½ lb. Monterey Jack cheese with jalapeno
Head of lettuce

2 tomatoes, thinly sliced
1 small jar roasted red peppers
Carmelized onions or sliced onions
4-6 Kaiser or sour dough rolls
Dijon mustard
Mayonnaise

Spread some mayonnaise and mustard on each roll. Divide up the meats, cheese, lettuce, tomato, peppers, and onion among each of the rolls.
You can also serve the meat, cheese and vegetables on a platter with the rolls and let people chose what they want.
Serve with garlic pickles.

"And in the sixth month the angel Gabriel was sent from God unto a city of Galilee, named Nazareth, to a virgin espoused to a man whose name was Joseph, of the house of David, and the virgin's name was Mary. And the angel came in unto her, and said, Hail, thou art highly favored, the Lord is with thee; blessed art thou among women. And when she saw him, she was troubled at his saying, and cast in her mind what manner of salutation this should be. And the angel said unto her, Fear not, Mary; for thou hast found favor with God, And behold, thou shalt conceive in thy womb, and bring forth a son, and shalt call his name Jesus…For with God nothing shall be impossible."
Luke 1:26-37

This is the feast day of Gabriel the Archangel, God's messenger. He interprets Daniel's dream, foretells John's birth to Zacharias and Elisabeth, and most importantly brings tiding to Mary about the impeding birth of the baby Jesus. Mary, unmarried, but betrothed, in those ancient days would produce the long awaited Messiah. I cannot imagine her feelings on hearing this. I am sure she was overwhelmed, but excited as she headed into the hills to the home of Zacharias and Elisabeth who themselves would be parents of John - *And the child grew, and waxed strong in spirit, and was in the deserts till the day of his shewing unto Israel.* (Luke1:80) We must thank Gabriel and all the angels for these miracles.

Angel Food Cake

1 angel food cake mix or store bought cake.

Frosting

1 box confectioner's sugar	½ cup strong coffee
1 stick butter, softened	½ cup cocoa
1 tsp. vanilla	

In a bowl beat together all the ingredients.
Spread on top of angel food cake and let it run down the sides.
Serve with ice cream.

"You have frequently asked me, dearest Innocent, not to pass over in silence the marvelous event which has happened in our own day. I have declined the task from modesty and, as I now feel, with justice, believing myself to be incapable of it, at once because human language is inadequate to the divine praise, and because inactivity, acting like rust upon the intellect, has dried up any little power of expression that I have ever had. You in reply urge that in the things of God we must look not at the work which we are able to accomplish, but at the spirit in which it is undertaken, and that he can never be at a loss for words who has believed on the Word."

These words written to Innocent (d 374) by St. Jerome (c 347-420) as a true believer who early on recognized that the Word was above all else. He translated the Bible from Greek and Hebrew to Latin in what is known as the *Vulgate*. He received a gift from God to bring the Bible to those of other tongues.

*"Every good and perfect gift is from above, coming down from the father of the heavenly lights."*James 1:17 Not only do we celebrate St. Jerome's feast day, but those of dear friends who always remember every birthday, wedding anniversary and holiday. They are there when you need a hug or to say a prayer. These are people who really care about you. They do not want to forget you, or you them. Friends are a gift, a gift from our Lord. Thank them for their friendship and all they do for you.

Baked Potatoes

Serves 4

4 baking potatoes
½ stick butter
4 cloves garlic, crushed
8 basil leaves, chopped
¼ cup sour cream

4 chives, snipped
4 strips bacon, cooked and crumbled
2 green onions, chopped
1 cup sharp cheddar cheese,
shredded

Put the potatoes in a microwave for 10 minutes. Remove, let cool for a couple of minutes. Make a slit in the top of each potato. Remove most of the potato pulp, reserving skins.
Preheat oven to 400°
In a bowl combine potato, butter, garlic, basil, sour cream, chives, bacon, green onions, and cheese.
Put the potato skins in a baking dish. Divide up potato mixture into each skin.
Bake 10 minutes, or until just browned. Serve immediately.

"Peter approached Jesus and asked him, Lord if my brother sins against me, how often must I forgive him? As many as seven times? Jesus answered, I say to you, not seven times but seventy-seven times."
Matthew 18:21-22

"How great a forest is set ablaze by a small fire! And the tongue is a fire."
James 3:5

Forgiveness is very difficult if you have been deeply hurt. Sometimes words are worst than physical abuse. There is the old saying *"Sticks and stones may break my bones, but words will never hurt me."* Words eat into you, and linger. You cannot forget them, no matter how hard you try. If you love someone enough, hopefully time will heal. You ask how can I? How can I forgive? Talk through it with others. Talk to the one you love. Think of Jesus who gave his life for us. Did he forgive those who put Him on the cross?

Meat Balls with Lemon Sauce

Serves 4

1 lb. ground beef	2 tbls. parsley, chopped
2 tbls. rice	1 ½ cups beef broth
¼ cup onion, finely chopped	2 tbls. mint, chopped
½ tsp. salt	2 egg yolks
1 tsp. pepper	¼ cup lemon juice

In a bowl combine the beef, rice, onion, salt pepper, parsley, mint, and ¼ cup broth. Make into small balls.
Bring the remaining broth to a boil. Drop the meat balls into the broth. Cook for 10-15 minutes. Reserve broth.
In a bowl beat the egg yolks with the lemon juice. Slowly add the broth, beating until slightly thickened.
Serve meatballs with lemon sauce and cooked rice.

October 2

"Keep me as the apple of the eye, hide me under the shadow of wings."
Psalm 17:8

When we think of the apple of the eye, we think of a favored person, a person who is cherished and loved. Don't you remember in school how someone might bring in an apple to please a teacher? In the fall my mother would take us to a cider mill where they sold cider and homemade donuts. They melted in your mouth. Then there would be baked apples, apple pie, apple brown Betty, and apples in curries. They are such a diverse food and can be used with all types of spices. Pork chops, apples, cranberries, a little dark rum and cinnamon makes a great dish. They are all comfort foods, just like being protected under the shadow of wings. Put your trust in God.

"How excellent is thy lovingkindness, O God! therefore the children of men put their trust under the shadow of thy wings."
Psalm 36:7

Apple Cake

¼ cup raisins
2 tbls. brandy
½ stick butter
1 cup sugar
2 eggs
1 cup flour
2 tsp. baking powder

1 tsp. salt
1 tsp. ground ginger
1 tsp. ground cinnamon
¼ tsp. nutmeg
3 apples, cored and diced
½ cup walnuts

Preheat oven to 350°
Soak the raisins in the brandy.
Cream the butter and sugar. Beat in eggs. Add flour, baking powder, salt, ginger, cinnamon and nutmeg.
Fold in raisins and brandy, apples and walnut.
Bake in floured tube pan for 35-40 minutes, or until a toothpick comes out clean.
Serve with applesauce, whipped cream, ice cream, or confectioner's sugar.

October 3

Walking down the street I am amazed how many homeless people there are even in what seem to be well-to-do neighborhoods. You see them pushing shopping carts filled with all they own. Even on the hottest days of summer, they wear winter clothes since they have no place to put them. Some look pretty well kempt, others certainly could use a shower. I don't find they beg so much, but rather they appear lost, lost in mind, lost in sickness, lost souls. Closing mental institutions has only brought about larger problems and more people on the street. As the economy keeps crashing I am afraid we will see much more of this. Reach out if you can and help your local organizations with their homeless shelters and food banks. They need our help more than ever in times of crises.

Fresh Vegetable Soup

Serves 4

2 red bliss potatoes, cubed	2 cups chicken stock
1 onion, chopped	1 cucumber, sliced
1 leek, chopped	½ lb. fresh peas
2 celery stalks, sliced	1 apple, peeled, cored and sliced
1 tsp. sea salt	2 cups cream
2 tsp. curry powder	Chives

Cook potatoes, onion, leek, celery, salt, curry and stock until vegetables are just tender. Cool. Pour into food processor with apple and cucumber until just blended. Stir in peas and cream.
Serve in bowls garnished with snipped chives.

October 4

"Most High, omnipotent, good Lord, To thee be ceaseless praise outpoured, And blessing without measure. Let creatures all give thanks to thee And serve in great humility.
"Canticle of the Sun"
Written by Francis of Assisi at St. Clare's Convent of St. Damian's

As children we stand in awe of St. Francis. This gentle man who devoted his life to the poor was born in 1182 and is honored on this day, the day of his death in 1226. In 1210 Pope Innocent III honored him with the Rule for the Order of Friars Minor. But his pity lay with the impoverished. Like St. Catherine he received the stigmata, the marks of Christ's wounds on his hands, feet and side. He is buried in the basilica in Assisi.

On my refrigerator hangs a picture of a beautiful statue of St. Francis. I still think of him, childlike, surrounded by animals and children. I guess that is why so many times I will end up in the Children's Chapel at the Washington National Cathedral. Besides St. Francis at the Cathedral, there is an exquisite kneeler with Noah's ark and a small statue of a young Jesus. James Quinn (1919 -) wrote a lovely hymn *Lord, Make Us Servants of your Peace,* using St. Francis' words.

"Lord make us instruments of your peace. Where there is hatred, let us sow love; where there is injury, pardon; where there is discord, union; where there is doubt, faith; where there is despair, hope; where there is darkness, light; where there is sadness, joy. Grant that we may not so much seek to be consoled as to console; to be understood as to understand; to be loved as to love. For it is in giving that we receive; it is in pardoning that we are pardoned; and it is in dying that we are born to eternal life. Amen"

Rice Salad

Serves 6

2 tbls. red wine vinegar
1 tbls. soy sauce
1 tbls. sugar
¼ cup olive oil
2 cups cooked rice
1 cup cooked wild rice

1 cup fresh peas
1 stalk celery, chopped
1 leek or 2 green onions, sliced
½ cup toasted slivered almonds
¼ cup parsley, chopped

Combine vinegar, soy sauce, sugar and olive oil in a bowl.
Toss in other ingredients.

October 5

"Go ye therefore, and teach all nations, baptizing them in the name of the Father, and of the Son, and of the Holy Ghost."
Matthew 28:19

A lawyer friend, even with a very bad back, travels frequently. Most recently the trips have been to the Baltic countries where he helped organize National Prayer Breakfasts with the leaders of the three countries. The progress that is being made to bring the citizens back into the fold, or encouraging them to continue as Christians, has been overwhelming. The President of Lithuania hosted the breakfast in the presidential palace, and was the keynote speaker. Less than twenty years ago this would have been unthinkable in a Communist country. Prayer breakfasts for political leaders in our country date back to 1942 when a group of Senators met for spiritual support. The first National Prayer Breakfast began in 1953 with President Eisenhower in attendance. The event is held annually on the first Thursday in February. Please pray for our leaders, show them wisdom, courage to make the right decisions, and above all to keep Jesus Christ in their hearts and minds.

Tomato Frittata

Serves 4

3 tbls. butter
7 eggs
1 leek, sliced
1 large tomato, finely chopped
¼ lb. baby spinach

2 tbls. chives, snipped
1 small wheel brie, thinly sliced
Parsley

Preheat the oven to 400°
Beat the eggs in a bowl.
Melt the butter an iron skillet.
Pour the eggs into the skillet and gently scrap sides of skillet to keep eggs from sticking.
As eggs are just beginning to set, sprinkle with leek, tomatoes, spinach and chive. Make a circle on the eggs with the brie.
Bake 10 minutes.
Serve garnished with the parsley.
Cheddar, Monterey Jack, feta or other types of cheese can be used.

October 6

"Sunset and evening star, And one clear call for me! And may there be no moaning of the bar, When I put out to sea, But such a tide as moving seems asleep, Too full for sound and foam, When that which drew from out the boundless deep Turns again home. Twilight and evening bell, And after that the dark! And may there be no sadness of farewell, When I embark; For tho' from out our bourne of Time and Place The flood may bear me far, I hope to see my Pilot face to face When I have crost the bar."

This lovely poem was written by Alfred Lord Tennyson (1809-92) and set to music by Hubert Parry. At the request of John M. Hay it was played at his funeral on July 5, 1905 in Cleveland. John Hay was a Secretary of State from Ohio. In 1978 I founded the John Hay Forum as the junior committee of the Council on World Affairs. We would sponsor meetings with speakers and attendees under forty. Our first speaker was Strobe Talbot, who later became Under Secretary of State. What impressed me was the dedication our small committee had to make this a better world and to understand what was going on. There were still signs that Communism could continue forever. Yet, there was hope, that darkness would turn to light, and peace could reign.

Pierogi

Dough

1 stick butter
1 cup flour

1/3 cup sour cream

Combine the ingredients in food processor until a ball forms.
On a floured board roll out the dough. Cut into circles with a glass

Filling

½ lb. ground lamb
2 green onions, chopped
1 hardboiled egg, chopped
¼ cup pignoli

8 green olives, chopped
Dash of cayenne
½ tsp. oregano
1 egg, beaten with 1 tbls. water

Preheat oven to 400°
Saute the lamb until just browned. In a bowl combine the lamb, green onions, egg, nuts, olives, cayenne and oregano.
Place a small amount of filling on each dough round. Fold over and seal. Brush with egg wash. Place on baking sheet and bake 12 minutes, or until golden.

"For a bishop as God's steward, must be blameless; he must not be arrogant or quick-tempered or addicted to wine or violent or greedy for gain; but he must be hospitable, a lover of goodness, prudent, upright, devout and self-controlled. He must have a firm grasp of the word that is trustworthy in accordance with the teaching, so that he may be able both to preach with sound doctrine, and to refuse those who contradict it."
The Letter of Paul to Titus 1:7-9

I first heard Archbishop Tutu speak at Trinity Church in Newport just prior to national elections. I regret I remember little of his sermon, except that at the end he exhorted us all to vote on Tuesday. In his country, South Africa, he did not have that privilege. Please remember if someone is elected, or not elected, to public office, every vote counts. Desmond Mpilo Tutu (b 1931) during the 1980s, was a major opponent of apartheid and spoke up for causes on poverty, human rights, and the oppressed. In 1984 he became the second South African to be awarded the Nobel Peace Prize. In 1986 he was elected and ordained the first black South African Anglican Archbishop of Cape Town, South Africa, and primate of the Church of the Province of Southern Africa. Archbishop Tutu chaired the Truth and Reconciliation Commission and is currently the chairman of The Elders. He has also received numerous other awards including the Albert Schweitzer Prize for Humanitarianism, and the Gandhi Peace Prize in 2007.

Chicken with Pomegranate Sauce

Serves 6

6 boneless chicken breasts
¼ cup olive oil
1 tbls. sea salt
1 orange, cut into 6 slices
1 cup orange juice

3 tbls. butter
2 tbls. flour
1 leek. sliced
1 pomegranate, peeled and diced
2 tbls. rosemary

Preheat oven to 350°
Rub the chicken breasts with the olive oil and sea salt.. Place each breast on an orange slice in a baking dish. Pour ½ cup orange juice over the chicken.
Bake 30 minutes.
Remove chicken from baking dish and reserve liquid.
In a pan melt the butter and stir in the flour. Add remaining orange juice and liquid from chicken. Stir until slightly thickened. Add leek, pomegranate and rosemary.
Serve the chicken with rice and pomegranate sauce.

"Be kind to one another, tenderhearted, forgiving one another, as God in Christ has forgiven you."
Ephesians 4:32

"Oh Lord what do I do? He got drunk, he said things that I cannot forget. He told me he was going to kiss her the way he always did; he would never dance with me again, only her. I have done nothing wrong. I have only loved him. Marriage is a sacred institution, a promise to love one another. Unfortunately sometimes we cannot forget and forgive. We have been abused by those we have trusted the most. Lord, accept us as we are. We are your faithful servants. Please don't let this ever happen again. If it does I will have to call 911. I have trusted, I have loved, I have kept Jesus walking beside me. He has not. I don't know if I can change him. I only know I have to protect myself, my children and those I truly love. Lord, please be with me and let me make the right decisions."

"Let us not grow weary in doing what is right, for we will reap at harvest-time, if we do not give up."
Galatians 6:9

Fettuccine with Shrimp

Serves 4

1 lb. fettuccine, cook according to directions
½ stick butter
4 green onions, chopped
4 garlic cloves, minced
1 pint cherry tomatoes

¼ lb. prosciutto
1 lb. shrimp, cooked and deveined
1 cup heavy cream
1 tsp. pepper
Parmesan cheese
¼ cup fresh basil chopped

Melt the butter in a skillet. Stir in onions and garlic. Add tomatoes, prosciutto, shrimp, cream and pepper.
Divide the fettuccine among 4 pasta plates. Top with shrimp sauce.
Garnish with parmesan cheese and basil.
1 lb. sliced asparagus can also be added.

"And their father Israel said unto them, if it must be so now, do this; take of the best fruits in the land in your vessels, and carry down the man a present, a little balm, and a little honey, spices and myrrh, nuts, and almond:"
Genesis 43:11

The story of Joseph is one of the first stories children learn in the Bible after the stories of Jesus. How can we forget a young boy being left by his brothers in a pit, and then becoming the right hand person to pharaoh? Later he is reunited with his father and family, and forgives his brothers for selling him to the Israelites. *"And it came to pass, when Joseph was come unto his brethren, that they stript Joseph out of his coat, his coat of many colours that was on him;"*
Genesis 38:23

Joseph and the Coat of Many Colors also became a smashing hit on Broadway as *Joseph and the Amazing Technicolor Dreamcoat*. This was the second play written by Andrew Lloyd Webber and Tim Rice, and was first performed in 1970.

Be strong like Joseph, have courage in your convictions, and *"Above all else, guard your heart, for it is the wellspring of life."*
Proverbs 4:23

Granola

4 cups rolled oats	½ cup maple syrup
1 cup almonds	½ cup canola oil
1 cup walnuts or pecans	1 cup dates
½ cup sesame seeds	1 cup raisins
1 cup coconut	1 cup dried apricots

Preheat oven to 300°
Place all the ingredients in a baking dish. Bake for1 hour, stirring each 15 minutes. Remove from oven. Cool. Store in sealed container.
Honey can be substituted for the maple syrup.

October 10

"The king's daughter is all glorious within; her clothing is of wrought gold. She shall be brought unto the king in raiment of needlework..."
Psalm 45:13

During my graduate year at the University of Pennsylvania several old friends were seniors. Having attended a small girls' school in New York without sororities and fraternities I only had a few occasions to attend sorority or fraternity parties. These friends all owned dinner jackets and evening gowns. On football nights the ladies would dress in gorgeous gowns and fix dinner. The men would dress in dinner jackets and bring the drinks. So little of this is done any more, but I am hoping with *"Dancing with the Stars"* and other TV shows elegant evenings might come back among the young. These evenings were filled with laughter, some intellectual stuff, but it was the camaraderie of friends with mutual interests. Sadly one of those friends died recently – too short a life. Her mother was grateful for our remembrances of her and sharing them with the family. But it never brings back an old friend. Treasure those moments and friendships. Even though many of my parent's friends are passing away, they still maintain friendships seventy years later. It's not the clothing we wear, but the friends we keep.

Fall Squash

Serves 6

2 medium yellow squash	2 tsp. thyme
2 medium zucchini	¼ cup dill, snipped
1 onion, chopped	1 tsp. salt
8 slices bacon, cooked and crumbled	1 tsp. pepper
	½ stick butter, melted
6 cloves garlic, minced	1 cup Gruyere cheese, grated

Preheat the oven to 350°
Slice the squash and zucchini. Place in a rectangular baking dish. Top with other ingredients.
Bake ½ hour, or until bubbling and just browned.

"Ah, holy Jesus, how hast Thou offended, That man to judge Thee hath in hate pretended? By foes derided, by Thine own rejected, O most afflicted. Who was the guilty who brought this upon Thee? Alas, my treason, Jesus, hath undone Thee. 'Twas I, Lord Jesus, I it was denied Thee: I crucified Thee. Lo, the Good Shepherd for the sheep is offered; The slave hath sinned, and the Son hath suffered: For man's atonement, while he nothing heedeth, God intercedeth. For me, kind Jesus, was Thine incarnation, Thy mortal sorrow, and Thy life's oblation: Thy death of anguish and Thy bitter passion, For my salvation. Therefore, kind Jesus, since I cannot pay Thee, I do adore Thee, and will ever pray Thee, Think on my pity and Thy love unswerving, Not my deserving."

Johann Heermann (1585-1647), a German poet and hymnist, was ordained in the Lutheran Church. Most of his life he was ill, but survived the plague. Following his first illnesses his mother vowed that if he survived, he would enter university and the ministry. His earliest poetry was in Latin, based on passages from the Gospels. Because of his illnesses he could sympathize with our Lord, and ask why me? Though in this hymn it is why thee? It is Christ that died for our sins. We are the guilty ones, please love us anyway Lord. Take pity on what we have done, never sway from our sides. As we sing this hymn during Holy Week, remember Christ was sacrificed for us.

Pistachio Pesto and Pasta

Serves 4

2 tbls. butter	1 lb. cheese ravioli
1 lb. wild mixed mushrooms	

Melt the butter in a skillet. Stir in mushrooms.
Cook ravioli according to instructions. Drain.
Serve ravioli with mushrooms and pesto sauce.

Pesto

1 cup fresh basil	½ cup fresh grated parmesan cheese
2 tbls. lime juice	½ cup shelled pistachios
1 tbls. olive oil	

Combine the ingredients, except pistachios, in a food processor. After processing add pistachios.

October 12

"O death, where is thy sting? O grave, where is thy victory? The sting of death is sin; and the strength of sin is the law. But thanks be to God, which giveth us the victory through our Lord Jesus Christ. Therefore, my beloved brethren, be ye stedfast, unmoveable, always abounding in the work of the Lord, forasmuch as ye know that your labour is not in vain in the Lord."
1 Corinthians 15:55-58

Life sometimes ends too quickly. One of my 9 cousins was the only one to get mixed up in drugs and alcohol. She married someone she met in rehab. Their son went through tumultuous times, but somehow graduated from high school and now is a Navy Seal. We are so proud of him and all those that serve in our Armed Services. My cousin was not so lucky. In her mid fifties she had a massive heart attack and died immediately. Drugs and alcohol do kill. If you know of someone with a problem try to get them to AA or rehab. Hopefully it will save a life. We can only lament afterwards.

Pear Salad

Serves 4

Walnut vinaigrette
½ lb. mixed spring greens
Carmelized pears

4 slices smoked bacon, cooked and crumbled
¼ lb. blue cheese

Pour the vinaigrette into a salad bowl. Toss with other ingredients.

Walnut Vinaigrette

¼ cup walnut oil
2 tbls. balsamic vinegar
2 tbls. honey

¼ cup walnuts
2 tbls. lemon juice

Combine the ingredients in a jar and shake well.

Carmelized Pears

2 tbls. butter
2 large ripe pears, peeled, seeded and sliced

2 tbls. brown sugar

Melt the butter in skillet. Stir in pears until tender. Add brown sugar.

"Christ is made the sure foundation, Christ the head and cornerstone, chosen of the Lord, and precious, binding all the Church in one; holy Zion's help for ever, and her confidence alone. All that dedicated city, dearly loved of God on high, in exultant jubilation pours perpetual melody; God the One in Three adoring in glad hymns eternally. To this temple, where we call thee, come, O Lord of Hosts, today; with thy wonted loving-kindness hear thy servants as they pray, and thy fullest benediction shed within its walls alway. Here vouchsafe to all thy servants what they ask of thee of gain; what they gain from thee, for ever with the blessèd to retain, and hereafter in thy glory evermore with thee to reign. Laud and honor to the Father, laud and honor to the Son, laud and honor to the Spirit, ever Three, and ever One, consubstantial, co-eternal, while unending ages run."

Words: Latin, c7th century, trans. John Mason Neale, 1851 Music: Westminster Abbey, Regent Square, Oriel, Urbs beata Jerusalem, Urbs coelestis

Edward the Confessor (c1003-66) was the last of the House of Wessex to rule England. In 1245 Henry III began building what was to become Westminster Abbey on the site of a Benedictine monastery. The Abbey is dedicated to Edward the Confessor and is the site of royal coronations, weddings, funerals, and the burial place of St. Edward, Queen Elizabeth I, and numerous other famous people. Daily worship is offered in the Abbey, but it is not a cathedral or church. Instead it is a Royal Peculiar under a Dean and Chapter and subject only to the Sovereign. The Feast of the Translation of St. Edward the Confessor occurs around this date and includes a Pilgrimage to the Shrine, evensong, and a Sung Eucharist.

Apple Fritters

2 cups flour	1 tbls. cinnamon
1 pint beer	½ tsp. nutmeg
6 apples	Vegetable oil
1 tbls. lemon juice	Confectioner's sugar
1 cup sugar	

Place the flour in a bowl, and make a well. Slowly stir in the beer. Let sit 1 hour. Peel and core the apples. Chop into small bitesize pieces. Sprinkle the apples with the lemon juice, sugar, cinnamon and nutmeg. Pour into the batter.
Heat oil in a skillet, about 3 inches. Drop the batter, using a large spoon, into the hot oil. Brown on all sides.
Sprinkle with powdered sugar before serving.

October 14

"People were bringing even infants to him that he might touch them; and when the disciples saw it, they sternly ordered them not to do it. But Jesus called for them and said, "Let the little children come to me, and do not stop them; for it is to such as these that the kingdom of God belongs. Truly I tell you, whoever does not receive the kingdom of God as a little child will never enter it."
Luke 18:15-17

A group of us gathered weekly on Long Island for a Bible Study group. These ladies ranged in age from about 40 to over 90. Several were very involved with the Billy Graham Crusade which came to Long Island while I was a member. The oldest lady would often close her eyes, and perhaps even dose off. But somehow as we finished she would always remind us of her love for children by reciting the passage above. At least three of these ladies have now gone to our Lord. We live only a fleeting time on earth and to ashes we will return. Savor every moment of each day, and take time to pray. Take time to pray for the children of the world, the elderly and sick.

Spaghetti

I can't think of any child who does not like spaghetti.

Serves 4

2 tbsp. olive oil	2 tbsp. fresh parsley
1 small onion, chopped	2 tbsp. Italian herbs
½ red pepper, diced	¼ tsp. cayenne
1½ pounds ground beef	1 tsp. chili powder
2 cloves garlic, minced	1 lb. spaghetti or linguine
1 15 oz. can diced tomatoes	Fresh grated Parmesan cheese
1 15 oz. can tomato sauce	

Heat the olive oil in a skillet. Add the onion and pepper and sauté until tender. Add the ground beef and brown. Add garlic, tomatoes, tomato sauce, parsley, herbs, and cayenne.
Simmer for ½ hour or more.
Cook the spaghetti according to the directions.
Serve the spaghetti with the meat sauce and sprinkle with grated cheese.

October 15

I spent nine of my early years growing up in the small town of New Castle, Delaware. Everyone knew each other. Children played in the streets. Only a few families had TVs and much of the laundry was done on the back porch and hung out in the garden to dry. Several doors down from us lived a couple with three sons. We were two girls and a boy, but our ages were almost identical. The father was a private school master. Both he and his wife were fantastic sailors. He did a number of the Bermuda races and she raced in Lightning class sailboats. As a guest member of the Royal Hellenic Yacht Club in Athens, Greece, she won the 1964 King's Cup and was awarded the trophy by King Constantine. Sadly these very special family friends died the same week in October. They lived life to its fullest. Their children are still some of our closest friends with two living nearby. Life is fleeting. Enjoy every moment. You do not know what will be around the bend. The Lord will strengthen you in all you do.

Coffee Mousse

Serves 4

1 envelope unflavored gelatin	2 tbls. Kahlua
¼ cup hot espresso coffee	2 tbls. dark rum
3 egg, separated	1 cup heavy cream
¼ cup sugar	1 tsp. vanilla
2 tbls. brandy	

Dissolve the gelatin in the coffee.
Beat the egg yolks and sugar until thickened. Stir in brandy, Kahlua and rum. Add gelatin.
Pour into soufflé dish. Refrigerate until thickened.
Beat egg whites until peaks form.
Beat cream until thickened.
Fold egg whites, cream and vanilla into soufflé. Refrigerate.
Can also be made in individual soufflé bowls.

October 16

"This is a true saying, If a man desire the office of bishop, he desireth a good work. A bishop then must be blameless, the husband of one wife, vigilant, sober, of good behavior, given to hospitality, apt to teach; Not given to wine, no striker, not greedy of filthy lucre; but patient, not a brawler, not covetous; One that ruleth well his own house...For if a man know not how to rule his own house, how shall he take care of the church of God?"
1 Timothy 3:1-5

Thomas John Claggett (1743-1816), was the first bishop of the Episcopal Church in the United States of America to be consecrated on American soil and the first bishop of the Episcopal Diocese of Maryland. He was born near Nottingham, Maryland and graduated from Princeton University. He was ordained a deacon in 1762 and consecrated bishop of Maryland in 1792 at Trinity Church, New York. In 1800 he was named chaplain of the United States Senate. He founded Trinity Episcopal Church in Upper Marlboro, Maryland in 1810 and consecrated Christ Church, Alexandria, Virginia, on January 9, 1814. Following their deaths, Bishop and Mrs. Claggett's remains were moved in 1898 to Washington National Cathedral, where a wood carving of his consecration was put on the bishop's stall.

I am a descendant of the Claggett family and feel very fortunate to have returned to my roots in Maryland, and join a very large roster of Claggetts (Clagget, Clagett). Bishop Claggett is an inspiration for all of us. Each time I pass his and Mrs. Claggett's plaques on the wall at the Cathedral I am reminded of his faithfulness, and serving our state as its first bishop.

Peanut Butter Cookies

2 sticks butter
1 cup peanut butter
1 cup sugar
1 cup brown sugar
2 eggs

1 tbls. milk
2 cups flour
1 tsp. baking soda
1 cup salted peanuts

Preheat the oven to 350°
Cream together the butter, peanut butter and sugars. Beat in eggs, milk, flour and baking soda. Fold in peanuts.
Drop by teaspoon on greased cookie sheet.
Bake 10 minutes.
For a real chocolate treat stick a Hershey's Kiss in each cookie as they come out of the oven and are still soft.

October 17

"And the manna was as coriander seed, and the color thereof as the color of bdellium."
Numbers 11:7

Coriander is a member of the parsley family. The seed is used in garam masala, a mix of Indian spices, in pastries, and also to reduce stress and stomach disorders. The ancient Egyptians thought it would bring about immortality. As you enjoy this curry let your body and mind be refreshed, and may you have abundance as the Israelites did when God gave them manna.

Several important events occurred on this date in history:
832 BC - the inauguration of the first temple in Jerusalem by King Solomon
539 BC - King Cyrus the Great of Persia marched into the city of Babylon to lead the Jews into Jerusalem after seventy years of exile.
1532 - Pope Clement VII issued a brief halting the Portuguese Inquisition, the tribunals used to prosecute heretics.

Chicken Curry

Serves 4

2 tbls. butter
2 celery stalks, chopped
1 medium onion, chopped
3 cloves garlic, minced
2 tbls. garam masala
1 tbls. curry powder
2 tbls. fresh grated ginger
1 tsp. coriander seed
1 tsp. cayenne
2 tsp. cumin
¼ cup flour

2 cups chicken stock
1 apple, peeled, cored and diced
½ cup raisins
1 tbls. lemon juice
3 boneless chicken breasts, cooked and diced
¼ cup cilantro, chopped
1 banana, smashed
1 cup peanuts
½ cup coconut
2 eggs, hardboiled and chopped
2 cups rice, cooked

Melt the butter in a skillet. Stir in celery and onion until tender.
Add garlic, garam marsala, curry, ginger, coriander, cayenne, cumin and flour.
Stir in chicken stock until slightly thickened.
Add raisins, lemon juice, and chicken breasts.
Simmer for 20 minutes.
Serve curry over rice. Garnish with cilantro, banana, peanuts, coconut and eggs.

October 18

"Forasmuch as many have taken in hand to set forth in order a declaration of those things which are most surely believed among us. Even as they delivered them unto us, which from the beginning were eyewitnesses, and ministers of the word; It seemed good to me also, having had perfect understanding of all things from the very first to write unto thee in order, most excellent Theophilus, That thou mightest know the certainty of those things, wherein thou hast been instructed."
Luke 1:1-4

Luke, our faithful physician, was probably born in Antioch. He is thought to have traveled extensively with Paul on his missionary trips. He wrote the third Gospel and some of Acts. His writings trace Jesus from his birth, right through his ascension, unlike the other Gospels. We are thankful for Luke, his poetry, his knowledge of medicine, and his love of his Lord. His words also became our hymns "And Mary said, *My soul doth magnify the Lord...*" (The Magnificat)

Paella

Serves 6

2 tbls. olive oil
1 lb. chorizo, sliced
2 leeks, sliced
2 cloves garlic, crushed
1 cup chicken stock
1 cup white wine
24 mussels, cleaned
12 clams

½ lb. smoked ham, diced
2 boneless cooked chicken breast
1 lb. shrimp, cooked, deveined and peeled
1 lb. lobster meat
15 oz. can artichoke hearts
½ lb. fresh peas
¼ tsp. saffron

Heat the olive oil and brown the chorizo.
Stir in leeks and garlic. Add stock, wine, mussels and clams.
Cover and cook until the mussels and clams open.
Add the other ingredients. Just heat.
Serve with rice, crusty bread, and a salad.

"Lord, now lettest thou thy servant depart in peace, according to thy word. For mine eyes have seen thy salvation, Which thou hast prepared before the face of all people; To be a light to lighten the Gentiles, and to be the glory of thy people Israel."
Nunc Dimitis Luke 2:29

This beautiful verse is often spoken at the end of evensong. Let us depart, but also let us be a light. *"And he said, It is a light thing that thou shouldest be my servant to raise up the tribes of Jacob, and to restore the preserved of Israel: I will also give thee for a light to the Gentiles, that thou mayest be my salvation unto the end of the earth."* Isaiah 49:6 We see in these words the foretelling of the coming of our Lord, the human that would open the eyes of the world to all that is good, and to rid us of evil. Like the night that comes which is darkness, the light comes to us as the truth – The Word.

Vegetarian Lasagna

Serves 6-8

12 lasagna noodles	15 oz. can artichoke hearts, drained
16 oz. tomato sauce	2 carrots, shredded
4 cloves garlic, minced	2 8 oz. packages cream cheese
1 tbls. fresh oregano	6 scallions, chopped
1 lb. broccoli, chopped	1 cup mozzarella
½ lb. baby spinach	1 cup parmesan cheese

Cook lasagna noodles according to directions. Drain.
Preheat oven to 350°
In a bowl combine the tomato sauce, garlic and oregano. Spread ½ cup of mixture on the bottom of a 9x13 baking dish. Spread 4 noodles over the tomato sauce.
In a bowl combine the cream cheese and scallions.
In another bowl combine the broccoli, spinach and artichoke hearts. Spread ½ mixture on top of noodles. Top with ½ cup tomato sauce and ½ cream cheese mixture. Top with 4 more lasagna noodles.
Repeat layer with ½ cup tomato sauce, rest of broccoli mixture and cream cheese.
Top with remaining 4 noodles and tomato sauce. Sprinkle with mozzarella and parmesan cheese.
Bake until bubbling about 40-45 minutes. Serve warm, cut into squares.

"For every creature of God is good, and nothing to be refused, if it be received with thanksgiving."
1 Timothy 4:4

Life can be lived long, and it can be shut off quickly. One of the legends of the Eastern Shore boat builders lived to be almost 90. Sadly, even as he was building another boat, his life was cut short by a speeding trooper's car. His sister and dog died too. This man built catboats, workboats, anything anyone needed. He used other people's plans, but also his own. Our beloved catboat Kit Kat has letters like the candy bar. Maynard loved the water, loved women, and could tell a good story. But he was the legend. Now he's gone to our Lord.

"All these trust in their hands: and every one is wise in his work."
Ecclesiasticus 38:31

Deviled Oysters

Serves 4

1 quart oysters, reserve ½ cup liquor	¼ cup parsley, chopped
1 large onion, chopped	4 chives, snipped
1 red pepper, chopped	½ tsp. salt
2 cloves garlic, minced	1 tsp. pepper
½ stick butter	1 tsp. Worcestershire sauce
2 tbls. flour	1/8 tsp. Tabasco sauce
1½ cups cream	½ cup fine bread or cracker crumbs
4 egg yolks, beaten	2 tbls. butter
Preheat oven to 350°	

In a skillet sauté the onion, pepper and garlic. Stir in flour. Add cream. Stir until slightly thickened.
Add liquor, egg yolks, parsley, chives, salt, pepper, Worcestershire sauce and Tabasco sauce. Fold in oysters.
Pour into a greased casserole, or individual ramekins. Sprinkle with bread crumbs and dot with butter. Bake 20 minutes, or until just bubbling and browned.

"When peace, like a river, attendeth my way, When sorrows like sea billows roll; Whatever my lot, Thou hast taught me to say, It is well, it is well with my soul. (Refrain:) It is well (it is well), with my soul (with my soul), It is well, it is well with my soul."

Horatio Spafford (1828-88) was a prosperous lawyer when the Great Chicago Fire took place on October 8, 1871. He had invested in buildings that were mostly destroyed by the fire. This was just after the death of his son. He decided to send his family to England, but the ship was struck by an iron sailing vessel and all four of his daughters perished. As he sailed to England to meet his wife, he wrote the hymn *It is Well with my Soul*. The Spafford's had two more children, one of whom also died. After all these losses the family led a group to Jerusalem in 1881 to set up a Christian utopian society known as the American Colony. They worked among the local people – with Jews, Muslims and Christians. Mr. Spafford died of malaria and was buried in Jerusalem.

Each time I read through Mr. Spafford's story tears well up in my eyes. How could a man, a good Christian man, he was a Presbyterian, continually lose most of his family and still keep the faith? The fact that he and his wife Anna were strong enough to found the American Colony shows that their strength came through the Lord. They set up soup kitchens, orphanages, hospitals, and performed whatever charitable work they could for people of every religion. Their heroism and bravery in ministering in Jerusalem, where Christ died for us, continues today with the Spafford's Children Center beside the walls of the Old City of Jerusalem.

Spice Cookies

4 cups flour

1 tsp. baking powder

1 tsp. ground cloves

½ tsp. ground allspice

¾ cup honey

1 cup dark Karo syrup

¾ cup sugar

½ stick butter

Preheat oven to 400°

In a sauce pan bring the honey, corn syrup and sugar to a boil. Heat until sugar is dissolved.

Add butter. Beat in flour, baking powder, cloves and allspice.

Drop by teaspoons onto a cookie sheet.

Bake 15 minutes.

"The Lord is my shepherd, I shall not want; He maketh me to lie down in green pastures; he leadeth me beside the still waters. He restoreth my soul; he leadeth in the path of righteousness for his name's sake. Yea, though I walk through the valley of the shadow of death, I will fear no evil: for thou art with me; thy rod and thy staff they comfort me. Thou preparest a table before me in the presence of mine enemies: thou anointest my head with oil; my cup runneth over. Surely goodness and mercy shall follow me all the days of my life; and I will dwell in the house of the Lord forever."
23rd psalm

The 23rd Psalm is read at funerals, but is memorized by all Christians in times of hope and in times of despair. The psalm can be read or sung, each with its own words piercing through to the core of our hearts. It may bring tears, tears of happiness, or tears of sadness. The psalm shows God as our protector and provider. The psalm is attributed to David as a young man and shepherd, reminding us also of Jesus the Good Shepherd in St. John's Gospel.

Sheep have been domesticated for thousands of years, using the meat and milk for food, the coat for clothing, and the fat for candles and cooking. During a trip to Chile I had the opportunity to visit a sheep farm. They demonstrated how the sheep were sheared. They turned them over them on their backs, held them tightly and clipped away, the process only taking a few minutes. At first I was slightly aghast at the handling of the animal, but it is done very humanely and the coat will grow back quickly. The shepherds and dogs are very protective of their flocks. Just as the Lord is to us. The Lord is our shepherd.

Kibbi

1½ cups burghul (crushed wheat)	½ tsp. sea salt
1 lb. ground lamb	1 tsp. pepper
¼ tsp. allspice	2 tbls. pignoli (pine nuts)
¼ tsp. nutmeg	¼ cup onion, chopped
¼ tsp. cayenne	1 cup olive oil

Combine all the ingredients, except oil, in a bowl. Divide the meat into 8 balls.
Heat the oil in a skillet.
Drop the balls into the skillet and brown, about 10 minutes.
Serve with rice and pita bread.

"When morning gilds the skies my heart awaking cries: May Jesus Christ be praised! When evening shadows fall, this rings my curfew call, may Jesus Christ be praised! When mirth for music longs, This is my song of songs; "May Jesus Christ be praised!" God's holy house of prayer Hath none that can compare With "Jesus Christ be praised!" No lovelier antiphon In all high heav'n is known Than "Jesus Christ be praised!" There to the eternal Word The eternal psalm is heard: "May Jesus Christ be praised!" Ye nations of mankind, In this your concord find; "May Jesus Christ be praised!" Let all the earth around Ring joyous with the sound: "May Jesus Christ be praised!" Sing, suns and star of space, Sing, ye that see His face, Sing, "Jesus Christ be praised!" God's whole creation o'er, Both now and evermore Shall Jesus Christ be praised! "

Robert Seymour Bridges (1844-1930) studied medicine at Oxford, and practiced medicine until lung disease forced him to retire in 1882. This lovely hymn was written c1800 and translated from the German by Mr. Bridges. He was a poet and became Poet Laureate in 1913. He also translated *Ah, Holy Jesus* and *Jesu, Joy of Man's Desiring*.

Today we also celebrate the life of James, brother of Jesus. During Jesus' life James was not sure who his brother really was. With the Resurrection there was little doubt He was the Messiah. *May Jesus Christ be praised*.

Almond Cake

2 sticks butter	2 tsp. baking powder
1 cup sugar	¼ cup milk
3 eggs	Zest of one orange
12 oz. can almond paste	2 tbls. Curacao
2 ¼ cups flour	¼ cup sliced almonds

Preheat oven to 350°
Cream the butter and sugar in a bowl. Add the eggs and almond paste. Stir in the flour, baking powder and lemon zest.
Pour into a greased tube pan.
Bake 50 minutes. Cool
Sprinkle with Curacao and almonds.

October 24

"And Saul, yet breathing out threatenings and slaughter against the disciples of the Lord, went unto the high priest, and desired of him letters to Damascus to the synagogues, that if he found any of this way, whether they were men or women, he might bring them bound into Jerusalem. And as he journeyed, he came near Damascus: and suddenly there was around about him a light from heaven: and he fell to the earth, and heard a voice saying unto him, Saul, Saul, why persecutest thou me? And he said, Who art thou, Lord? And the Lord said I am Jesus whom thou persecutest: it is hard for thee to kick against the pricks. And he trembling and astonished said, Lord, what wilt thou have me to do? And the Lord said unto him, Arise and go into the city, and it shall be told thee what thou must do...And Saul arose from the earth; and when his eyes were opened, but he saw no man: but they led him by the hand, and brought him into Damascus. And he was three days without sight, and neither did eat or drink...and putting his hands on him said, Brother Saul, the Lord even Jesus, that appeared unto thee in the way as thou camest, hath sent me (Ananias), that thou mightest receive thy sight, and be filled with the Holy Ghost. And immediately there fell from his eyes as it had been scales: and he received sight forthwith, and arose, and was baptized...And straightway he preached Christ in the synagogues, that he is the Son of God..."
Acts 9

The conversion of Saul from an evil and cruel man to St. Paul, one of the Lord's strongest supporters and missionary makes us realize how much we want to be like him. Paul traveled to Cyprus, Asia Minor, Macedonia and Greece. In Jerusalem he was arrested for protesting Jewish law. As a Roman citizen he could be tried by Emperor Nero. He later was beheaded, for preaching Christianity. He who had been at the stoning of St. Stephen, he who converted, lost his life for us too.

Baba Ganoush

3 eggplant	¼ cup lemon juice
1 tbls. olive oil	½ tsp. sea salt
1/3 cup tahini paste	3 jalapeno, seeded and chopped
3 cloves garlic, minced	

Preheat oven to 400°. Place eggplant on a greased baking sheet. Roast for 30 minutes. Cool. Chop into chunks. Peel the skins.
In a food processor combine the olive oil, tahini, garlic and jalapeno. Add the eggplant. Place in a bowl and stir in lemon juice and salt. Serve with pita bread.

"Be patient therefore, brethren, unto the coming of the Lord. Behold, the husbandman waiteth for the precious fruit of the earth, and hath long patience for it, until he receive the early and latter rain. Be ye also patient; stablish your hearts: for the coming of the Lord draweth nigh."
James 5:7-8

When my husband came home I could tell something was wrong. His company had filed for bankruptcy a while ago. Employees, some of them long timers had been let go, shelves were half empty, and morale low. He thought he was the next to go. The next day he sent an email to the owner, telling him at age 64 he would have no insurance, had no pension from elsewhere, no trust funds, nothing to live on. Luckily they came to a compromise – an hourly wage, health benefits, and a commission. The waiting for the final decision was agonizing, but waiting patiently and thinking through his future, my husband was able to weather a very trying couple of days, for both of us. Now we pray the company will survive in these bad economic times. Be patient. *Good things come to those who wait, and trust in God.*

Breakfast Burrito

Serves 4

4 large flour tortillas, warmed
7 scrambled eggs
½ lb. chorizo, cooked
¼ lb. Monterey Jack cheese with jalapeno
1 red pepper, sliced

1 red onion, sliced
Salsa
Sour cream
Guacamole
Fried tortilla chips

Place each tortilla on a plate.
Divide up the eggs, chorizo, cheese, red pepper and onion in the middle of the tortilla.
Roll up tortilla from each side. Turn over.
Serve with salsa, sour cream, guacamole and tortilla chips.

"God is working his purpose out as year succeeds to year: God is working his purpose out, and the time is drawing near; nearer and nearer draws the time, the time that shall surely be, when the earth shall be filled with the glory of God as the waters cover the sea. From utmost east to utmost west, wherever foot hath trod, by the mouth of many messengers goes forth the voice of God; give ear to me, ye continents, ye isles, give ear to me, that earth may be filled with the glory of God as the waters cover the sea."

Arthur Campbell Ainger (1841-1919) attended Eton and Cambridge, and later taught at Eton until he retired in 1901. He composed several songs for Eton and the hymn above. His repetition of "with the glory of God as the waters cover the sea" reminds us that God's Word is spread worldwide, not just for us to hear, but for everyone. God does work His purpose out. It is not ours to chose, but the Lord's on His own time. *"And we know that all things work together for good to them that love God, to them who are the called according to the will of God.* Romans 8:28

Apricot Bars

2 sticks butter   2 cups flour
½ cup sugar

Preheat oven to 350°
Combine the ingredients in a bowl.
Press into a greased 9x13 baking dish.
Bake until golden, about 25 minutes.

Topping

1¼ cups dried apricots   1 tsp. baking powder
1 cup water   ½ tsp. salt
2 cups brown sugar   1 tsp. vanilla
4 eggs   1 cup chopped walnuts or pecans
2/3 cup flour

Cook the apricots and water on simmer for 10 minutes. Drain water.
Beat the brown sugar and eggs in a bowl. Add the other ingredients. Spread over crust.
Bake 30 minutes. Cool, cut into squares and sprinkle with powdered sugar.

"Also when they shall be afraid of that which is high, and fears shall be in the way, and the almond tree shall flourish, and the grasshopper shall be a burden, and desire shall fail; because man goeth to his long home, and mourners go about the streets."
(Ecclesiastes 12:5)

My mother-in-law died on this date. I never really knew her, as she had been bedridden for years. Sadly she decided one day she no longer wanted to walk. I think when I came into George's life she realized how much she was missing, but then it was too late. Her Parkinson's had advanced and she could no longer walk. I guess I don't understand why she wanted to be taken care of this way – an invalid for the rest of her life. I want to run, to play tennis, to sail, to carry my grandchildren. God gave us feet to walk on, not to be immobile. I want to be taken up on wings of eagles, to soar, and to walk in the footsteps of our Savior. I will only let Him take care of me.

Apple/Almond Flan

1 stick butter
1½ cups flour
¼ cup almonds
¼ cup sugar
1 egg yolk

1 tbls. cold water
¼ teaspoon almond extract
4 large apples, peeled, cored and sliced
¼ cup currants or raisins

Preheat oven to 375°
To make the pastry put the butter, flour, almonds, sugar, egg yolk, water and almond extract in a food processor. Process until a ball is formed. Roll out into a circle to fit a flan baking tin. Arrange apple slices so they overlap in the circle. Sprinkle with currants. Cover with topping.
Bake for 25-30 minutes, or until apples are tender.
Sprinkle with powdered sugar, or leave plain. Can also be served with ice cream or whipped cream.

Topping

1 cup plain flour
¼ tsp. allspice
½ stick butter

4 tbls. sugar
½ cup sliced almonds

Combine all the ingredients in a bowl. Roll out pastry and form into a circle same size as flan tin. Chill for 15 minutes.

October 28

"We three kings of Orient are; Bearing gifts we traverse afar, Field and fountain, moor and mountain, Following yonder star.
Refrain: O star of wonder, star of light, Star with royal beauty bright, Westward leading, still proceeding, Guide us to thy perfect light.
Born a King on Bethlehem's plain Gold I bring to crown Him again, King forever, ceasing never, Over us all to reign. (r) Frankincense to offer have I; Incense owns a Deity nigh; Prayer and praising, voices raising, Worshipping God on high. (r) Myrrh is mine, its bitter perfume Breathes a life of gathering gloom; Sorrowing, sighing, bleeding, dying, Sealed in the stone cold tomb. (r) Glorious now behold Him arise; King and God and sacrifice; Alleluia, Alleluia, Sounds through the earth and skies. (r)"

John Henry Hopkins (1820-1891), the son of the first Episcopal bishop of Vermont and eighth Presiding Bishop of the United States, like his father became an Episcopal minister. He wrote *We Three Kings* (The Quest of the Magi) for a Christmas Pageant at Union Theological Seminary in New York. Reverend Hopkins was also an author, book illustrator, stained glass window designer, and editor of the *Church Journal* out of New York.

In a little over a month we will begin the Advent season – the awaiting of the Christ child. After his birth three wise men found Him lying in a manger, guided by a star, a glorious star – the Light – that would forever change this world. He didn't need gifts, He only had to spread the Word. The Word that God has brought His only Son into the world, to save us all from sin. To bring love, hope and peace to a world gone astray.

Potato Strata

Serves 4

2 lbs. Yukon gold potatoes	1 egg
1 lb. wild mushrooms, sliced	1 cup heavy cream
1 large leek, sliced	¼ tsp. nutmeg
½ lb. Gruyere cheese, grated	Butter

Preheat oven to 350°
Slice the potatoes thinly and place in a buttered casserole. Top with mushrooms, leeks and cheese. In a bowl beat together the egg, cream and nutmeg.
Pour over potatoes. Dot with butter.
Bake 25 minutes, or until potatoes are bubbling and slightly browned.

"How amiable are thy tabernacles, O Lord of Hosts!"
Psalm 84:1

"How lovely is thy dwelling place, O Lord of hosts, to me!"
Scottish Psalter 1650

My teen years were spent on Long Island. We attended the lovely New England St. John's Church in Cold Spring Harbor. This historic church was built in 1835 on a lake overlooking the harbor. The Tiffany windows, the simplicity of the interior and the plaques dedicated to former parishioners and clergy spoke about the legacy this church has. The last Sunday of October is celebrated as St. John's Day. I still have a number of the pins that were given out in honor of the church. I was fortunate to be confirmed and married there. In 1991 I came to the Lord, taking Bible study classes, becoming a Lay Eucharistic Minister and serving on the Altar Guild. Christ began to work in me, changing my heart and mind about so many things. I could now truly look up to God and let Him take me in his arms. I suffered many bumps after that, He took my hand, and I somehow got through. Christ is there for all of us. Just learn to let Him lead you.

Seafood Salad

Serves 4

½ cup mayonnaise
½ cup sour cream
2 tbls. Dijon mustard
2 tbls. fresh tarragon
1 lb. lobster meat
1 lb. shrimp, cooked and deveined
1 cup fresh peas
1 leek, sliced

2 stalks celery, sliced
1 red pepper, julienne
Salt and pepper to taste
Baby spinach
4 hardboiled eggs, halved
Thin lemon slices

In a bowl combine the mayonnaise, sour cream, mustard, and tarragon.
Fold in the lobster, shrimp, peas, leek, celery, pepper and salt and pepper.
Serve on a bed of spinach and garnish with eggs and lemon slices.

October 30

Christ Our Lord You suffered and were tempted. You are powerful to come to the aid of those who are assailed by the devil, For you are the support of Christian people. O Lord, protect with Your Right Hand those who trust in Your Name. Deliver them from the Evil One, and grant them everlasting joy. Amen
St. Gregory of Khandzta (759-861)

Tomorrow is Halloween or All Hallows. Halloween has always been a fun filled day, but some chose to wear the costumes of devils or other evil people. When you are young you can't wait to find the special costume to wear to school and the parade and trick or treating that night. In Cleveland we were fortunate to belong to the Cleveland Skating Club. Each year after the big show, they would sell off some of their costumes. My daughter loved finding these priceless bargains. I even picked up a dress I called my "Mary had a little lamb". I'd put it on Halloween, with high heels, and red lipstick. You can imagine the comments I'd get from the dads, but my daughter thought it was fun I'd dress up too. Other years I made her costumes. One she really enjoyed was the black and white costume, like the clown.

Gregory of Khandzta was born into a well-to-do Kartly, Georgia family. From an early age he determined to give up this lifestyle and founded several monasteries in his county. His feast day is celebrated by the Georgian Orthodox Church on October 18th.

Pumpkin Soup

Serves 8 or more

2 32 oz. cans pumpkin	¼ cup apple cider
4 carrots, peeled and sliced	½ tsp. ground nutmeg
2 leeks, sliced	½ tsp. ground cloves
4 celery stalks, sliced	1 tbls. fresh grated ginger
4 cloves garlic, crushed	½ tsp. cinnamon
6 cups chicken stock	2 cups heavy cream

Combine all the ingredients, except cream in a large pot. Bring to a boil. Simmer 15 minutes.
Add cream. Heat.
Serve in bowls and garnish with chives or parsley.

October 31

"He shall fly away as a dream, and shall not be found; yea, he shall be chased away as a vision of the night. The eye also which saw him shall see him no more; neither shall his place any more behold him."
Job 20:8-9

Last night I had a dream. I was on the beach, Nantucket perhaps? Coming out of the water were several men carrying a shrouded gurney. I had dreamed the same dream two years before when a dear friend died. Now I awoke anxiously, not knowing who it might be this time. As I took bridge lessons with my Long Island friends my mind went blank at just about twelve noon. It was if I had blacked out. I didn't say anything, but did find it hard to concentrate the rest of the afternoon. When I got home my daughter called to say her grandfather Holmes had died. I pray I never have this dream again. I don't want to lose another friend or family member. Among the many awards Mr. Holmes received during his lifetime was the Humanitarian Award from the National Conference of Christians and Jews. May all those we have lost rest in peace, and be remembered for the life they lived on earth.

Madeleines

Makes 12

1¼ cups flour
1 tsp. baking powder
2 eggs
½ cup sugar

1 tbls. lemon or orange juice
Zest of 1 lemon or orange
6 tbls. unsalted butter, melted

Preheat oven to 375F
Grease a 12 cup madeleine cake tin.
Sift flour and baking powder together.
In a bowl beat the eggs and sugar together until the mixture is thick.
Fold in the zest and juice. Alternately fold in some of the flour mixture and then the melted butter. Let stand for 10 minutes, then spoon into the tin.
Bake for 15 minutes, and rotate the tin halfway through.
Dust with confectioer's sugar before serving.

November 1 (All Saint's Day)

"I sing a song of the saints of God…and I mean, God helping, to be one too."

Growing up my favorite hymn besides *Fairest Lord Jesus* was "*I Sing a Song of the Saints of God.*" I guess when you are young you dream a lot about what you are going to be when you grow up. The music was written by John Henry Hopkins (1861-1945) of Grand Isle Vermont. How glorious a place on Lake Champlain to hum about saints. The words were written by Lesbia Scott (1898 – 1986) for her children. No wonder I loved them as a child!

I was never one of the saints. Instead my life took many paths, some easy, but most putting me through great hurtles. Why is it some people have all the good luck of leading an easy life – making enough money to survive, not going through a divorce, have great children, and just being successful and happy? Thank goodness for finding God, and trying to live a more saintly life. Otherwise I would have just been lost in the crowd.

I have always tried to do good – help others, give generously of time and when I had it, money. I have called on others to assist me, and each time they have been very godly people. I am blessed.

Wasabi Whipped Potatoes

Serves 6-8

6 large red bliss potatoes, cubed
¾ cup cream
½ stick butter
1 tsp. kosher salt

1½ tsp. pepper
2 tbls. wasabi paste
1 small leek, sliced

Boil the potatoes until tender. Drain
Place all the ingredients in a bowl and whip until smooth.
Green onions can be substituted for the leeks.

November 2

"All of us who were baptized into Jesus Christ were baptized into His death...We were therefore buried with Him through baptism into death in order that, just as Christ was raised from the dead...we too may live a new life."
Romans 6:3-4

"Then Peter said unto them, Repent, and be baptized every one of you in the name of Jesus Christ for the remission of sins, and ye shall receive the gift of the Holy Ghost. For the promise is unto you, and to your children, and to all that are afar off, even as many as the Lord our God shall call."
Acts 2:38-39

Baptisms are most often held on All Saints' Sunday and Easter Eve. My godson was christened in a lovely church in Richmond. Church banners led the procession. Families ogled and awed over the babies, and the singing reached a crescendo. That godson is now married with his own daughter who was recently baptized. At baptism not only do we welcome a child, or an adult, into the Christian Church, but we too renew our vows. *"Will you who witness these vows do all in your power to support these persons in their life in Christ?" "We will."*

Beef Wellington

Serves 6

2 ½ lbs. beef tenderloin	½ lb. liver pate
6 tbls. butter	Salt and pepper
1 leek, chopped	1 package puff pastry
½ pint duxelle mushrooms, finely chopped	1 egg yolk, beaten with 1 tbls. water

Preheat oven to 425°
Place the beef rubbed with 2 tbls. butter in a baking dish, and bake 10 minutes. Remove from dish. Cool. Reserve beef juice.
Melt 2 tbls. butter in a skillet and sauté the leek and mushrooms for 3 minutes .
Roll out the puff pastry and place the beef in the center
In a bowl combine the remaining butter and pate. With a knife smooth onto the beef. Top with mushroom mixture.
Fold the puff pastry completely around the beef and seal. Brush with egg wash. Put the beef into a baking dish and bake for 25 minutes, or until puff pastry is golden.
Serve with a currant or Bordelaise sauce.

November 3

"Have you not known? Have you not heard? The Lord is the everlasting God, the Creator of the ends of the earth. He does not faint or grow weary; his understanding is unsearchable."
Isaiah 40:28

As a dear family friend's condition got worse from her breast cancer, I would visit her, always walking into her room as she listened to the Christian radio station. Back then I was into classical and 60s music. Now I realize how much a part of my life is listening to the Christian stations, especially as I travel. I do have to admit I really enjoy the music more than listening to sermons, or readings, but I will take whatever I can get in the area I am traveling. Thank you, dear friend for your faith in the Everlasting God. Thank you for helping me find him. Your generosity and love will never be forgotten, though you are now long gone from us.

"For all flesh is as grass, and all the glory of man as the flower of grass. The grass withereth, and the flower thereof falleth away: But the word of the Lord endureth forever. And this is the word which by the gospel is preached unto you."
1 Peter 1.24-25

Chicken Picatta

Serves 4

2 tbls. olive oil
1 shallot, minced
4 boneless chicken breasts
¼ cup lemon juice

1 cup heavy cream
2 tbls. capers
Salt and pepper to taste

Heat the olive oil in a skillet. Saute the shallot.
Add the chicken breasts. Brown on both sides.
Add the other ingredients.
Serve with rice, noodles, or couscous.

November 4

"For unto us a child is born, unto us a son is given..."
Handel's *Messiah*

A miracle happened today. A new and precious life came into being – my first grandchild – Little Ned. He is almost too perfect – angelic rounded face, blue eyes, and a head of dark hair. How blessed I am and for his parents, and the fact his great grandparents are still living. Ned's countenance just radiates, he beams like the morning or evening star. God thank you for all that you bestow upon us, especially new life. Christmas will be upon us in a little over a month when we remember how you gave life to your son, our Savior, Jesus Christ.

Little Ned's Birthday Cupcakes (Courtesy of Ned Grieg)

24 giant cupcakes

8 cups cake flour, sifted
2 tbls. and ¾ tsp. baking powder
2 tsp. kosher salt
6 sticks unsalted butter, softened
6 cups cane sugar
12 egg yolks
2 tbls. vanilla extract

2 tbls. almond extract
3 cups whole milk
12 egg whites
½ cup cane sugar
1 lb. coconut shredded
½ lb. white chocolate, grated

Preheat oven to 335°
Combine the flour, baking powder and kosher salt in a mixing bowl.
Cream the butter and sugar until fluffy. Add the egg yolks, one at a time. Add the vanilla, milk and almond extract alternately by thirds with the flour mixture. Scrape bowl sides at least three times.
In a separate bowl beat egg whites until stiff. Add ½ cup sugar. Fold into batter. Fold coconut and white chocolate into batter.
Divide between 24 paper lined tins. Bake 30 minutes, or until toothpick comes out clean. Cool. Frost cupcakes and dust with extra coconut.

Cream Cheese Frosting

2 lbs. cream cheese
3 sticks butter
1 tbls. vanilla extract

1 tbls. key lime juice
3 lbs. confectioner's sugar
Pinch of kosher salt

Combine the cream cheese, butter, vanilla, salt and key lime juice. Slowly add confectioner's sugar.

November 5

"Therefore, the prisoner of the Lord, beseech you that ye walk worthy of your vocation wherewith ye are called. With all lowliness and meekness, with longsuffering, forebearing one another in love; endeavouring to keep the unity of the Spirit in the bond of peace. There is one body, and one Spirit, even as ye are called in one hope of your calling; One Lord, one faith, one baptism, One God and Father of all, who is above all, and through all, and in you all."
Ephesians 4:1-6

We need to give ourselves to the Lord. Let Him make decisions for us. Yesterday we went through one of the ugliest national election that I have ever known. There was much divisiveness, even within the parties. Citizens voted against party lines. However, in this passage we are asked to show unity. The new President and other elected officials will have to reach across party lines and unite this great country of ours. This will be a mean task, one that will require much prayer, thought, and hope. Not only has our country gone through difficult times, but the rest of the world is embraced in a recession, the Stock Market keeps falling, a lot of people are without jobs and losing their homes. O Lord we do pray for this country and its leaders, and the world.

"Be of good courage and he shall strengthen thine heart: wait, I say, on the Lord "
Psalm 27:14

Vegetable Omelet

Serves 4

2 tbls. butter
½ red pepper, diced
½ green pepper, diced
2 green onions, chopped
1 medium tomato, chopped
7 eggs, beaten

½ lb. Monterey Jack cheese
Salsa
Guacamole
Sour cream
Warm tortillas

Melt the butter in a skillet. Saute the peppers, onions and tomatoes until just tender.
Add the eggs, scraping the sides of the skillet.
Slide the finished omelet out of the pan and flip onto a cutting board.
Sprinkle the cheese on the eggs. Serve with salsa, guacamole, sour cream and warm tortillas.

November 6

"He shall judge thy people with righteousness, and thy poor with judgment. The mountains shall bring peace to the people, and the little hills, by righteousness. He shall judge the poor of the people, he shall save the children of the needy, and shall break in pieces the oppressor. They shall fear thee as long as the sun and moon endure, throughout all generations. He shall come down like rain upon the mown grass: as showers that water the earth. In his days shall the righteous flourish; and abundance of peace so long as the moon endureth. He shall have dominion also from sea to sea, and from the river unto the ends of the earth. They that dwell in the wilderness shall bow before him; and his enemies shall lick the dust. The kings of Tarshish and of the isles shall bring presents: the kings of Sheba and Seba shall offer gifts. Yea, all kings shall fall down before him: all nations shall serve him. For he shall deliver the needy when he crieth; the poor also, and him that hath no helper. He shall spare the poor and needy, and shall save the souls of the needy."
Psalm 72:2-13

There was a recent article in a local paper about students who, instead of receiving well paying jobs, opt to start their own foundations or work with the poor. I really commend them as we do not know what the future brings. These are troubling economic times, but when young people can reach out to those who cannot receive an education, can barely feed themselves, let alone buy clothes, we know there are people with good hearts. They are godly people who want to make a change in the world. They don't walk by a beggar, they may take him to a shelter or give him money. Walk in the ways the Lord has taught us. Save the souls of the needy.

Stuffed Acorn Squash

Serves 4

2 acorn squash, cut in half lengthwise, seeds removed
2 tbls. cinnamon
½ cup brown sugar

1 cup dried cranberries
1 cup spicy pecans
½ stick butter

Preheat the oven to 350°
In a pot of boiling water cook the acorn squash until just tender.
Place the squash on a baking sheet.
Divide up the ingredients among the 4 squash.
Bake for 10 minutes.

November 7

"My heart is inditing a good matter; I speak of the things which I have made touching the king; my tongue is the pen of a ready reader."
Psalm 45:1

As a writer I often find days when nothing comes to mind. Try as I might my mind is blank. I don't know why as I am always doing things to enrich it – cooking, laughing, traveling, being with family and friends. So I ask God for inspiration. My morning prayers include my wish list. Or I go out into the garden, walk on the beach, or look up at that full moon, or the bright sunlight. I need to be where I see light. My office window looks out on the garden and is filled with light. The dark mornings of fall do not help as I am an early riser and would like to write. Somehow the inspiration is not there. However I can praise and thank the Lord for a new day. He will speak to me and inspire me to praise Him.

Seafood Crepes

12 crepes

Crepes

1 cup flour	¼ tsp. salt
3 eggs	1 tbls. chives, snipped
2 tbls. butter, melted	1 tbls. parlsey
1½ cups milk	

Combine the ingredients in a bowl.
Heat some butter in a skillet. Using a ladle pour a large spoonful of batter into the pan. Swirl so it meets the sides. Turn crepe as soon as it puffs. Reserve on plate and continue cooking other crepes.

Filling

1 stick butter	1 tbls. tarragon
½ cup flour	½ lb. small shrimp
2 cups half and half	½ lb. crab or lobster meat
1 tbls. curry	

Melt the butter in a sauce pan. Stir in flour and half and half. Add curry and tarragon. Fold in seafood.
Spoon equal portions of the seafood on each crepe. Roll up. Serve immediately.

November 8

"For as the rain cometh down, and the snow from heaven, and returneth not thither, but watereth the earth, and maketh it bring forth and bud, that it may give seed to the sower, and bread to the eater: So shall my word be that goeth forth out of my mouth: it shall not return unto me void, but it shall accomplish that which I please, and it shall prosper in the thing whereto I sent it."
Isaiah 55:10-11

In a previous life I wrote a series of newsletters entitled "The Diplomat". Each issue focused on a particular country, its etiquette and protocol, and doing business. While living in Cleveland years ago I had the opportunity to help someone who is now a good friend, defect from Romania. When I moved to Washington I made contact with the Romanian Embassy, and was asked to attend many events. I got to know the cultural attaché, and through her was able to arrange a trip to Romania to do my newsletter. This was not long after the "Velvet Revolution" and a number of officials were a result of the old regime. The media was highlighting the problems of orphans as adoptees, many with acute medical problems, and the gypsies. Because of this situation and since I was a guest of the Romanian government, they wanted to make sure I painted a rosy picture of the present situation. This was a difficult assignment. I arrived in a blizzard, totally unprepared, no boots, but a heavy coat. The streets were icy and snowy. And of course my first impressions of downtown Bucharest were the hideous Communist concrete buildings. But I took a deep breath, my hostess lent me her mother's green rubber boots, and I somehow managed to see a country just coming out of Communism. However, it was depressing visiting state offices and receiving glowing pictures of how the economy was growing, and that Bucharest would soon again be the "Paris" of Eastern Europe.

My saving grace was visiting monasteries, Brasov, the Village Museum, and the royal treasures. These are a proud people with a long history. Once a very wealthy country, Romania had rich natural resources, including gold and salt. The wide boulevards in Bucharest attested to its charm. But it was at one monastery that I knew the faith had been kept, and during the repression religion was secretly kept in people's hearts. I met Father Lawrence. On this coldest of days, he wore only a robe and sandals, yet he escorted us to the magnificent murals (all outside) on the monastery grounds. He then asked if he could sing. All of a sudden his voice carried amazing Gregorian chants. I was filled with the Lord. He took us to his room for cold coffee as that was all he had. I gave him a small donation. He said that would take care of food for a month. We kept in touch for several years, and then no more. How I long to meet him again. A man so godly, yet so humble like our Lord.

314

"Lord Jesus Christ, Son of God, have mercy on me, a sinner."
Jesus Prayer from the Eastern Orthodox Church

Ghiveciu (Romanian Veal Stew)

Serves 10-12

½ cup olive oil
3 lbs. boneless veal, cut into bite size chunks
2 tbls. sea salt
1 tbls. pepper
½ cup flour
2 large onions, sliced
4 cloves garlic, minced
1 eggplant, peeled and sliced
8 red bliss potatoes, sliced
½ lb. cabbage, shredded
1 acorn squash, peeled, cut into bite size pieces, and seeds removed

1 red pepper, sliced
½ lb. celeric, peeled and sliced
1 lb. cauliflower florets
½ lb. green beans
3 tomatoes, sliced
½ cup fresh peas
¼ lb. raisins
4 bay leaves
1 tbls. thyme
1 tbls. marjoram
½ tsp. cayenne
4 cups beef stock
1 cup red wine

Preheat oven to 350°
In a bowl combine the flour, salt and pepper. Dredge the veal.
Heat the olive oil in a skillet and brown the veal on all sides.
Oil a large casserole dish. Layer the onions, garlic, eggplant, potatoes, cabbage, acorn squash, pepper, celeric, cauliflower, and veal in the dish.
Sprinkle with herbs.
Pour the wine and stock over the veal and vegetables.
Cover tightly and bake 1 hour.
Remove from oven and add green beans, tomatoes, peas, and raisins.
Bake for 15 minutes.
Serve with a salad and crusty bread.

November 9

"Then I looked and heard the voice of many angels surrounding the throne, and the living creatures and the elders; they numbered myriads of myriads and thousands of thousands, singing with full voice, "Worthy is the Lamb that was slaughtered To receive power and wealth and wisdom and might And honor and glory and blessing!" Then I heard every creature in heaven and on earth and under the earth, and in the sea, and all that is in them singing, "To the one seated on the throne And to the Lamb be blessing and honor and glory and might forever and ever!" And the four living creatures said "Amen!" And the elders fell down and worshipped."
Revelation 5: 11-14

The last night I was in Romania I went out for dinner and then to hear the Madrigal Singers. I had heard Madrigal singers before in school, but never these which are a Romanian national treasure. They truly sang as angels. Magnificently dressed, the voices harmonized like no other group I have ever heard. The music was not just Romanian, but encompassed every European nationality. This was like a dream, soaring up to heaven and back. You just wanted them to continue on forever. We do not fall down and worship these singers, but we do worship our risen Lord. He is the king over all and greatly to be praised.

Zama

Zama is a traditional Romanian soup.

Serves 4-6

½ stick butter
1 onion, chopped
¼ cup flour
1 teaspoon pepper
1 teaspoon salt
4 boneless chicken breasts
1 tsp. red pepper

1 garlic clove, minced
2 lb string beans
6 cups water
¼ cup parsley, chopped
¼ cup dill, chopped

Melt the butter in a large pot. Saute the onion for about 2 minutes.
Combine the flour, salt and pepper in a bowl. Dredge the chicken in flour mixture.
Add the red pepper, water, chicken, garlic, green beans and cook for a half hour.
Pour into a soup tureen or separate soup bowls.
Garnish with parsley and dill.

November 10

"A mighty fortress is our God, a bulwark never failing; Our helper He, amid the flood of mortal ills prevailing: For still our ancient foe doth seek to work us woe; His craft and power are great, and, armed with cruel hate, On earth is not his equal. Did we in our own strength confide, our striving would be losing; Were not the right Man on our side, the Man of God's own choosing: Dost ask who that may be? Christ Jesus, it is He; Lord Sabaoth, His Name, from age to age the same, And He must win the battle. And though this world, with devils filled, should threaten to undo us, We will not fear, for God hath willed His truth to triumph through us: The Prince of Darkness grim, we tremble not for him; His rage we can endure, for lo, his doom is sure, One little word shall fell him. That word above all earthly powers, no thanks to them, abideth; The Spirit and the gifts are ours through Him Who with us sideth: Let goods and kindred go, this mortal life also; The body they may kill: God's truth abideth still, His kingdom is forever."

Martin Luther (1483-1546) was born in Germany. He is known as the "Father of Protestantism", for church reform, and a hymnist. He challenged the Roman Catholic Church and later was excommunicated. He translated The Bible into the vernacular (German) allowing the people to be able to read it. *A Mighty Fortress Is our God* is based on Psalm 46. He also wrote *From Deepest Woe I Cry*, based on Psalm 130. As you sing these hymns remember how Luther changed the world by publishing his 95 Theses and that salvation is a gift of God, just believe in Jesus as the Messiah. A favorite quote of his is *"The fewer the words, the better the prayer."*

Mushroom Soup

Serves 4

½ stick butter
1 pound mushrooms, sliced
½ cup celery, chopped
1 cup onion, chopped
2 cups chicken stock

2 cups cream
2 tbls. Sherry
Fresh chives, basil or parsley, chopped

Melt the butter in a saucepan. Stir in mushrooms, celery and onion. Simmer for 5 minutes.
Add stock and cream. Cook until warm.
Serve in individual bowls. Splash with sherry and herbs.
Can be served chilled.

November 11

"Blest be the King Whose Coming is in the Name of God!"
Advent Hymn by Frederico J. Pagura

Martin of Tours (316-397) was born in Upper Pannonia (Hungary) to pagan parents. He was part of the Imperial cavalry. One night during a freezing rain he lent part of his cloak to a beggar. Later he had a vision of Christ appearing in the cloak, and was baptized. Believing Christians did not fight, he asked to be discharged from the military. He was declared a coward. Instead he would stand in the battle lines, holding only a cross, and the enemy would surrender. After his military career he became of disciple of St. Hilary of Poitiers. He traveled to Italy and Dalmatia, and for ten years was a hermit. He met St. Hilary again, and through him started Liguge, the first monastery in France. He became bishop of Tours, France. From the late 4th century to the late Middle Ages, most European Christians fasted for 40 days, a period called "Quadragesima Sancti Martini," which means "the forty days of St. Martin" in Latin. This fasting time later became our Advent.

Frederico J. Pagura (b 1923-) is co-president of the Ecumenical Movement for Human Rights in Argentina, a past president of the Latin American Council of Churches, and the Council of Methodist Bishops of Latin America and the Caribbean.

Ginger Cookies

1 stick butter
1 cup brown sugar
1 egg
1 cup molasses
2 ½ cups flour
2 tsp. baking soda

1 teaspoon ground cinnamon
1 tbls. ground ginger
2 tbls. fresh grated ginger
½ tsp. ground cloves
½ teaspoon salt

Preheat oven to 375°
Cream the butter and sugar in a bowl. Beat in the eggs and molasses. Add the other ingredients.
Drop by spoonfuls onto an ungreased baking sheet.
Bake 12 minutes.

.

November 12

"In Christ there is no East or West, In Him no South or North…"

John Oxenham (William Arthur Dunkerley) (1852-1941) was an English journalist, novelist and poet. He wrote these words for the *Pageant of Darkness and Light* at the London Missionary Society's exhibition "The Orient in London," which ran from 1908 to 1914. I love to hear children sing this tune as it is from a spirited African-American spiritual written by Harry Thacker Burleigh (1866-1949). He began composing in 1899 and wrote over 300 pieces. We are one big family, and nothing will separate us from the love of Christ.

"My faith looks up to Thee, Thou Lamb of Calvary, Savior divine! Now hear me while I pray, take all my guilt away, O let me from this day be wholly Thine! May Thy rich grace impart Strength to my fainting heart, my zeal inspire! As Thou hast died for me, O may my love to Thee, Pure warm, and changeless be, a living fire! While life's dark maze I tread, And griefs around me spread, be Thou my Guide; Bid darkness turn to day, wipe sorrow's tears away, Nor let me ever stray from Thee aside. When ends life's transient dream, When death's cold sullen stream over me roll; Blest Savior, then in love, fear and distrust remove; O bear me safe above, a ransomed soul!"

Also born on this day was Ray Palmer (1808-87) author of *My Faith Looks up to Thee, Thou, Lamb of Calvary*. Give yourself to the Lord. We are challenged, we are tested, gone down to the depths, but you will always, forever be by our side.

Fried Rice

Serves 8

3 tbls. peanut oil
½ lb. pork tenderloin, diced
2 jalapeno, seeded and diced
2 cloves garlic, minced
4 cups cooked rice
2 tbls. soy sauce

8 green onions, sliced
1 cup peas
½ lb. small shrimp, cooked
4 eggs, beaten
¼ cup cilantro, chopped
1tsp. chili powder

Heat the oil in a wok. Add the pork, jalapeno and garlic. Cook 4 minutes.
Add the rice and soy sauce. Stir in shrimp, onions and peas. Push to one side of wok. Pour in eggs. Cook for 2 minutes.
Combine pork mixture and eggs, and cook until eggs are no longer liquid.
Serve immediately and garnish with chili powder and cilantro.

"Almighty God, you have given us grace at this time with one accord to make our common supplication to you; and you have promised through your well-beloved Son that when two or three are gathered together in his Name you will be in the midst of them: Fulfill now, O Lord, our desires and petitions as may be best for us; granting us in this world knowledge of your truth, and in the age to come life everlasting. Amen."

"Where two or three are gathered together in my name, there am I in the midst of them."
Matthew 18:20

God is omnipresent. He is the one who leads the way. He does fulfill what we ask for. He forgives our sins. He loves us every day.

Saint John Chrysostom (c. 347–407) was a student of Greek language and writings, and turned early to the Lord. Becoming a hermit he starved himself, standing daily and memorizing the Bible which led to poor health. However he was determined to serve the church, was ordained and later became archbishop of Constantinople, where he also founded several hospitals. He was considered one of the great preachers of his time, and his sermons were often on St. Paul's writings and Genesis. After his death he was given the Greek surname chrysostomos, meaning "golden mouthed", or in English Chrysostom. He is also called John of Antioch.

Chicken Salad

Serves 4

4 chicken breasts, cooked and cubed	1 cup pecans
15 oz. can artichoke hearts, drained	1 tbls. fresh grated ginger
½ cup mayonnaise	1 tsp. curry powder
½ cup sour cream	½ tsp. salt
2 stalks celery, chopped	Baby fresh greens
4 green onions, chopped	Fresh parsley or cilantro

In a bowl combine the chicken, artichoke hearts, mayonnaise, sour cream, celery, onions, pecans, ginger, curry powder and salt.
Place the baby greens on individual plates.
Top with salad. Garnish with parsley or cilantro.

November 14

"The elders which are among you I exhort, who am also an elder, and a witness of the sufferings of Christ, and also a partaker of the glory that shall be revealed: Feed the flock of God which is among you, taking the oversight thereof, not by constraint, but willingly; not for filthy lucre, but of a ready mind; Neither as being lords over God's heritage, but being examples to the flock. And when the chief Shepherd shall appear, ye shall receive a crown of glory that fadeth not away."
1 Peter 5:1-4

Samuel Seabury (1729-1796) graduated from Yale, studied medicine in Edinburgh, was ordained a deacon by the bishop of Lincoln and priest by the Bishop of Curlisle in 1753. Rev. Seabury was consecrated in Aberdeen, Scotland as the first American Episcopal bishop and first bishop of Connecticut on November 14, 1783. At that time the United States had only recently won its independence from Great Britain. Since he could not take his oath of allegiance to King George III of England, he was concsecrated in the Scottish Episcopal Church. However, he was required to study the Scottish Rite of Holy Communion, not the English. Even today the Episcopal Church in the United States continues in the Scottish tradition. Bishop Seabury became the second Presiding Bishop of the Episcopal Church, USA.

Sauteed Shrimp

Serves 6

¼ cup olive oil
2 green onions, chopped
4 cloves garlic, minced
2½ lbs. shrimp, cooked, peeled and deveined
1 pint cherry tomatoes
½ lb. baby spinach

¼ lb. arugula
15 oz. can artichoke hearts, drained
1 small jar roasted peppers
1 cup white wine
Juice of 1 lemon
¼ tsp. cayenne
½ cup basil, chopped

Heat the olive oil in a skillet. Stir in the onions and garlic. Saute the shrimp for 2 minutes. Add the other ingredients.
Serve over linguine.
Can be served warm or chilled.

November 15

"We have gifts that differ according to the grace given us."
Romans 12:6

During the fall churches prepare for their annual stewardship campaigns. A lot of people do not like to ask for money, but there are others who kindly give of their time, their love for Christ and the Church, and the knowledge that for a church to grow and expand outreach programs and ministries, tithing is essential. In several places in the Bible ten per cent is asked, but it is what comes from the heart, the joy of giving. This is not a tax, but a contribution to the church. *"Every man according as he purposeth in his heart, so let him give; not grudgingly, or of necessity: for God loveth a cheerful giver."* 2 Corinthians 9:7 Even more so during these economic tough times the churches depend on these cheerful givers. Please be one of them. Pray for what you can give.

Apple Tart

Pastry

1 stick butter	¼ cup water
1¼ cups flour	2 tbls. sugar
3 oz. cream cheese	

Preheat oven to 400°
Combine the ingredients in a food processor until a ball forms. Roll out on a floured board to the size of pie plate. Place in pie plate. Bake 10 minutes.

Filling

½ cup almonds	1 cup heavy cream
4 large apples, peeled, cored and sliced	3 egg yolks
	¼ cup bourbon or rum
2 tbls. sugar	

Sprinkle the almonds on the pie crust. Top with apples. Sprinkle with sugar. Beat the egg yolks until thickened. Add cream and bourbon. Pour over apples. Bake for 25-30 minutes, until just browned.

November 16

"Now concerning the times and the seasons, brothers and sisters, *you do not need to have anything written to you. For you yourselves know very well that the day of the Lord will come like a thief in the night. When they say, 'There is peace and security', then sudden destruction will come upon them, as labour pains come upon a pregnant woman, and there will be no escape! But you, beloved,* *are not in darkness, for that day to surprise you like a thief; for you are all children of light and children of the day; we are not of the night or of darkness. So then, let us not fall asleep as others do, but let us keep awake and be sober; for those who sleep sleep at night, and those who are drunk get drunk at night. But since we belong to the day, let us be sober, and put on the breastplate of faith and love, and for a helmet the hope of salvation. For God has destined us not for wrath but for obtaining salvation through our Lord Jesus Christ, who died for us, so that whether we are awake or asleep we may live with him. Therefore encourage one another and build up each other, as indeed you are doing."*
1 Thessalonians 5:1-11

I love Advent, awaiting the coming of the birth of Jesus. I love humming the hymns *"Lo, He comes with clouds descending"* or *"Come thou long expected Jesus."* Keep on track, never sway from the real meaning of Advent. The one thing I don't appreciate is how early the stores get ready for Christmas. For some, Halloween isn't yet over, and they're putting out Christmas merchandise. Can't Christmas be like it was when I was a child? You got a beloved doll, a party dress, and a stocking with an orange, some dates, a candy cane, and maybe a small present or two. Now, it's let's see how much we can spend and how many presents we can buy. Let us be sober, open our eyes, to the real meaning of Jesus' coming.

Pumpkin Risotto

Serves 4

2 tbls. butter
2 cups arborio rice
3 cups chicken stock, heated

1 15 oz. can pumpkin
2 tbls.fresh sage

Melt the butter in a sauce pan. Stir in the rice. Gradually add stock. When the stock is almost absorbed, put a lid on pan. Let sit 10 minutes.
Stir in pumpkin and sage.
Ground cinnamon, ginger and nutmeg can be substituted for the sage.

"But he, being full of compassion, forgave their iniquity, and destroyed them not: yea, many a time turned he his anger away, and did not stir up all his wrath. For he remembered that they were but flesh, a breath that goes forth and does not return."
Psalm 78:38-39

St. Basil's Cathedral looms over Moscow right next to the Kremlin. The cathedral was commissioned by Ivan IV (Ivan the Terrible) and built from 1555-1561 to commemorate the capture of the Khanate of Kazan. In 1588 Tsar Fedor Ivanovich added a chapel above the grave of Basil Fool for Christ, the Russian Orthodox saint for whom the cathedral is named. The circumstances under which the cathedral was built do not testify to the spirituality of the people of that time. Yes, I can only assume the cathedral was built to the glory of God. Ivan was the first tsar and consolidated Russia into an empire rather ruthlessly. He was prone to outbursts, and in one rage murdered his son and heir. He also is believed to have had Metropolitan Philipp, St. Philipp II, murdered for his outspokenness. Somehow I do not picture Ivan as a devout Christian and following in the path of Basil.

In my living room is a beautiful little music box, a replica of St. Basil's Cathedral in Moscow. The music box and other ornaments are handmade and benefit Russian orphans through a group in Alexandria, Virginia. The colors, the chapels, the crosses, speak of the uniqueness of this incredible building. Let us remember its purpose, not who commissioned it.

Eggplant Casserole

Serves 8

2 tbls. olive oil
1 medium onion, sliced
3 cloves garlic, chopped
1 medium eggplant, cubed
4 medium tomatoes, sliced
1 medium zucchini, sliced
1 red pepper, sliced
1 yellow pepper, sliced
¼ cup parsley, chopped
1 tsp. sea salt
¼ cup basil, chopped
1 tbls. fresh ground pepper

Heat the olive oil in a large skillet. Add the onion cook until tender. Stir in the garlic. Add remaining ingredients.
Bring to a boil. Cover. Simmer for about 10 minutes, or until vegetables are tender.
Fresh grated parmesan cheese can be used as a garnish.

"With the Lord on my side I do not fear. What can mortals do to me.?
Psalm 118:6

"By him therefore let us offer the sacrifice of praise to God continually, that is,
the fruit of our lips giving thanks to his name."
Hebrews 13:15

I have never met Carl Harrison, only read about the ministry he and his wife
have accomplished for over 30 years. This amazing man was born in China to
missionary parents. When he was five the Japanese invaded and he and his sister
spent the remainder of the war in a military internment camp. His family fled in
1944 and returned to Pennsylvania. During college he learned about Wycliffe
International. He spent years in Brazil living among two indigenous tribes,
learning their language, and translating the Bible into the Guajajara language.
His first task was the New Testament, and later after much pressure, the Old
Testament. Today The Bible has been translated into over 2400 languages. Let
us continue to follow in Mr. Harrison's footsteps and preach the Word of our
Lord.

Bread Pudding

Serves 6

6 cups French or Challah bread, cubed	1 cup walnuts, pecans or almonds
3 cups milk	1 cup raisins or currants
4 eggs	2 apples, peeled, cored and chopped
½ cup sugar	1 tbls. cinnamon
½ cup brown sugar	½ tsp. fresh grated nutmeg
Zest of 1 orange	½ tsp ground ginger
	½ tsp. ground cloves

Preheat oven to 350°
Soak the bread in a large bowl with the milk for 20 minutes.
In another bowl beat the eggs, sugars and zest.
Pour the egg mixture over the bread. Add nuts, raisins, apples and spices.
Pour into a buttered baking dish. Sprinkle with additional sugar.
Bake 30-40 minutes until top is crusty.
Serve with whipped cream or ice cream.

"Open thou mine eyes. That I may behold wondrous things out of thy law."
Psalm 119:18

At the University of Pennsylvania I worked on my Master's in education. One of the young ladies I met was only a freshman, but we became fast friends, and shared a lot in common. After receiving her degree from Penn she went on to Jefferson Medical School where she received a degree in ophthalmology, becoming very prominent in her field. One summer when my daughter was quite young, she visited us on Nantucket. Other nieces and nephews were playing together, everyone enjoying a beautiful summer day. I will never forget when she asked if any of the children wore sun glasses? I said "no". She replied children's eyes are very sensitive, and as they grow older their eyes will deteriorate much faster, unless they wear sunglasses. How blind we are. We think about us as parents wearing them, but not protecting our own children.

Beef Tenderloin with Mushroom Sauce

Serves 4

4 beef tenderloin, about ½ lb. each

Cook the tenderloins on a grill or under the broiler until desired pinkness. Serve the tenderloins with mushroom sauce.

Mushroom Sauce

½ stick butter	½ cup beef broth
2 green onions, sliced	½ cup Port
2 cloves garlic, crushed	½ teaspoon black pepper
1 lb. portabella mushrooms, sliced	

Melt the butter in a skillet. Saute the onions for about 3 minutes. Add the garlic and mushrooms. Cook until the mushrooms are just tender. Add the broth and Port. Simmer for 15 minutes. Add pepper.

"Praise, my soul, the King of heaven; to his feet thy tribute bring; ransomed, healed, restored, forgiven, evermore his praises sing: Alleluia, alleluia! Praise the everlasting King. Praise him for his grace and favor to our fathers in distress; praise him still the same for ever, slow to chide and swift to bless: Alleluia, alleluia! Glorious in his faithfulness. Father-like, he tends and spares us; well our feeble frame he knows; in his hand he gently bears us, rescues us from all our foes. Alleluia, alleluia! Widely yet his mercy flows. Angels, help us to adore him; ye behold him face to face; sun and moon, bow down before him, dwellers all in time and space. Alleluia, alleluia! Praise with us the God of grace."

Henry Francis Lyte (1795-1847) was born in Scotland, but educated at Trinity College, Dublin. He was a clergyman and hymnist. He died at a very young age, probably of consumption. My other favorite hymns of his are *Abide with Me* and *God of Mercy, God of Grace. Abide with Me* was completed just about the time of his death in Nice, and was sung at his memorial service in Brixham, England.

Mincemeat Pie

½ lb. beef suet
4 cups currants
2 cups dried cranberries
1 cup slivered almonds
1 cup candied fruit
½ cup chopped figs
4 apples, peeled, cored and finely chopped

1¼ cups sugar
1 tsp. ground nutmeg
1 tsp. ground allspice
1 tbls. ground cinnamon
½ tsp. ground cloves
2 cups brandy
1 cup dry Sherry

Combine all the ingredients in a bowl. Cover the bowl and set aside in a cool place for at least three weeks, not in the refrigerator. Check each week and add more brandy and Sherry.

2 pie crusts

Preheat oven to 400°
Bake the pie crusts for 10 minutes.
Divide the mincemeat between the two crusts.
Bake 30-35 minutes.
Serve with hard sauce or ice cream.
A latticework top crust is also pretty. Just buy two extra crusts and cut strips.

"Blessed are the pure in heart for they shall see God."
Matthew 5:8

From the time I was a little girl I loved spending summers on Nantucket with my grandmothers. I also had a lovely neighbor, never married, who had served as a Major in the Army Nurse Corps. She talked about serving overseas during the Second World War. She also taught me to make cranberry chutney. I loved spending time with her. She towered over me, always standing straight and tall. Faith has left us, but not her memories and her little house with the white picket fence. She gave so much to others and they loved her in return.

Blueberry Pie

Pie Crust

1¼ cups flour   ½ cup almonds
¼ cup sugar   3 tbls. cream cheese
1 stick butter

Combine the ingredients in a food processor.
Roll out on a floured board to the size of your pie plate.
Preheat oven to 400°. Bake ten minutes

Filling

2 pints blueberries   1½ tbls. lemon juice
½ cup sugar   1 tbls. cornstarch
½ cup brown sugar

In a bowl combine the blueberries, sugar, brown sugar, and lemon juice. Pour into the pie crust. Spoon the topping on blueberries.
Bake pie at 425° for 10 minutes and 35 minutes at 350°

Topping

½ stick butter   ¼ tsp. nutmeg
½ cup flour   ½ tsp. allspice
½ cup sugar   ¼ tsp. cloves
1 tsp. cinnamon   ½ cup rolled oats

Combine the ingredients in a bowl.

November 22

"Holy God, we praise Thy Name; Lord of all, we bow before Thee! All on earth Thy scepter claim, All in Heaven above adore Thee; Infinite Thy vast domain, Everlasting is Thy reign. Hark! the loud celestial hymn Angel choirs above are raising, Cherubim and seraphim, In unceasing chorus praising; Fill the heavens with sweet accord: Holy, holy, holy, Lord."
Hymn sung at the funeral of John F. Kennedy November 25, 1963 and written by Ignaz Franz 1774

The question is always "where were you when President John F. Kennedy was assassinated?" I remember it so well, lo these many years later. We were seated in study hall at the Cathedral School of St. Mary, which I attended for three years. Someone came in to tell us the news. Shock. Disbelief. How could this happen? As a young teenager the death of President Kennedy was such an incredible loss. We all looked up to this handsome man with a gorgeous wife. How could anyone take him away? Even today questions arise about his assassination. His memory lives on. Just visit Arlington National Cemetery and see the flame and how it affects all ages, even those who were not yet born. Years later while I was waiting to pick my daughter up after school, a mother ran to all the cars announcing there had been an attempt on President Reagan's life. Thankfully he survived. Pray for our country and its leaders.

Fish Chowder

Fish chowder was one of President Kennedy's favorite meals.

Serves 6-8

¼ lb. salt pork, rind removed, diced
½ stick butter
2 leeks, sliced
6 red bliss potatoes, diced
2 cups fish or chicken stock
1 tsp. sea salt
1 tbls. pepper

2 lbs. cod or haddock, cut into small chunks
2 cups half and half
2 cups heavy cream
2 tbls. tarragon, chopped
Chives and parsley for garnish

Heat the salt pork in a large pot until crispy. Remove the pork and add butter. Saute the leeks until just tender. Add the potatoes and stock. Cook the potatoes until tender, about 10 minutes. Stir in salt and pepper.
Add cod and cook 5 minutes. Add half and half, cream and tarragon. Simmer until warmed.
Serve in bowls. Garnish with chives and parsley.

"Let there be light, and there was light. And God saw the light, that it was good: and God divided the light from the darkness, And God called the light "day", and the darkness he called "night", And the evening and the morning were the first day."
Genesis 1:3-5

Recently I was going through some of my books, cleaning them out, and arranging them according to topics. One of the books I hadn't looked at in a long while, was trying to organize one's life, written almost twenty years ago by an old friend. I started glancing through the book, looking around at my disheveled office, the piles everywhere, boxes of old pictures to be sorted, unpaid invoices, wrapping paper, everything in one little room! My sincere vow, once this book is published, is to clean up my mess. I always feel better when the house is clean, but why does my office always look like a cyclone went through it. Only three days ago we had tornado warnings. Thank you Lord they did not strike the Eastern Shore. Why is it someone else who opens our eyes, let's us see the light, and not we ourselves? I am not blind. I just have too many things on my mind. I need to get organized, and get out of the darkness!

Chicken Quesadillas

Serves 4

8 tortillas
2 tbls. olive oil
1 large red onion
2 tomatoes, sliced
4 jalapeno, seeded and chopped

2 large cloves garlic, minced
2 cups cooked boneless chicken breast
½ cup cilantro, chopped
½ lb. Monterrey jack, grated

Preheat oven to 400°
Heat the olive oil in a skillet. Saute the onions until tender. Stir in the tomatoes, jalapeno and garlic.
Lay 4 of the tortillas on a large baking sheet. Evenly divide up the other ingredients on each tortilla. Cover with 4 remaining tortillas. Place another baking sheet on top. Press down.
Bake 10 minutes.
Serve with salsa, guacamole, and fried tortilla chips.

November 24

"O Lord, how manifold are Thy works! In wisdom hast thou made them all; the earth is full of Thy riches."
Psalm 104:24

Thanksgiving is a time to give thanks to God for all that He has given us. Too many people celebrate it more as a time to socialize, watch football games, and eat and drink too much. They forget the true meaning. We are blessed to live in a country of abundance, but beneath the surface there are people starving and living in dire poverty, who cannot afford to celebrate. We must take care of them too; to give them hope, something to live for. Soup kitchens and shelters provide some relief, but that is not enough. As the world food crisis continues to grow we must find other ways to sustain ourselves. Cutting back on eating will not only keep us in better shape, but provide for those in need. Help others, not just yourself. Celebrate the freedom and abundance of this country.

Pumpkin Pie

Pie Crust

1 ¼ cups all purpose flour
2 tbsp. sugar
1 stick unsalted butter

¼ cup cold water
1 3 oz. package cream cheese
½ cup slivered almonds

Combine the flour, sugar, butter, water and cream cheese in a food processor. Roll the dough out into a circle to fit a 9" pie plate. Press the dough into the pie plate. Dot with the almonds.

Filling

1 (15 ounce) can pumpkin
½ stick butter
3 eggs
½ cup sugar
1 cup heavy cream
½ teaspoon allspice
1 tbs. fresh grated ginger

¼ teaspoon cloves
1 teaspoon ground cinnamon
½ teaspoon freshly grated nutmeg
1 cup pecans, almonds or walnuts
1 cup cranberries

Preheat oven to 375°
Combine the ingredients, except nuts and cranberries, in a bowl.
Spoon into the pie crust.
Sprinkle nuts and cranberries over top. Bake about ½ hour.

"When they found Him on the other side of the sea, they said to him, "Rabbi when did you come here?" Jesus answered them, "Very truly, I tell you, you are looking for me, not because you saw signs, but because you ate your fill of the loaves. Do not work for food that perishes, but for the food that endures for eternal life, which the Son of Man will give you. For it is on him that God the Father has set his seal." Then they said to him, "What must we do to perform the works of God?" Jesus answered, "This is the work of God, that you believe in him whom he has sent." So they said to him, "What sign are you going to give us then, so that we may see it and believe you? What work are you performing? Our ancestors ate the manna in the wilderness; as it is written, "He gave them bread from heaven to eat." Then Jesus said to them, "Very truly I tell you, it was not Moses who gave you the bread from heaven, but it is my Father who gives you the true bread from heaven. For the bread of God is that which comes down from heaven and gives life to the world." They said to him, "Sir, give us this bread always." Jesus said to them, "I am the bread of life. Whoever comes to me will never be hungry, and whoever believes in me will never be thirsty."
John 6:25-35

As we celebrate this Thanksgiving season we are so thankful for what God has given us. It's not the material things in life, but the spiritual, and the bounty which comes from the land. God gave manna to the Jews, yet they still rebelled. Sir Walter Raleigh brought potatoes to the Irish, but they rotted and famine encompassed the land. Here in this country we have had droughts and floods. Yet, on the fourth Thursday of November we sit down to a bountiful table with family and friends, thanking God for giving us the bread of life that we may never be hungry or thirsty.

Baked Brie

1 round of Brie
½ cup cranberries or currants
½ cup pecans or walnuts
1 tsp. cinnamon
¼ tsp. nutmeg

1 tbls. fresh ground ginger
1 shot rum or bourbon.
1 can crescent rolls, rolled out flat into a circle, to fit around Brie
1 tbls butter

Remove Brie from refrigerator one hour before using.
Preheat oven to 400°
Place the round circle of rolled dough into pie plate. Put Brie in middle.
Sprinkle with cranberries, pecans, spices and bourbon.
Fold sides of dough up to cover Brie. Pinch seams together. Put butter on top.
Bake 12-15 minutes, until browned. Serve with crackers or French bread slices.

November 26

"O for a closer walk with God, a calm and heavenly frame, a light to shine upon the road that leads me to the lamb!...So shall my walk be close with God, calm and serene my frame; so purer light shall mark the road that leads me to the lamb."
William Cowper

GOD moves in a mysterious way, His wonders to perform; He plants his footsteps in the sea, And rides upon the storm. Deep in unfathomable mines Of never failing skill He treasures up His bright designs And works His sovereign will. Ye fearful saints, fresh courage take; The clouds ye so much dread Are big with mercy and shall break In blessings on your head. Judge not the Lord by feeble sense, But trust Him for His grace; Behind a frowning providence He hides a smiling face. His purposes will ripen fast, Unfolding every hour; The bud may have a bitter taste, But sweet will be the flower. Blind unbelief is sure to err And scan His work in vain; God is His own interpreter, And He will make it plain.
Olney Hymns (1779) 'Light Shining out of Darkness'

William Cowper (1731-1800) was an English poet and hymnist. He translated Homer's *Iliad* and *Odyssey* into blank verse. He was committed to an insane asylum and later had several more attacks. How remarkable, this man who trained to be a lawyer, could write of God with such sincerity and love. Obviously God was in his heart, no matter the trauma he was going through. Listen to his words and walk with God.

Apple Muffins

½ cup canola or vegetable oil	1 tsp. cinnamon
1 cup sugar	¼ tsp. ground cloves
2 eggs	½ tsp. ground ginger
1 tsp. vanilla	½ tsp. ground nutmeg
1 1/3 cups flour	1 apple, finely chopped
1 tsp. baking soda	½ cup raisins or currants
½ tsp. salt	½ cup chopped walnuts or pecans

Preheat oven to 325°
In a bowl combine the oil and sugar. Beat in the eggs. Add the other ingredients.
Grease muffin tins, or put in liners.
Divide batter between the 12 muffin tins.
Bake 50-60 minutes, or until a toothpick comes clean.

"Peace I leave with you; My peace I give unto you; not as the world giveth, give I unto you."
John 14:27
"You shall go out with joy and be led forth with peace."
Isaiah 55:12

After a several year hiatus in getting the Middle East Peace talks resumed, President Bush gathered leaders from almost fifty different groups in Annapolis in 2007. Hope was that the Israelis and Palestinians could sit side by side and discuss a strategy to end the conflict in that region. Unfortunately the talks once again only led to handshakes, and no real resolution.

During my senior year in college my roommate was Iranian. We often talked about the Middle East and if there ever would be peace. I shall never forget her telling me, "There will never be peace." Just look at The Bible. There was never peace in the Old Testament, only war. Look at us who observe Ramadan, we go crazy not eating all day. Do you think this will lead to peace? Never"

I truly wish there could be a solution, but as we enter a new age of warfare, I can only pray that someone does not create a bomb that destroys this magnificent planet. We need to pray for peace in this world. Give our leaders strength to know what is best. It is not war. It is not hatred. It is love and hope and forgiveness.

Lamb Stew

Serves 8

¼ cup flour
1 tbls. Italian herbs
3 lbs. lamb shoulder, boneless, and cubed
3 tbls. olive oil
1 large onion, chopped
3 celery stalks, chopped
3 carrots, chopped
4 cloves garlic, minced
8 red bliss potatoes, cubed
1 tbls. rosemary
2 bay leaves
½ cup water
1 ½ cups red wine

Preheat oven to 350°
Combine the flour and herbs on a plate. Dredge the lamb cubes.
Heat the olive oil and brown the lamb.
Place all the ingredients in a covered baking dish.
Bake 1 hour, or until meat is tender.

November 28

"We gather together to ask the Lord's blessing; He chastens and hastens His will to make known. The wicked oppressing now cease from distressing. Sing praises to His Name; He forgets not His own. Beside us to guide us, our God with us joining, Ordaining, maintaining His kingdom divine; So from the beginning the fight we were winning; Thou, Lord, were at our side, all glory be Thine! We all do extol Thee, Thou Leader triumphant, And pray that Thou still our Defender will be. Let Thy congregation escape tribulation; Thy Name be ever praised! O Lord, make us free!"

As children one of the first songs we learn at Thanksgiving besides *Over the River and Through the Woods* is *We Gather Together*. Thanksgiving is a time for friends and family to gather together, to ask God's blessing for what they have. The country's earliest settlers had so little, but developed this land into the most prosperous in the world. No other country can boast about the fertileness, productivity and diversity of what can be grown here. However we must learn to appreciate our abundance. It is not endless. There are droughts, hurricanes, flooding, and other natural and manmade disasters. Be thankful and preserve what we have for future generations.

Theodore Baker (1851-1934) translated this hymn from German, written in 1694. The song was originally written for a Dutch victory in 1597.

Sweet Potato Souffle

Serves 4

4 sweet potatoes	½ tsp. nutmeg
½ cup cream	Zest of 1 lemon or orange
¼ cup brandy	4 egg yolks, beaten
½ stick butter	½ cup walnuts or pecans
1/8 tsp. cayenne	

Preheat oven to 350°
Bake the sweet potatoes for 1 hour. Remove the skins and mash in a bowl. Add the other ingredients.
Pour into a buttered casserole.
Bake 25 minutes, or until just puffy and golden.

November 29

"Bless the Lord, O my soul, and forget not all His benefits."
Psalm 103:2

As we were about to sit down for Thanksgiving dinner, we held hands to say grace. I looked at the candelabra and in horror realized that we were having an earthquake, a minor one, but even so enough to make the candles shake. We were so lucky. Only sixty-eight years earlier the city of San Francisco had been destroyed. We lived on Broadway and dinner was only a few streets below. I do admit we had drunk some wine, since our host and several other guests worked for a couple of wineries in the Napa Valley. This was one of many meals we would spend with them, the others making complete meals from Gourmet. I am very thankful the Lord blessed us that day, keeping us safe from harm, and allowing me now to pursue my cooking pastime by writing cookbooks.

Turkey with Cornbread Stuffing

For a 16 lb. turkey

1 lb. herb or hot sausage, crumbled	1 cup cranberries
1 stick butter	2 tbls. poultry seasoning
1 large onion, chopped	1 tbls. Italian herbs
4 apples, cored and chopped	1 tbls. sea salt
Homemade or store bought cornbread, cut into cubes	1 tbls. pepper
	½ cup parsley, chopped

Preheat oven to 350°
Cook the sausage in a skillet until browned. Remove.
Melt the butter in the skillet. Saute onions and apples until just tender.
Add the other ingredients.
Stuff both cavities of the turkey.
Rub the turkey with sea salt.
Bake 20 minutes to the pound.

"And Jesus, walking by the sea of Galilee, saw two brethren, Simon, called Peter, and Andrew his brother, casting a net into the sea: for they were fishers. And he saith unto them, Follow me, and I will make you fishers of men. And they straightway left their nets and followed him."
Matthew 4:18-20

First Andrew was a follower of John, then Jesus. He was also present when Jesus blessed the five loaves of bread and two fish to feed five thousand people. The miracle opened the eyes of those who came to think of him as a prophet. However Andrew and Peter followed Jesus as two of his closest disciples, treating him not as a prophet, but their Lord and Savior. Andrew is thought to have been martyred on an x-shaped cross. His symbols are a fish and the x-shaped cross. Let us be like the twelve disciples and walk with Jesus every day. Let Him call out to you, let Him take your hand, let Him guide you along the path of life.

Baked Rockfish (Striped Bass)

Serves 6

2 ½ lbs. rockfish filets
2 leeks, sliced
2 large tomatoes, diced
½ yellow pepper, julianne
½ red pepper, julianne
1 pint mushrooms, sliced

¼ cup parsley, chopped
1 tsp. salt
1 tsp. pepper
½ cup dry white wine
2 tbls. lemon juice

Preheat oven to 350°
Place the fish in a buttered baking dish.
Sprinkle all the ingredients on the fish.
Bake ½ hour
Serve with rice and garnish with parsley and lemon slices.

"Let love be genuine; hate what is evil; hold fast to what is good; love one another with mutual affection; outdo one another in showing honor.
Romans 12:9-10

My maternal grandparents were married in 1917. My grandfather served in the Army achieving the rank of Colonel. On retiring they settled on a farm north of Baltimore. Here they raised cattle, pigs, chickens and Chesapeake Bay Retrievers. Hartley oversaw the farm and lived down the hill from the main house. As children we loved to visit the farm, playing with the Retriever puppies that would grow into hunting dogs; swimming in the pond, even though there were snapping turtles; sledding down the big hill in the winter; or sitting around a fire in the den. Sometimes we'd be joined by aunts, uncles and cousins. Often there was a party on the terrace. If a dinner took place we might be relegated to the guestroom for dinner. Azzie did the cooking, but we were allowed to lick the bowls. Back then children did not attend funerals. Instead we stayed home with Azzie while my parents went to my godmother's funeral. Life seemed so simple then, just after the Second World War. Families dressed for dinner, used their best silver and linens, and sat down as a family. Let us return to civility and spend more time with family and enjoying a meal.

Roast Duck

Serves 4

1 duck 5-6 lbs.	1 orange, cut into slices
Kosher salt	2 celery stalks, chopped
1 apple, sliced	1 onion, sliced

Preheat the oven to 350°
Stuff the duck with the apple, orange, celery and onion. Rub the duck with salt. Bake 20 minutes to the pound, or until duck is crispy. Serve with orange sauce.

Orange Sauce

4 large oranges, peeled, and sectioned, save zest	¼ cup honey
¼ cup water	¼ cup Grand Marnier

In a sauce pan bring the oranges, zest, water and honey to a boil. Simmer 30 minutes. Stir in the Grand Marnier.

December 2

"Now Jacob's well was there (Sychar). Jesus therefore, being wearied with his journey, thus sat on the well: and it was about the sixth hour. There cometh a woman of Samaria to draw water: Jesus saith unto her, Give me to drink...Then saith the woman of Samaria unto him, How it that thou, being a Jew, asketh drink of me, which am a woman of Samaria? For the Jews have no dealings with the Samaritans? Jesus answered and said unto her, if thou knowest the gift of God, and who it is that saith to thee, Give me to drink; thou wouldest have asked of him of him, and he would have given thee living water."
John 4:6-10

One of the things most Americans do not understand are cultural differences, especially in the Middle East. We need to realize it takes time to make friendships, sitting down with people, drinking cups of tea, and not rushing. Probably the best book out there right now to explain this is *Three Cups of Tea* by Greg Mortenson. Mr. Mortenson had attempted to climb K2, one of the highest peaks in the world. Getting lost while returning to civilization, he arrived in a small village in Pakistan. He realized without education villages like this could never move forward, leaving behind uneducated children, not only boys, but girls. He spent time getting to know the villagers, drinking tea with them, sleeping in their homes, and forming binding friendships. He went on to build over forty schools in Pakistan and Afghanistan before and after 9/11. We need more people like Mr. Mortenson, not the government throwing money at warlords, and expecting something to be done, and a country rebuilt. We need people who can take the time to build trust, spend little money, drink of the living water, and live a saintly life by giving to others.

Apple Butter Bread

Makes 1 loaf

1 stick butter	2 tsp. cinnamon
1 cup sugar	2 tbls. milk
2 eggs	½ cup raisins
¾ cup apple butter	½ cup pecans or walnuts
2 cups flour	

Preheat oven to 350°
In a bowl cream the butter and sugar. Stir in the other ingredients.
Pour into a a greased and floured bread pan.
Bake 1 hour, or until toothpick comes out clean.

December 3

"Where cross the crowded ways of life, Where sound the cries of race and clan Above the noise of selfish strife, We hear your voice, O Son of Man. Till sons of men shall learn Your love And follow where Your feet have trod, Till, glorious from Your Heaven above, Shall come the city of our God!"

This hymn was written by Frank Mason North (1850-1935), a Methodist Episcopal minister. The hymn certainly speaks to all of us, no matter what our conditions are. Follow Jesus and you will come to the city of God.

Dr. North lived much of his life in New York City and saw the deplorable conditions that people of all ages suffered working in factories, mines, or other industries. He, along with other clergy worked for social reform that even to this day, has improved conditions for most workers, at least in this country. In 1892 he became Corresponding Secretary of the New York City Church Extension and Missionary Society and was editor of the *Christian City*, published in New York City.

Chocolate Mousse

Serves 4

2 eggs

3 egg yolks

½ cup sugar

2 tbls. Grand Marnier

6 oz. semi-sweet chocolate

2 oz. cold water

Zest of 1 orange

Juice of 1 large orange

1 package unflavored gelatin

1 cup whipping cream

In a bowl beat the eggs, egg yolks and sugar until thickened. Add the Grand Marnier.

Melt the chocolate and water in a sauce pan. Add the orange zest.

In another sauce pan combine the orange juice and gelatin. Heat, but do not bring to a boil. Add to the egg and sugar mixture. Fold in the chocolate.

Beat the whipping cream until peaks form.

Fold into the chocolate.

Pour into a oufflé dish or individual molds. Chill.

Serve with whipped cream.

December 4

"Come, ye faithful, raise the strain of triumphant gladness; God hath brought forth Israel into joy from sadness; Loosed from Pharaoh's bitter yoke Jacob's sons and daughters, Led them with unmoistened foot through the Red Sea waters. 'Tis the spring of souls today; Christ has burst His prison, And from three days' sleep in death as a sun hath risen; All the winter of our sins, long and dark, is flying From His light, to Whom we give laud and praise undying."

John of Damascus (c 676-c 749), a Syrian monk, founded a monastery at Mar Saba south of Jerusalem. He received his education from a Sicilian priest, Cosmas, who had been taken prisoner during a raid on Italy and was sold in the Damascus market to John's father. John was the Chief Administrator to the Saracen caliph of Damascus, a post once held by his father. During his tenure the veneration of icons was prohibited by Emperor Leo III. John wrote *Apologetic Treatises against those Decrying the Holy Images,* attacking the Emperor. The Emperor became aware of this, and John was dismissed from his post with the caliph, who then cut off his right hand, which he had used for his writing. Somehow through prayer before an icon of the Virgin Mary his hand was restored. The caliph offered to restore his position, but John retired to the Mar Saba monastery. Sir Arthur Sullivan of Gilbert & Sullivan fame wrote the music for the hymn.

Baklava

1½ cups sugar
2 tbls. lemon juice
¾ cup honey
1½ cups water
16 oz. package phyllo dough
2 sticks butter, melted

4 cups ground walnuts
2 tsp. ground cinnamon
½ tsp. ground nutmeg
½ tsp. ground cloves

Preheat oven to 350°
Grease a jelly roll pan.
In a sauce pan boil the sugar, water, lemon juice for 5 minutes. Stir in the honey. Combine the walnuts and spices in a bowl.
Roll out the phyllo into seven layers. Brush each layer with the butter and place 1st layer in the jelly roll pan. Sprinkle with ½ cup the walnut mixture. Place next phyllo on top. Repeat. Brush remaining butter on top. With a sharp knife cut pastry into diagonal lines ½ in. deep and 2 inches apart. Then cross diagonally so diamond shape is formed. Bake 1 hour, or slightly longer until golden brown. Pour honey syrup over the baklava. Cut into diamond shaped serving pieces.

"In the Bleak midwinter, Frosty wind made moan, Earth stood hard as iron, Water like a stone. Snow had fallen, snow on snow, Snow on snow, in the bleak midwinter, Long ago. Our God, heaven cannot hold Him, nor earth sustain; Heaven and earth shall flee away When he comes to reign. In the bleak midwinter A stable place sufficed The Lord God incarnate, Jesus Christ. Angels and archangels May have gathered there, Cherubim and seraphim Thronged the air; But his mother only, In her maiden bliss, Worshipped the beloved With a kiss. What can I give him, Poor as I am? If I were a shepherd, I would bring a lamb; If I were a wise man, I would do my part, Yet what can I give him: Give my heart."

Christina Rossetti (1830-94) wrote this poem in 1872. Gustav Theodore Holst (1874-1934) added the music in 1906. I have always found this hymn hauntingly beautiful, but my favorite part, even as a child was asking me to give the Lord my heart. What could be more touching? I did not have to think about a present, where to buy it, wrap it, and what it would be. I only had to give him what was within me. His mother only had to give him a kiss.

Walter Chalmers Smith (1824-1908), writer of *Immortal, Invisible, God Only Wise* was also born on this date. He was a clergyman of the Free Church of Scotland, a poet and hymnist.

Meatloaf

Serves 4

1 lb. ground beef
½ lb. ground pork
1 small onion, chopped
¼ cup ketchup
1 egg
1 teaspoon fresh ground pepper

2 cloves garlic, minced
1 cup fresh bread crumbs
2 tbls. Italian herbs or parsley
1 tbsp. Worcestershire sauce
2 slices bacon

Preheat oven to 350°
Combine all the ingredients, except the bacon in a bowl. Spoon into a bread pan.
Cross bacon strips on top.
Bake 30 minutes.
Serve with garlic mashed potatoes and/or macaroni and cheese.

December 6

"And He saith unto them, Why are ye fearful, O ye of little faith? Then He arose, and rebuked the winds and the sea; and there was a great calm. But the men marveled saying, What manner of man is this, that even the winds and the sea obey Him?"
Matthew 8:26-27

St. Nicholas was Bishop of Myra in Turkey. He is thought to have rescued three girls from prostitution, three sailors from drowning, and to have brought back to life three boys who were murdered by a butcher. He brings presents to children in the Scandinavian countries, and is the patron of sailors. The legend of the gift giving comes from the story of St. Nicholas meeting a very poor man who could not provide a dowry for his three daughters. Secretly as each daughter came of age St. Nicholas provided a purse with gold coins for the girl. St. Nicholas' remains were supposedly removed to Bari, Italy.

In parts of Europe children receive gifts, coins and food in shoes. I wish in this country we could go back to the more humble ways of giving. While visiting the Collegiate Church of St. Nicholas in Galway I was touched by the simple plaques and banners dedicated to those who have worshipped in this historic church built c 1320. Christopher Columbus may have worshipped here in 1477. Banners hang in honor of those who fought with the Connaught Raiders during the Peninsular Wars (1808-14) and the lovely Celtic cross honors those who perished during World War I. Amid the hustle and bustle of downtown Galway this ancient simple stone church serves as a beacon of hope in memory of St. Nicholas.

St. Nicholas Day Cookies

2 sticks butter	4 tsp. cinnamon
1 cup Crisco	½ tsp. nutmeg
2 cups brown sugar	½ tsp. ground cloves
½ cup sour cream	4 ½ cups flour
½ cup sugar	½ cup chopped nuts
½ tsp. baking soda	

Cream the butter and brown sugar. Sift together the flour, soda and spices. Add the sour cream alternately with sifted dry ingredients. Stir in the nuts. Knead the dough into rolls, 2 inches thick.
Wrap in plastic and refrigerate for a few hours or overnight. Cut into slices and bake at 375° for 10 to 12 minutes.
4 sticks of butter can be used instead of the butter and Crsico.

December 7

"Lift high the cross, the love of Christ proclaim"
George Kitchin and Michael Robert Newbolt

"And no man hath ascended up to heaven, but he that came down from heaven, even the Son of man which is in heaven. And as Moses lifted up the serpent in the wilderness, even so must the Son of man be lifted up: That whosoever believeth in him should not perish, but have eternal life. For God so loved the world, that he gave his only begotten Son, that whosoever believeth in him should not perish, but have everlasting life."
John 3:13-16

Each time I sing this hymn I am uplifted. Uplifted thinking how our Lord died for our sins. How he sacrificed himself for us the sinners. How each day we must go out, seek out unbelievers and let them open their eyes to see the living Lord, so they might come to worship the King.

George William Kitchin (1827-1912) studied at Oxford and was ordained in 1859. Dr. Kitchin was the first chancellor of the University of Durham, and was also Dean of Durham and Winchester Cathedrals.

Baked Cod

Serves 6

2½ lbs. cod filets
½ cup white wine
2 tbls. olive oil
2 tbls. butter
½ lbs. baby spinach
4 cloves garlic, minced

1 pint shitake mushrooms
1 tsp. sea salt
1 tsp. pepper
2 tbls. lemon juice
6 slices smoked bacon, cooked and crumbled

Preheat the broiler.
Place the fish in a baking dish and pour the wine and olive oil on top.
Bake 10 minutes, or until fish is just browned.
In a skillet melt the butter and stir in spinach, garlic and mushrooms. Add the salt, pepper, lemon juice and remaining liquid from the cod. Stir in the bacon.
Spoon over the cod.
Put back under boiler for 2 minutes.
You can also add parmesan cheese.

December 8

"The law of the Lord is perfect, converting the soul: the testimony of the Lord is sure, making wise the simple."
Psalm 19:7

The Shakers were a group of people who left England to escape prosecution. They lived simple, spartan lives. The founder, Ann Lee, and her husband moved to the Hudson River area, having to escape from New York as the Revolutionary War was just about to begin and some thought she was a British spy. They settled in a place called Niskeyuna, and only survived winters because of the local Mohicans who thought Ann was "The Good Woman." Despite many ups and downs the Shakers eventually numbered about 6000 people. Unfortunately because men and women lived and worshipped separately, the sect gradually died out. Some of their traditions, mainly furniture and songs remain. One of these is *Simple Gifts* which Aaron Copeland used in Appalachian Spring, and in 1963 Sydney Carter wrote *I Danced in the Morning*.

'Tis the gift to be simple, 'tis the gift to be free, 'Tis the gift to come down where we ought to be, And when we find ourselves in the place just right, 'Twill be in the valley of love and delight. When true simplicity is gained, To bow and to bend we shan't be ashamed, To turn, turn will be our delight, Till by turning, turning we come round right."
Joseph Brackett, Jr. (1797-1882)

Cheese Puffs

1 8 oz. package cream cheese
¼ cup mayonnaise
4 green onions, finely chopped
¼ tsp. Tabasco sauce

¼ lb. prosciutto, cut into small pieces
1 cup parmesan cheese
Thin sliced white bread
Butter

Preheat the broiler.
Combine the cream cheese, mayonnaise, onions and Tabasco in a food processor. Transfer to a bowl and combine with prosciutto and cheese.
With a biscuit cutter cut out 40 round circles of the bread. Place on a cookie sheet. Butter one side. Place under the broiler until just browned.
Remove from the oven and top with cheese mixture.
Place under the broiler again until just browned and bubbling. Serve immediately.

December 9

"Now When Jesus was born in Bethlehem of Judea in the days of Herod the king, behold, there came wise men from the east to Jerusalem...for out of thee shall come a Governor, that shall rule my people Israel."
Matthew 2:1, 6

When I taught at Episcopal Academy in Merion, the second grade boys participated in the Christmas pageant. Each year the decision as to which one would play Mary had to be carefully considered by the staff of the Lower School. Usually it was left up to me! Parents would even call in. But it was time for the boys to learn memorization of St. Matthew and favorite Christmas hymns. The boys all had costumes, sets were on the stage, and parents beamed at their little ones. Unfortunately, not long after I left the school several parents, including a Jewish couple protested that the pageant should no longer be performed. Because (if I can remember back) of four parents, the pageant was no more. This was a strong Episcopal school with daily chapel, and active participation by students and faculty. Christmas is a time to share, to let voices ring out, and share our love for Christ and each other. Those parents should not have sent their children to this school. A Christian upbringing is essential to a child and his parents. Episcopal is now co-ed. Gone are the days of my angelic boys. I still have the little statue one boy gave me – a little boy with a bouquet of flowers hidden behind his back. I also remember the name of that child. He's grown now. I wonder what he's doing, how many children he has, and whether he is instilling in them the Christian values that he was taught? I miss my little boys, except now I have a grandson.

Chocolate Chip Cookies II

2 sticks butter	1 tsp. baking soda
1½ cups brown sugar	½ tsp. salt
½ cup sugar	1½ cups rolled oats
2 eggs	1 cup chocolate chips
2 tbls. milk	1 cup dried cranberries
1 tsp. vanilla	1 cup pecans
1¾ cups flour	

Preheat the oven to 375°
In a bowl cream the butter and sugars. Add the eggs, milk and vanilla. Beat in the flour, baking soda, and salt. Stir in the oats, chocolate chips, cranberries, and pecans.
Drop by rounded teaspoons on an ungreased baking sheet. Bake 10 minutes, or until golden.

December 10

"Watch therefore, for ye know neither the day nor the hour wherein the Son of man cometh."
Matthew 25:13

At Christmas I love to watch the expressions of the children. Some don't know anything about Christmas, except for presents. They don't know about the coming of our Lord. It is important to teach them at an early age that it is not presents that they await but the baby Jesus whose birthday we will celebrate. As soon as you mention birthdays their eyes will open wider and you can see they understand. But once again you have to tell them it's not presents. They have other things to look forward to, being with family and friends, yes some presents and a cake with candles. Explain to them how Jesus was born in a manger with only his mother and Joseph and the animals present. No gifts, only the acknowledgement that his mother had been sent word by the angel Gabriel that her son was the Son of God, who was to change our world forever.

Christmas Coffee Cake

Batter

1 stick butter	1½ cups flour
1 cup sugar	1 teaspoon vanilla
2 eggs	1 cup pecans
1 cup sour cream	½ jar mincemeat
1½ tsp. baking powder	Candied green and red cherries

Preheat oven to 350°
Melt the butter in a large sauce pan over low heat. Remove from heat.
Beat in the sugar, eggs, sour cream, baking powder, flour, vanilla and pecans.
Fold in the mincemeat.
Pour into a greased 9" square baking dish. Spoon the topping over the batter. Garnish with cherries.
Bake 45 minutes, or the top is golden and a toothpick comes out clean.

Topping

¼ cup brown sugar	2 tbls. cinnamon
¼ cup sugar	

Combine ingredients in a small bowl

December 11

"Silent night, holy night. All is calm, all is bright Round yon virgin mother and child Holy infant so tender and mild Sleep in heavenly peace Sleep in heavenly peace. Silent night, holy night. Shepherds quake at the sight, Glories stream from heaven afar, Heav'nly hosts sing alleluia: Christ the Saviour is born, Christ the Saviour is born. Silent night, holy night Son of God, love's pure light, Radiant beams from thy holy face, With the dawn of redeeming grace: Jesus, Lord, at thy birth, Jesus, Lord, at thy birth."
Joseph Mohr 1816

As the Christmas season approaches we think of that holy night when our lord was born. Christmas services, Christmas concerts, and Christmas Eve we sing this beloved song by Joseph Mohr (1792-1848). There is not a dry eye. It is so emotional, so beautiful, hoping the night will be calm, and the New Year too. The original lyrics of the song *Stille Nacht* were written in German by the Austrian priest Josef Mohr and the melody was composed by the Austrian headmaster Franz Xaver Gruber. The carol was first performed in the Church of St. Nicholas in Oberndorf, Austria on December 24, 1818. Mr. Mohr was an illegitimate child, and when he decided to enter the priesthood, had to receive permission from the pope. He later founded a children's school in Wagarin where he was the parish pastor.

Rolled Veal

Serves 4

¼ cup flour
1 tbls. Italian herbs
2 cloves garlic, crushed
3 tbls. butter
1 tbls. olive oil

1 lb. very thin veal scaloppini (at least four good slices)
4 slices prosciutto
4 slices parmesan cheese
3 tbls. Port

Preheat oven to 350°
Combine the flour, Italian herbs and garlic on a plate. Dredge the veal in the flour mixture.
Heat an iron skillet with the butter and olive oil. Brown the veal on each side. Remove from the skillet.
Place one slice of prosciutto and one slice cheese on each scaloppini. Roll up and secure with a toothpick.
Bake the veal for 10 minutes. Remove veal. Stir the Port into the drippings. Pour over veal. Serve with pasta and a salad.

December 12

"That I may know Him., and the power of his resurrection, and the fellowship of his sufferings, being made conformable unto his death."
Philippians 3:10

That is my fervent wish. That I may know Him more and more each day. And that the world will come to know Him. Do not hide your devotion to God. Display it with a cross, or holding, or reading the Bible in public. Do not be ashamed. We are the ones who must reach out, especially to the young. Embrace them in our arms, give them hope, not despair. They are our future.

When I moved to the Eastern Shore I did not have a church or know a lot of people. The first Sunday at Christ Church everyone opened their arms to me and introduced themselves. Shortly thereafter, a neighbor across the street knocked on the door. Both she and her husband are actively involved in their church, have gone on missions, and participate in Bible study groups. Several months later I became reacquainted with a lady who had been in my Nantucket Bible Study Group. These were all Christians who gave freely of themselves and shared their beliefs with others. All of them had found the Lord. Oh how I am blessed to live in a beautiful place with fervent believers. Thank you Lord for letting me make the choice to move here.

Mango Salsa

1 large mango, peeled and diced
¼ cup cilantro, chopped
¼ cup red onion, chopped

¼ cup red pepper, chopped
¼ cup lime juice
2 tbls. olive oil

Combine the ingredients in a bowl. Chill.
Serve with chips, or use with grilled chicken or fish, especially swordfish.

"For all the saints, who from their labors rest, Who Thee by faith before the world confessed, Thy Name, O Jesus, be forever blessed. Alleluia, Alleluia! Thou wast their Rock, their Fortress and their Might; Thou, Lord, their Captain in the well fought fight; Thou, in the darkness drear, their one true Light. Alleluia, Alleluia! O may Thy soldiers, faithful, true and bold, Fight as the saints who nobly fought of old, And win with them the victor's crown of gold. Alleluia, Alleluia! And when the strife is fierce, the warfare long, Steals on the ear the distant triumph song, And hearts are brave, again, and arms are strong. Alleluia, Alleluia! But lo! there breaks a yet more glorious day; The saints triumphant rise in bright array; The King of glory passes on His way. Alleluia, Alleluia!"

This favorite hymn is sung on All Saint's Day and celebrates those who gave their lives for Christ. Each day we should walk in their footsteps, doing good deeds, giving of ourselves to God and others, knowing that the future brings good tidings. When you take communion remember Bishop How and his work for the church. William Walsham How (1823-1897) was an English bishop and founded the East London Church Fund. In 1863-1868 he published a *Commentary on the Four Gospels* and wrote a manual for Communion.

Beef Tenderloin with Balsamic Sauce

Serves 6

6 beef tenderloin
1 tbls. sea salt
2 tsp. garlic salt

1 tbls. pepper
Blue cheese

Rub the tenderloin with the salt, garlic and pepper.
Grill on a BBQ to desired pinkness.
Serve with balsamic sauce and a spoonful of blue cheese.

Balsamic Sauce

½ cup balsamic vinegar
½ stick butter

¼ cup honey
¼ cup fresh chopped basil

Bring the balsamic vinegar to a boil until the liquid is reduced by half.
Stir in butter, honey and basil.

December 14

"Take my life, and let it be consecrated, Lord, to Thee. Take my moments and my days; let them flow in ceaseless praise. Take my hands, and let them move at the impulse of Thy love. Take my feet, and let them be swift and beautiful for Thee. Take my voice, and let me sing always, only, for my King. Take my lips, and let them be filled with messages from Thee. Take my silver and my gold; not a mite would I withhold. Take my intellect, and use every power as Thou shalt choose. Take my will, and make it Thine; it shall be no longer mine. Take my heart, it is Thine own; it shall be Thy royal throne. Take my love, my Lord, I pour at Thy feet its treasure store. Take myself, and I will be ever, only, all for Thee."

Dear Lord, for a woman, this is one of the most poignant hymns. Women played such an important role in Jesus' short life. To have a female compose this hymn offers our love for the Lord, and that we are His. We know he is always with us, but for us to give every part of our body and soul lifts us to a new high. We can soar with eagles, we can achieve. We are the Lord's. He made us, and we shall follow in his footsteps. Women and children, are as much God's own, as men. Please never forget that.

Frances Ridley Havergal (1836-1879) was a poet and wrote several hymns - *Like A River Glorious, I Gave My Life for Thee"* and *Who Is on the Lord's Side?* Her father and brother were both ministers and also musically talented.

Spinach Souffle

Serves 4

½ stick butter
¼ cup flour
1 cup half and half
4 eggs, separated
½ cup parmesan cheese

½ cup sharp cheddar cheese
¼ tsp. nutmeg
2 tbls. dill, snipped
½ lb. fresh baby spinach

Preheat oven to 400°
Melt the butter in a sauce pan. Stir in flour and half and half until thickened.
Add the egg yolks, cheeses, nutmeg, dill and spinach.
Beat the egg whites until stiff. Fold into the spinach mixture.
Pour into a greased soufflé dish.
Bake 40 minutes. Do not open oven. Serve immediately.

"But it shall be one day which shall be known to the Lord, not day, nor night; but it shall come to pass that at evening time it shall be light…And the Lord shall be king over all the earth, in that day shall there be one Lord, and his name one."
Zechariah 14:7-9

There is something special about a winter sky. The evening sky is all aglow – red, purples, pinks, blue and sunlight peaking through the clouds. Oh how glorious God has made the earth and all that surrounds it. The Lord's creation overflows with His majesty and beauty. Look up, not down, seek that which is the Lord's and never turn back. See the light and sing out *May Jesus Christ be praised.*

The last book of the Old Testament concludes with the destruction of Jerusalem, but that the Lord shall be king over the whole earth, the Light of the world. This book foretells the coming light – the light of the Messiah that will save mankind. In Zechariah 9:9 *"Rejoice greatly, O daughter of Zion; shout, O daughter of Jerusalem: behold thy king cometh unto thee: he is just and having salvation; lowly and riding upon an ass, and upon a colt the foal of an ass."*

Baked Oysters

Serves 4

1 quart oysters, reserve 2 cups liquor
½ stick butter
1 large leek, chopped
2 cloves garlic, minced
¼ cup flour
2 cups cream
1 cup grated parmesan cheese

¼ cup parsley, chopped
4 chives, snipped
½ teaspoon salt
1 tsp. pepper
1 tsp. Worcestershire sauce
1/8 tsp. Tabasco sauce
8 Ritz crackers, crushed
Butter

Preheat oven to 350°
Melt the butter in a large pan. Saute the leeks and garlic. Stir in the flour and cream. Add liquor. Cook until just slightly thickened.
Add cheese, parsley, chives, salt, pepper, Worcestershire, and Tabasco.
Place the oysters in a buttered casserole. Pour the sauce over the oysters.
Sprinkle with crackers and dot with butter.
Bake 15 minutes, or until bubbling.
Serve with rice.

December 16

"Joyful, joyful, we adore thee, God of glory, Lord of love…"
Ludwig van Beethoven

Each time I hear these words, or the tune, my eyes well up and think back on the concert Leonard Bernstein conducted at the Berlin Wall on December 25, 1989. The wall had come down in November, now Germany was once again one country. Thank you Mr. Bernstein for conducting Beethoven's 9th Symphony on Christmas Day, and that Christians throughout Germany could rejoice.

Ludwig van Beethoven (1770-1827) was a German composer and pianist. His father was a court musician and tenor, and encouraged Beethoven's musical talent. He played his first concert when he was only eight years old. In his 20s he moved to Vienna and studied under Joseph Haydn. His hearing quickly deteriorated, but he composed and conducted, even when he became completely deaf. His hymns, his symphonies, concerti, and chamber music are played throughout the world. How could a man, who had lost his hearing, compose such incredible uplifting music? He obviously had a lot of faith.

Glazed Carrots

Serves 6

12 carrots, peeled and thinly sliced, lengthwise
½ stick butter
¼ cup dark brown sugar

¼ cup dark rum
¼ tsp. nutmeg
2 tbls. fresh grated ginger

In a skillet melt the butter. Stir in the brown sugar, rum, nutmeg and ginger. Add the carrots and saute for 2-3 minutes.
Serve warm.
Maple syrup or honey can be substituted for the brown sugar.

December 17

"Spikenard and saffron; calamus and cinnamon; with all trees of frankincense; myrrh and aloes; with all the chief spices."
Song of Solomon 4:14

The smells of Christmas permeate throughout the house. Yes, it's still a week away, but there are cookies, pies, puddings and cakes to bake. We are fortunate to have freezers, saving us time to bake ahead. Friends gather to do a cookie exchange. Ladies break bread over tea or luncheons. Each night parties fill our calendar. However, it is when we think of these rich spices, that we remember the purpose of Christmas. How Christ was born in a manger to a young mother and a carpenter father. Shepherds watched their flocks by night. Three wise men came bearing gifts of frankincense, gold and myrrh. A star shone in the East. A child was born, a savior for all mankind, who would give up his life for us, so that we could be saved from sin. Rejoice, Jesus Christ is Lord!

"We three kings of Orient are, bearing gifts we traverse afar...gold and frankincense and myrrh..."
John Henry Hopkins

Pumpkin Ice Cream Pie

1 graham cracker pie crust
1 pint vanilla or butter pecan ice cream
1 15 oz. can pumpkin
1½ cups sugar
½ tsp. salt
2 tsp. cinnamon
½ tsp. ground ginger
¼ tsp. ground cloves
1 tsp. vanilla
1 pint whipping cream
1 tbls. butter
1 cup sliced almonds
¼ cup sugar

Spread the ice cream in the bottom of the pie crust. Freeze.
In a bowl combine the pumpkin, sugar, salt, cinnamon, ginger, cloves, and vanilla.
In another bowl beat ½ pint whipping cream until peaks form. Fold into the pumpkin mixture. Pour the mixture over the ice cream. Cover and freeze for at least 4 hours.
In a small sauce pan heat the butter, almonds and sugar until almonds are just browned.
Beat the remaining whipping cream until peaks form.
Serve the pie with whipped cream and top with almonds.

December 18

"Come, O thou Traveler unknown, Whom still I hold, but cannot see…Thy Name is Love."

"And he (Jacob) rose up that night, and took his two wives, and his two women servants, and his eleven sons, and passed over the ford Jabbok… And Jacob was left alone; and there wrestled a man with him until the breaking of the day. And when he that he prevailed not against him, he touched the hollow of his thigh; and the hollow of Jacob's thigh was out of joint, as he wrestled with him. And he said, Let me go, for the day breaketh, And he said, I will not let thee go, except thou bless me. And he said unto him, What is thy name? And he said Jacob. And he said, Thy name shall be called no more Jacob, but Israel, for as a prince hast thou power with God and with men, and hast prevailed."
Genesis 32:22-28

Charles Wesley (1707-1788) is one of the most beloved hymnists. He wrote more than a thousand hymns and was one of the founders of the Methodists. Among my favorite hymns are *Jesus Christ is Risen Today*; *Come Thou Long Expected Jesus*; *Lo, He comes with Clouds Descending; Hark the Herald Angels Sing; Love Divine, All Love Excelling; and O for a Thousand Tongues to Sing.* We are truly thankful for this Englishman who gave us heavenly words. His hymn *"O Thou Traveler Unknown"* is based on this Biblical passage. God and Jacob each want to know who the other is. God gives Jacob his new name Israel meaning *"he who struggles with God."* Jacob also wants to know God's name, and God finally gives in and tells him it is *"Love."*

Sweet Potato Bisque

Serves 4

½ stick butter
2 leeks, chopped
4 sweet potatoes, peeled and quartered

2 cups chicken stock
2 cups heavy cream
½ tsp. nutmeg

Melt the butter in a pan. Saute leeks. Add sweet potatoes and stock.
Cook until sweet potatoes are tender, about 20 minutes.
Place in food processor until blended.
Stir in cream and nutmeg. Serve warm or chilled.

"And Jacob sod pottage: and Esau came from the field, and he was faint: And Esau said to Jacob, Feed me, I pray thee, with that same red pottage; for I am faint: therefore was his name called Edom. And Jacob said, Sell me this day thy birthright. And Esau said, Behold, I am at the point to die; and what profit shall this birthright do to me? And Jacob said, Swear to me this day; and he swear unto him: and he sold his birthright unto Jacob. Then Jacob gave Esau bread and pottage of lentils; and he did eat and drink, and rose up, and went his way: thus Esau despised his birthright."
Genesis 25:29-34

We love to think families should get along, but all it takes is a brother, or someone else to inherit an estate, and bitter feelings blast out. No longer do siblings speak to each other, and hatred breeds animosity that even time may not heal. Money and envy truly are at the root of all evil. Mend family wounds that scar not only you, but for generations or more to come.

Fried Lentils with Cilantro Sauce

1 cup dried lentils	1 jalapeno, seeded and chopped
3 cups water	1 tbls. fresh grated ginger
½ cup cilantro	½ tsp. salt
1 tbls. fresh grated coconut	Vegetable oil

Bring water and lentils to a boil. Cover and simmer for about 30 minutes, until lentils are tender. Drain. Reserve 1 cup water.
In a food processor combine the lentils, water cilantro, coconut, jalapeno, ginger and salt.
Pour vegetable oil into a skillet so that it is about 2 inches deep. Heat.
Form the lentil mixture into balls. Drop into hot oil until they are browned on all sides.
Place on rack with paper towel.

Sauce

1 cup sour cream or yogurt	½ tsp. salt
¼ cup cilantro, chopped	1 tsp. cumin
¼ tsp. Tabasco or cayenne	

Combine the ingredients in a bowl. Serve with fried lentils.
Add more cayenne for a hotter sauce.
Chopped cucumber can be added to the sauce.

December 20

"Oh little town of Bethlehem, How still we see thee lie; Above thy deep and dreamless sleep the silent stars go by: Yet in thy dark streets shineth the everlasting Light. The hopes and fears of all the years are met in thee tonight. For Christ is born of Mary, and gathered all above while mortals sleep, the angels keep their watch of wondering love. O morning stars, together proclaim thy holy birth, and praises to God the King, and peace to men on earth."
Phillips Brooks 1868; music by Lewis Henry Reiner

I love the Christmas carols. We can hum them, dreaming about the birth of our Lord. Think how quiet Bethlehem might have been that night, though a stable might have animals cooing, mooing and neighing. But from above the angels watched, guarding Mary and Joseph as they awaited the birth of baby Jesus. As I read about Phillips Brooks (1835-93) "The Prince of the Pulpit" who gave incredible sermons at Trinity Church in Boston, I wish there were more preachers like him today. There are those who try to teach the Gospel, those who try to make us laugh at a bad joke, those full of brimstone and fire, and a few who can enlighten our day or path.

Strawberry Torte

Serves 8

1 stick butter	¼ cup milk
1½ cups sugar	½ cup walnuts or pecans
4 eggs, separated	2 cups heavy cream
1 cup flour	1 pint strawberries
1 tsp. baking powder	

Preheat oven to 325°
Cream the butter and ½ cup sugar. Beat in the egg yolks. Stir in the flour, baking powder, and milk.
In a separate bowl beat the egg whites until peaks form. Gradually add remaining cup of sugar.
Combine the batter and egg whites.
Divide the butter mixture between two cake pans. Sprinkle one pan with walnuts.
Bake 30 minutes. Cool.
Place cake without nuts on a cake plate. Spread with half of whipped cream and half of strawberries.
Place nut cake on top with nuts on top. Spread with remaining whipped cream and strawberries.

December 21

"But Thomas, one of the twelve, called Didymus, was not with them when Jesus came. The other disciples therefore said unto him, We have seen the Lord. But he said unto them, Except I shall see in his hands the print of the nails, and put my finger into the print of the nails, and thrust my hand into his side, I will not believe. And after eight days again his disciples were within, and Thomas with them: then came Jesus, the doors being shut, and stood in the midst, and said, Peace be unto you. Then saith he to Thomas, Reach hither thy finger, and behold my hands; and reach hither thy hand, and thrust it into my side: and be not faithless, but believing. And Thomas answered and said unto him, My Lord and my God." Jesus saith unto him, Thomas because thou hast seen me, thou hast believed: blessed are they that have not seen, and yet have believed."
John 20:24-29

Doubting Thomas. A person who truly loved the Lord, but needed to touch and know that He had died for all of us. He carried on the work of the apostles, possibly traveling to India and dying there.

On this date in 1988 Pan Am flight 103 crashed after a terrorist bomb blew it up over Lockerbie, Scotland. A friend from Cleveland was supposed to have been on that flight, but because of business could not leave out that day. When I saw him just a year later, for the first time after that awful disaster, I greeted him warmly. He was thankful to be alive, but had lost several coworkers. Their lives cannot be brought back, only memories. And now as we watch how terrorism continues to dominate the world scene, we do pray for peace, and hope, and love among all peoples. May they see how our Lord, even though our faith does have doubters, trusts us to believe in Him.

Ice Cream with Raspberry Sauce

Serves 4

1 quart of your favorite ice cream	¼ cup corn syrup
2 pints raspberries	¼ cup Curacao

Puree the raspberries, corn syrup and Curacao in a food processor.
Serve over ice cream.
Save a few raspberries for garnish.
Whipped cream can also be served for a few more calories.

December 22

"Rejoice in the Lord always: and again I say Rejoice. Let your moderation be known unto all men. The Lord is at hand. Be careful for nothing; but in everything by prayer and supplication with thanksgiving let your requests be known unto God. And the peace of God which passeth all understanding, shall keep your hearts and minds through Christ Jesus."
Philippians 4:4-7

Christmas is almost here. There is much laughter, tasting from spoons, and the aroma of sweet puddings, cakes and pies baking in the oven. Joy is in the air, no heaviness, only the singing of carols and awaiting the birth of our Lord. The celebration of Christmas brings together old family traditions and new when more members are added.

Christmas Pudding

1 lb. currants	2 cups flour
1 cup brandy	2 tsp. baking soda
6 slices challah bread, broken into small pieces	1 tsp. salt
	1 tsp. ground nutmeg
1 cup apple cider	2 tsp. cinnamon
1 lb. raisins	2 tsp. ground mace
½ lb. candied orange peel	1 tsp. ground ginger
½ lb. candied lemon peel	½ teaspoon ground cloves
½ lb. citron	1 lb. suet
½ lb. dates	2 cups brown sugar
2 cups walnuts	6 eggs

Preheat oven to 300°
Soak the currants in brandy for 30 minutes. Soak the bread in apple cider.
Combine the currants, raisins, orange peel, lemon peel, citron, dates and walnuts in a bowl. Stir in the flour, baking soda, salt and spices. Add the suet, bread, brown sugar, and eggs.
Grease 2 pudding molds. Spoon the mixture into the molds.
Cover with moistened parchment paper. Secure with rubber bands.
Place molds in pans filled with boiling water. Cover molds and pans with aluminum foil. Steam for 5 hours, adding more water if needed.
Remove from the oven. Pour ½ cup brandy over each mold. Cover and keep in a cool place.
Before serving pudding, steam for at least another hour. Remove the pudding from the mold. Serve with hard sauce.

December 23

"The Son of Man will come at an hour when you are not expecting Him."
Luke 12:40

We wait impatiently for the Lord. We are like little children, too itchy to stay seated for any length of time. For we do not know when he will come. We don't even know what we might be doing at that time. Will I be sitting at my computer writing another book? Crazy in the kitchen cooking up a storm to develop a new recipe? Painting another room? Sitting on the beach with a favorite book? Or reading my daily lessons and saying morning prayers? The time does not matter. What matters is that we accept Him, that we know we have found Him. That he is our Savior and Redeemer. *"Our help in ages past and our hope for years to come."* Don't wait. Actively seek the Lord.

Christmas Bread

2 packages yeast	1 stick butter, melted
½ cup warm water	Zest of 1 orange
2 cups milk, scalded	Zest of 1 lemon
½ cup sugar	½ cup raisins
1/8 tsp. cardamom seed	½ cup dried cranberries
2 tsp. salt	1 cup candied fruit
8 cups flour	1 cup walnuts, almonds or pecans

Dissolve the yeast in the warm water. Stir in milk and sugar. Add salt and cardamom. Beat in 4 cups of flour. Stir in the butter. Gradually beat in remaining 4 cups flour, orange and lemon zest.
Shape into a ball. Place in a buttered bowl. Cover. Let rise until doubled in size.
Punch down dough. Divide in two. Braid. Place on a baking sheet. Press the raisins, cranberries, fruit and nuts into the dough.
Preheat oven to 375°
Bake 15 minutes.
Turn heat to 350°. Bake 20 minutes or until golden brown.
Serve with butter or cream cheese.

December 24 – Christmas Eve

"Refrain: Go tell it on the mountain Over the hills and far away Go tell it on the mountain That Jesus Christ is born.
The shepherds all were watching Over their sheep at night When a guiding star shone from heaven And the followed that holy light (r) They found a lovely manger Where the humble Christ was born And God sent out salvation On that blessed Christmas morn (r) He brought with Him forgiveness He live to show us the way He came to redeem all creation And to wash all our sins away (r)"

This lively Afro-American spiritual is one that most children learn at a very early age at Christmas. The hymn dates back to c 1865 and has been recorded by numerous artists. I love to hear it sung in church by the children. This is truly a Christmas song proclaiming the nativity. Go tell it everywhere, spread the word that Jesus Christ is born.

Christmas Eve has always been a special time for my family. We dress in elegant clothes, dine at home or the club, stuff our Christmas stockings, attend church and think about what the next morning will bring. Little did I guess that years ago my father and now husband would walk back from the club behind the rest of us. Finally, almost at the house, George asked dad for my hand. He got his courage up, and did it! It wasn't until Christmas morning, as he looked for a small package under the tree that he proposed in front of my whole family! The little box contained a gold bracelet, a cigar wrapper, and a note saying "this is good until we get to Tilghman's." Tighman's is our hometown jewelry store! Two months later, along with my daughter, we found the perfect engagement ring. God sent this man to be part of my life, as baby Jesus was sent for us.

Eggnog Ice Cream

½ cup sugar
4 egg yolks
3 cups heavy cream
1 cup milk

2 vanilla beans or 1 tsp vanilla
1 tbls. rum
1 tbls. brandy
¼ tsp fresh grated nutmeg

In a bowl beat the egg yolks and sugar until thickened. Stir in the cream, milk vanilla, rum, brandy, and nutmeg.
Place in an ice cream maker and mix until thickened, about 20-25 minutes.
Place in the freezer for at least two hours before using. Can be sprinkled with more nutmeg before serving.

December 25

"Therefore the Lord himself will give you a sign. Behold, a young women shall conceive and bear a son, and shall call his name Immanuel."
Isaiah 7:14

"We will be glad and rejoice."
Isaiah 25:9

For a number of years now we have spent Christmas through New Year's Day with my parents in Florida. This is a lovely break before winter truly sets in. A walk on the beach, time with family and friends, a good book to read, a place to refresh the body and soul. The waves roll in, the heron perch nearby, and the osprey screech, protecting their nests. Dophins can be seen gracefully and playfully swimming, oblivious to those watching. As a boat appears on the horizon the wind picks up, billowing the sails, and sending its crew careening forward. How lucky we are to enjoy the peace and quiet, far from the city with bright lights and lots of noise. We are blessed, Lord. You made the beauty of the earth. Let us enjoy each moment. Let us rejoice. A child has been born, your Son and our Savior.

On Christmas Eve or Day we serve Oysters Rockefeller. Sadly most of the oysters no longer come from the Chesapeake Bay, but from North Carolina, Florida, Texas, or other places.

Oysters Rockefeller

1 quart oysters, drained (about 24 oysters), drained
1 large package fresh baby spinach
Juice of one lemon

4 green onions, chopped
½ teaspoon Tabasco sauce
½ cup fresh grated Parmesan cheese

Preheat oven to 400°
Wash and dry the spinach. Place in a 13 by 9 baking dish. Sprinkle with lemon juice, Tabasco and green onions
Divide up the oysters on the spinach
Sprinkle with grated cheese
Bake for about ten minutes, or just bubbling.

December 26

"And cast him (Stephen) out of the city, and stoned him, and the witnesses laid down their clothes at a young man's feet, whose name was Saul. And they stoned Stephen, calling upon God, and saying, Lord Jesus "receive my spirit." And he kneeled down, and cried with a loud voice, "Lord lay not this sin to their charge." And when he had said this he fell asleep."
Acts 7:58-60

December 26 is remembered as the day Saint Stephen was stoned to death, our first Christian martyr. Sadly this occurs the day after Christmas when we have celebrated the birth of our Lord. St. Stephen was a Jew, but spoke Greek. We do not know much about his life, other than the fact he was brought before the Sanhedrin for his preaching and then accused of blasphemy.

This day is also remembered for King Wenceslas. The story is about a king who goes out to give alms to a poor peasant on the Feast of St. Stephen. His page is about to give up following him in a blizzard, but he is warmed by stepping in the king's footprints. The story is based on the life of Saint Wenceslaus I, Duke of Bohemia (907-935), who was also known as Svaty Vaclav. The hymn *Good King Wenceslas* was written by an Englishman, John Mason Neale, c 1849.

King Wenceslaus Soup

Serves 6

2 cans black beans, drained
1 ham bone
2 quarts water
½ stick butter
2 stalks celery, chopped
½ green pepper, chopped

1 medium red onion, chopped
1 tsp. cumin
1 tsp. chili powder
½ tsp. cayenne
1 cup sherry

Cook the ham bone in water until ½ liquid remains.
In a skillet melt the butter. Stir in the
onions, celery and pepper. Cook until tender. Stir in beans and remaining liquid.
Simmer for 1 hour, or until beans are tender.
Put in a food processor with cumin, chili and cayenne.
Serve in bowls with a pitcher of sherry.

December 27

"In the beginning was the Word, and the Word was with God, and the Word was God. The same was in the beginning with God. All things were made by him; and without him was not any thing made that was made. In him was life; and the life was the light of men. And the light shineth in darkness; and the darkness comprehended it not. There was a man sent from God, whose name was John. The same came for a witness, to bear witness of the Light, that all men through him might believe. He was not that Light, but was sent to bear witness of that Light. That was the true Light, which lighteth every man that cometh into the world. He was in the world, and the world was made by him, and the world knew him not. He came unto his own, and his own received him not. But as many as received him, to them gave he power to become the sons of God, even to them that believe on his name: Which were born, not of blood, nor of the will of the flesh, nor of the will of man, but of God. And the Word was made flesh, and dwelt among us, (and we beheld his glory, the glory as of the only begotten of the Father,) full of grace and truth. John bare witness of him, and cried, saying, This was he of whom I spake, He that cometh after me is preferred before me: for he was before me. And of his fulness have all we received, and grace for grace. For the law was given by Moses, but grace and truth came by Jesus Christ. No man hath seen God at any time, the only begotten Son, which is in the bosom of the Father, he hath declared him. John 1: 1-18

John and his brother James were two of Jesus' first disciples, when he found them by the Sea of Galilee. John witnessed Jesus' transfiguration, the Last Supper, and was there at Gethsemane. John is "the disciple Jesus loved." He was also one of those who witnessed Jesus' resurrection. John traveled with Peter to Jerusalem and Samaria. He is thought to have died in Ephesus. He is the author of the Fourth Gospel, three of the Epistles, and the Book of Revelation. As we read these Books, remember John. Jesus loves all of us.

Pecan Crescents

2 cups flour
2 sticks butter
1 cup pecans, chopped
½ cup confectioners' sugar

½ tsp. salt
1 tsp. vanilla
½ tsp. almond extract

In a bowl combine the ingredients. Wrap the dough in plastic wrap and refrigerate 2 hours.
Preheat oven to 375°. Form the dough into balls. Roll out on a floured board in a crescent shape by bending not quite in half. Bake on cookie sheet for 12-15 minutes. Cool. Roll in confectioners' sugar.

December 28

"That the LORD called Samuel: and he answered, Here am I. And he ran unto Eli, and said, Here am I; for thou calledst me. And he said, I called not; lie down again. And he went and lay down. And the LORD called yet again, Samuel. And Samuel arose and went to Eli, and said, Here am I; for thou didst call me. And he answered, I called not, my son; lie down again. Now Samuel did not yet know the LORD, neither was the word of the LORD yet revealed unto him. And the LORD called Samuel again the third time. And he arose and went to Eli, and said, Here am I; for thou didst call me. And Eli perceived that the LORD had called the child."
I Samuel 3:4-8

How many times does the Lord have to speak to us before we listen? Why do we tune him out and only when we are in dire straits do we finally turn to him? The Lord is always there, always with us. Take time each day, it doesn't matter when, although I like the early morning to spend a few quiet moments with God. He is a good and loyal God, he hears our every word, and knows our ever move. Let him speak to you. *"Here, I am Lord."* Remember that beautiful hymn by Dan Schutte (1947-) and sing it whenever you want Him to know your presence.

Apple Pie

Pie Crust

Filling

1 cup walnuts, almonds or pecans	2 tsp. cinnamon
4 apples, sliced	¼ tsp. ground nutmeg
Juice of ½ lemon	1 tsp. ginger
¼ cup sugar	¼ cup flour
¼ cup brown sugar	½ stick butter, softened
¼ cup maple syrup	

Preheat oven to 400°
Bake the pie crust for 10 minutes. Let cool.
Line the crust with the nuts and apples.
In a bowl combine the sugars, syrup, spices, flour and butter. Spread over the apples.
Bake 30 minutes, or until just golden. Serve with ice cream, cheddar cheese wedges, or whipped cream.

December 29

"The strife is o'er, the battle done; The victory of life is won; The song of triumph has begun: Alleluia!
Refrain: Alleluia! Alleluia! Alleluia!
The powers of death have done their worst; But Christ their legions hath dispersed; Let shouts of holy joy outburst: Alleluia! (r) The three sad days are quickly sped; He rises glorious from the dead; All glory to our risen Head! Alleluia! (r) He closed the yawning gates of hell; The bars from heaven's high portals fell; Let hymns of praise His triumphs tell! Alleluia! (r) Lord, by the stripes which wounded Thee, From death's dread sting Thy servants free, That we may live, and sing to Thee: Alleluia! (r)"

Alleluia, the year is almost past. What have we accomplished to make us better Christians? Have you gotten out in the community and volunteered? Did you help a sick person and ask for prayers to heal him (her)? Did you find time to play with your children (grandchildren), read to them, and put them to bed? Did you take time to pray, or find a quiet moment to appreciate and thank God for all he has given you? If not, it is not too late. Please don't say there is always tomorrow. Do it today. Sing praises to the Lord, fall down and worship Him, and know He is always there for you, for me, for everyone.

Francis Pott (1832-1909) attended Oxford and was ordained in 1856. He served as curate at several churches, but is best known as a hymn translator. *The Strife is O'er* comes from Latin words written in 1695, and may date back to the 12th century.

Wild Rice Casserole

Serves 8-10

2 cups wild rice
5 cups chicken stock
½ stick butter, melted
1 cup dried or fresh cranberries

1 leek, chopped
1 cup dried apricots
1 cup slivered almonds

Preheat oven to 350°
Combine the ingredients in a buttered casserole.
Cover and bake 1 hour, or until rice is just tender.
Serve with maple syrup.

December 30

Tomorrow we celebrate the last day of the year. For years old friends gave a New Year's Eve party in their New York apartment. Up to 150 people might appear during the course of the evening. The parties were always black tie. Food was in abundance, and a rum punch forever served. At midnight the host would rev up his organ, and we would sing a resounding *Auld Lang Syne*. Most of the party goers were members of the Canterbury Singers and the Blue Hill Troop. You couldn't help but feel exhilarated and on a high. As the year comes to a close we do not know what might happen in the future. We do know however, that God is always with us. He does not change. We do, sometimes for the better, sometimes for the worst. *"Jesus Christ, the same yesterday and today, and forever."*

Oyster Stew

Serves 6

6 slices bacon, cooked and crumbled, reserve drippings	1 quart oysters with liquor
1 stick butter	2 cups milk
1 large leek, sliced	2 cups heavy cream
2 large potatoes, peeled and diced	¼ cup white wine
1 stalk celery	½ cup fresh parsley, chopped
	½ tsp. Old Bay seasoning

Melt the butter and bacon drippings in a large pot.
Stir in the leek, potatoes and celery.
Add the oyster liquor and milk. Bring to a boil. Simmer until potatoes are tender.
Stir in cream, white wine, parsley, Old Bay, and oysters.
Heat until just warmed.
Serve garnished with parsley or dill.

"For God louede so the world that he yaf his oon bigetun sone, that ech man that beliueth in him perische not, but haue euerlastynge lijf."
Wyclif Bible translation John 3:16

John Wycliffe (c1320s-1384) explained that scripture contains all truth and, being from God, is the only authority. There is only one church, and Christ is the head of it. Mr. Wycliffe translated the New Testament into English. He was buried in the Lutterworth churchyard. In 1428 the English bishop removed his remains, burned them and threw them into the river Swift at the command of the pope. This man, who acted and preached so much like the original apostles, died a martyr as so many before him had done in the name of the Lord.

SCRIPTURE CAKE

Scripture Cake originated in England, later coming to America.

½ cup Judges 5:25, last clause	½ cup butter
2 cups Jeremiah 6:20	2 cups sugar
2 tablespoons I Samuel 14:25	2 tablespoons honey
6 Jeremiah 17:11, separated	6 eggs
1½ cups I Kings 4:22	1½ cups flour
2 teaspoons Amos 4:5	2 teaspoons baking powder
Pinch of Leviticus 2:13	¼ teaspoon salt
½ cup Judges 4:19	½ cup milk
2 cups Nahum 3:12, chopped	2 cups figs
2 cups Numbers 17:8	2 cups almonds
2 cups I Samuel 30:12, chopped	2 cups raisins
II Chronicles 9:9	2 teaspoons cinnamon, ½ teaspoon cloves, 1 teaspoon nutmeg, ½ teaspoon ginger

Preheat the oven to 300°.
Grease a 10 inch tube pan.
Whip together the Judges, Jeremiah, and I Samuel until light.
Beat the 6 egg yolks of Jeremiah 17 and add the Kings, Amos, Chronicles, and Leviticus, alternating with Judges.
Fold in Nahum, Numbers, and Samuel.
Beat Jeremiah 17's 6 egg whites until stiff and fold into the rest of the batter.
Pour into the pan and bake 2 hours.

A

AA, 287
Acts 1:15-26, 57
Acts 2:2-4, 177
Acts 2:36, 177
Acts 2:38-39, 308
Acts 4:13, 148
Acts 4:33, 263
Acts 5:30, 175
Acts 6:7, 246
Acts 7:58-60, 363
Acts 12:12, 272
Acts 20:35, 143
Acts 24:16, 218
Acts 27:25-26, 183
Acts 28:31, 183
Advent, 318, 323
Agnes, St., 23
Agnus Dei, 247
Alexander, Cecil, 97
All Hallows, 305
Almonds
Almond Scones, 16
Swordfish Almondine, 219
Aloe Vera, 195
Andrew, 337
Anger, 58
Annapolis, 214
Anselm, 113
Appetizers
Artichoke Dip, 218
Baked Brie, 332
Baked Brie with Apricots, 10
Basil Parmesan Polenta, 146
Big Ga's Stuffed Bread, 147
Cheese Puffs, 68, 345
Crab Cream Cheese Dip, 165
Crab Dip, 172
Crab Spread, 157
Crab Spring Rolls, 143
Cucumber Dip, 188
Easy Crab Dip, 264
Hummus, 210
Oysters Rockefeller, 362

Pate, 74
Smoked Salmon Blini, 118
Stuffed Portabella Mushrooms, 22
Apples
Apple/Almond Flan, 302
Apple Butter Bread, 339
Apple Cake, 277
Apple Fritters, 211, 288
Apple Pancakes, 115
Apple Pie, 365
Apple Muffins, 333
Apple Raspberry Crisp, 57
Apple Tart, 322
Apple Trees, 32
Applesauce Cake, 93
Apricots
Apricot Pudding, 32
Apricot Trees, 32
Baked Brie with Apricots, 10
Aquinas, Thomas, 30
Arlington Cemetery, 64
Artichokes
Artichoke Dip, 218
Asparagus
Asparagus Crab Casserole, 126
Asparagus Risotto, 13
Asparagus Souffle, 224
Augustine of Hippo, 241
Avocado
Avocado Salsa, 72

B

Bach, J.S., 73, 211
Baker, Henry William, 184
Baker, Theodore, 335
Bakewell, John, 79
Ballintubber Abbey, 11
Baltic Countries, 280
Bananas
Banana Bread, 88, 179
Sauteed Bananas, 135
Baptism, 308
Baring-Gould, Sabine, 4

Barley
Barley Pilaf, 21
Barley Soup, 228
Basil Parmesan Polenta, 146
Bates, Katherine Lee, 186
Beans
Bean and Corn Salsa, 33
Black Beans and Rice, 8
Green Beans with Dill, 169
Green Beans with Mustard Seeds, 142
Haricots Verts, 94
Herbed Green Beans, 4
King Wenceslaus Soup, 363
Old Fashioned Baked Beans, 166
Oriental Green Beans, 90
Tarragon Green Beans, 205
White Bean Salad, 12
Beef
Beef Fajitas, 215
Beef Hash, 100
Beef Tenderloin, 121, 269, 326, 350
Beef Tournados, 235
Beef Wellington, 308
Beef with Portabella Sauce, 139
Chili, 84
Meatballs with Lemon Sauce, 276
Meatloaf, 342
Spaghetti, 137, 289
Stroganoff, 217
Sweet and Sour Meatballs, 52
Beets
Orange Beets, 198
Roasted Beet Salad, 267
Benedict, St., 82
Bernard of Montjoux, 150
Bible Study Groups, 138
Birth, 310
Bishop Whipple's Pudding, 48

Bishops, 48
Blueberries
Blueberry Pie, 328
Blueberry Salad, 236, 240
Blueberry Sorbet, 187
Boberg, Carl, 230
Bonhoeffer, Dietrich, 37
Borthwick, Jane Laurie, 251
Boy Scouts, 84
Brackett, Joseph, 345
Brahms, Johannes, 129
Breads
Almond Scones, 16
Apple Butter Bread, 339
Apple Muffins, 333
Banana Bread, 88, 179
Big Ga's Stuffed Bread, 147
Bread Pudding, 325
Bread Salad, 41
Christmas Bread, 360
Christmas Coffee Cake, 347
Cinnamon French Toast, 15
Cornbread, 193
Focaccia, 54
Herb and Cheese Biscuits, 152, 176
Irish Bread, 78
Pashka, 87
Raisin Bread, 206
Rosemary French Bread, 107
Spoon Bread, 35, 242
Strawberry Bread, 221
Tomato and Basil Flatbread, 161
Tsoureki, 101
Brie
Baked Brie with Apricots, 10
Bridges, Matthew, 197
Broccoli
Broccoli Salad, 51
Brooks, Philips, 357
Brown, Katharine Kennedy, 199
Brownies, 132
Byrom, John, 61

C
Cabbage
Red Cabbage, 77, 153
Cakes
Angel Food Cake, 274
Apple
Apple Cakes, 277
Applesauce Cake, 93
Bourbon Cake, 42
Carthage, 136
Devil's Food Cake, 83
Honey Cake, 270
Pound Cake, 24
Scripture Cake, 368
Cancer, 20
Candy
Divinity Candy, 67
Whisky Fudge, 251
Canticle of the Sun, 279
Catherine of Siena, 244
Carrots
Glazed Carrots, 353
Sauteed Carrots, 11
Cashew Rice, 82
Cereal
Granola, 284
Ceviche, 108
Cheese
Blue Cheese Salad, 49
Cheese Puffs, 68, 345
Cherries
Cherry Cobbler, 216
Cherry Pie, 55
Chesapeake Bay, 227, 232, 264
Chicken
Chicken Carbonara, 86
Chicken Curry, 292
Chicken Fried Rice, 192
Chicken in Tomato Sauce, 209
Chicken Leek Mushroom Pie, 129
Chicken over Fettuccine, 196
Chicken Paprika, 9
Chicken Picatta, 309
Chicken Quesadillas, 330
Chicken Salad, 249, 320
Chicken Stew, 171

Chicken with Dumplings, 259
Chicken with Pomegranate Sauce, 282
Chinese New Year Stir Fry, 44
Coq au Vin, 27
Coronation Chicken Salad, 155
Grilled Chicken Penne, 150
Grilled Chicken with Green Sauce, 5, 177
Honey Chicken, 99
Lemon Roasted Chicken, 141
Spicy Chicken, 53
Stuffed Chicken with Basil Sauce, 246
Children, 168, 213, 248
Chinese New Year, 44
Chocolate
Chocolate Baker's Frosting, 83
Chocolate Mousse, 47, 340
Christmas, 346, 347, 348, 354, 359, 360, 361, 362
1 Chronicles 29:3, 16
Chrysotom, St. John, 320
Claggett, Thomas John, 291
Clams
Cheese Ravioli with Clams, 265
Clam Chowder, 162
Clams in Wine Sauce, 134
Pasta with Clam Sauce, 81
Cleveland, 53, 127, 281
Coconut Coffee Cake, 85
Cod
Baked Cod, 344
Cod with Tomatoes, 158
Coffee
Coffee Mousse, 290
Coffee Pudding, 25
Coffee Supreme, 130
Coleslaw, 58
Colossians 3:15-17, 194

Colossians 3:24, 77
Constitutional Convention, 262
Cookies
Cookies
Chocolate Chip, 248, 346
Ginger Cookies, 318
Madeleines, 306
Peanut Butter Cookies, 291
Pecan Crescents, 364
St. Nicholas Day Cookies, 343
Shortbread, 168
Walnut Cookies, 123
Coriander, 292
1 Corinthians 3:10, 269
1 Corinthians 6:10, 120
1 Corinthians 10:31, 75
1 Corinthians 11:23-26, 107
1 Corinthians 12:31, 14
1 Corinthians 13:4-7, 49
1 Corinthians 13:4-8, 13, 270
1 Corinthians 13:7, 213
1 Corinthians 15:55-58, 287
2 Corinthians 1:8, 90
2 Corinthians 9:8, 198
2 Corinthians 13:11-14, 126
2 Corinthians 9:15, 239
Corn
Baked Polenta, 131
Bean and Corn Salsa, 33
Corn and Shrimp Chowder, 109
Corn Relish, 225
Cornbread, 193
Spoon Bread, 35
Succotash, 96
Colossians 3:2, 40
Colossians 3:14, 198
Couscous
Couscous Salad, 73, 114
Cousins, 33, 287
Cowper, William, 333
Crab
Asparagus Crab Casserole, 126

Crab and Lobster Cakes, 207
Crab Cream Cheese Dip, 165
Crab Cakes over Salsa, 195
Crab Dip, 172
Crab Quiche, 185, 231
Crab Souffle, 203
Crab Spread, 157
Crab Spring Rolls, 143
Easy Crab Dip, 264
Maryland Crab Imperial, 223
Risotto with Crab, 98
Seafood Frittata, 46
Shrimp, Crab Casserole, 122
Veal Thermidor, 20
Cranmer, Thomas, 82
Croatia, 271
Crosby, Fanny, 85
Crusades, 198
Cucumbers
Cucumber Dip, 188
Cucumber Salad, 194
Cucumber Soup, 260
Tomato Cucumber Bisque, 230
Currants
Red Currant Sauce, 7
Warm Currant Sauce, 75
Curry
Chicken Curry, 292
Vegetable Curry, 95
Cuttyhunk, 201

D
Daughters, 52, 118
Day by Day, 5, 130
Depression, 90
de Giardini, Felice, 104
De Sales, St. Francis, 31
da Vinci, Leonardo, 107
Desserts
Apple Raspberry Crisp, 57
Apricot Pudding, 32
Baklava, 341
Birthday Cake, 213

Bishop Whipple's Pudding, 48
Blueberry Sorbet, 187
Bourbon Cake, 42
Brownies, 132, 183
Cherry Cobbler, 216
Chocolate Mousse, 47, 340
Christmas Pudding, 359
Coffee Mousse, 290
Coffee Pudding, 25
Coffee Supreme, 130
Crème Brulee, 175
Devil's Food Cake, 83
Divine Bars, 112
Eggnog Ice Cream, 361
Fruit with Rum Sauce, 181
Heavenly Pudding, 3
Hot Lemon Souffle, 156
Ice Cream with Raspberry Sauce, 358
Lemon Bars, 119
Little Ned's Birthday Cupcakes, 310
Meringues, 199
Pear Pie, 29
Pecan Tarts, 17
Peanut Butter Pie, 40
Pound Cake, 24
Rice Pudding, 26
Sauteed Bananas, 135
Scripture Cake, 368
Syllabub, 56
Trifle, 184
Deuteronomy 8:3, 8, 228
Deuteronomy 15:11, 278
Deuteronomy 32:4, 225
Disasters, 19, 160, 242, 254, 255, 258, 264
Diseases, 70, 192, 309
Divinity Candy, 67
Divorce, 42, 158, 219
Dix, William Chatterton, 253
Doane, Rt. Rev. William, 139
Docherty, Rev. George, 131
Doddridge, Philip, 179
Dressings

Pesto Dressing, 41
Drinking, 66
Drinks
Sangria, 66
Vodka Punch, 234
Duck
Roast Duck, 75, 338
Dudley, Gov. Thomas, 116
Duffield, George, 189
Dykes, John Bacchus, 71

E
Earth Day, 114
Ecclesiastes 3:1-8, 157
Ecclesiastes 5:18-19, 7
Ecclesiasticus 6:14,16, 127
Ecclesiasticus 38:31, 295
Ecclesiasticus 44:1-15, 64
Edward of Wessex, 288
Eggplant
Eggplant Casserole, 262, 324
Eggs
Eggnog Ice Cream, 361
Eggs Benedict, 61
Eggs Florentine, 110
Seafood Frittata, 46
Spinach Frittata, 23
Vegetable Omelet, 311
Eisenhower, Dwight, 4, 280
Elizabeth, Queen, 155
Elliott, Charlotte, 267
Ephesians 1:16, 17
Ephesians 2:10, 100
Ephesians 3:19-21, 41
Ephesians 4:1-6, 311
Ephesians 4:32, 283
Ephesians 5: 15-17, 138
Ephesians 5:20, 27
Ephesians 6:10-19, 28
Epiphany, 8
Exodus 16:11-13, 91
Exodus 20:3, 13
Exodus 23:10-11, 210
Ezekial 27:15, 171

F
Faber, Frederick William, 181
Faith, 28
Family, 14, 156, 161, 356
Farjeon, Eleanor, 46
Fathers, 84, 164, 191, 202
Fawcett, John, 161
Fettuccine
Chicken over Fettuccine, 196
Fettuccine with Shrimp, 283
Pasta and Smoked Salmon, 45
Figs
Figs in Honey, 65
Fig Pudding, 173
Fire, 135
Flag Day, 167
Flounder
Flounder with Vegetables, 182
Fortunatus, Vanantius, 101
Forgiveness, 276
Fosdick Harry, 146
Fourth of July, 186, 187
Francis of Rome, 70
Francis, St., 279
Franz, Ignaz, 329
Friends, 16, 17, 22, 39, 42, 89, 141, 144, 149, 156, 157, 159, 162, 163, 165, 166, 172, 175, 209, 233, 237, 243, 250, 255, 259, 268, 280, 309
Fruit
Apple Raspberry Crisp, 57
Apricot Pudding, 32
Brie with Apricots, 10
Cherry Pie, 55
Figs in Honey, 65
Fruit Soup, 1367
Lamb with Fruit, 247
Lemon Squares, 50
Pear Pie, 29
Mango Sauce, 39
Strawberry Salsa, 127
Strawberry Torte, 357

G
Gabriel, 274
Galatians 2:20, 62
Galatians 5:1, 167
Galatians 6:2, 278
Galatians 6:9, 283
Galatians 16:6, 25
Gardens, 204
Garlic, 69
Garlic Soup, 69
Gazpacho, 149
Genesis 1-3, 67
Genesis 1:3-5, 330
Genesis 2:15-17, 55
Genesis 6:12, 17, 258
Genesis 7:8-22, 264
Genesis 7:11, 68
Genesis 8:1, 258
Genesis 8:11, 19
Genesis 25:29-34, 356
Genesis 28:14, 161
Genesis 32:22-28, 355
Genesis 33:5, 209
Genesis 38:23, 284
Genesis 43:11, 284
George, St., 229
Georgia, 222
Gerhardt, Paul, 73
Gifts, 25
Goose
Roast Goose, 7
Grandparents, 151, 182, 269, 338
Stuffed Grape Leaves, 103
Grasshopper Pie, 120
Green Salad with Onion Vinaigrette, 140
Green Beans with Mustard Seeds, 142
Greenwich, 39, 121, 268
Gregory of Khandzta, 305
Gregory the Great, 247

H
Haddock
Pesto Haddock, 227
Halibut
Halibut with Vegetables, 258

Handel, George Frederick, 56, 310
Harrison, Carl, 325
Havergal, Frances Ridley, 351
Haydn, Joseph, 92
Heavenly Pudding, 3
Hebrews 4:12, 262
Hebrews 13:6, 98
Hebrews 13:8, 367
Hebrews 13:12, 53
Hebrews 13:15, 325
Hebrews 13:20-21, 367
Heermann, Johann, 286
Hell, 83
Hernnaman, Claudia Frances, 51
Honey
Honey Cake, 270
Honey Crullers, 117
Hopkins, John Henry, 307, 354
How, William, 350
Howe, Julia Ward, 149
Hymns
A Mighty Fortress, 317
Ah, Holy Jesus, 286
Amazing Grace, 3
America, 186
Ancient of Days, 139
All Glory, Laud and Honor, 94
All Hail the Power, 6
Awake My Soul, 179
Battle Hymn of the Republic, 149
Be Still, My Soul, 106
Bless be the King, 318
Christ for the World, 185
Christ is Made the Sure Foundation, 288
Come Labor On, 251
Come, O Thou Traveler, 355
Come Ye Faithful, 341
Crown Him with Many Crowns, 197
Eternal Father, Strong to Save, 125
Fairest Lord Jesus, 307
Faith of our Fathers, 181

Fight the Good Fight, 63
For All the Saints, 350
Glorious Things of Thee are Spoken, 92
Go Tell it on the Mountain, 361
God Moves in a Mysterious Way, 333
God of Grace, 146
Good Christian Friends Rejoice, 26
Hail Thee, Festival Day, 101
Hail, Thou Once Despised, 79
He is Risen, 97
Here, I am Lord, 365
Holy God We Praise Thy Name, 329
How Bright Appears the Morning Star, 224
How Great Thou Art, 230
How Firm a Foundation, 249
Immortal, Invisible, 342
In the Bleak Midwinter, 342
Jesu, Joy of Man's Desiring, 211
I am the Bread of life, 206
I Come to the Garden, 86
I Sing a Song, 307
I want to walk as a Child, 178
I'll Praise my Maker, 170
In Christ There is No East or West, 44, 319
Jesus Loves Me!, 24
Joy to the World, 56
Just as I am, 267
Lift high the Cross, 344
Lord of All Hopefulness, 203
Lord Who throughout these Forty Days, 51
Morning has Broken, 46
My Country 'Tis of Thee, 187
My Faith Looks up to Thee, 319

Now, Thank We all our God, 115
O For a Closer Walk with God, 333
O God, Our Help, 200
Oh Little Town of Bethlehem, 357
O Sacred Head, Sore Wounded, 73
On Eagle's Wings, 11
Only Thy Presence, 85
Praise My Soul, 327
Praise to the Lord, 153
Rock of Ages, 225
Silent Night, 348
Stand Up for Jesus, 189
Take My Life, 351
The King of Love, 184
The Strife is o'er, 366
The Tie that Binds, 161
'Tis the Gift, 345
We Gather Together, 335
We Three Kings, 354
What a Friend We have in Jesus, 259
What Child is This, 253
Where Cross the Crowded Ways, 340
Ye Watchers and Ye Holy Ones, 224
Hypocrites, 76

I
Idols, 190
India, 260
Innocent, 275
International, 39, 53, 120, 171, 220
Introduction to the Devout Life, 31
Irish Bread, 78
Isaiah 7:14, 362
Isaiah 25:9, 362
Isaiah 30:15, 160
Isaiah 40:11, 59
Isaiah 40:28, 309
Isaiah 41:12-13, 254
Isaiah 41:31, 208
Isaiah 43:18-21, 236
Isaiah 49:6, 294
Isaiah 53:6, 36

Isaiah 54:13, 118
Isaiah 55:10-11, 314
Isaiah 55:12, 334
Isaiah 56:7, 112
Isaiah 65:15-25, 141
Isaiah 65:18-19, 99.

J
Jambalaya, 105
James 1:17, 275
James 1:17-27, 58
James 3:5, 276
James 5:7, 240
James 5:16, 175
Jamestown, 116
Jews, 215
Joan of Arc, 152
Job 3:11-12, 108
Job 12:7, 133
Job 20:8-9, 306
John, 364
John 1:1-18, 364
John 2:4, 66
John 3:16, 368
John 4:6-10, 339
John of Damascus, 341
John 5:4, 70
John 5:37-38, 76
John 6:7, 9
John 6:16-21, 201
John 6:25-35, 332
John 6:35, 206
John 9:24-25, 3
John 14:1, 72
John 14:3, 144
John 14:6, 159
John 14:27, 334
John 15:1-8, 66
John 15:12, 235
John 15:13, 120
John 15:13-14, 120
John 18:37, 12
John 19:20, 205
John 20:11-17, 23
John 20:19-24, 145
John 20:24-29, 358
John 20:28, 145
John 21:17, 106
1 John 4:16, 93
1 John 5:21, 190
3 John 1:4, 118

John the Baptist, 242
Johnson, James Weldon, 170
Joncas, Michael, 11
Joshua 1:7, 45
Joshua 1:9, 180
Joy to the World, 56
Julian, St., 130
Justice for Children, 168, 219

K
Kennedy, John F., 329
King, Martin Luther, 96
Kitchin, George William, 344

L
Lamb
Braised Lamb Shanks, 59
Grilled Leg of Lamb, 36, 106
Kibbi, 297
Lamb Kebabs, 138
Lamb Soup, 38
Lamb Stew, 18, 334
Lamb with Currant Sauce, 263
Lamb with Fruit, 247
Lamb with Port Sauce, 268
Pierogi, 281
Lambs, 36, 59
Lamentations 3:54-57, 242
Lawrence, Brother, 194
LeCompte, Rowan, 78
Leeks
Braised Leeks, 79
Leek Soup, 6
Leek Tart, 212
Lemons
Hot Lemon Souffle, 156
Lemon Bars, 119
Lemon Roasted Chicken, 141
Lemon Squares, 50
Lent, 51, 62
Lincoln, Abraham, 35, 169
Lobster

Crab and Lobster Cakes, 207
Lobster and Scallop Pie, 243
Lobster Bisque, 245
Lobster Casserole, 252
Lobster Crepes, 244
Lobster Salad, 186
Lobster Sauce, 20
Lobster Souffle, 233
Lobster Stew, 154
Lobster with Pasta, 89
Seafood Frittata, 46
Seafood Pizza, 60
Long Island, 60, 75, 289
Lord's Prayer, 103
Lovage, 250
Love, 17, 41, 49, 65
Luke, 293
Luke 1:1-4, 293
Luke 1:26-37, 80, 274
Luke 1:36, 33
Luke 2:29, 294
Luke 4:23, 237
Luke 5:24-26, 39
Luke 6:38, 80
Luke 6:48
Luke 8:2, 205
Luke 9:2, 163
Luke 10:25-37, 255
Luke 10:27, 13
Luke 10: 30-34, 42
Luke 10:38-42, 212
Luke 11:1, 5
Luke 12:6-12, 72
Luke 12:40, 360
Luke 14:13, 266
Luke 16:10, 226
Luke 18:15-17, 289
Luke 18:24, 121
Luke 19:38, 12
Luther, Martin, 317
Lyte, Henry Francis, 327

M
Maine, 154
Mango
Mango Sauce, 39
Mark 2:13-17, 266
Mark 3:25, 169
Mark 9:23-24, 190

Mark 12:42-44, 140
Mark 13:28-31, 173
Mark 16:1-6, 205
Mark 16:15, 222
Mark's St., 272
Marriage, 219
Martha, 212
Martin of Tours, 318
Mary Magdalene, 205
Maryland Hunt Cup, 119
Matthew, 266
Matthew 1:1, 116
Matthew 2:1, 6, 346
Matthew 2:9-10, 8
Matthew 4:1-2, 51
Matthew 4:18-20, 337
Matthew 4:28, 193
Matthew 5:16, 261
Matthew 5:8, 328
Matthew 6:19-21, 121
Matthew 6:34, 22, 54
Matthew 7:7, 265
Matthew 7:8, 257
Matthew 8:11, 44
Matthew 8:26-27, 343
Matthew 9:20, 192
Matthew 11:28, 38
Matthew 13:31-32, 142
Matthew 14:25-33, 231
Matthew 16:18, 225
Matthew 18:9, 83
Matthew 18:20, 44, 320
Matthew 18:21-22, 276
Matthew 19:4-6, 65, 235
Matthew 20:21, 23, 178
Matthew 21:33-46, 226
Matthew 22:36-40, 49
Matthew 25:13, 347
Matthew 25:14, 208
Matthew 25:34-36, 30
Matthew 28:17-20
Matthew 28:19, 280
Matthias, 57
May Day, 123
McGraw, Dr. Myrtle, 248
Meat
BBQ Pork Chops, 204
Beef Fajitas, 215
Beef Hash, 100
Beef Tenderloin, 121,
269, 326, 350

Beef Tournedos, 235
Beef Wellington, 308
Beef with Portabella
sauce, 139
Braised Lamb Shanks, 59
Braised Pork Chops, 253
Chili, 84
Grilled Lamb, 106
Kibbi, 297
Lamb Kebabs, 138
Lamb Stew, 18
Lamb with Currant Sauce,
263
Lamb with Port Sauce,
268
Lamb with Fruit, 247
Meatballs with Lemon
Sauce, 276
Meatloaf, 342
Pork Stew, 80
Roast Pork with Salsa, 72
Rolled Veal, 348
Spaghetti, 137
Stroganoff, 217
Stuffed Grape leaves, 103
Stuffed Peppers, 76
Stuffed Veal, 113
Sweet and Sour
Meatballs, 52
Veal Meatballs, 70
Veal Stew, 315
Veal Thermidor, 20
Venison Stew, 71
Memorial Day, 152
Michelangelo, 67
Mincemeat
Mincemeat Pie, 327
Mohr, Joseph, 348
Monsell, John Samuel
Bewley, 63
Morning, 46, 173
Mortenson, Greg, 339
Mothers, 52, 59, 128,
175, 252
Mozart, Amadeus, 29
Mushrooms
Cream of Mushroom
Soup, 116
Mushroom Soup, 317
Stuffed Portabella
Mushrooms, 22

Mussels
Mussel Salad, 214
Mussel Soup, 180, 201
Stuffed Mussels, 30
Mustard Seed, 142

N
Nantucket, 137, 151, 180,
183, 193, 207, 234, 240,
245, 257, 306, 328
National Prayer
Breakfast, 280
National Society of
Colonial Dames, 116
Neale, John Mason, 26
Neander, Joachim, 153
Nehemiah 5:10-11, 215
Nehemiah 8:10, 290
New Castle, 105, 290
New Year, 367
Newport, 53, 261, 282
Newton, John, 3, 92
Nicene Creed, 188
Nicholas, St. 343
St. Nicholas Church,
Galway, 343
Nicolai, Philipp, 224
Niebuhr, Reinhold, 174
Noel, Caroline Maria, 102
North, Frank Mason, 340
Notre Dame Cathedral, 29
Numbers 11:7: 292
Numbers 11:5, 69
Nuts
Almond Scones, 16
Candied Pecans, 124
Cashew Rice, 82
Pecan Crescents, 364
Pecan Tarts, 17

O
Offero, St. Christopher,
208
Old Irish Blessing, 202
Olives, 210
Onions
Baked Onions, 104
Onion Tart, 238
Oranges
Orange Salad, 200
Oxenham, John, 319

Oyster Bay, 68
Oysters
Baked Oysters, 352
Oyster Stew, 367
Oysters Rockefeller, 362

P
Pagura, Frederico, 318
Palm Sunday, 94
Palmer, Ray, 319
Pan Am 103, 358
Pancakes
Apple Pancakes, 115
Baked Pancake, 62
Dessert Pancakes, 92
Paprika
Chicken Paprika, 9
Parents, 270
Pashka, 87
Pasta
Lobster with Pasta, 89
Pasta and Smoked
Salmon, 45
Pasta with Clam Sauce,
81
Tortellini Soup, 19
Pate, 74
Patience, 111, 131
Patrick, St., 78
Paul, St. 182
Peace, 18
Peanuts
Peanut Butter Cookies,
291
Peanut Butter Pie, 40
Peanut Soup, 64
Pecan Tarts, 17
Pears
Pear Pie, 29
Pear Salad, 287
Pentecost, 177
Peppers
Rice with Peppers, 28
Stuffed Peppers, 76
Perronet, Edward, 6
Peter, St. 182
1 Peter 1:24-25, 309
1 Peter 3:2-5, 156
1 Peter 4:8-11, 191
1 Peter 4:10, 25
1 Peter 5:1-4, 321

2 Peter 3:9, 131
Pesto
Pesto Dressing, 41
Phelps, Michael, 231
Philadelphia, 42, 89, 285,
326, 346
Philippians 3:10, 349
Philippians 3:10-14, 37
Philippians 4:4, 34
Philippians 4:4-7, 359
Philippians 4:6, 38
Philippians 4:7, 15
Philippians 4:19, 196
Pies
Apple Pie, 365
Apple Tart, 322
Blueberry Pie, 328
Cherry Pie, 55
Grasshopper Pie, 120
Mincemeat, 327
Peanut Butter Pie, 40
Pear Pie, 29
Pecan Tarts, 17
Pumpkin ice Cream Pie,
354
Pumpkin Pie, 331
Red, White and Blue Pie,
167
Pistachios
Pistachio Puffs, 43
Pistachio Pesto and Pasta,
286
Pizza
Grilled Vegetable Pizza,
226
Salmon Pizza, 256
Seafood Pizza, 60
Plumptre, Edward, 34
Pork
BBQ Pork Chops, 204
Braised Pork Chops, 253
Pork Stew, 80
Roast Pork with Salsa, 72
Pott, Francis, 366
Potatoes
Baked Potatoes, 275
Potato Delight, 31
Potato Muffins, 34
Potato Salad, 190
Sweet Potato Bisque, 355
Sweet Potato Souffle, 335

Wasabi   Whipped
Potatoes, 307
Praise, 6
Prayer, 5, 103, 130
Proverbs 3:5-6
Proverbs 4:1-6, 164
Proverbs 4:23, 284
Proverbs 15:15
Proverbs 17:6, 168
Proverbs 17:17, 17
Proverbs 17:22, 105
Proverbs 18:24, 89
Proverbs 20:11, 248
Proverbs 22:6, 52
Proverbs 31:10-29, 252
Providence, 42
Psalms
1:3, 204
6:2, 163
9:14, 162
16:6, 182
16:11, 162
17:8, 277
18:6, 98
19:1, 122
19:7, 345
19:14, 246
23, 184, 297
27:1, 62
27:14, 35, 311
30:11, 201
31:1-5, 159
32:11, 74
33:20-21, 114
36:7, 276
37:3-5, 223
40:1, 111
44:22, 176
44:23-26, 217
45:1, 313
45:8, 195
45:13, 285
46:1, 50
46:10, 132
47:8, 152
50:2, 60
55:19, 166
62:7-12, 238
66:12, 135
71:17, 234
72:2-13, 312

73:26, 47
78:23-29, 221
78:38-39, 324
89:9, 232
90:12, 20
91:4, 11
91:9-10, 84
95:5, 239
100, 8, 271
102:1-2, 109
103:1-5, 78
103:2, 336
104:13-15, 273
104:23-26, 227
104:24, 216, 331
107:29-30, 165
118:6, 325
119:18, 326
119:103, 124
121, 81
121:8, 269
122:1, 154
126:2, 172, 268
128:3-4, 219
130:6, 46
133:1, 245
137:1, 182
145:8, 260
147:3, 157, 217
149:1-6, 243
149:3, 10
150, 134
Puddings
Apricot Pudding, 32
Bishop   Whipple's
Pudding, 48
Bread Pudding, 325
Christmas Pudding, 359
Coffee Pudding, 25
Fig Pudding, 173
Heavenly Pudding, 3
Rice Pudding, 26
Pumpkin
Pumpkin Ice Cream Pie,
354
Pumpkin Pie, 331
Pumpkin Risotto, 323
Pumpkin Soup, 305

Q
Quails, 91

Baked Quail, 91
Quiet, 132
Quinn, James, 93, 279

R
Rainbow, 122
Raspberries
Apple Raspberry Crisp,
57
Ice Cream with Raspberry
Sauce, 358
Rejoice, Ye Pure in Heart,
34
Requiem, Mozart's, 29
Revelation 5:11-14, 316
Revelation 12:7-11, 152
Revelation 12:7-9, 229
Revelation 19:12, 197
Revelation 21:5, 74
Rice
Black Beans and Rice, 8
Cashew Rice, 82
Chicken Fried Rice, 192
Fried Rice, 319
Rice Casserole, 63
Rice Pudding, 26
Rice Salad, 279
Rice with Peppers, 28
Wild rice Casserole, 366
Richard of Chichester, 95
Riley, John A.L., 224
Rinkart, Martin, 115
Rippon, John, 249
Risotto
Asparagus Risotto, 13
Pumpkin Risotto, 323
Risotto with Crab, 98
Rockfish
Baked Rockfish, 220, 337
Rockfish Delight, 261
Rockfish   in   Tomato
Sauce, 125
Stuffed Rockfish, 239
Romania, 220, 314, 315,
316
Romans 1:11-12, 25
Romans 6:3-4, 308
Romans 6:4, 86
Romans 8:28, 150, 233
Romans 8:35-39, 176
Romans 12:6, 322

Romans 12:9-10, 338
Romans 13:10, 151
Romans 14:17-18, 263
Rosemary French Bread,
107
Rossetti, Christina, 342
Rule of St. Benedict, 82
Russia, 222

S
St. Basil's, 324
St.   Mary's   Collegiate
Church, 263
St. Peter' Basilica 110
Salads
Baby Greens Salad, 241
Berry Salad, 222
Blue Cheese Salad, 49
Blueberry Salad, 236, 240
Bread Salad, 41
Broccoli Salad, 51
Chicken Salad, 249, 320
Coleslaw, 58
Couscous Salad, 73, 114
Cucumber Salad, 194
Greek Salad, 237
Green Salad with Onion
Vinaigrette, 140
Lobster Salad, 186
Mussel Salad, 214
Orzo Salad, 197
Orange Salad, 200
Pear Salad, 287
Potato Salad, 190
Rice Salad, 279
Roasted Beet Salad, 267
Spinach Salad, 163
Strawberry Salad, 124
Veggie Pasta Salad, 266
Salmon
Pasta   and   Smoked
Salmon, 45
Salmon and Pasta, 178
Salmon on the BBQ, 250
Salmon Pizza, 256
Salmon with Herb Sauce,
14
Salmon   with   Mango
Sauce, 39
Salsa
Avocado Salsa, 72

Bean and Corn Salsa, 33
Corn Salsa, 195
Mango, 349
Strawberry Salsa, 127
Tomato Salsa, 174
Salvation Army, 4, 199
1 Samuel 3:4-8, 365
1 Samuel 10:1, 155
1 Samuel 16:18, 214
1 Samuel 22:47, 225
San Francisco, 69, 134, 272
Sandwiches
Winery Sandwiches, 273
Sangria, 66
Sauces
Balsamic Sauce, 350
Blue Cheese Sauce, 121
Cilantro Sauce, 356
Clam Sauce, 81
Currant, 263
Green Sauce, 5
Herb Sauce, 14
Lobster Sauce, 20, 164
Mango Sauce, 39
Mint Sauce, 106
Newburg, 202
Pesto, 227
Pomegranate, 282
Port, 268
Red Currant, 7
Warm Currant Sauce, 75
Scallops
Ceviche, 108
Grilled Scallops, 191
Lobster and Scallop Pie, 243
Scallops, Shrimp ,Pasta, 272
Seafood Pizza, 60
Shrimp and Scallop Scampi, 229
Schutte, Dan, 365
Scones
Almond Scones, 16
Scott, Lesbia, 307
Scriven, Joseph, 259
Seabury, Samuel, 321
Seafood
Baked Cod, 344
Baked Oysters, 352

Baked Rockfish, 220, 337
Baked Sole with Lobster Sauce, 164
Baked Trout, 97, 111
Ceviche, 108
Clams in Wine Sauce, 134
Cod with Tomatoes, 158
Corn and Shrimp Chowder, 109
Crab and Lobster Cakes, 207
Crab Cakes over Salsa, 195
Crab Quiche, 185
Crab Souffle, 203
Fettuccine with Shrimp, 283
Fish Chowder, 329
Flounder with Vegetables, 182
Grilled Scallops, 191
Grilled Swordfish Kabobs, 159
Halibut with Vegetables, 258
Jambalaya, 105
Lobster and Scallop Pie, 243
Lobster Bisque, 245
Lobster Casserole, 252
Lobster Crepes, 244
Lobster Souffle, 233
Lobster with Pasta, 89
Maryland Crab Imperial, 223
Mussel Salad, 214
Paella, 293
Pasta and Smoked Salmon, 45
Past with Clam Sauce, 81
Pesto Haddock, 227
Risotto with Crab, 98
Rockfish Delight, 261
Rockfish in Tomato Sauce, 125
Salmon on the BBQ, 250
Salmon Pizza, 256
Salmon with Mango Sauce, 39
Sauteed Shrimp, 321

Scallops, Shrimp Pasta, 272
Seafood Casserole, 232
Seafood Chowder, 151, 257
Seafood Crepes, 313
Seafood Frittata, 46
Seafood Pizza, 60
Seafood with Newburg Sauce, 202
Shrimp and Scallop Scampi, 229
Shrimp Casserole, 208
Shrimp/Crab Casserole, 122
Smoked Salmon Blini, 118
Stuffed Mussels, 30
Stuffed Rockfish, 239
Summer Shrimp, 189
Swordfish Almondine, 219
September 11, 254, 255
Sermons, 83
Serve, 77
Shakers, 345
Shrimp
Corn and Shrimp Chowder, 109
Fettuccine with Shrimp, 283
Paella, 293
Sauteed Shrimp, 321
Scallops, Shrimp and Pasta, 272
Seafood Pizza, 60
Shrimp and Scallop Scampi, 229
Shrimp Casserole, 208
Shrimp/Crab Casserole, 122
Summer Shrimp, 189
Smith, Captain John, 223
Smith, Samuel, 187
Smith, Walter Chalmers, 342
Smoked Salmon Blini, 118
Sole
Baked Sole with Lobster Sauce, 164

Solzhenistyn, Alexander, 217
Son-in-law, 27
Song of Solomon, 2:1-2, 123
Song of Solomon 2:3, 32
Song of Solomon 2:13, 65
Song of Solomon 4:11, 43
Song of Solomon 4:13, 250
Song of Solomon 8:5, 32
Soups
Clam Chowder, 162
Cream of Mushroom Soup, 116
Cucumber Soup, 260
Fish Chowder, 329
Fresh Vegetable Soup, 278
Fruit Soup, 136
Garlic Soup, 69
Gazpacho, 149
King Wenceslaus, 363
Lamb Soup, 38
Mushroom Soup, 317
Mussel Soup, 180, 201
Peanut Soup, 64
Pumpkin Soup, 305
Seafood Chowder, 257
Spinach Soup, 37
Sweet Potato Bisque, 355
Tomato Bisque, 102
Tomato Cucumber Bisque, 230
Tortellini Soup, 19
Zama, 316
Zucchini Soup, 128
Spaghetti, 137, 289
Spinach
Spinach Frittata, 23
Spinach Souffle, 351
Spinach Soup, 37
Spinach Salad, 163
Spoon Bread, 35
Sports, 109
Squash
Fall Squash, 285
Stuffed Acorn Squash, 312
Stephen, St. 363
Stews

Lamb Stew, 18, 334
Oyster Stew, 367
Pork Stew, 80
Venison Stew, 71
Stewardship, 322
Still, 106
Stone, Samuel John, 117
Strawberries
Strawberry Bread, 221
Strawberry Salad, 124
Strawberry Torte, 357
Stress, 50, 98, 194
Struther, Jan, 203
Suicide, 90
Swordfish
Grilled Swordfish Kabobs, 159
Swordfish Almondine, 219

T
Tabbouleh, 133
Taylor, J. Hudson, 143
Temptation, 55
Tennyson, Lord Alfred, 281
Teresa, Saint of Avila, 157
Thanksgiving, 331, 332, 335, 336
Theodulph, St., 94
1 Thessalonians 5:1-11, 323
1 Thessalonians 5:12
2 Thessalonians 2:15
Thomas, 358
Thomerson, Kathleen, 178
Tiffany Windows, 68
St. Tikhon, 21
1 Timothy 3:1-5, 291
1 Timothy 6:2, 63
1 Timothy 6:7,10, 207
2 Timothy 2:3, 4
2 Timothy 3:10, 199
Timothy 4:8, 158
Tindley, Rev. Charles, 96
Titus 1:7-9, 282
Toolan, Mercy Sister, 206
Tomatoes
Stuffed Tomatoes, 170

Tomato and Basil Flatbread, 161
Tomato Bisque, 102
Tomato Cucumber Bisque, 230
Tomato Frittata, 280
Tomato Pie, 144
Tomato Quiche, 160
Tomato Salsa, 174
Toplady, Augustus, 225
Traditions, 10
Travel, 39
Trinity, 104
Trout
Baked Trout, 97, 111
Trust, 72
Tsoureki, 101
Turkey
Turkey with Cornbread Stuffing, 336
Tuttiet, Laurence, 174
Tutu, Archbishop Desmond, 282
Twelfth Night, 7

U
United States Naval Academy, 214

V
Valentine's Day, 43, 47
van Beethoven, Ludwig, 353
Veal
Rolled Veal, 348
Stuffed Veal, 113
Veal Meatballs, 70
Veal Stew, 315
Veal Thermidor, 20
Vegetables
Bean and Corn Salsa, 33
Black Beans and Rice, 7
Braised Leeks, 79
Broccoli Salad, 51
Chinese New Year Stir Fry, 44
Dalmatian Coast Vegetables, 271
Eggplant Casserole, 262, 324
Fall Squash, 285

Fresh Vegetable Soup, 278
Fried Lentils, 356
Glazed Carrots, 353
Green Beans with Dill, 169
Grilled Vegetable Pizza, 226
Grilled Vegetables, 148
Haricots Verts, 94
Herbed Green Beans, 4
Onion Tart, 238
Orange Beets, 198
Oriental Green Beans, 90
Red Cabbage, 77, 153
Sauteed Carrots, 11
Spinach Frittata, 23
Spinach Souffle, 351
Spinach Soup, 37
Stuffed Peppers, 76
Stuffed Acorn Squash, 312
Stuffed Tomatoes, 170
Succotash, 96
Sweet Potato Souffle, 335
Tarragon Green Beans, 205
Tomato Frittata, 280
Tomato Pie, 144

Vegetable Curry, 160, 95
Vegetable Omelet, 311
Vegetable Primivera, 145
Vegetable Tart, 254
Vegetarian Lasagna, 294
Veggie Pasta Salad, 266
White Bean Salad, 12
Zucchini Soup, 128
Venison Stew, 71
Vietnam, 45
Vodka Punch, 234
Volunteers, 140
Von Schlegel, Katherina, 106

W
Waltz Evenings, 10
Warner, Anna Bartlett, 24
Washington, George, 35
Washington National Cathedral, 4, 74, 78, 112, 177, 279, 291
Watts, Isaac, 200
Webber, Andrew Lloyd, 284
Wenceslaus, King, 363
Wesley, Charles, 170, 355
Wesley, John, 170

Westminster Abbey, 99, 155, 288
Whipple, Bishop Henry, 48
Wilberforce, William, 3, 238
Williams, Roger, 93
Wilmington, 80
Winchester Cathedral, 100
Winter, 38
Wolcott, Samuel, 185
Wycliffe, John, 368

Y
Yale Whiffenpoofs, 36
YMCA, 218
Yorktown, 114

Z
Zechariah 9:9, 352
Zechariah 14:7-9, 353
Zechariah 14:20, 119
Zucchini Soup, 128

About the Author

Katie Moose, born in Baltimore, is a descendant of the Clagett (Claggett) family of Maryland, and many old New England whaling families. Born a Barney she has been unable to trace her lineage to Captain Joshua Barney, the famous Naval hero of the War of 1812.

She has lived in many of the U.S.' great architectural, historical and waterside gems – Annapolis and Easton, MD; New Castle, DE; Newport and Providence, RI; Cold Spring Harbor, NY; Nantucket, MA; San Francisco; Philadelphia; Greenwich, CT; Alexandria, VA; Washington, DC; and New York City.

Mrs. Moose is the author of "Annapolis: The Guidebook", "Eastern Shore of Maryland: The Guidebook", "Chesapeake's Bounty", Chesapeake's Bounty II, New England's Bounty, "Nantucket's Bounty"; Maryland's Western Shore: The Guidebook" and several publications on the fiber optic telecommunications business, and is a consultant on international business and protocol. Her hobbies include gourmet cooking, fine wines, history, sailing, genealogy, theology and travel.

Conduit Press

Please send me____copies of God's Bounty @ $18.95

Please send me ____copies of Chesapeake's Bounty @ $16.95

Please send me____copies of Chesapeake's Bounty II @ $17.95

Please send me____ copies of New England's Bounty @ $17.95

Please send me ___copies of Nantucket's Bounty@$17.95

Please send me____ copies of Maryland's Western Shore: The Guidebook @ $15.95

Please send me____ copies of Eastern Shore of Maryland: The Guidebook @ $16.95

Postage:
1st book___$4.00
Each additional book____$1.00

Please autograph book
to_____

Make check payable to Conduit Press

Conduit Press
307 Goldsborough Street
Easton, MD 21601
Ship or deliver the cookbooks and guidebooks to:

Name_____

Address_____

_____

Telephone_____

Phone: 410-820-9915   Email:kamoose@goeaston.net